Being Political

Being Political

Genealogies
of
Citizenship

Engin F. Isin

University of Minnesota Press
Minneapolis / London

"Waiting for the Barbarians," by Constantine P. Cavafy, from *Collected Poems,*
edited by George Savidis and translated by Edmund Keeley and Philip Sherrard, is
reprinted as the epigraph to chapter 1 by permission of Princeton University Press.
Copyright 1975, 1992 by Edmund Keeley and Philip Sherrard.

Published by the University of Minnesota Press
111 Third Avenue South, Suite 290
Minneapolis, MN 55401-2520
http://www.upress.umn.edu

Library of Congress Cataloging-in-Publication Data

Isin, Engin F. (Engin Fahri), 1959–
    Being political : genealogies of citizenship / Engin F. Isin.
       p.   cm.
    Includes bibliographical references and index.
    ISBN 0-8166-3271-5 (alk. paper) — ISBN 0-8166-3272-3 (pbk. : alk. paper)
    1. Citizenship.   2. Aliens.   I. Title.
    JF801 .I75 2002
    323.6—dc21

                               2001004576

To the memory of my mother, Gülten Silman Işın (1929–1995)

Contents

Preface

This book assembles a series of genealogical investigations on citizenship as alterity. The "history" of citizenship has often been narrated by dominant groups who articulated their identity as citizens and constituted strangers, outsiders, and aliens as those who lacked the properties defined as essential for citizenship. In every age since the Greeks, citizens have narrated their own stories by establishing lineages between themselves and the glory and magnificence of ancient Greek citizens who are thought to have originated citizenship. Yet, Greek citizenship was as invented and inherited as any other: the Greek citizens also looked backward to a heroic age of the Orient, and Greek citizenship was hardly as original as they and subsequent generations claimed. Nevertheless, European aristocracies during the sixteenth and seventeenth centuries and the bourgeoisie in the eighteenth and nineteenth centuries "revived" the Greeks in their own image. Throughout centuries an unstable combination of solidaristic, agonistic, and alienating strategies and technologies of citizenship, such as stigmatization, marginalization, heroization, ritualization, racialization, professionalization, universalization, confraternization, and mediatization, constituted citizens as those who managed to inculcate virtues through others as strangers and outsiders. Slaves, women, peasants, artisans, prostitutes, vagabonds, sansculottes, workers, and squeegeers were constituted as problematized beings, interpellated and enticed to conduct themselves in just and virtuous ways conducive to social, political, and spatial orders envisioned by citizens.

While the images of being political given to us by citizens are well documented, the way strangers and outsiders constituted themselves as being political is much less so. *Being Political* investigates those moments of becoming political, when strangers and outsiders question the justice adjured on them by appropriating or overturning those same strategies and technologies of citizenship. *Being Political* is not about politics. It is about citizenship and otherness as conditions of politics. It assumes an ontological difference between politics and the political. Being political, among all other ways of being, means to constitute oneself simultaneously with and against others as an agent capable of judgment about what is just and unjust. Citizenship and otherness are then really not two different conditions, but two aspects of the ontological condition that makes politics possible. *Being Political* aims to make it more difficult to refer to historical forms of citizenship as though there were an unbroken continuity between "us" and "them" by questioning the narratives given to us by citizens and recovering some moments of strangers, outsiders, and aliens becoming political; in a sense, it aims to make us strangers to ourselves.

An invitation from Simon Fraser University in Vancouver to deliver a Koerner Lecture on citizenship in November 1993 was among the original sparks to write this book. I am grateful to Judy Oberlander of the City Program for the invitation and the subsequent meetings with various activists in the city. I am also grateful to many political activists in Toronto, Vancouver, Berlin, Montreal, İstanbul, Ankara, London, and Liverpool for sharing their thoughts on being political. I owe much to my comrades during a fifty-five-day strike at York University in 1997. Besides discovering new ways of becoming political by walking, talking, and writing together, our collective experience sharpened my thoughts about the academic profession and its contemporary entrapments. Paul Axelrod, Linda Briskin, Eduardo Canel, Jon Caulfield, Warren Crichlow, Gene Desford, Craig Heron, Pablo Idahosa, Roger Keil, Janice Newson, David Noble, Linda Peake, and Tricia Wood were an inspiration in our shared struggle. Writing *Citizenship and Identity* with Tricia Wood immediately after that strike was a notably rewarding experience for writing this book. So was undertaking research on Toronto with Myer Siemiatycki.

The research on which this book is based was funded at various stages by the Social Sciences and Humanities Research Council of Canada (SSHRC), the Faculty of Arts, and the Division of Social Science at York University, Toronto. I am grateful to reviewers, who wish to remain anonymous, and who have made critical interventions that saved me from many embarrassments. I am most grateful to David Burchell, who read the manuscript and made significant interventions, and to Barry Hindess for reading and providing invaluable comments on the first chapter. Bryan Turner, Saskia Sassen, Edward Soja, Gerard Delanty, Eleonore Kofman, and Nikolas Rose have been most supportive. The University of Cambridge and the University of Liverpool were exemplary hosts in my stays during the final months of writing. I immensely benefited from discussions with graduate students who were the members of the "built thought" seminar group at York University: Feyzi Baban, Darryl Burgwin, Antonio Gómez-Palacio, Elvan Gülöksüz, Jennifer Keesmaat, Tom Kemeny, Jamie Paquin, Mark Shwarzman, and Cheryl Teelucksingh. I am grateful to Fuat Keyman and Ahmet İçduygu for inviting me to an international conference on "citizenship, state, and identity in a globalizing world" that was held in Ankara in June 2000. I benefited from discussions with them and other participants, especially Ayşe Çağlar, Nilüfer Göle, Jan Nederveen Pieterse, John Rex, and Bobby Sayyid. Remarkably, but perhaps fittingly, another invitation from western Canada, this time from the University of Victoria, provided the spark to finish the book. I am grateful to Warren Magnusson and Rob Walker for inviting me to a workshop on the "political and the governmental" that was held in August 2000 as well as for their thoughts on the political. I am also grateful to and have benefited from the contributions of the workshop participants, Richard Ashley, Michael Brown, Mitchell Dean, Michael Dillon, Christine Helliwell, Barry Hindess, Timothy Luke, Karena Shaw, Mariana Valverde, and Reg Whitaker. I am also grateful to Urs Stäheli for inviting me to a conference on "Inclusion/Exclusion and Identity" that was held on March 1–3, 2001, at the Centre for Interdisciplinary Research, University of Bielefeld, Germany. I would like to thank Ernesto Laclau and Dorothea Nolde for their genuine and critical engagement with my ideas during this conference.

As for broader intellectual affinities and debts, Weber claimed that his intellectual milieu was dominated by Marx and Nietzsche, and that one could judge the intellectuals of that milieu very largely by the stand they took in relation to these two, so that anyone "who does not confess that he could not do the most important part of his own work without these two deceives himself and others." Almost a century later, would it be an exaggeration to make the same claim for Foucault and Bourdieu and Weber as the link between them and Marx and Nietzsche?

Carrie Mullen and her assistant Robin A. Moir at the University of Minnesota Press were absolutely fantastic as editors. When I met Carrie in 1997, I had already abandoned this book after a rough draft. She re-invigorated and encouraged me to return to it, and her support did not waver. Even when she must have doubted my ability to deliver it, she never let on, saving me from my own demons. I would also like to thank Linda Lincoln for her superb editing of this manuscript.

I am grateful to my father, Talât Işın, and my sister, Alev, and my brother-in-law Tümer Tüğberk for their support and their impeccable hospitality during stays in Kyrenia, Cyprus (geographically between ancient Salamis and Soli), at which I was able to work on the manuscript. I am grateful to my sister and brother-in-law Ute and Ian Nunes for their unflinching support. I am also grateful to my father-in-law, William Ruppert, for his generosity during a stay in Campbellford, Ontario, at which I was able to complete a draft. The generous hospitality of Güven and Yiğit Gülöksüz for a stay in their summer residence, which is located literally a few hundred meters away from the Myndos gate where the ancient Greek warriors, peasants, merchants, artisans, and slaves, under the watchful gaze of the Mediterranean gods, battled for the rights to Didyma and Halikarnassos, was most appreciated.

Yiğit Gülöksüz and Shoukry Roweis, those two warriors of grand politics who never met and whom I have had only few contacts with during the last decade or so when this book took shape, were nonetheless crucial in the assemblage of this author. I hope they will take *Being Political,* for all its flaws, as a small consolation for their dedication to my becoming a scholar without a scholastic habitus.

Evelyn Ruppert has been a true comrade all along the paths that led to this book and my deepest gratitude and debt are to her, which cannot be expressed by words. As well, my chapter on the cosmopolis has benefited immensely from her ongoing research into the moral economies of cities in Canada, America, and Britain. I am also grateful to her for reading and providing extensive and invaluable comments on various drafts of the manuscript.

Liverpool, April 2000
Toronto, May 2001

City as a Difference Machine

Citizens
Strangers
Outsiders
Aliens

Why this sudden restlessness, this confusion?
(How serious people's faces have become.)
Why are the streets and squares emptying so rapidly,
everyone going home so lost in thought?
Because night has fallen and the barbarians have not come.
And some who have just returned from the border say
there are no barbarians any longer.
And now, what's going to happen to us without barbarians?
They were, those people, a kind of solution.
  —Constantine Cavafy, "Waiting for the Barbarians"

Every age since the ancient Greeks fashioned an image of being political based upon citizenship. That citizenship has expressed a right to being political, a right to constitute oneself as an agent to govern and be governed, deliberate with others, and enjoin determining the fate of the polity to which one belongs is well recognized. Such images as the heroic warrior-citizen of the Greek polis, the patrician-citizen of the Roman civitas, the merchant-citizen of Christianopolis, and the bourgeois-citizen of the metropolis are deeply entrenched in Western memory and experience.

The virtuous image of the Greek citizen exercising his rights and obligations in the agora, the austere image of the Roman citizen conducting himself in the forum, and the stirring image of medieval citizens receiving

1

their charter in front of the guildhall have such a hold on the Western imagination of being political that they blur the boundaries between history and the present. Yet behind such seemingly timeless images, there lie intense struggles, conflicts, and violence to wrest the right to becoming political from dominant groups, which have never surrendered it without struggle. The Greek warriors struggled with the kings to wrest rights to the polis; the peasants, in turn, struggled with the aristocracy for the same rights; the plebeians in Rome struggled with the patricians; the medieval artisans struggled with the merchants and nobles. The bourgeoisie did not surrender the rights to the metropolis to the worker-citizen without struggle. Such social struggles often determined the content (rights and obligations) and extent (criteria of inclusion) of citizenship. Yet, rather than focus on these conflicts and struggles, nineteenth- and twentieth-century social and political thought often focused on the consequent images of citizenship. What the peasants demanded, the plebeians dreamed, the artisans claimed, and the workers sought have been of less concern. For good reason. We have been given these images by the victorious citizens themselves, who established narrative continuities and affinities between themselves and historical forms of citizenship.

The images of being political bequeathed to us come from the victors: those who were able to constitute themselves as a group, confer rights on and impose obligations on each other, institute rituals of belonging and rites of passage, and, above all, differentiate themselves from others, constructing an identity and an alterity simultaneously. Throughout history, citizenship has been associated with particular forms of identity: aristocrats, warriors, merchants, nobles, and the bourgeoisie claimed the rights to being political, constituting themselves as citizens. While the conditions of being a citizen were fundamentally different in every epoch, since the ancient Greeks every epoch emulated that original version invented by the Greeks. While being ambiguous about the Greek polis as their other, Roman citizens nonetheless thought of themselves somehow as inheritors of the Greek ideal of citizenship and developed rituals and rites that constituted the civitas as emulation. During the fourteenth and fifteenth centuries, when the Italian city republics were being formed by the nobility and merchants, citizens consciously appealed to antiquity and found symbols, rites, rituals, and images that established them as legitimate inheritors of citizenship as an ancient institution. Early modern nobility, too, developed its envy and lusted after antiquity in its claim for legitimate roots. Similarly, such associations are so deeply etched in our bodies that perhaps we do not recognize the bourgeoisie's triumph as its claim of "citizenship" as a historical entitlement: a class whose name inherits the institution. This is not an instance of traditions weighing like a nightmare on the living, as Marx (1852, 300) wrongly thought, but the appropriation of traditions by the victors, who sought to establish themselves as legitimate inheritors.

If, then, there is a harmonious unity and unbroken continuity in the images we are given of citizenship, it is not because of a natural growth, but a strategic emulation and appropriation—invention—of tradition that has made it possible. *Being Political* is animated by a skepticism toward these harmonious and continuous narratives given to us by citizens. At the very least, investigating citizenship historically ought to require contrasting the claims of citizens against the claims of their others. For citizens to establish themselves as virtuous, there ought to have been those who "lacked" their virtues. Against whom did citizens define themselves? How were strangers and outsiders constituted in relation to citizens? Rather than focusing on the glorious images given to us by the victors, would it not be more revealing to problematize the margins or points of contact where the inside and outside encounter, confront, destabilize, and contest each other?

Being Political is a series of genealogical investigations on citizenship from the perspective of its alterity. But this means neither focusing on the "excluded" nor making the "subaltern" speak. While nineteenth- and early twentieth-century scholars did not bother to either apologize or remark that women, metics, slaves, and artisans were excluded from ancient and medieval forms of citizenship, by the end of the twentieth century, such apologetic admissions have become a norm. We now encounter in almost every discussion of citizenship that while ancient citizenship was "revolutionary," it *did* exclude those groups. But did it? The logic of exclusion assumes that the categories of strangers and outsiders, such as women, slaves, peasants, metics, immigrants, refugees, and clients, preexisted citizenship and that, once defined, it excluded them. The logic of exclusion presupposes that the excluding and the excluded are conceived as irreconcilable; that the excluded is perceived in purely negative terms, having no property of its own, but merely expressing the absence of the properties of the other; that these properties are essential; that the properties of the excluded are experienced as strange, hidden, frightful, or menacing; that the properties of the excluding are a mere negation of the properties of the other; and the exclusion itself (or confinement or annihilation) is actuated socially (Karskens 1991, 84). By contrast, the focus on otherness as a condition of citizenship assumes that in fact citizenship and its alterity always emerged simultaneously in a dialogical manner and constituted each other. Women were not simply excluded from ancient Greek citizenship, but were constituted as its other as an immanent group by citizens. Similarly, slaves were not simply excluded from citizenship, but made citizenship possible by their very formation. The alterity of citizenship, therefore, does not preexist, but is constituted by it. The closure theories that define citizenship as a space of privilege for the few that excludes others neglect a subtle but important aspect of citizenship: that it requires the constitution of these others to become possible. The problem with the logics of exclusion and enclosure is that they assume that such identities as "woman" and "immigrant" preceded citizenship and were excluded from it. Becoming political involves questioning such essential categories as "woman" or "immigrant" as given and assumes that they were produced in the process of constituting citizenship and that they are internally, not externally, related to it. This assumption has significant consequences for investigating citizenship.

As various groups constituted themselves as citizens throughout history, they also invented various categories, classifications, and identities to govern themselves and others. Taken together, they make up a very complex terrain of contested identities. Rather than attempting to document this complex terrain, and for other reasons we shall discuss later, *Being Political* focuses on *immanent* others and is concerned only tangentially with the constitution of *transitive* or distant others, such as barbarians (Balsdon 1979; Dench 1995; Hall 1989; Kristeva 1991; Veyne 1993). It is concerned with the construction of identities that are immanent in the political field and constitute an integral part of it. For example, while it is concerned with how the Greeks constituted citizens against and with slaves or peasants, it is less concerned with whom the Greeks called barbarians. Similarly, while concerned with how the Roman patricians created categories to define the plebeians, it is less concerned with how the Romans constructed the Greeks or the barbarians as their distant others. Nor is it concerned with the constitution of Islam during the Crusades in the Middle Ages (Tyerman 1998). Rather, it is concerned with the rise of groups and their identities, such as the patricians, merchants, craftsmen, and professionals, that are immanent in the city. Making this distinction enables various categories of otherness to be investigated historically, rather than relying on a universal or dialectical distinction of inside/outside, which, as we shall see, is itself strategic, and thus political (see Walker 1993).

This is a choice whose rationale we shall discuss in more detail later.

For now what we need to emphasize is that while our received view of the origins of citizenship comes from how dominant groups defined themselves against distant others, aliens, and barbarians, the dominant groups have never been inclined to give an account of their dominance. Rather, the dominant groups have always been inclined to naturalize their "superiority" and the "inferiority" of the dominated, interpreting the struggles that resulted in their domination as epic struggles against transitive and distant aliens and barbarians. As a result, their dominated others appear as the distant and transitive (barbarians), rather than the near and immanent (strangers, outsiders, and aliens). That is among the reasons why citizenship has been interpreted as a unique occidental institution whose conditions were lacking in the Orient. At the root of the occidental conception of citizenship lies the invention of the oriental city as its Other and the distinction between (civilized) peoples with cities and (barbarian) peoples without cities.

Inventing the Occidental City: Synoecism and Orientalism

The orientalist narrative of the origins of cities goes something like this. Over a vast span of time, human groups throughout the world ostensibly underwent little change: they lived in small tribes as hunters and gatherers. Then, about 10,000 B.C., the pace of change began to accelerate. Over the next few millennia, in the "fertile crescent" of the Near East, in the foothills of the Indus Valley, and in the valleys of the Nile and the Yellow Rivers, tribes developed a capacity for producing their own food by cultivating wild grasses and domesticating certain indigenous animals. As these tribes became more sedentary, the capacity to produce their own food led to the capacity to store and ration the produce. Then, beginning with the astonishingly early settlements of the eighth millennium B.C., at the "walled oasis city" of Jericho, in Palestine, at Hacılar and Çatal Höyük in the Konya plain of south-central Anatolia, and at Jarmo in the foothills east of the Tigris, a significant change took place around 3000 B.C.: the tribes "settled together" and the city was born.

Or, alternatively, thus was the occidental city invented. For what this nutshell account illustrates is a particular, orientalist view of the origins of cities. In the nineteenth and twentieth centuries, the question of the origins of cities held the greatest fascination for many archaeologists and historians who were intrigued by the emergence of "city-states" in the great river valleys of the Tigris and Euphrates, the Nile, the Indus, and the Yellow Rivers (Soja 2000, 19–24). The origins of these early cities became even more gripping when years of painstaking interpretive struggles suggested that in each of these valley locations, the momentum that led tribes to "settle together" in increasingly large, dense, and differentiated settlements came ostensibly from within. Only later, as economy and society became more complex (i.e., "civilized"), did patterns of exchange, tenuous at first, begin to create links between them. That the emergence of the earliest Chinese states in the Yellow River valley is sufficiently isolated from developments in the Near East and India added further weight to the view that all these early manifestations are likely to have been sui generis (Maisels 1990). Moreover, although the ancient Mesoamerican civilizations flourished much later, from A.D. 250 to A.D. 1500, the Mayans, Teotihuacán, Aztecs, and Toltecs, as well as the ancient Incas, were considered civilizations based on city-states, having developed independently of other civilizations (Southall 1998, 45–53). The question that arose about the origins of these cities was concerned with how their independent rise was possible. The debate in the twentieth century focused primarily on whether this rise represented an "urban revolution" (Childe 1985) or an "urban implosion" (Mumford 1961); whether it was caused by an agrarian revolution or whether the city itself led to an agricultural explosion (Jacobs 1969). More recently, following Jacobs, Soja (2000, 24–27) has suggested a provocative inversion of the urban origins thesis by putting cities first, rather than seeing them as consequences of other factors. By focusing on more recent archaeological studies, especially on Jericho and Çatal Höyük, Soja concludes that these early "cities" were not simply proto-urban aberrations, but "represent a revolutionary leap in the social and spatial scale of human societies and culture, with scale being measured not just in numbers of people but in the intensity and geographical extent of human interaction" (46). For Soja, "The stimulating interdependencies and cultural conventions created by socio-spatial agglomeration—moving closer together—were the key organizing features or motor forces driving virtually everything that followed" (46).

There is no doubt that the question of the origins of cities will continue to fascinate historians and urbanists. The objective of the genealogical investigations into the question of being political as logics of citizenship and alterity is not to dwell on the question of the "origins" of cities in diverse valleys around the world. We are concerned with how the question of origins is often framed, which reveals a latent assumption: that the city was always a *unified* agglomeration of tribes "settling together." Even the recent provocative inversion of Soja essentially accepts a universal definition of the city as a spatial agglomeration, a settling together or synoecism. In fact, by appealing to Lefebvre (1996, 87, 100), Soja elevates synoecism into a general principle underlying a universal conception of the city, connoting "the economic and ecological interdependencies and the creative—as well as occasionally destructive—synergisms that arise from the purposeful clustering and collective habitation of people in space in a 'home' habitat" (2000, 12). The question that arises from this definition is that it takes the invention of the occidental city as a unified agglomeration as given, an invention that originated with the ancient Greek citizens who wrote histories of their own cities from the perspective of settling together or "synoecism," and transforms it into an essentialism. As we shall see later, synoecism was an invented tradition of dominant groups— citizens—in the ancient Greek poleis (von Reden 1998). It is from this perspective that the origins of cities were interpreted and extended back to other ancient civilizations by fitting evidence to them. They were also extended forward to medieval cities, which provided a complete, universalized history of the occidental city. Since the Greek poleis and medieval cities were fit into an occidental trajectory, the problem then became how to explain the difference between "oriental" and "occidental" cities. For Max Weber this difference eventually hinged on citizenship: that "oriental" cities never dissolved their tribal bonds, but the "occidental" cities dissolved them and invented the city as an association. To develop an interpretation of citizenship as alterity requires a critique of synoecism and orientalism in the origins of cities.

Weber, Synoecism, Orientalism

While Weber's work has been associated with what may be called sociological orientalism (a way of dividing the world into essentially two "civilizational" blocs, one having rationalized and secularized, and hence modernized, the other remaining "irrational," religious, and traditional), his emphasis on synoecism (a way of seeing the city, and later the state, as embodying spatial or political unification) has never been subjected to a critique. An important reason for this is that his conception of citizenship as the unique aspect of occidental capitalism has been far less discussed and emphasized than his emphasis on rationalization and religion. For his critics, Weber's designation as the major sociological progenitor of orientalism rests on three assumptions: first, that he shared the orientalist view of the superiority of the Occident over the Orient; second, that his comparative causal account of the uniqueness of the Occident rested on an internalist research program that discarded or downplayed the role of colonialism and imperialism in blocking the development of the Orient; and, third, that the religion-based civilizational aspect of Weber's comparative sociology ascribed a unity, autonomy, and primacy to religion and culture that drew him to the orientalist perspective (Nafissi 1998, 98).

From Rodinson (1966, 99–117) and Said (1978, 259) to Dean (1994, 79–89), Turner (1974, 1996, 257–86), and Springborg (1992, 9), the critics of Weber have focused on his theses on the origins of modern capitalism and his interpretation of why oriental societies "failed" to develop modern capitalism. The critics have invariably converged on issues of the rationalization of law, state administration and commerce, an ethic of acquisition, and an ethic of ultimate values as the essential differences between the oriental and occidental cultures, religions, societies, and economies, issues that originally appeared in Weber's (1905) celebrated *The Protestant Ethic and the Spirit of Capitalism*. While this critique has been useful in highlighting how Weber's work connects up with broader themes of orientalism, the fact that Weber later identified the city as a locus of citizenship as being the unique character of the occident that led to the development of capitalism has remained an unexplored issue. This theme is also remarkably absent among sympathetic discussions of Weber's work on the city, such as those by Momigliano (1970), Finley (1981), Murray (1990), and Colognesi (1995). Even a more recent review of Weber's construction of the Orient by Love (2000b) fails to make the connection between his conception of citizenship and its ostensible lack in the Orient. Thus, elective affinities between synoecism and orientalism that constitute the basis of Weber's conception of the difference between occidental and oriental cities remain curiously unexplored. That for Weber the absence of autonomous cities and citizenship was the root cause of the "failure" of oriental societies to develop capitalism and that this was connected with synoecism is what we need to explore in further detail.

By always defining the city in terms of five *essential* characteristics (fortification, market, autonomous law and administration, association, and autocephaly), Weber argued that what made the occidental city unique was that it arose from the establishment of a fraternity, brotherhood in arms for mutual aid and protection, and the usurpation of political power (1927, 319). In this regard, Weber always drew parallels between the medieval "communes" and ancient "synoecism." For Weber, "The polis is always the product of such a confraternity or synoecism, not always an actual settlement in proximity but a definite oath of brotherhood which signified that a common ritualistic meal is established and a ritualistic union formed and that only those had a part in this ritualistic group who buried their dead on the acropolis and had their dwellings in the city" (320). As we shall see below, while Weber consistently emphasized that some of these characteristics emerged in China, Japan, the Near East, India, and Egypt, he insisted that it was only in the occident that all were present and appeared regularly. From this he concluded that "[m]ost importantly, the associational character of the city and the concept of a burgher (as contrasted to the man from the countryside) never developed [in the Orient] at all and existed only in rudiments" (1921, 1227). Therefore, "a special status of the town dweller as a 'citizen,' in the ancient medieval sense, did not exist and a corporate character of the city was unknown" (1227). He was convinced that "in strong contrast to the medieval and ancient Occident, we never find the phenomenon in the Orient that the autonomy and the participation of the inhabitants in the affairs of local administration would be more strongly developed in the city . . . than in the countryside. In fact, as a rule the very opposite would be true" (1228). For him this difference was decisive: "All safely founded information about Asian and oriental settlements which had the economic characteristics of 'cities' seems to indicate that normally only the clan associations, and sometimes also the occupational associations, were the vehicle of organized action, but never the collective of urban citizens as such" (1233).

As we shall see in more detail below, Weber provided two reasons for why the city as confraternity arose only in the Occident. First, since the occidental city emerged as a defense group, the means of warfare belonged to the group. For Weber, whether a group owned the means of warfare or was furnished by an overlord was as fundamental as whether the means of production were the property of the worker or the capitalist (1927, 320). Everywhere in the Orient the development of the city as a brotherhood in arms was prevented by the fact that the army of the prince or overlord was older than the city. Why? Because in their origins and development, for India, China, the Near East, Egypt, and Asia, the question of irrigation was crucial. "The water question conditioned the existence of the bureaucracy, the compulsory service of the dependent classes, and the dependence of subject classes upon the functioning of the bureaucracy of the king" (321). That royal power was based on monopoly of martial capital was the foundation for the distinction between the Orient and the Occident. "The forms of religious brotherhood and self equipment for war made possible the origin and existence of the city" (321). While elements of analogous developments occur in India, China, Mesopotamia, and Egypt, the necessity of water regulation, which led to the formation of kingship monopoly over the means of warfare, stifled these beginnings.

The second obstacle preventing the development of the city in the Orient was the persistence of magic in oriental religions. They did not permit the formation of ritualistic communities and hence the city. The magical barriers between clans, tribes, and peoples, which were still known in the ancient polis, were eventually set aside and so the establishment of the occidental city was made possible (Weber 1927, 322–23). What makes the occidental city unique was that it allowed the association or formation of groups based on bonds and ties other than lineage or kinship.

In various studies between *The Agrarian Sociology of Ancient Civilizations* (1909) and *Economy and Society* (1921), Weber's argument that the city as a locus of citizenship was the characteristic that made the Occident unique and his reliance on synoecism and orientalism appeared more consistently and with more urgency than his emphasis on rationalization (Käsler 1979, 42). Thus, a more detailed analysis is in order before we develop a critique.

For Weber, at first glance, the occidental city presented striking similarities to its Near and Far Eastern counterparts (1921, 1236). Like the oriental city, it was a marketplace, a center of trade and commerce and a fortified stronghold. Merchant and artisan guilds could also be found in both cities (1917, 33–35). Even the creation of autonomous legal authority could be found in both cities, though to varying degrees. Moreover, all ancient and medieval cities, like their oriental counterparts, contained some agricultural land belonging to the city. Throughout the ancient world, however, the law applicable in cities differed from rural areas. In the occidental city, particularly in the occidental medieval city, such difference was essential, whereas it was insignificant and irregular in the ancient oriental city. The ancient city almost always arose from a confluence and settling together of strangers and outsiders. While Weber used this as evidence of why the city always manifested a social and cultural differentiation, he often underlined its unity over diversity (1921, 1237). While he recognized that the urban population consisted of very diverse social groups, what was revolutionary in the occidental city was the free status of this distinct population. The fact that the city was a center of trade and commerce led rulers to free bondsmen and slaves to pursue opportunities for earning money in return for tribute (1238). The ancient occidental city arose as "a place where *the ascent from bondage to freedom* by means of monetary acquisition was possible" (1238). The principle that "city air makes man free," which emerged in central and north European cities, was an expression of the unique aspect of the occidental city. "The urban citizenry therefore usurped the right to dissolve the bonds of seigniorial domination; this was the great—in fact, the *revolutionary*—innovation which differentiated the medieval occidental cities from all others" (1239). Through time, however, in many of the European cities, patrician families became differentiated from the rest of the citizens and coalesced into a powerful class of knightly nobility. The feudal nobility settled in rural areas and did not acknowledge the knightly nobility based in cities. Nevertheless, the internal differentiation of the medieval city continued with more intensity and fierceness than the differentiation between urban and rural nobility. Hence, "At the close of the middle ages and at the beginning of modern times, nearly all Italian, English, French and German cities—insofar as they had not become monarchical city states as in Italy—were ruled by a council-patriciate or a citizen corporation which was exclusive towards the outside and a regime of notables internally" (1240). The common quality of the ancient polis and the medieval commune was therefore an association of citizens subject to a special law exclusively applicable to them. In ancient Asia, Africa, or America, similar formations of polis or commune constitutions or corporate citizenship rights were not known.

Despite his emphasis on the internal differentiation of the occidental city, however, when Weber made comparisons with the oriental city, he overlooked its differentiation in favor of a unity signified by its corporate status: "The fully developed ancient and medieval city was above all constituted, or at least interpreted, as a fraternal association, as a rule equipped with a corresponding religious symbol for the associational cult of the citizens: a city-god or city-saint to whom only the citizens had access" (1921, 1241). A significant difference between the occidental city and the ancient oriental city was that in the former there was no trace of magical and animistic castes. It was the belief of ancient citizens that their cities originated as free associations and confederations of tribes (1242). But Weber never explained why the beliefs of the ancient Greek citizens should be taken as given. That the polis was a settling together of tribes was *their* narrative. Weber incorporated this narrative with a twofold move: first, he considered synoecism as the origins of cities; and, second, he interpreted the rise of the plebs as the origins of citizenship. So while the polis was a confederation of noble families and was religiously exclusive in its origins, it was later to dissolve clan ties and invent citizenship. Weber saw an identical trajectory in the occidental medieval city, especially in the south, which was originally, for Weber, a federation of noble families. Yet the entry of the plebs into citizenship lessened the significance of membership in clans or tribes; rather, membership was defined along spatial and occupational lines. Yet, the ancient polis never became a fraternized association. Weber maintained that in fact it was on its way to becoming an association, but it was incorporated into the Hellenistic and Roman kingdoms. "The medieval city, by contrast, was a commune from the very beginning, even though the legal concept of the 'corporation' as such was only gradually formulated" (1243). As we shall see later, this was not the case.

Weber thus believed that in the ancient oriental city, the magical and clan ties persisted regularly, while in Greek poleis and medieval cities, they were progressively dissolved and replaced by spatial and occupational relationships. In Greek poleis this becomes visible beginning with colonization, which required the settling together of strangers and outsiders to become citizens. As well, the change in the martial organization of the polis from heroic warfare to hoplitic warfare intensified the dissolution of clan ties. Although many Greek poleis maintained such ties for a long time, they became more ritualistic and less significant in the everyday life of politics. Similarly, the warrior associations of the wandering Germanic tribes in Europe after the fall of the Roman Empire were organized around leadership and martial prowess, rather than clan ties. The development of spatial units such as the "hundreds" as a method of distributing obligations impeded a clan development. "When Christianity became the religion of these peoples who had been so profoundly shaken in all their traditions, it finally destroyed whatever religious significance these clan ties retained; perhaps, indeed, it was precisely the weakness or absence of such magical and taboo barriers which made the conversion possible. The often very significant role played by the parish community in the administrative organization of medieval cities is only one of many symptoms pointing to this quality of the Christian religion which, in dissolving clan ties, importantly shaped the medieval city" (Weber 1921, 1244). By contrast, the oriental city never really dissolved the tribal and clan ties.

For Weber all cities in world history were founded by the settling together of strangers and outsiders previously alien to that space. Chinese, Mesopotamian, Egyptian, Mycenaean, Minoan kings founded cities, relocated them, and in them settled immigrants and recruited people. In such cities the king who controlled the warfare apparatus retained absolute power. An association failed to develop and the urban residents maintained their tribal identities (Weber 1921, 1244). "Under such circumstances no legal status of urban citizenship arose, but only an association for sharing the burdens and privileges of those who happened to inhabit the city at any given time" (1245). In the ancient polis, membership in one of the tribal associations remained a distinguishing mark of the citizen with full rights, entitled to participate in the religious cult and qualified for all offices that required communication with the gods. The ancient tribe remained an association insofar as it was artificially created rather than being an expression of descent or lineage. The north European medieval cities were different. The resident joined the citizenry as an individual, and as an individual swore the oath of citizenship (1246). His membership was not in a tribe or clan, but in a city association. All the same, both ancient and medieval cities were able to extend citizenship to outsiders. "In all Asian cities, including the Near Eastern ones, the phenomenon of a 'commune' was either absent altogether or, at best, present only in rudiments which, moreover, always took the form of kin-group associations that extended also beyond the city" (1248).

The majority of Weber's interpretations on Islam, India, Judea, China, and the Near East rely on separate studies he undertook on these cultures, and thus each requires more detailed discussion. Although Weber did not undertake a special study on Islam comparable to those of Judaism, China, and India, which we shall discuss below, he made several scattered but significant comments on Islamic cities. Bryan Turner (1974) has undertaken the most penetrating analysis of these scattered comments. For Weber, it was the urban piety of certain status groups— artisans and merchants—in autonomous cities that was characteristic of the rise of European capitalism (Turner 1974, 94). While Christianity played a fundamental part in the development of the associational character of the occidental city, Islam impeded the development of such a character with its emphasis on clan and kinship (97). So, in oriental cities one finds a collection of distinct and separate clan and tribal groups that do not join in common action, a tribalism that Christianity helped break in Europe. "The internal development of a rich and autonomous guild and associational life within the city was closely connected with the legal and political freedom of the city from the interference of the patrimonial, or feudal officials. Not only were cities legal persons, they were also independent political agents" (97). They fought wars, concluded treaties, and made alliances. Their autonomy was fundamentally connected with their martial independence. "It was in the city that urban piety, legal autonomy, occupational associations and political involvement developed;

hence, the autonomous city had very important connections with the rise of European capitalism. In Islam, Weber argued, it was the combination of a warrior religiosity with patrimonialism which limited the growth of autonomous cities and which in consequence precluded the growth of urban piety within the lower middle classes" (98).

For Turner, although Weber mistakenly overstated the importance of the warrior nobles in shaping Islamic ethos, contemporary historical research gives ample evidence for Weber's thesis that Islamic cities were internally fissiparous and externally controlled by patrimonial rulers. "The result was that Islamic cities did not produce a rich life of independent burgher associations" (98).

But was the ostensible fissiparousness of the Islamic city any more divisive than the factionalism of the polis or the medieval city? Turner agrees with Weber that it was, arguing that the fact that Islamic cities were aggregates of subcommunities rather than socially unified communities is illustrated by the very geography of the great cities of Islam, Cairo, Damascus, Aleppo, and Baghdad. These cities were divided into quarters or districts and each district had its homogeneous community and markets. The social solidarity of these districts, or "villages" within cities, sometimes reflected the religious identity of its inhabitants (Turner 1974, 99–100). "As Weber rightly observed, the continuity of clan and tribal organization within the city context imported rural feuding arrangements into urban life" (100). The city was the focal point of Islamic government, trade, and religion, yet this focal point of Islamic culture lacked corporate institutions, a civic culture, and a set of socially binding forces. Urban life was a precarious balance of social forces, a balance of contending quarters, sedentarized tribes, sects, and legal schools (103). "Islamic guilds were not, therefore, organizations created by workmen to protect themselves and their craft; they were organizations created by the state to supervise the craft and workmen and above all to protect the state from autonomous institutions" (103). The guilds were a facet of patrimonial control. The Islamic city lacked "group feeling" and also failed to provide corporate institutions that would protect individuals (104). But, as Southall (1998, 228–29) emphasizes, this sharp distinction overlooks some structural similarities between Islamic guilds and their occidental counterparts. While guilds as self-governing and self-regulating bodies, controlling standards of production, conditions of work, and criteria of entry, did not exist in Islamic cities, local authorities on behalf and by appointment of the ruler were required to control occupations by enlisting the help of guild leaders and notables (Southall 1998, 228). In many cities this led to craft and merchant guilds in which local notables, just like their occidental counterparts, exercised power and exerted control.

Similarly, Eldem, Goffman, and Masters (1999) argue against Weber's typology of cities in the context of the Ottoman city. In their studies they have found that "there does not exist a *typical* Ottoman, Arab, or Islamic city that imposes fundamentally unique and thus ghettoizing characteristics upon all such urban centers and their inhabitants" (15). Moreover, they also found that the civic unity that was ostensibly missing in the Ottoman city was present albeit in different forms and there were already syncretic and hybridized civic cultures: "The colonies of Europeans in early modern Istanbul (the labyrinthine Galata and Pera), Izmir (the exposed Street of the Franks), and Aleppo (the semi-fortified khans) each took different forms as they followed the distinctive cultural controls of their particular milieus" (15). As a result, such outsider groups not only enriched each of these Ottoman cities but also contributed to the formation of a particular civic culture. As more studies become available, clearly the orientalist picture of Islamic cities will undergo radical transformation.

Weber recognized that craft and merchant guilds existed in India during the period in which the great salvation religions originated. The position of the guilds was quite comparable to that occupied by guilds in the cities of the medieval Occident. But "The uniqueness of the development of India lay in the fact that these beginnings of guild organization in the cities led neither to the city autonomy of the occidental type nor, after the development of the great patrimonial states, to a social and economic organization of the territories corresponding to the 'territorial economy' of the Occident" (1917, 33). Instead, a caste system developed that was totally different from that of the merchant and craft guilds in at least three respects. First, the caste system regulated the social distance between members of different castes, and membership was essentially hereditary (34–35). Second, that apprentices socialized in the guilds of the Occident under a master enabled the transition of the children to occupations other than those of their parents. Third, despite violent struggles among themselves, the guilds in the Occident displayed a tendency toward fraternization (35). Castes, however, made fraternization impossible because of inviolable barriers against commensalism (36).

For Weber this last difference—fraternization—between the caste and guild was decisive, leading him to make perhaps his clearest statement about the origins of occidental citizenship. Weber mentions a letter by Paul to the Galatians in which Paul reproaches Peter for having eaten in

Antioch with the Gentiles and for having withdrawn and separated himself afterward. For Weber this emphasis on shattering the ritual barriers and refusing to regard any people as pariah means the origins of commensalism are specifically Christian, which cut across nations and groups. "The elimination of all ritual barriers of birth for the community of the eucharists, as realized in Antioch, was, in connection with the religious pre-conditions, the hour of conception for the occidental 'citizenry.' This is the case even though its birth occurred more than a thousand years later in the revolutionary *coniurationes* of the medieval cities. For without commensalism—in Christian terms, without the Lord's Supper—no oathbound fraternity and no medieval urban citizenry would have been possible" (1917, 37–38).

As regards the Chinese civilization, for Weber, cities were a major impediment to the development of capitalism, despite the fact that many other conditions were already there for its development. But ancient cities and medieval cities and emerging states in the Occident were vehicles of financial rationalization, of a money economy, and of politically oriented capitalism. "In China, there were no cities like Florence which could have created a standard coin and guided that state in monetary policies" (1916, 13). For Weber, "In contrast to the Occident, the cities in China and throughout the Orient lacked political autonomy. The oriental city was not a 'polis' in the sense of Antiquity, and it knew nothing of the 'city law' of the Middle Ages, for it was not a 'commune' with political privileges of its own" (13).

The cities in the Orient never aimed at gaining a charter that might, at least in a negative way, guarantee the freedom of the city. "This was hardly possible along occidental lines because the fetters of the sib were never shattered. The new citizen, above all the newly rich one, retained his relations to the native place of his sib, its ancestral land and temple" (1916, 14). While craft and merchant guilds developed in Chinese cities, they never coalesced into an oath-bound political association formed by an armed citizenry. The city could not function as a corporate body.

Weber explained this in terms of the different origins of the occidental and oriental city. The ancient polis originated as an overseas trading city, however strong its base in landlordism. But China was predominantly an inland area. The prosperity of the Chinese city did not depend upon the enterprising spirit of its citizens in economic and political ventures, but rather upon the imperial administration, especially the administration of rivers. On this point, Weber remarked that just as in Egypt the sign of government is the Pharaoh holding the lash in his hand, so the Chinese character identifies governing with the handling of a stick (1916, 16). But the essential point is that "[o]ur occidental bureaucracy is of recent origin and its past has been learned from the experiences of the autonomous city states. The imperial bureaucracy of China is very ancient" (16).

Ultimately, the legal foundations beneficial to the development of capitalism were absent in China because the cities and guilds had no politico-martial capital of their own. Chinese authorities repeatedly reverted to liturgical controls, but they failed to create a system of guild privileges comparable to that of the West during the Middle Ages. The lack of political associational character of the city in turn was explained by the early development of a bureaucratic organization in the army and civil administration (Weber 1916, 20).

To conclude, the occidental city was foremost a sworn confraternity and for Weber this *was* the decisive basis for the development of capitalism. Everywhere it became a territorial corporation and officials became officials of this institution. The occidental city was an institutionalized association in which the citizen was an active creator of law to which he was subject. For the medieval city to develop into a sworn association, two circumstances were of central importance. First, at a time when the economic interests of citizens urged them toward an association, this was not frustrated by magic or religious barriers. Second, a broader power enforcing the interests of a larger association was absent (Weber 1921, 1249). While Weber saw essential affinities between the ancient Greco-Roman polis and the medieval corporation, he believed that the latter diverged from the former by being a confraternity exclusively devoted to peaceful means of acquisition, rather than warfare. Ultimately, that is why economic capitalism would emerge rather than being stifled by the political capitalism of the ancient polis (Love 1991).

Weber isolated two types of medieval corporation: spontaneous and derived. The spontaneous corporation emerged as a political association of citizens in defiance of legitimate powers. Formal recognition by these powers came only later. The derived corporation was formed by such powers as a result of a charter or grant of limited and limiting rights. The latter existed right from the beginning of the eleventh and twelfth centuries, while the former came only later (1921, 1250). Many large medieval cities were ostensibly constituted as "spontaneous" associations through swearing an oath of citizenship (1250–51).

The real home of de facto or spontaneous corporations as sworn confraternization was Italy (Weber 1921, 1252). The meaning of sworn confraternity can therefore best be understood by analyzing medieval Italian cities. Many early associations in the city were formed with fixed duration to be dissolved at the end of its period, for example, in Genoa, while others were indefinite but could be dissolved. A permanent confraternity was formed only when all those groups that claimed authority and usurped martial capital in the city were included. The confraternity was above all a *unification* of all local landowners. It was formalized for the purposes of defense, settling disputes, and administration of justice. Other purposes included the regulation of trade and commerce. Only the members of the corporation could engage in trade and commerce in the city. The city association also determined the obligation owed to the lord and the martial organization. Masses of citizens were forced to join the sworn confraternization. "The noble and patrician families, which had founded the association would administer an oath to all inhabitants qualified by land-ownership; those who did not agree to take it were forced into exile" (1253). The initial *coniurationes* still observed political and legal feudal ranks and customs, but soon abandoned them in favor of distinctly urban political and legal customs (1253–54). The political achievement of the *coniurationes* was the dethroning of royal authority. In addition to acquiring political citizenship rights, many of them explicitly banned the building of castles near their spaces. The legal achievement of the *coniurationes* was the creation of special law that excluded irrational or traditional means of evidence and their substitution with rational evidence. Nevertheless, the urban nobility still maintained a knightly style of life and maintained ties with feudal associations (1255).

The northern European cities lacked a knightly nobility based in cities and therefore could not benefit from their martial capital to usurp power from the lords and royalty. Instead, the guild typically represented the association in the north. The guild was an association of mutual protection that clans and tribes provided in the ancient polis. The guild also provided social needs by organizing festivals, feasts, and meals (Weber 1921, 1256). The city did not originate in the guild, but the guild originated in the city. Still, in only a small number of cities, the occupational, crafts, and merchants guilds were dominant. It was mostly noble families that seized power initially. Also, guilds were not the only associations in the city. Religious associations were also important (1257). These diverse associations habituated the citizens in forming coalitions in the pursuit of common interests, and by providing models for political leadership, which was entirely absent in the ancient or medieval oriental city (1258). The confraternization of these varied, overlapping, and at times conflicting occupational, religious, crafts, and merchants guilds and associations did not occur smoothly or similarly in many medieval cities. But once confraternities began usurping powers, they spread throughout Europe with relative uniformity as the charters and grants that were used to seize power from the royal and feudal authorities were copied and imitated throughout (1259). Among the most important achievements of this movement were autonomous law and administration. In the beginning, active membership in the association was bound up with possessions of urban land, which was inheritable and transferable. Later other kinds of property also became subject to municipal taxation (1260). Thus was born modern occidental citizenship.

Against Weber

We have isolated synoecism and orientalism as perspectives from which Weber interpreted the origins of the occidental city and citizenship. For Weber, that the development of the city as a locus of citizenship was impeded in the Orient by the presence of magic ties of the sib association was as much his premise as his conclusion. He approached ancient China already "knowing" that the sibs were the bearers of central religious concerns and were very powerful. He approached ancient India already assuming that the castes were carriers of a specific style of life, and that they determined the individual's fate. While he recognized that the clan and sib ties were not as powerful in the ancient Near East as they were in ancient India and China, he still saw them as impediments to the emergence of confraternity. As Turner (1996, 268) argued, Weber's studies on Islam, India, China, and Judea were not isolated, original, or innovative researches, but developed in the context of an established and prestigious tradition of orientalism. Weber's increasingly urgent and obstinate search for the origins of modern capitalism was situated in a general understanding of an ontological difference between the Orient and the Occident. Orientalism guided Weber to draw sharper and sharper distinctions between occidental and oriental cities and, in the process, provided a unified and homogeneous account of both. Citizenship became both the embodiment and the expression of the uniqueness of the occidental city. This ontological orientation meant that Weber never acknowledged that kinship and magic ties were never fully dissolved in ancient poleis and civitates or medieval cities, and that factionalism and fissiparousness were endemic conditions in both. As we shall see, the ancient Greek poleis and Roman civitates maintained their clans and tribes. Even in later stages, membership was a mixture of clan and kinship ties, as well as occupational and spatial ones. Ultimately, the intensity of familial and religious ties persisted in the city. The European medieval city, too, especially in the south, was essentially a federation of noble families. The harmony and unity attributed to the ancient polis and medieval corporations in Weber's work overlooked the otherness of citizenship, its strangers and outsiders. Being a quintessential citizen himself (for Weber described himself as a bourgeois, i.e., a citizen), perhaps he was not nearly as skeptical and questioning about the narratives passed down to him by citizens and so did not consider it a problem to bequeath the same.

For Weber the second main reason for the absence of the city as a sworn association in the Orient was the monopolization of martial capital. The necessity of river regulation and an irrigation policy in the Near East, Egypt, and China led to the development of royal bureaucracies, which monopolized martial capital. The royal administration recruited, equipped, and fed the soldier, and the soldier was separated from the ownership of martial capital (Weber 1921, 1261). Under such conditions, an association of citizens capable of usurping power from the king was not possible. In other words, martial capital that enabled the ancient and medieval landowning groups to dethrone the king was not available to the landowning groups in the ancient Orient. By contrast, the presence of self-equipped armies in the Occident meant that the king was much more reliant on the loyalty of his warriors than on an army constituted of soldiers employed by a royal administration.

This thesis of the persistence and omnipotence of theocratic government in the Orient was crystallized later in the twentieth century as "oriental despotism" (Wittfogel 1957). From this perspective, the necessity of irrigation and water regulation in Mesopotamia, Egypt, India, and China, which required financing and coordinating large projects and disciplining masses of men, forced the development of a ruling class responsible for these activities. These large-scale undertakings enabled the kings and the ruling classes to monopolize martial capital and to build bureaucratic administrations. Warriors simply became soldiers who were the officers of the royal army, which through the monopoly of force dominated subjects. In other words, the rule of the king and the royal bureaucracy was, though not total, omnipotent. Under such conditions, although certain rights were secured by the subjects, neither an association of subjects as citizens nor a special status for them was possible (Weber 1921, 1261). But the "explanations" of "oriental despotism" arising from the necessity of irrigation and the rise and persistence of a theocracy are now empirically questioned and the foundations of Weber's theses are seriously flawed (Clarke 1997; King 1999; Love 2000a, 2000b; Springborg 1992). But this is not the argument we shall follow and elaborate upon.

Weber contra Weber

This critique of Weber's orientalism and synoecism does not necessarily mean rejecting his historical sociological investigations. As both Turner (1996, 285) and Dean (1994, 89–90, 91) recognized, in his empirical investigations, Weber was often nuanced, subtle, and, above all, pluralistic and sensitive to internal differentiations of the city. He also struggled to break away from both orientalism and synoecism. In fact, as Colognesi (1995) recognized, a significant shift occurs between *The Agrarian Sociology of Ancient Civilizations* (1909) and *Economy and Society* (1921). Colognesi correctly noted that Weber considered ancient and medieval cities closer to each other in 1920 than in 1909, placing more emphasis on structural similarities between them than on their differences. The "later" Weber apparently became more urgently concerned with establishing essential differences between the occidental and oriental cities than with drawing out differences and similarities between different types of cities. In this, the later Weber seems to have gone against his better judgment. A note on method hastily added to his 1909 account, almost as an afterthought, suggested that "[a] genuinely analytic study comparing the stages of development of the ancient polis with those of the medieval city would be welcome and productive. . . . Of course . . . such a comparative study would not aim at finding 'analogies' and 'parallels,' as is done by those engrossed in the currently fashionable enterprise of constructing general schemes of development. The aim should, rather, be precisely the opposite: to identify and define the individuality of each development, the characteristics which made the one conclude in a manner so different from that of the other. This done, one can then determine the causes which led to these differences" (1909, 385). That Weber failed to follow his own methodological orientations raises a number of questions about the excessive focus in the twentieth century on his methods, assuming that there was a straightforward homology between his investigations and his methodological writings.

If we reject Weber's orientalism and synoecism but recognize that his historical sociological investigations still remain refreshingly provocative, especially on ancient Greek, Roman, and medieval European cities and citizenship as the foundation of modern capitalism, it seems there are two avenues open for us. First, we could retrace the steps of Weber, beginning with his early sociology of ancient citizenship, and identify the individuality of each city-citizenship type, in a manner he suggested above, by taking into account the most recent specialist scholarship, and critically updating and revising his findings. To be blunt, after years of emphasis on his theses of rationalization, religion, and capitalism, this would be a refreshing avenue to follow (see Springborg 1992). In fact, viewed from the historical sociological investigations he undertook, later controversies among the specialist historians in the twentieth century, whether it is the Hans Baron thesis on the "civic humanism" of fifteenth-century Florence or the controversies surrounding the rule of peasants in fifth-century Athens, Weber indeed appears prescient, sophisticated, and purposeful because of his "comparative" ethos.

Second, while building on Weber's specific and concrete histories, we could not only critically interrogate them, but also alter the question that framed these histories, asking how and against whom citizenship was defined as a group identity and what kinds of strategies and technologies of citizenship were assembled to make citizens, strangers, and outsiders.

Being Political attempts to follow the second avenue. It develops a critique of the founding narrative of citizenship with its twin assumptions of synoecism and orientalism. Rather than taking the Orient as its frame of reference for comparison, it develops an interpretive analytics of groups and explores forms of citizenship defined against its strangers and outsiders in different configurations of space, from the polis to the cosmopolis. To put it differently, rather than taking the narratives provided by citizens as given and rather than comparing citizens with barbarians and aliens, *Being Political* investigates the immanent strangers and outsiders of the city. What follows is a brief outline of its underlying interpretive analytics and the sources it draws from.

Ways of Being Political: Solidaristic, Agonistic, Alienating

That human beings struggle for recognition and that in doing so form associations with other human beings, and that by virtue of this sociation they group themselves and others need not be a universal or transcendental conception. It is how a specific—occidental—experience has been interpreted beginning with the ancient Greeks. It is an interpretation of that experience that constituted human beings as social and political beings—social because such association has been considered an inescapable condition of being human, and political because human beings have become "conscious" of this condition, and hence have constituted themselves as agents capable of changing it. As yet, whether we wish it or not, we cannot step outside that experience. But we can interrogate and problematize it, call its unity, naturalness, and continuity into question, and interpret that interpretation itself as a game (Bourdieu 1980; Tully 1999, 162–63). To do so required an analytics of groups that, while drawing upon that experience, enabled our investigations to expose and stretch its limits.

That is perhaps why investigating social groups—how human beings associate with each other to form assemblages with meaning, durability, and borders—has been one of the most troubling questions of social and political thought. Two questions have particularly troubled thought from Aristotle and Baldus de Ubaldis to Simmel, Tajfel, and Bourdieu. Do groups possess properties that are different in any significant way from the aggregate of the properties of individuals? This first question concerns whether agents can attribute meanings to groups. Do groups have some of the properties of individuals, such as continuity, identity, and conduct through time and space? (Harré 1993). This second question concerns whether agents can attribute action to groups. To what extent can we consider groups acting on each other? Under what conditions do human beings associate with each other and form groups and how do these groups generate sources of self? To these questions two answers have been most dominant: an individualist view that denies the existence of groups and a collectivist view that denies the autonomous actions of individuals. Without developing a relational conception of group formation that rejects both individualism and collectivism, genealogical investigations on citizenship as alterity encounter irresolvable difficulties.

Groups as Solidaristic Multiplicities

Although it is true that, in the last analysis, individuals interact with individuals, they do not necessarily interact with each other as individuals, but as members of either well-defined, or in the process of being defined, social groups (Tajfel 1981, 228). It is equally impossible to find instances where there are purely interpersonal (any social encounter between two or more individuals in which all interaction is determined by their respective individual characteristics) or intergroup (any encounter between individuals that is determined by their membership in different social groups) relationships. Rather, differences in terms of the nature of the relationship between and among individuals always lie somewhere between these two impossible extremes (Tajfel 1981, 240). Being political is inconceivable in these two extremes as the former generates an image of an individual without affiliations and the latter an image of automatons.

Yet, to say that multiple identifications form the basis of groups makes matters more complex. The number and variety of situations that an individual will perceive as being relevant in some ways to her group identity increases when she recognizes an available group identification, the extent of the positive or negative evaluations associated with this identification, and the extent of economic, social, cultural, and symbolic capital invested in it (Tajfel 1981, 239). Moreover, there are certain situations where individuals are forced, coerced, compelled, cajoled, or ensnared into group identifications, however weak and unimportant to them may be their initial affiliation. By contrast, other situations can function as agents of activation or creation of group identifications by mobilizing certain attributes or properties of the agent (239). Such strategies as coercion, mobilization, stigmatization, seduction, or excommunication, or technologies such as enrollment, membership, or assembly implicates agents in games of recognition, affiliation, association, and dissociation with political consequences insofar as their conduct is shaped through them.

That is why the definition of being social provided by Mead as "the capacity of being several things at once" can be extended to being political (1932, 49). In fact, perhaps paradoxically, the more social a being is the more personal *and* political she becomes (Simmel 1922, 138–40). As Simmel observes, "the larger the number of groups to which an individual belongs, the more improbable is it that other persons will exhibit the same combination of group-affiliations, that these particular groups will 'intersect' once again in another individual" (140). This is perhaps the sense in which each individual is unique: "As the person affiliated with a social group, he surrenders himself to it. A synthesis of such subjective affiliations creates a group in an objective sense. But the person also regains his individuality, because his pattern of participation is unique" (141). Multiple group affiliations therefore become tactical resources through which individuals activate distinction and constitute uniqueness through strategies (intentional but nonsubjective orientations) and technologies (mechanisms and instruments of the conduct of conduct) in which they are implicated. Hence individuality is "that particular set of constituent elements which in their quality and combination make up the individual" (141).

Thus, while groups are certainly formed by social and political beings, under what conditions do the affiliations that constitute their beings arise? As Elias observes, "The problem is how and why human beings perceive one another as belonging to the same group and include one another within the group boundaries which they establish when saying 'we' in their reciprocal communications, while at the same time excluding other human beings whom they perceive as belonging to another group and to whom they collectively refer as 'they'" (1976, xxxvii). But Elias invokes the logics of exclusion and enclosure as the foundations of alterity. By contrast, from a relational perspective, social categorization and classification are systems of orientation and stakes in the struggles that create and situate individuals in certain positions *within* the social space. The logics of alterity embody differentiation and distinction, not only as strategies of exclusion, but as strategies of elective affiliation, recognition, incorporation, and congregation. Moreover, strategies and technologies are not always or even only toward affiliation, but also dissociation and even estrangement (Lévinas 1999). While the struggle for recognition and sources of the self and esteem arise from identifications and affiliations always under certain systems of classification and categorization, these systems often embody a combination of solidaristic, agonistic, and alienating strategies and technologies. Elias is, therefore, closer to the mark when he suggests that between two groups, "If the power differential is great enough, a member of an established group may be quite indifferent to what outsiders think about him or her, but it is hardly ever indifferent to the opinion of insiders—of those who have access to power resources in whose monopolistic control he or she participates or seeks to participate and with whom he or she shares a common pride in the group, a common group charisma" (1976, xl).

The conditions for solidaristic, agonistic, and alienating assemblages— how strategies and technologies such as affiliation, identification, dissociation, and misrecognition are assembled—are therefore matters of genealogical investigation and cannot be determined theoretically.

Groups as Agonistic Multiplicities

While it is possible that "a collection of individuals who perceive themselves to be members of the same social category, share some emotional involvement in this common definition of themselves, and achieve some degree of social consensus about the evaluation of their group and their membership in it" (Tajfel 1982, 485), such a consensus is neither the primary nor the only basis of a group. Agonistic encounters arise from multiple-group affiliations because either in their means or ends, several social groups may overlap. What determines the intensity of agonism engendered by such encounters is whether the groups an individual is affiliated with are concentric or overlapping. Either way, the formation of social groups requires the presence and recognition of other groups, which give rise to solidaristic, agonistic, and alienating orientations simultaneously. The danger with accepting an ostensible consensus as the basis of a group is that whether a group exists or not is itself an instrument of social struggle (Becker 1966). Agon, or contest, can be more significant than consensus as a basis for group formation. For this reason a distinction made by Bourdieu between classification struggles (in which different individuals argue for or against the existence of certain groups in society) and group struggles (in which individuals struggle for recognition and their interests) is an important analytical distinction. While these two types of struggle reinforce and overlap with each other, they cannot be reduced to each other. Failing to distinguish them results in either objectivism or subjectivism.

How do we then recognize the presence or absence of social groups and whether they have active or passive properties? There have been two prevalent approaches to answering this question and it is useful to identify them as ways of *avoiding* how to think about groups. Objectivism assumes that the classification of individuals into groups on the basis of criteria or attributes such as occupation, sexuality, ethnicity, race, employment, income, or education can correspond to groups as they exist in reality. Objectivism leads to varieties of essentialism where certain categories of individuals are expected to act according to their properties, such as being "black," "Hispanic," or "woman." Subjectivism assumes that individuals classify themselves according to their consciousness of the social world, as though there is a sovereign will to determine one's own position in social space and that will is conscious of that choice. Both views hypostatize groups with discrete boundaries and properties. Yet, social groups are not things but relations. As Tajfel states with some flair, the existence of a group for its members is a "complex sequence of appearances and disappearances, of looming large and vanishing into thin air" (1982, 485). Groups never exist statically as given, but they come into existence when their potential designations as such have acquired a reality. Moreover, a group defined by outsiders, which may have no meaning for its members, and one that has a meaning for them may not correspond to each other. A robust distinction between *hypothetical* and *real* groups becomes crucial for investigating citizenship and its alterities.

As discussed, objectivism treats individuals as objects that can be classified, while subjectivism denies the real existence of groups unless individuals have consciousness of such groups. From the objectivist perspective, groups as described by categories and classifications exist in reality. The difficulty with this is, as many scholars have shown, that the variety of individuals in the real world becomes impossible to classify into discrete groups. This difficulty in classification then leads some to claim that there are no real social differences among individuals and that there is no such thing as social groups. Thus, Bourdieu is correct to claim that those who argue that groups exist in reality and those who argue that groups are nothing other than analytical constructs actually hold the same notion of reality as directly given to the intuition of everyday experience. By contrast, "it is possible to deny the existence of groups as homogeneous sets of economically and socially differentiated individuals objectively constituted into groups, and to assert at the same time the existence of a space of differences based on a principle of economic and social differentiation" (Bourdieu 1987, 3). If so, how does one proceed, especially with a historical analysis of group formation?

The distinction between hypothetical and real groups is necessary: the former is the work of symbolic or classification struggles, while the latter is the result of the practical and political work of organizing and mobilizing. Any homology between groups as hypothetical constructs and groups as real entities is a result of both conceptual and practical work. The hypothetical group can be characterized as a group of individuals who, by virtue of their similar social positions, experience similar conditions of existence and are endowed with similar dispositions. The conceptual work classifies these individuals who, being subject to similar conditions, tend to affiliate with each other and are inclined to perceive themselves as members of a group, to assemble as a group, and thus to reinforce their affiliations and identifications. But such an assembly is the practical and political work of organizing and mobilizing. Just because an authority can empirically classify individuals does not mean that these individuals will act as a group struggling through strategies and technologies. Marx did make such a distinction but did not follow it through consistently. He assumed the practical existence of hypothetical groups, while such groups must be seen as only probable real groups whose constituent individuals are likely to be brought together and mobilized on the basis of their similar dispositions (Bourdieu 1987, 6–7). All the labor of group making involves a recognition that a group as such does not exist, that groups form only as a result of specific practical work, but that such work is likely to succeed only when it is supported by real experiences.

Aware that Marx had made such an important distinction but had not followed it through, Weber (1918, 287–88) appears to have used a more robust conception of groups. For Weber, group formation is inextricably bound up with relations of power, defined as the possibility of an agent or a group of agents to realize their will in a social action, even against the resistance of others who are participating in the action. Weber also recognized forms of capital other than economic to be constitutive of social groups. "On the contrary, the emergence of economic power may be the consequence of power existing on other grounds. Man does not strive for power only in order to enrich himself economically" (1921, 926–40). As is well known, Weber conceived that relations of power materialize through at least three spheres: juridical, economic, and social. At the intersection of these three spheres, each individual occupies a situation that conditions his life chances for accumulating wealth, gaining status, and exercising power. A group for Weber is neither a community nor a category, but a possible basis for social action. A group arises when a number of people share similar (but not identical) life chances and own capital under the conditions of commodity or labor markets. Because Weber argues that the market is the decisive element, which presents a common condition for life chances, the ownership of property becomes crucial. While a robust conception of groups seems latent in Weber, he did not elaborate his theoretical conception of social groups any further (Scott 1996).

To sum, a group could be said to exist only "when there are agents capable of imposing themselves, as authorized to speak and to act officially in its place and in its name, upon those who, by recognizing themselves in these plenipotentiaries, by recognizing them as endowed with full power to speak and act in their name, recognize themselves as members of the group, and in doing so, confer upon it the only form of existence a group can possess" (Bourdieu 1987, 15). It is through the work of representation that individuals impose their vision of the world or the vision of their own position in that world toward developing their identification with or membership in a group. In the reality of the social world, in the everyday experiences of individuals, there are no clear group boundaries. Group identifications or affiliations and disassociation or differentiations are multiple, fluid, and overlapping. The institutionalization of organizations capable of representing different groups tends to create more durable, recognizable, and visible group boundaries. The struggles of everyday life become political struggles through a presentation of self that draws from various group identifications. As we shall see, symbolic power is crucial in politicizing struggles. Symbolic power is the power to make groups and to consecrate or institute them in particular through various strategies and technologies. It is the power to make something exist in the objectified, public, or formal state, which only previously existed in an implicit or embodied state; this happens only when the group is named, designated, or selected as such (Becker 1966). The power of naming usually comes with the power of representing since the group must now be represented with its organizations, leaders, and spokespersons. Groups can never be homogenous and unified entities with an absolute overlap of interests among their constituent members. Even solidaristic assemblages are internally differentiated and are afflicted by agonistic assemblages. The harmony, unity, and homogeneity that are attributed to groups are always a result of its dominant members being able to inculcate such a vision and represent the group as harmonious. In fact, the more internally differentiated a group becomes, the more its dominant segment becomes interested in differentiating itself from other groups. This is the fundamental reason why we must be skeptical about claims made by citizens about the harmony, unity, and homogeneity of the polity they claim to represent.

Alterity: Citizens, Strangers, Outsiders, Aliens

At the core of investigating citizenship as alterity, then, lies a relational conception of group formation. Solidaristic, agonistic, and alienating strategies and technologies constitute ways of being political insofar as they enable agents to take up positions via each other and articulate forms of sociation and identification. These relationships are not simply inclusory or exclusory but dialogical. Ways of becoming political, such as being citizens, strangers, outsiders, and aliens, do not exist in themselves, but only in relation to each other. While we may agree with Elias that "Much can be gained from a better understanding of the dynamics of established-outsider figurations and thus of the problems involved in the changing position of groups in relation to each other, of the rise of groups into the position of monopolistic establishment from which others are excluded, and the decline or fall from such a position to another where they themselves are, in some respects, among the excluded outsiders," we must also recognize that these figurations embody not only logics of exclusion, but logics of alterity (1976, xliv–xlv). We have seen that a relational perspective on group formation insists that no social group forms in isolation from others, and therefore the processes underlying the ways in which it *constitutes* itself with other groups are crucial to the manner in which it is defined by its members (Tajfel 1981, 165). Different social groups always orient toward each other and form their identities from this orientation (Tajfel 1981, 223). The fate of one social group is inextricably tied to that of at least one other, and often many others.

We have also argued that group identity does not exist as an immutable or given fact of life. It is created out of social realities, it changes with them, and it always includes views about "others" without which life narratives would lose both their meaning and their function (Tajfel 1981, 226). In the formation of groups, narrative strategies value certain attributes and devalue others. These values become virtues in the process of the construction of myths and images, and of what is feasible in the undertaking of action. The result is the achievement of certain positionings toward other groups and the strategic government of its internal differentiations. Group identity is that part of an individual's self-image that derives from his knowledge of his membership in a social group (or groups), together with the value and emotional significance attached to that membership (Tajfel 1981, 255).

While the logics of exclusion would have us believe in zero-sum, discrete, and binary groups, the logics of alterity assume overlapping, fluid, contingent, dynamic, and reversible boundaries and positions, where agents engage in solidaristic strategies such as recognition and affiliation, agonistic strategies such as domination and authorization, or alienating strategies such as disbarment across various positions *within* social space. The logics of exclusion would have us believe that the formation of identity involves establishing opposites and others whose actuality is always subject to the continuous interpretation and articulation of their difference from the group (Lévinas 1978, 156–62). But the logic of exclusion based on establishing opposite others is only one among countless strategies open to the formation of identities. That is why it is important to distinguish between the logics of alterity that constitute strangers and outsiders as immanent identities and the logics of exclusion and enclosure that constitute aliens or barbarians as transitive or exterior identities (Lévinas 1969, 212–14).

To investigate citizenship as alterity, certain categories of otherness that make citizenship itself possible must be considered, which are grouped into three overlapping but distinct forms: strangers, outsiders, and aliens. For Simmel the stranger is not a wanderer who comes today and goes tomorrow, but rather one who comes today and stays tomorrow (1908c, 143). This conception of the stranger captures its principle of immanence, its interiority to social space. The stranger is the potential wanderer, who although an insider, interacts as though he is an outsider. If wandering is detachment from a particular place, belonging is its opposite, attachment to a place, and estrangement is a synthesis of attachment and detachment, wandering and belonging. Being estranged from a group is a condition of both being a member of the group and being distant from it. This membership involves being estranged as well as being recognized. A group consolidates and stabilizes its identity by distinguishing itself from different modes of being. But the differences against which an identity consolidates itself contain their own drives to identity, and these may well take a form that will destabilize, disturb, and disrupt the security of the identity that a group seeks. For Connolly, "These alter-drives, then, are required for the stabilization of an identity, but they can also emerge as threats to the same identity. When these pressures intensify, one or both of the parties involved may move to consolidate its identity by defining a range of difference as evil, irrational, perverse, abnormal, or heretical. Identity requires difference, but difference also threatens to destabilize identity" (1993, x–xi). The stranger is near and far at the same time (Simmel 1908c, 148). Between nearness and distance a tension arises because a drive toward identity has the effect of highlighting difference.

The difference between strangers and outsiders is subtle but still significant. While both are immanent, strangers are often implicated in a combination of solidaristic and agonistic strategies and technologies, and outsiders often in a combination of agonistic and alienating strategies and technologies. As we shall see, merchants and artisans in the polis or sansculottes and workers in the metropolis are examples of strangers. While estranged from citizenship, they were nonetheless considered as belonging to the city and they could associate with citizens via solidaristic or agonistic strategies and technologies. By contrast, slaves in the polis, vagabonds in the eutopolis, or refugees in the cosmopolis were constituted as outsiders, neither belonging to the group nor interacting with it, but belonging to and necessary for the city in which citizens and strangers associated. They were typically, though not always, constituted via agonistic and alienating strategies and technologies.

By contrast, aliens constitute a category that is entirely outside the realm of sociation and association, whether solidaristic, agonistic, or alienating. The logic of exclusion constitutes others as aliens, often as transitive enemies with othering strategies. The group constitutes them as enemies and a relationship is oriented toward effacement insofar as institutional, formal, and informal mechanisms of everyday life of the group are concerned. For ancient Greeks and Romans, "barbarians" were such aliens. For modern Europeans, "orientals" have served the same purpose. For contemporary Eurocentrism, "Islam" has become its alien Other. While aliens are important to group formation and for strategies of othering, for citizenship and alterity as conditions of being political, groups constituted as aliens are of only passing concern for three reasons. First, since our focus is the immanent groups in the city, it would become unwieldy to investigate the impact of distant othering on these groups. Second, there has been overwhelming attention paid to broader categories of othering in postcolonial, oriental, and cultural studies, partly spurred by Edward Said's *Orientalism* and we have already discussed some aspects of that literature in the context of Weber's orientalism. The third reason is more theoretical and less pragmatic and concerns the notion of the political. In Western traditions of political thought there has been an overwhelming emphasis on being political based upon a friend versus enemy "dialectic," whose best known proponent was Carl Schmitt (1932a, 1932b). From our perspective, however, the friend versus enemy dialectic is in fact not a condition, but a nonrelation as far as politics is concerned. By contrast, being political means to constitute relationships between oneself and others either via affiliation and identification, or agon and estrangement. These relations are political insofar as groups orient toward each other without the intent of elimination or effacement (i.e., without constituting each other as enemies). Alienating strategies that constitute aliens and barbarians as enemies, while serving certain purposes as frames of reference and identity, are not necessarily a primary focus of the formation of political and social beings. That is also why it is unproductive to insist, as Mouffe (1998) does, on the usefulness of confronting and coming to terms with the concept of the political articulated by Schmitt (1932a). For the binary friend-enemy dialectic articulated by Schmitt as the foundation of politics is fundamentally flawed and misses the complex character of group formation. As Žižek argues, Schmitt disavows the political by his insistence on the primacy of external politics (relations between sovereign states) over internal politics (inner social antagonisms): "[I]s not the relationship to an external Other as the Enemy a way of disavowing the *internal* struggle that traverses the social body?" (1999, 241 n. 21).

That is why the analytical distinction between solidaristic, agonistic, and alienating strategies advanced here is crucial for investigating the political. While it is true that the relationships that constitute groups involve domination, that does not mean that the object of these relationships is elimination or even subservience. Whether the relationship is solidaristic (affiliation, sociation, identification), agonistic (conflict, competition, resistance, tension), or alienating (exclusion, estrangement, oppression, expulsion), it involves the conduct of conduct, or the government of the self and the other. The formation of citizens, strangers, and outsiders involves relations of power and is not a benign or innocuous process; it triggers the formation of multiple, overlapping, and conflicting wills. Foucault's Nietzschean genealogies have problematized the modern orientation to subjectivity and responsibility. Instead of viewing them as universal norms, Foucault emphasized how they are historically formed and how the maintenance of affirmative wills constantly requires the production of the other, which denies and resists them. These dualities constantly engender and sustain each other (Connolly 1993, 236). Yet, Foucault's Nietzschean genealogies typically investigated how power/knowledge constituted "strangers" and "outsiders" and overlooked the moments in which strangers and outsiders constituted themselves as being political by overturning various strategies and technologies of citizenship in which they were implicated and thereby constituted themselves differently from the dominant images given to them (Mahon 1992; Frijhoff 1999). Those moments of becoming political are also the subject of genealogical investigations in this book.

Strategies and Technologies of Citizenship

While domination is a form of interaction and fundamental to being political, among various objects of exercising power, it is often not the most important or coveted action (Simmel 1908a, 96). For when domination is absolute, when power differentials between two groups are too great, the dominant group does not need the dominated group to constitute its identity. When the power differentials are small enough and when the dominated pose a possible threat, then the dominant constitutes the dominated as an object of difference (Elias 1976, xxxi). "What makes the domination of a group, a caste, or a class, together with the resistance and revolts which that domination comes up against, a central phenomenon in the history of societies is that they manifest in a massive and universalizing form, at the level of the social body, the locking together of power relations with relations of strategy and the results proceeding from their interaction" (Foucault 1982, 226). That is when the question of government as the conduct of conduct arises and that is when being political and governmental imply each other. While domination, authority and differentiation, obedience and opposition are implicated in each other in orientations toward the other, these are often interpreted by members in other terms, such as good versus evil, virtue versus vice, black versus white, inferior versus superior, healthy versus unhealthy. Members of dominant groups aim to constitute themselves as virtuous and aim to govern the conduct of their selves and others in a manner that repels vice and encourages virtue. As we shall see later, *aristocracy* in archaic Greece meant the rule of the best (Nagy 1985). The term *noble* still retains its double meaning of higher rank and a highly valued attitude. "This is the normal self-image of groups who in terms of their power ratio are securely superior to other interdependent groups" (Elias 1976, xv). For Elias, "the more powerful groups look upon themselves as the 'better' people, as endowed with a kind of group charisma, with a specific virtue shared by all its members and lacked by the others" (xvi). The dominant groups often develop strategies and technologies to adjure the dominated to recognize that they lack virtue. For Elias the principal aspect of established-outsider figuration is that the dominant group attributes to its members superior human qualities and excludes all members of the other group from contact with its own members (1976). The existence and functioning of stereotypes illustrate the ways in which identities are formed in intergroup situations (Tajfel 1981, 225). The dominant group tends to attribute to its outsider group as a whole the "bad" characteristics of that group's worst segments or characteristics of the dominated within the dominant group, what Elias calls anomic minority (xix). By contrast, its virtuous and noble attributes derive from the dominant segments of the dominant group. But both Elias and Tajfel draw too sharp a line between the dominant and the dominated, as if, again, there were discrete and binary boundaries between them.

This way of interpreting group formation becomes clearly problematic in that most used notion of minority groups. Louis Wirth, for example, defines minority "as a group of people who, because of their physical or cultural characteristics, are singled out from the others in the society in which they live for differential and unequal treatment and who therefore regard themselves as objects of collective discrimination" (1945, 245). For Wirth, "The members of minority groups are held in lower esteem and may even be objects of contempt, hatred, ridicule, and violence. They are generally socially isolated and frequently spatially segregated" (245). However, "When the sentiments and attitude of such disadvantaged groups become articulate, when the members become conscious of their deprivations and conceive of themselves as persons having rights, and when they clamor for emancipation and equality, a minority becomes a political force to be reckoned with" (246). Noting a great variation of minority groups across the world, Wirth argues that "[i]t is not the specific characteristics, therefore, whether racial or ethnic, that mark a people as a minority but the relationship of their group to some other group in society in which they live. The same characteristics may at one time and under one set of circumstances serve as marks of dominant status and at another time and under another set of circumstances symbolize identification with a minority" (249–50). It is much more important, therefore, to understand the nature and origins of the relationship between dominant group and minority group than it is to know the marks by which people are identified as members of either. The development of an adequate typology of minorities in Western nation-states must, therefore, take into account the general types of situations in which minorities find themselves and must seek to grasp the relational aspects of their constitution (253). While Wirth clearly holds a subtle and relational conception of groups, he still assumes the existence of essential attributes that define groups prior to their formation. So for Wirth, characteristics or attributes are static but how they are interpreted is dynamic and relational.

For Elias, by contrast, even attributes such as "sex," "race," "ethnicity," and "age" are incidental, arbitrary, and unessential but strategic. The ability of one group to constitute the other as inferior is a function of a specific figuration, which two groups form with each other (1976, xx). "Differentials of cohesion and integration as an aspect of power differentials have probably not received the attention they deserve" (xxii). The mechanics of differentiation cannot be understood without exploring the part played by a person's image of his group's standing among others and, therefore, of his own standing as a member of his group (xxiii). Participation in the formation of group identity means submitting to the attributes that are valued within the group or group-specific norms. The rights that arise from belonging to a group are matched by the obligation to subject oneself to its norms. "At present the complex polyphony of the movement of rising and declining groups over time—of established groups which become outsiders or, as groups, disappear altogether, of outsider groups whose representatives move as a new establishment into positions previously denied them or, as the case may be, which become paralysed by oppression—is still largely concealed from view" (xxxv). While affective experiences and fantasies of individual people are not arbitrary—that they have a structure and dynamics of their own—does not mean that there is an overarching rationality of action among members of groups. Rather, there are multiple, intersecting, and overlapping rationalities that may appear irrational from a specific perspective but entirely rational from another (xxxvi).

To conclude, *Being Political* considers citizenship as that kind of identity within a city or state that certain agents constitute as virtuous, good, righteous, and superior, and differentiate it from strangers, outsiders, and aliens who they constitute as their alterity via various solidaristic, agonistic, and alienating strategies and technologies. Citizenship exists through its alterity and strategies, and technologies of citizenship are about the dialogical constitution of these identities via games of conduct. Thus, citizenship at any given moment and space cannot be defined without investigating strategies and technologies as modes of being political that implicate beings in solidaristic, agonistic, and alienating orientations of being political, constituting them as citizens, strangers, outsiders, and aliens. Ways of being political combine these modes and orientations through which beings are constituted as citizens, strangers, outsiders, or aliens.

Forms of Capital: Martial, Economic, Cultural, Social, Symbolic

How does a group constitute itself as virtuous, righteous, and superior, and thereby cast a shadow on other groups as those lacking these attributes? We have noted that the explanations of power differentials with the appropriation of economic capital are limited (Elias 1976, xviii). They disregard what Elias calls "figurational" aspects of power differentials arising from differences in the degree of group organization. By figuration Elias means a field of forces that evolve in orientation with each other. While the ability to constitute otherness is based on a certain solidarity achieved within the group, the symbolic capital to define otherness diminishes or is even reversed when a group is no longer able to maintain its own identity (xxi). By contrast, the power to define otherness increases when a group is able to make the members of the other groups recognize their view as the inner voice of their vision (xxiv). "Often enough the very names of groups in an outsider situation carry with them, even for the ears of their own members, undertones of inferiority and disgrace" (xxiv). This often undermines the ability of groups with less capital to mount resistance and counterforce. The key strategy is to conceal that the inferior status of the dominated group derives not from the very conditions of their stranger or outsider situation and the oppression associated with it, but from the characteristics that the dominant group attributes to it. It is almost as if power is most effective when it conceals itself. "Just as established groups, as a matter of course, regard their superior power as a sign of their higher human value, so outsider groups, as long as the power differential is great and submission inescapable, emotionally experience their *power* inferiority as a sign of *human* inferiority" (xxvi). Elias gives special emphasis to duration as a source of the cohesion and integration of groups. That is why familial lineages always play a significant role in the formation of groups. There are certain bonds that develop only among human beings who have lived together through a group process of some duration (xxvii–xxxix).

The strategies and technologies that arise in the formation of groups are not haphazard or accidental processes, but occur under definite social and economic conditions that enable groups to appropriate different forms of capital (Bourdieu 1994a, 136–37). In everyday usage, the word *capital* generally describes an asset owned by an individual as wealth. Capital might then denote a sum of money to be invested in order to secure a rate of return, or it might denote the investment itself: a financial instrument, or stocks and shares representing titles to means of production, or the material means of production themselves. As is well known, in political economy the usage is a little broader. Capital denotes any asset of whatever kind that can be used as a source of income, even if potentially. A house, for example, can be an individual's capital, as could the education or expert training that enables a higher income. In general, then, capital is an asset that can generate an income flow for its owner. But if we understand capital as a thing and merely an asset, we misunderstand its essentially social character. Because for an asset to have value expressed in capital, there must exist definite social conditions that give rise to such value (Harvey 1982). If we live in a social order where "education" has no value, that is, there are no institutions in which such education can be brought into the market for exchange for income, then education cannot be an asset. How things acquire value and become assets that can generate income depends on existing social conditions.

It is by means of different forms of capital that groups enact rituals, rules, norms, and institutions that are necessary for their reproduction and growth. When agents appropriate capital, it enables them to occupy strategic positions in social space vis-à-vis affiliations or identifications. Capital has a twofold character: it is a resource inscribed in strategic possibilities available to an agent and it is the principle underlying regularities of group formation (Bourdieu 1983, 241). Unlike money earned instantaneously in a lottery, capital takes time and space to accumulate. It requires accumulated dispositions, ideas, institutions, transmission from one generation to another, inertia, and patient acquisition. Capital is therefore not a thing, but accumulated labor (Marx 1867; 1963, 85). But its accumulation and appropriation is never the sole objective or motive. Rather, in the complex layers of group formation, individuals enter into definite relationships with each other and form associations, identifications, and affiliations that allow them to narrate and script their lives as relatively stable and durable projects. In a very significant sense, the cognitive entities that we call groups are temporary names for these projects that make social life possible. Becoming implicated in strategies and technologies that constitute these projects is that moment of being political. At the moment that an individual orients toward others as citizens, strangers, or outsiders, he or she appropriates different forms of capital inscribed in available tactics, strategies, technologies, and conducts in order to pursue various projects. It is because capital is not a thing but a relationship that it takes different forms and investigating these forms at any given time becomes crucial for investigating group formations. Being political presupposes the appropriation of at least one form of capital.

Various distinct forms of capital were isolated during the genealogical investigations on citizenship as alterity assembled in *Being Political*. While these cannot be defined without reference to the specific relations through which they were realized, a brief description of each is a useful segue into a discussion of different states in which capital exists. While, for example, martial capital involves forces of coercion and violence (Bourdieu 1994b, 5), it cannot be reduced to what Weber considered as "means of warfare." It includes or is inscribed in various strategies and technologies that are embedded in the terrain of violence. Similarly, while money can be converted to economic capital with relative ease and may be institutionalized as property, the conditions under which such conversions occur are complex and often require other forms of capital, such as cultural capital, which is convertible to money under certain conditions but is institutionalized as educational or training qualifications. Social capital consists of social obligations and may be institutionalized in certain rituals. While it bestows a status to its holder, ranging from titles to credentials and prestige, this status may exist in a symbolic state as socially recognized prestige or it may be institutionalized in the name of a family, tribe, party, or school (Bourdieu 1983, 249). The amount of social capital possessed by a given agent depends on the number of networks and affiliations that agent can effectively mobilize and on the amount of capital possessed by each of those with whom the agent is affiliated. Such affiliations are products of constant effort, which include rituals of consecration and gifts to enhance mutual knowledge and recognition. "The reproduction of social capital presupposes an unceasing effort of sociability, a continuous series of exchanges in which recognition is endlessly affirmed and reaffirmed" (Bourdieu 1983, 250). Symbolic capital consists of images, expressions, knowledge, ideas, information, and beliefs that mobilize the views of the dominant as well as the dominated (Bourdieu 1991, 166–67).

Thus, it is important to make a distinction not only between different forms, but also between states of capital in which they exist. Bourdieu identifies three states: embodied, objectified, and institutionalized (1983). The *embodied* state takes the form of dispositions, habits, outlooks, ideas, feelings, and mentalities; the *objectified* state takes the form of cultural commodities, such as books, dictionaries, objects, films, and records; and the *institutionalized* state takes the form of educational qualifications, certificates, and diplomas.

Embodied capital is accumulated in the body and requires cultivation, inculcation, and assimilation. The ancient Greek chariot warriors, for example, went through enormous amounts of practice and drills to acquire fighting skills in their bodies. Yet, embodied capital not only requires that individuals invest enormous time and energy to acquire it, but also presupposes that they already embody qualities necessary in order to make such investment. A Greek boy who was not born into a citizen family did not develop the style of life and reasoning of a warrior that would enable him to practice for chariot fighting. Cultural capital cannot be accumulated beyond the appropriating capacities of an agent. Thus, Bourdieu describes embodied capital as "the work of acquisition is work on oneself . . . with all the privation, renunciation, and sacrifice that it may entail" (1986, 244). This is analogous to Foucault's technologies of the self, which enable individuals to effect by their own means or with others a certain number of operations on their own bodies and souls, thoughts, and conduct, so as to transform themselves in order to attain happiness, purity, wisdom, perfection, or immortality (Foucault 1988, 18). The two principles of embodied capital, then are first, that its acquisition requires governing oneself and, second, that it cannot be transmitted instantaneously, like money, property, or titles of nobility. These two principles point toward the relationship between capital and group formation: because the logic of capital accumulation provokes already inherited qualities, agents occupying specific positions tend to reproduce those positions. The objective possibilities open to an agent to shift position are limited because of the inherited qualities of embodied capital.

The objectified state of capital can only be defined in relation to its embodied state. Although, for example, commodities have exchange values and thus are accessible to any agent with economic capital, their use value presupposes embodied capital, that is, taste, habitus, and disposition. Thus while the material appropriation of cultural commodities presupposes economic capital, their symbolic appropriation presupposes cultural capital. "Everything suggests that as the cultural capital incorporated in the means of production increases . . . so the collective strength of the holders of cultural capital would tend to increase" (Bourdieu 1983, 247). Cultural capital exists as symbolically and materially active capital only insofar as it is appropriated (Gouldner 1979, 23).

The institutionalized state of cultural capital takes the form of recognized and consecrated qualifications. For example, academically sanctioned capital confers on its holder a conventional, constant, and legally guaranteed value with a relative autonomy to its bearer, as well as the effective cultural capital she possesses at any given time. By conferring institutional recognition on the cultural capital possessed by any given individual, the academic qualification also makes it possible to compare qualification holders and even to exchange them. Its institutionalized state makes it possible for cultural capital to realize itself in the market with conversions into economic and social capital (Bourdieu 1983, 248).

Being political implicates agents in the appropriation of different forms of capital whose overall volume and combination position them in specific trajectories. The regimes guiding the transformation of different forms of capital generate different trajectories of becoming political. As Bourdieu emphasizes, while there are some commodities that economic capital gives immediate access to without invoking other forms of capital, many commodities are appropriated only through a combination of different forms of capital (1983, 252). Thus, economic capital is merely a possibility, which, without other forms of capital, may not be realized at all. Therein lie the moments of being and becoming political, since capital is accumulated labor. Any form of capital by itself remains unrealized. What transforms anything into capital is the labor of conversion. The expenditure of labor that is spent on conversion of one form of capital into another determines the value. The best measure of cultural capital, for example, is the amount of time devoted to acquiring it, because the transformation of economic capital into cultural capital presupposes an expenditure of time that is made possible by the possession of economic capital (Bourdieu 1983, 253). The regimes of accumulation are therefore specific combinations of different forms of capital, the principles of their transformation to each other that obtain within the specific figuration of groups, and specific strategies and technologies by which these groups are constituted.

The regimes of accumulation become effective in fields, circumscribing and delimiting the appropriation and circulation of different forms of capital. A field is where one form of capital is converted into another, which is always the site of struggles in which agents seek to maintain or alter the distribution of the forms of capital specific to it. What determines the position in social space is the form and volume of capital that an individual mobilizes or appropriates. The distribution of the various forms of capital determines the overall structure of that social space (Bourdieu 1987, 4). Agents are positioned in the overall social space according to the overall amount of capital they appropriate, the composition of their capital, and their social trajectory, that is, the evolution over time of the volume and composition of their capital (Bourdieu 1987; Bourdieu and Wacquant 1992, 99). A field constitutes agents as political in the sense that an agent becomes implicated in various strategies to pursue projects only in and through a field.

Bourdieu often uses spatial metaphors to describe the field: "a network, or a configuration, of objective relations between positions. These positions are objectively defined, in their existence and in the determinations they impose upon their occupants, agents or institutions, by their present and potential situation in the structure of the distribution of species of power (or capital) whose possession commands access to the specific profits that are at stake in the field, as well as by their objective relation to other positions (domination, subordination, homology, etc.)" (Bourdieu and Wacquant 1992, 97). While using a spatial language (i.e., relations, positions, occupants, or situation), Bourdieu has been unable to investigate fields spatially and considers them as aspatial boundaries, such as the "political field" (1981), the "cultural field" (1993), and the "philosophical field" (1988). Yet when one says that individuals take their positions in social space, these positions also have their equivalence in material space. Bourdieu recognized this: "To account more fully for the differences in life-style between the different fractions—especially as regards culture—one would have to take account of their distribution in a *socially ranked geographical space*. A group's chances of appropriating any given class of rare assets (as measured by mathematical probability of access) depend partly on its capacity for the specific appropriation, defined by the economic, cultural, and social capital it can deploy in order to appropriate materially or symbolically the assets in question, that is, its position in social space, and partly on the relationship between its distribution in geographical space, and partly on the relationship between its distribution of the scarce assets in that space" (Bourdieu 1979, 124). While, therefore, Bourdieu recognizes that the distribution of capital and social struggles "take place" not only in social space but also in material space, he produces a flawed image when he assumes a straightforward homology between the social space and material space: "Social space tends to be translated, with more or less distortion, into physical space, in the form of a certain arrangement of agents and properties" (1997, 134). While the relations that describe different groups and the distance that separates them have equivalent material properties, this equivalence should not be translated into a homology "with more or less distortion." While the multidimensional geometric space that Bourdieu describes has its equivalence in material space, the structure of material space restructures social space in complex but nonhomologous ways. The relationship between social and material space in investigating group formation is a crucial analytical issue that we cannot simply bypass as it also enables us to critically interrogate orientalism and synoecism as the founding perspectives of occidental citizenship. While a lengthier consideration of the relationships between social and material spaces in group formation is necessary, the following brief section will serve to illustrate at least the basis from which my genealogical investigations proceeded by considering spatial strategies and technologies as constitutive aspects of groups.

Space Is the Machine

Must a relational conception of group formation take into account how space structures groups? Just as a distinction was made between hypothetical and real groups, we also need to make a distinction between symbolic space and material space: that human beings inhabit two spaces simultaneously. But these two spaces are neither distinct nor homologous. Nor can each be read off from the other. The first is a discontinuous experience of expressive forms, signs, and symbols, which create a cognitive space; the second is a continuous material space of objects, which we inhabit *and* move through. The former is symbolic space and the latter is material space (Hillier 1996, 396). There is a third space, where these two spaces are mediated, created, produced, symbolized, and materialized, but these two spaces remain as the conditions that enable the formation of groups in the third space (Soja 1996, 60–70). Just as groups bring themselves into real existence through work, including organizing, arranging, and communicating, they also bring themselves into existence in material space by building, congregating, assembling, and confronting. All this work involves the creation and production of space (Lefebvre 1974; Soja 1996, 26–52). The formation of groups involves, in a fundamental way, the production of these three spaces (Allen 1999). To put it in another way, groups cannot materialize themselves as real without realizing themselves in space, without creating configurations of buildings, patterns, and arrangements, and symbolic representations of these arrangements. Yet, first and second spaces are necessary but not sufficient conditions under which hypothetical groups may be transformed into real groups. If the formation of groups involves creating relatively durable relationships that are maintained and projected through time, third space is the means by which such durability and persistence are materialized.

How do buildings, configurations, patterns, and arrangements through which groups realize themselves affect the very nature of the relationships that form these groups? How do buildings, configurations, patterns, and arrangements themselves become strategies and technologies of government and differentiation of groups? A tradition of critical urban thought has produced valuable insights on these questions (Castells 1983; Deutsche 1996; Gottdiener 1994; Harvey 1996; Harvey 1993; Magnusson 1996; Smith and Katz 1993; Soja 1989, 1996). More precisely, that space is a condition of being political, and that spaces of citizenship as expressions of being political always involve buildings (Pantheon, pnyx, guildhall), configurations (forum, plaza), and arrangements (agora, gymnasia, assembly) has been a premise of critical urban studies for some time now. But within that tradition there are those who categorically deny that social relations can be effected by spatial relations (Saunders 1981). There are those who emphatically defend that spatiality is fundamental to the formation of social relations (Soja 1989). And there are those who make a difference between necessary and contingent relations and argue that abstractions about how social relations are structured in a given point in time focus on necessary relations that do not have spatial reference (Sayer 1992). While this tradition has been useful for raising the issue of space in social and political thought, its analytical depth remains inadequate for undertaking genealogical investigations on how groups realize themselves through spatial strategies and technologies. This tradition remains locked into social scientific styles of thought, which are ahistorical, presentist, and explanatory, as opposed to genealogical and investigative. At any rate, this issue is far too complex to receive justice within my scope here (Deutsche 1996, 78; Gottdiener, 1984). My beginning point, however, is Simmel's thoughts on space as a segue into developing an analytics of space for investigating citizenship and its alterities.

When Simmel describes the stranger as the synthesis of detachment and attachment, he adds that "[t]his is another indication that spatial relations not only are determining conditions of relationships among men, but are also symbolic of those relationships" (1908c: 143). Yet Simmel was not entirely clear whether he thought space to be a necessary condition of group formation or a cause of social relations (1908b). At times he was emphatic that if a historical interpretation emphasizes spatial factors, such as the size of a kingdom or the concentration or dispersal of its population as the forces for its political and social organization, it risks the danger of confusing causes with conditions since he thought "space always remains the actually ineffectual form, in whose modifications real energies are manifested, but only in the way that language expresses thought processes, which occur *in* words but not *through* words" (1908b, 137). But he also considered space as a cause because in it "we possess the clearest documentation of the real forces" (1908b, 137, 138). The formation of groups relies on several fundamental qualities of space. They are important for ascertaining the forms of sociation and group formation.

To the extent that a social group inhabits a space, it possesses a character of uniqueness or exclusivity that is not normally attainable in other ways. Space becomes its defining characteristic as a group. For individuals acting *as* members of this group it may simply mean acting in that space. For certain types of association space becomes their fundamental aspect (Simmel 1908b, 138–39). The state is such an association and its formation involved intense struggles for achieving this, which came to be reflected in its strategies of sovereignty (Bartelson 1995). The city as an association is also based on this principle, though historically it has been much more permeable than the state. Even during periods such as those when ancient Greek and medieval cities are thought to have possessed spatial characteristics of states, their territories were much more permeable and fluid than the modern state. But often the absolute claim to a space is less common. Rather, various groups and associations claim functional jurisdiction over a spatial extent and struggle simultaneously for their rights to that space. Medieval guilds, for example, created a quilt of rights and obligations that were defined over the same space of the city. Some did collide over rights and some existed simultaneously without overlapping claims. Exclusivity or multiplicity displayed by the relations of the group to a particular spatial configuration is therefore often the root of the group's symbols and structure.

Another quality of space that affects the formation of groups is that of boundaries, which range from legal designations to demarcations such as rivers, mountains, streets, landmarks, and buildings. Such boundaries allow groups to conceive of themselves as groups, marking themselves off against other groups and assembling themselves together (Simmel 1908b, 141). But since every group includes members with multiple group affiliations, the boundaries of groups are always permeable, fluid, overlapping, multiple, and intersecting. Nonetheless, the consciousness of boundedness becomes essential for the group to realize itself as a group. Boundaries enable individuals to act as members of groups but be perceived as though they were acting as individuals. It is neither countries nor districts that bind one to another; rather, it is their inhabitants, who exercise reciprocal effects on each other. Thus, "the boundary is not a spatial fact with sociological consequences, but a sociological fact that forms itself spatially" (Simmel 1908b, 143).

For social groups, space also engenders a capacity to fix their content. Whether a group is able to fix objects that are essential to its identity and durability or is prevented from establishing determinate forms affects its structure. This is the crucial difference between nomadic and diasporic groups or sedentary groups. "The spatial immovability of an object of interest creates certain forms of relationships that group around it" (Simmel 1908b, 146). The significance of fixed spatiality as a pivotal point for social relationships emerges whenever the contact or union of otherwise independent objects can only occur at one particular location. For religious groups, for example, a pivotal point such as a church or a mosque is essential. This fixed point in space becomes a pivotal point for the relationships and the cohesion of the faithful, so that communal rather than isolated, religious forces are developed. Conversely, the forces emanating from such a center also awaken a consciousness of belonging to that which it represents.

Whether groups stand near to or far from each other has a significant impact on how they orient toward each other. Two groups that are formed by the very same interests, forces, and convictions will change their structure and character according to whether their members have spatial contact with each other or are separated from one another. The proximity or distance among the members of a group or between two groups has considerable impact on the relationships they constitute. But proximity and distance are not absolute properties. The form and content of the relationship between two or more groups demand a degree of spatial proximity or distance (Simmel 1908b, 152). While two neighboring groups may develop complete indifference toward each other, two or more other groups may develop intense relationships of domination, rivalry, and agonistic association. When considering proximity and distance as properties of space, other issues also enter into account, such as conversational versus visual proximity, sense of smell, and speech recognition. Similarly, whether a dominated group is concentrated within a larger dominant group or is dispersed has important consequences. As we shall see, the bourgeoisie distinguished itself from the working classes in the nineteenth century by, among other things, attributing superiority to its healthy habits, such as cleanliness, and inferiority to the unclean manners expressed in the sights, sounds, and smells of the dangerous classes. Similarly, the nobility in the fifteenth century developed ways of speech that it valorized over base forms of speech and attributed the difference to inferiority. These principles of differentiation disrupted the spatial proximity with which various groups intermingled before such distinctions were drawn. For Simmel, the reception of Africans among Americans and Jews among Germans were impeded because of this repulsion (1908b, 156). But Simmel overlooks that these orientations toward sights, sounds, and smells were not natural or immutable universal orientations, but agonistic strategies.

So far the above discussion of the properties of space and their consequences for group formation has assumed a rather static formation: habitation, boundaries, location, and distance are regarded as static properties of space. As complicating as these properties undoubtedly are, still a more complicating property of space is that formed by movement. What forms of sociation appear from wandering groups? How do groups realize themselves over a distance? How do groups maintain and reproduce their identities when some of their members move? Simmel believed that the immanent restlessness of human beings, which provokes stimulation through distance, finds its form in nomadism and wandering. That nomadism or wandering originates from a will to difference makes it a basis of group formation. For some groups nomadism results in restless movement as diasporic groups. For others it may mean restless change and transformation without spatial movement as sedentary groups. Simmel believed that sedentary groups rely strongly on agonistic strategies within themselves while nomadic groups become more reliant on solidaristic strategies (1908b, 161). But wandering is entirely different from traveling. While the former relies on solidaristic strategies and technologies, traveling generates groups that are ephemeral and unstable, however meaningful the identifications and affiliations they may engender. That when traveling, identity becomes unstable and fluid, creating a weakened sense of obligations and rights and enhancing inner insecurities, demonstrates how important spatial properties are in the formation of groups and the formation of stable identities (165). But the form and content of traveling are very different in different epochs. In medieval and early modern Europe, kings, judges, courts, craftsmen, scholars, students, and merchants ceaselessly moved and traveled to maintain integration and cohesiveness with their respective groups. By contrast, modern traveling, such as tourism, is less about achieving cohesion and more about interface and interaction. Thus, restless mobility and wandering can create different forms of sociation between insiders and outsiders, citizens and strangers.

While Simmel was right to think that the properties of space, such as habitation, boundaries, location, distance, and movement, were inherently social, his dispersed arguments that space cannot generate and restructure social relations must be called into question. Similarly, Saunders (1981) and Urry (1996) argued that Weber also seemed to have held the same view about space. Yet, as has been discussed, Weber's crucial distinction between occidental and oriental conceptions of association hinged upon the difference between confraternal forms based on the spatial principle versus forms of association based on the kinship principle. For Weber the emergence of the Greek polis as an association of warriors could only be explained by the dissolution of clan and kinship ties and their replacement by spatial (i.e., nontribal and nonkinship) relations, as was evidenced in the reforms of Kleisthenes in the fifth century B.C. Athens. It must be pointed out that orientalism and synoecism are themselves spatial perspectives that enabled Weber to account for the unique origins of occidental citizenship.

That it is only through their realization in space that we can recognize groups and that the socially produced properties and regularities of space, such as habitation, boundaries, location, distance, and movement, effect the character of groups is a plausible enough statement. But using it in genealogical investigations is immensely difficult. While Soja (1996, 34) is right to argue that Lefebvre was one of the first to theorize difference and otherness in explicitly spatial terms and associated his spatial theorization with his critique of representations of power and power of representations, Lefebvre's imprecise approximations remain inadequate for genealogical investigations. Moreover, as we shall see later, Lefebvre made significant historical errors, some of which were related to his uncritical appropriation of synoecism in occidental thought. By contrast, the language (space syntax) developed by Bill Hillier and his associates was useful for my investigations of the strategies and technologies of group formation (Hillier 1989, 1996, 1999; Hillier and Hanson 1984; Hillier, Hanson, and Graham 1987). A very brief discussion of their findings from various research studies and two fundamental consequences for undertaking genealogical investigations follows.

Appropriately enough, their researches began some twenty years ago with the recognition that, by arranging relations through patterns of movement and encounter and through buildings, boundaries, paths, markers, and zones, social groups acquire a definite spatial presence or order (Hillier and Hanson 1984). But the language through which groups form identifications and differentiations does not merely represent or express spatial metaphors. Rather, since spatial arrangements are inherent in the formation of groups, this language embodies their spatial origins. Unlike what Simmel thought about space as a medium akin to language, metaphors such as insider-outsider, inhabitant-stranger, boundary, orientation, and action indeed have qualities that originate from spatial arrangements and this has profound consequences for investigating groups. This was one of Gaston Bachelard's notable insights (1964, 211–31). Two such consequences were fundamental for my genealogical investigations on citizenship and its alterities.

First, space is an arrangement (or configuration) of objects that orients inhabitants (or citizens or insiders) toward strangers (or outsiders and aliens) in a way that allows agents to form solidarities, affinities, and identifications (subjectivities) by using contiguous proximity and similarity (spatial relations) or analogy and difference (transpatial relations) as strategies and technologies (Hillier and Hanson 1984, 141–42). By creating boundaries that are fluid but relatively stable, that demarcate the insides and outsides, space engenders or endangers solidarities of two essential types. Solidarities through space involve identifications and affinities via contiguity and encounter. To realize these solidarities requires recognizing not the separateness or difference of the inside, but the continuity between the inside and the outside. By contrast, transpatial solidarities involve identifications and affinities via analogy and isolation. To realize these solidarities requires the reproduction of an identical pattern by agents who remain spatially separated from each other, but socially bound with each other. The formation of groups involves social and spatial processes simultaneously but inseparably that become visible only through specific strategies and technologies of otherness.

Second, space is a configuration that generates and modulates encounters among and between groups (Hillier and Hanson 1984, 143–47). Encountering, congregating, assembling, avoiding, interacting, dwelling, and conferring are not attributes of individuals, but configurations formed by groups. These relationships between groups depend on a structured pattern of co-presence and co-absence (Hillier 1996, 29). The objective of citizens (insiders) is never to exclude strangers and outsiders from their space, but to conduct their conduct through space (Hillier and Hanson 1984, 140). Space as configuration is not merely a means through which individuals form groups, but it develops its own properties and regularities that can also act as a system of constraints on encounters. By virtue of its sui generis logics, space becomes an object in the struggle for domination and differentiation (Hillier and Hanson 1984, 199). As groups realize themselves in space, they engage in strategies by inventing various technologies that alter configurations and properties of space so as to fragment, weaken, destabilize, constrain, immobilize, segregate, incarcerate, or disperse other groups as much as possible while increasing their own solidarities (Hillier and Hanson 1984, 241).

Thus, in their encounters and interactions that constitute space (configurations of objects expressed in boundaries, buildings, zones, insides, and outsides) agents simultaneously form themselves and others as groups (expressed in citizens-citizens, citizens-strangers and citizens-outsiders, citizens-aliens logics). Space understood as a configuration is thus never simply a passive background of becoming political. It is a fundamental strategic property by which groups, nations, societies, federations, empires, and kingdoms are constituted in the real world, and, through this constitution, structured as "objective" realities. Space as configuration can have no definite shape or form independent from the groups that constitute and are constituted by it and the strategies and technologies that are embodied in its constitution. We speak of "space" merely as a convention. More cumbersomely but accurately, it is perhaps more appropriate to speak of the "spatialization of virtue" (Osborne and Rose 1999). While the affinities should be recognizable, it is beyond my scope here to contrast my usage of space as a machine with "abstract machines" (Deleuze and Guattari 1980), "diagrams" (Foucault 1975), "figurations" (Elias and Scotson 1994), and "fields" (Bourdieu 1979). Nonetheless, the metonym "space is the machine" draws attention to the relational and configurational aspect of group formation, where the machine is understood not as a mechanical construct but as an assemblage (cf. Molotch 1976, 1999). The city is a difference machine insofar as it is understood as that configuration that is constituted by the dialogical encounter of groups formed and generated immanently in the process of taking up positions, orienting themselves for and against each other, inventing and assembling strategies and technologies, mobilizing various forms of capital, and making claims to that space that is objectified as "the city." Neither groups nor their identities exist before the encounter with the city. "Women," "peasants," "Africans," "hooligans," "prostitutes," "refugees," "workers," "bourgeois" do not encounter each other in the city as though they existed before that encounter, but they constitute each other via the encounter (Sennett 1994). Nor does the city exist in a pre-defined shape or form as unity. The city is neither a background to these struggles *against which* groups wager, nor is it a foreground *for which* groups struggle for domination. The city is the battleground *through which* groups define their identities, stake their claims, wage their battles, and articulate citizenship rights and obligations. The city as an object of thought and experience emerges out of these practices and has neither the unity, nor the cohesion, nor the shape that has been attributed to it. The city as a difference machine relentlessly provokes, differentiates, positions, mobilizes, immobilizes, oppresses, liberates. Being political arises qua the city and there is no political being outside the machine.

Conclusion

Although this chapter has discussed some theoretical issues, its aim was neither to develop a "theory" of group formation, nor even a "method," but rather to outline some analytical principles regarding citizenship as alterity. Moreover, these analytical principles arise from doing genealogical investigations and, during the process, encountering and confronting a few thinkers who are helpful on these specific issues. While these analytical principles arose from writing this book, they should be regarded neither as consistent nor comprehensive, but rather as specific and contingent principles concerning the problems addressed in *Being Political*.

Nevertheless, how this interpretive analytics of groups has taken us away from the Weberian and traditional concerns with citizenship needs to be emphasized. The critique that emerges here is not necessarily of Weber's synoecism and orientalism. Rather, it is to illustrate that Weber and subsequent Western social and political thought advanced historical claims about the occidental city that become problematic when synoecism and orientalism are abandoned. The critique, therefore, is of synoecism and orientalism only insofar as it illustrates how they enabled the advancement of these claims, rather than critiquing them as perspectives. By abandoning synoecism and orientalism, new pathways open for investigation and, possibly, new interpretations of citizenship. The ostensible differences between the oriental and occidental cities are no longer objects of analysis. Nor is the oriental city subjected to a *unified* frame of reference for contrasts and comparisons. Nor is an unbroken continuity in the history of citizenship a given, immutable fact. Rather, the continuity of the narrative established by citizens themselves now becomes what can be critically investigated. We are now free, as it were, to focus on the internal differentiations of the city and how in different moments it was a locus of being political.

Although he was not interested in the city as a locus of citizenship, nonetheless Mumford came closest to holding a relational conception of the city in history and was absolutely right to believe that many aspects, such as its size, density, and heterogeneity were incidental, not essential, aspects of the city (1961). For Mumford the city was a configuration of social groups, layered one after another through centuries. Mumford was perhaps the best archaeologist of the city that the twentieth century witnessed. Yet Mumford was unable to free himself from a perspective that relentlessly cornered him into recovering the good or evil of the city, rather than seeing that one was not possible without the other. That the city was a crucial condition of citizenship in the sense that being a citizen was inextricably associated with being *in* the city was obvious to Mumford. That over the centuries struggles over citizenship have always taken place "over" the city too was also obvious. But that the city was neither a background to these struggles *against which* groups have wagered, nor a foreground *for which* groups have struggled for hegemony was less so. That the city was the battleground *through which* groups defined their identities, staked their claims, waged their battles, and articulated citizenship rights, obligations, and principles was not at all obvious to Mumford.

The group configurations explored here—polis, civitas, Christianopolis, eutopolis, metropolis, and cosmopolis—are neither sequential, nor ideal, nor unified types, displacing or replacing each other in the order of time. Rather, these group configurations are moments articulated into the history of the city, leaving behind their material traces and sediments. Like archeological classifications of different moments of the city into stages such as Troy I, Troy IVa, and Troy IVb or Çatal Höyük VIa and Çatal Höyük VIb, these group configurations coexist, but in an incongruent yet juxtaposed manner. Indeed, while the chapters of this work focus on main group configurations, there are many more variations, layers, and moments articulated into the history of the city yet to be investigated.

Polis

Women
Peasants
Slaves
Metics
Mercenaries
Raiders
Traders

O Perses, follow justice; control your pride.
For pride is evil in a common man.
Even a noble finds it hard to bear;
It weighs him down and leads him to disgrace.
The road to justice is the better way,
For Justice in the end will win the race
And Pride will lose; the common man must learn
This fact through suffering. The god of Oaths
Runs faster than an unjust verdict; when
Justice is dragged out of the way by men
Who judge dishonestly and swallow bribes,
A struggling sound is heard; then she returns
Back to the city and the home of men,
Wrapped in a mist and weeping, and she brings
Harm to the unjust men who drove her out
But when the judges of a polis are fair
The citizen and outsiders alike,
Their polis prospers and her people bloom;
Since Peace is in the land, her children thrive;
Zeus never marks them out for cruel war.

—Hesiod, *Works and Days*

53

Both Greek and Roman citizens produced a bewildering array of categories for identifying themselves and others. These categories often changed and their meaning was always contested. As is well known, beginning at the highest level of generality, Greek citizens divided all humankind into two mutually exclusive and antithetical categories: Greeks and barbarians (Cartledge 1993, 11). Cartledge argues that while in the seventh and sixth centuries the Greeks did not actually use the word *barbarian* or engage in such a general "othering," by the fifth century inventing the barbarian was well under way (38–39). For Cartledge, a major factor for the invention was that the majority of slaves were by origin barbarian (41). As we shall see, while slavery existed in Greece well before citizens invented the barbarians (Hartog 1988), the dramatic rise of slavery was closely associated with the rise of "democratic" citizenship. Hence, there is an intimate connection between the invention of citizenship and of barbarians. At any rate, while this general category has received the most historical curiosity and attention (Hall 1989), Greek citizens created four major categories below it, all revolving around citizenship: men-women, citizen-foreigner, free-slave, and god-mortals. For Cartledge, "The Greeks thus in various ways constructed their identities negatively, by means of a series of polarized oppositions of themselves to what they were not" (12–13). But this view invokes the logic of exclusion. *Some* "Greeks" may have defined their identities negatively, but many categories such as citizen-slave, citizen-women, citizen-merchant, and citizen-craftsman were a good deal more complicated than being merely negative oppositions. The use of *xenos* is indicative of this complexity. It was the most general Greek word for a stranger or outsider who was not a member of the polis, whether Greek or barbarian. Typically, however, a linguistic distinction was drawn according to the context between *xenoi* for Greek aliens and *barbaroi* for non-Greek aliens. To complicate matters further, Spartans refused this custom and used *xenoi* regardless of the origin of the stranger (Cartledge 1993, 47). However, resident aliens, merchants, traders, craftsmen, and slaves were not designated with the negative category of *xenoi*, but were classified by their own special categories.

Thus, it would be misleading to focus on the immanent categories of alterity that the "Greeks" created as negative identities. Instead, we need to examine the conditions under which the immanent categories of alterity such as women, mercenaries, metics, merchants, raiders, and craftsmen were created. As well, various grading schemes were devised that classified citizens themselves. An essential basis of these identities was that the city was the principal axis of differentiation: the right to the city and its institutions, rituals, rites, cults, festivals, religion, and heroes determined the position of citizens, strangers, and outsiders in the social and spatial order, and generated principles governing their conduct.

"Greek Citizen"?

Since the discovery of ancient Greek texts in the twelfth and thirteenth centuries in Europe, Greek culture has been held in awe by the "western civilization" (Vidal-Naquet 1995). As we have seen, there is a fundamental sense in which the "Greeks" are regarded as the inventors of a game that "we" still play: the city-citizen game of democracy (Tully 1999, 163–69). Moreover, since these first discoveries every age has created its own version of the "Greeks" (Bernal 1994). Much of this fascination, though, remains focused on a few texts that extolled the virtues of Greece in its "classical" era: Homer, Aristotle, Plato, Herodotus, and Thucydides. The omnipresence of their histories in our present appears immutable and overwhelming (Golden and Toohey 1997). If we are to gain anything from their narratives, we ought to distance ourselves from them by making them strangers to ourselves. Ironically, this is an ancient Greek strategy of citizenship.

Yet, this is a major task and here we can only glimpse what that task might involve. Let us begin by pointing out how fragile, short, isolated, and tentative was the classical age of the Greeks. When one considers the entire history of ancient Greece from the first settlement in Crete by Minoans around 3000 B.C. to the Macedonian conquest of the Greek poleis in 322 B.C., the period between the emergence of politics and citizenship around the eighth century B.C. and its eventual "decline" in the fourth is remarkably short. While citizenship makes its appearance in periods of Greek history known as the archaic (750–500 B.C.) and classical (500–400 B.C.), it must surely be placed within that broader history. Moreover, as we shall see, even within that very short span, citizenship was contested and questioned. Finally, among hundreds of Greek poleis, each had a discontinuous and tenuous trajectory regarding citizenship, lapsing into tyranny here and oligarchy there. It is with these enormous qualifications that we must use the term "Greek citizen."

Considering citizenship within the context of broader Greek history renders the distinction made between occidental and oriental cities ever more problematic. In contrast to historians of the late nineteenth and early twentieth centuries, late twentieth-century historians began to recognize that Greek history unfolded within the context of oriental civilizations and in many ways was an extension of them (Bernal 1994;

Cartledge 1993). Like other ancient civilizations, the early Greeks, Minoans (3000–1100 B.C.) and Mycenaeans (1600–1150 B.C.) developed palace-based cultures. In both Mycenae and Crete, the hereditary kings ruled "cities," though the status and nature of these cities are far from clear. Judging from the archaeological remains of some colossal defensive walls and palaces, these kings must have amassed enormous power and used the forced labor of subjects (Weber 1921, 1282–83). It appears that these kings, like their oriental counterparts, had a certain affinity for cities and their attendant benefits of power and domination. Since their power appears formidable, the image of the individual that dominates these societies was one who obeyed: an "individual" was a subject. In this way, the Minoans and Mycenaeans display the characteristics of the oriental cultures in terms of the power of the royal class.

But the affinities extend beyond the Minoan and Mycenaean cities. The grand orientalist narrative claimed that while Mycenaean cities were ruled by kings, toward the end of their span, the emergence of a new type of warfare based on self-equipped warriors resulted in the gradual decline of the kingship and its eventual dethroning. In a sense, what made Greeks occidental was their ability to dethrone the kings. As the narrative went, until the emergence of warriors, the monopoly of kings, in Greece and elsewhere, had always rested on their ability to coordinate and finance war. This narrative gave us the memorable metaphor of the "oriental" city as a war machine (Mumford 1961). The main outlines of the narrative are as follows. Until the rise of warriors who owned their own equipment, the kings were always able to separate the soldiers from martial capital, thereby establishing power over them and their subjects (Finer 1997a, 316). But the self-equipped and self-financed warrior was essentially the owner of martial capital. The power relationship was reversed (Drews 1983, 129–30). The kings could no longer assume the obedience of soldiers, but had to secure their loyalty. "It was probably the rise of knightly warfare, with the attendant military independence of noble families who maintained their own chariots and followings and who themselves owned ships, that shattered the monopoly of the kings" (Weber 1921, 1285).

This pattern gradually emerged toward the end of the so-called "dark ages" (1100–750 B.C.), when the growth of cities had stagnated across the Near East and the Mediterranean. By the middle of the eighth century B.C. a new formation—polis—made its appearance, which was associated with the disappearance of the monopoly of the kings and the appearance of noble landowners. Fustel de Coulanges and Weber interpreted this moment as the rise of the ancient patrician city (Fustel de Coulanges 1864, 235–37; Weber 1921, 1287). Although as a general pattern the aristocracy maintained some residences outside the city, it primarily resided in the city, which was a collection of villages and farm lots. The aristocracy also differentiated itself and its style of life by designating its status as citizenship: it was no longer subject to the kings, but it was also different from the peasants, slaves, and serfs. The city was a fraternity of the nobles as citizens and was organized as a standing army of warriors. Vernant argues that "[t]he city-state can thus be defined as a system of institutions which allows a privileged minority (the citizens) exclusive access to landed property within a definite area. In this sense the economic basis of the polis was a particular form of land appropriation" (1974, 16). The right to the city as both appropriation and inhabitation became a condition of citizenship, and hence, a condition of being political. Anyone, including the artisans, merchants, traders, and free peasants, not belonging to the polis was economically and socially at the mercy of the nobles, who were organized as warrior-citizens (Weber 1921, 1290).

This was the first phase in the march toward democracy. The second phase began, principally in Athens, around the sixth century B.C. In essence, a new image of citizenship was brought about by peasants, craftsmen, tradesmen, and other free but nonnoble groups of the poleis who challenged the aristocracy (Wood 1988). Within a relatively short time, in Athens and in other poleis, though in varying degrees, the powers of the aristocratic families were dramatically challenged. The decisive factor in this dramatic challenge was the rise of hoplitic warfare—a new technique of warfare where a formation of equipped warriors as infantry (hoplites) replaced the heroic warrior. The new hoplites were largely drawn from the peasantry in the rural demes of the polis. By virtue of the new force they possessed, the peasant-warriors demanded a greater share in the polis assembly, where the nobility had exclusively made many decisions. Anyone who could equip and train himself could become a member of the hoplite and a citizen, with the right to participate in the assembly. Thus, the ownership of large tracts of land ceased to be a necessary condition of citizenship.

The new order was the rule of the demos, which opened up new avenues for wealth, status, and power for the already relatively wealthy groups of nonnoble citizens who owned money, slaves, ships, or trading or economic capital. It allowed them to gain a share in the assembly and in the offices beside aristocratic families, whose position was mainly based on landed property (Weber 1921, 1312). Moreover, not only were groups of tradesmen and people of small fortunes defined as strangers to these offices (though this was challenged at least in Athens to an extent), but women, slaves, and serfs were also constituted as outsiders. In other words, the decisive change in the Greek political game was not a transfer of power from the nobility to the masses, but the emergence of a new group of peasant-warriors, who challenged the nobility and acquired the right to the political assembly and its attendant benefits (Wood 1988).

The new citizenship practice had two significant consequences for the polis as a political association. The first was the rise of spatial relationships, replacing entirely the clan and other ties. The new citizenship was essentially a synoecism of citizens in demes, which were spatial districts of the polis. The deme became the basis for allocating rights and duties in the polis. For one to become a citizen, one had to be registered in a deme at birth: one was born into citizenship; neither wealth, nor status, nor power, nor even clan ties could determine citizenship. The polis was governed by the demes. Consequently, this spatial government replaced the ad hoc law, where the determination of just and unjust was based on personal power, with an instituted law, where just and unjust were determined by deliberation in the assembly by deme representatives (Weber 1921, 1312–13).

The second consequence was the replacement of notables, who ruled by virtue of their office, with functionaries of the demos, elected or chosen by lot for short terms, and responsible to the assemblies and sometimes removable (Weber 1921, 1314). As has been noted, these functionaries were compensated for their time, which made participation in the assembly possible for a large mass of nonnoble citizens.

These are the broad outlines of two transformations—from kingship to the warrior-citizen and from the warrior-citizen to the peasant-citizen—that constitute the basis of the grand orientalist narrative of occidental citizenship. This narrative argues that with these two transformations, the Greeks were able to invent citizenship and diverge from the oriental trajectory. There are good reasons to be skeptical if not strongly critical of this narrative.

Orientalizing Polis

While the ancient Greeks seem to have considered their own histories continuous with the Minoans and Mycenaeans, modern orientalists have been intent on differentiating them very sharply. Is that because neither set of histories is consistent with the grand narrative of water and river regulation? Perhaps. Obviously, Minoan civilization was a coastal culture based on naval power. There was no need for water regulation, at least in the manner of the Yellow River, Mesopotamia, the Indus River, or the Nile. Yet, from archaeological studies we learn that Crete was dominated by great palaces, which were residences of kings and rulers, centers of control and administration, and at the same time places of storage for tribute. On the island of Crete there were many different palace-based cities, each with its own leader, but it seems likely that Knossos was the seat of an overlord. The cities such as Pahiastos, Mallia, and Zakro evidently show marked similarities to the royal palaces of other parts of Asia Minor with perceptible Mesopotamian and Hittite influences. Every Minoan city shows evidence of deep cleavages between the dominant and the dominated groups. Minoan religion was centered on deities, and there is evidence of rites of consecration and sacred symbols of sovereignty. Crete also seems to have existed in a peaceful state until about 1700 B.C. without being threatened by "barbarians." This is evidenced in the lack of fortifications in its palace-based cities. Crete, then, if we follow the orientalist logic, was in a perfect condition, lacking the necessity of water regulation and lacking major outside threat, to develop the occidental polis. Why the Minoans did not develop the occidental polis would, then, be a fair question to ask Weber. Given his analysis and the evidence available to him, it was possible to pose this question, but it seems it did not occur to him.

In addition, Minoan religion also embodies characteristics of oriental religions. At the head of Minoan civilization was the Minos, who ruled from Knossos after establishing himself as the leader of old tribal associations and other dynasties. The names and titles of the Minos, his priestly offices, and divine attributes reveal the sacred character of kingship. Greek tradition implies an identification of the king with the bull-god, which interprets the Minos as an immanent god, like the Egyptian pharaoh. However, there is evidence that the bull-god was an anthropomorphic manifestation of a celestial being, the Zeus of antiquity, and the Minos was thought of as his chosen protégé and delegate. So it is clear that the Minoan kingship was similar to those of Mesopotamia, rather than that of Egypt. Were other cities in Crete ruled by the Minos in Knossos? It might be possible to answer this question were scholars able to solve the Linear A script, which was used to record transactions in the Minoan palaces. As in Egypt and Asia, the palace was the vital element in the king's rule, not simply because he lived there, but because it was the instrument of his power—private dwelling, council chamber, temple, government offices, law courts, and military headquarters. The palace was to the king what the sanctuary was to the god. Whether Minoans were Greeks or not (and certainly later Greek traditions from Homer to Theognis thought that they were), the more we learn about them, the less is the distance that separates the Orient from the Occident.

Similar questions concerning the orientalist narrative of citizenship based upon a lack of theocratic government and sacred religion can also be raised about Mycenaeans. As tradition has it, around 1500 B.C. the island of Crete fell to Achaean warriors, and the palace of Knossos was destroyed. Achaeans, centered on the fortified city of Mycenae, were in some respects very different from the Minoans. They were warriors whose political culture centered around massive fortified palaces with elaborate monuments and tombs such as Mycenae, Tiryns, Gla, and (across the Aegean) Troy, and they displayed remarkable similarities to another warrior culture, the Hittites. (Later Greeks, whose own cities and fortifications were much more modest, called these walls "cyclopean" because they thought only super human beings could have erected them.) Each of these fortified cities was ruled by a local lord, the *basileus*, who held authority from the *wanax* or king (McDonald and Thomas 1990). Major fortresses like Mycenae and Tiryns were centers of kings who fought in chariots at the head of companions, who dined at the royal table and were recompensed with land, slaves, and cattle (Weber 1909, 154). The fortress was surrounded by settlements of artisans and craftsmen. At the heart of each fortified city was the palace, organized around a large, rectangular room called the *megaron*, with a low, circular hearth in the center and a throne to one side. The king was like Agamemnon in Homer: a supreme ruler of the heights of Mycenae, whose position was "hereditary in a family made prominent by wealth in cattle and marked out as favoured by the gods by success in war and equity in judgement" (Weber 1909, 151). Since tradition was the only source of law, a *wanax* had to rely on the aid of a council of elders, recruited from great families ennobled by wealth and martial prowess. Land was distributed on a graded system of ownership depending on class. At the top was the warrior class, who were aristocrats, followed by the local administrators, then the priests, the foot soldiers, and finally the peasants, craftsmen, and traders. It appears that economic and social life was strictly controlled. The *wanax* and the *basileus* had a monopoly on metals, and had also at their disposal great stocks of every sort of commodity brought as tribute to the palace. All the land belonged to the king, the temples, or the nobles, or was common land, belonging to the villages. Arms and chariots could be personal or royal property. Although the Homeric poems depict the rural population as simply a mass of slaves and serfs, there were also free peasants, who were severely oppressed by the martial aristocracy (Scully 1990; Weber 1909, 155).

That Achaean-Mycenaean civilization was founded on the prominence of the warriors is nowhere more symbolically represented than in excavated tombs: they wore their arms even to the grave. They lie enclosed in breastplates, shields as tall as themselves lie beside them, and of their life apart from war they have left only records of hunting, the warrior's leisure. In such a culture, the ruler's position above the rest depended on his superiority in war, and religion itself could only mark a martial leader as one whom the gods considered their equal and worthy of protection. Thus, Weber insisted, the warrior-king of the Mycenaean era based his claim to power on his might and success as a fighter. He ruled not because the gods wanted him as their delegate, high priest, and supreme judge, speaking divinely inspired truth and justice, but because he was the most valiant and successful of the warriors, whom the gods assisted by allowing him the martial supremacy that was the origin of his power.

But, if that was so, we can ask the question of citizenship and its occidental uniqueness with more urgency and perhaps asperity. If Weber could look upon India, China, Judea, and Mesopotamia as oriental cultures and religions that "failed" to develop citizenship, surely we can ask the same question of Mycenaeans about a millennium later. Why did Mycenaeans, despite very favorable conditions, fail to develop the occidental polis? That they were about to do so is a teleological answer that begs the question. Is there a better answer given by the Mycenaeans themselves, whose voice is embodied in their script, which was not available to Weber in the early twentieth century?

While Minoan Linear A script still remains a mystery, the Mycenaean Linear B, which is in part based on Linear A, has been recovered from Mycenae, Thebes, Pylos, and from the period of Mycenaean occupation of Knossos (Palmer 1963; Vernant 1962). While tablets in Linear B were discovered in the early twentieth century, they were not deciphered until the 1950s (Ventris and Chadwick 1956). These tablets reveal a world of inventories, assessments, deliveries, records of distributions of materials for production and the goods produced, and specifics about land and herds (Palmer 1963). They also reveal a world of the king and the administration of the palace as well as its religious aspects (Chadwick 1976).

At first, the political and religious world of Mycenaean cities appears very similar to that of oriental cities. As the interpreter of the divine will and mediator between god and man, the Mycenaean king inherited characteristics of the Minoan and Near Eastern kingships: divine sanction was a privilege granted to a whole family and passed on by inheritance. Weber had held that this approach to theocratic kingship was circumscribed by the warrior aristocracy, exercising control through the assembly of elders, which collaborated with the king in every decision he made. For Weber, here as elsewhere, the ownership of martial capital was decisive: despite the power of *wanax,* he was not the sole supplier of arms to the warrior caste; *basileus,* too, could raise tribute and booty to maintain horses and arms. *Wanax* could not maintain an absolute power over *basileus* in the manner of Mesopotamian and Egyptian kings, because he did not have total control over martial capital.

Thus, the picture that emerges from the Mycenaean tablets—that the political struggle in Mycenaean culture revolved around the relations among fortified cities, each with its own king, the *basileus*—is not very different from that which was held by Weber. If the legitimacy of the king's rule over *basileus* had to be maintained continuously, and this had made the *wanax* rule very volatile, why, then, did the occidental polis not crystallize? While Weber believed that the fundamental weakness of the oriental theocracies was that they were not able to keep the king's power in check, this simultaneously raises the question of why the Mycenaeans were not able to develop the occidental polis.

To address that question, it would be fascinating to explore the Homeric epics from the point of view of citizenship as alterity. The significance of the Homeric epics is that they give us a mythical but eminently possible synthetic view of Minoan, Mycenaean, and early Greek warriors and their style of life. But it is very hard to know how categories such as "women," "peasants," "craftsmen," and "merchants" in Mycenaean cities functioned and how the warriors defined themselves against these forms of otherness. This is an irony because we are precisely interested in how dominant groups constructed their identities against the dominated. There are references in Mycenaean records to "followers," who were presumably the entourage of the king, as well as to their slaves, clothes, a distinctive style of dress, and access to the use of chariots. There is also reference to the *damos,* a word that was transformed into one of the most illustrious of concepts, *demos* in the classical Greek polis. For Mycenaeans it presumably meant "the people" or even perhaps "all others." It may have also meant the plot holders or peasants. There are also references to crafts, which included shepherd, goatherd, and ox driver; woodcutter, carpenter, mason, bronzesmith, and potter; carder, spinner, and weaver;

bath attendants and serving women. The differentiation of tasks is revealing: while both men and women appear as garment workers, only
women manufactured cloth and only men were fullers. Similarly, whereas the grinding and measuring of grain were women's work, only men
made bread. While Mycenaean documents display some differentiation
of categories, they do not reveal how they functioned. Nor is it possible to
understand how these categories emerged and how these identities were
constructed. What appears certain is that while the warriors had a distinct identity constructed against others, this identity was not yet expressed in "citizenship" or any other associational form. Rather, the
image that one gains is one of heroic warriors who considered themselves as independent lords warring within the realm of the king. Is it the
case, as Scully claimed, that while the polis in Homer is not yet a "state" in
the sense of the classical polis, it is still more than an autonomous *oikos*?
While in the Homeric polis, *politai* are not citizens but inhabitants of a
polis in the sense that the citizens are not conscripted, taxed, or governed
by a constitution, the polis already appears as a named political space and
citizenship as some kind of claim to such space (Scully 1990, 1–2).
Similarly, Homeric critics have begun to interpret the resolution of the
Iliad at the end of the epic as a reflection of a new spirit that emerges
from the heroic tradition and culminates in the ethos of the polis. Nagy,
however, argues that such an ethos is already emergent in the structure of
the *Iliad* (1997, 194).

Be that as it may, we cannot focus here on the Homeric poems. But
the remarkable story that emerges from the brief discussion above on
Minoan and Mycenaean cities is that the narrative of the occidental city
and citizenship is not only pervaded by external inconsistencies, as argued earlier, but also suffers from its own assumptions when applied to
ostensibly occidental times and places. Especially its twin pillars, the
ownership of the means of warfare and theocratic religions, are unable
to explain the failure of the crystallization of citizenship in Minoan and
Mycenaean cities, where presumably the conditions were most favorable. That said, however, a focus especially on Mycenaean cities with the
help of Homer reveals some very interesting developments in the emergence of new forms of government, conduct, and technologies of the
self. A warrior ethic, with its focus on prowess and skill, emerges as an
art of governing oneself. The emergence of the cult of physical perfection and the mighty warrior caste, securely dominant, aspiring to a no-
bler state, are intimately related to the articulation of polis, citizenship,
and politics.

Romancing Polis

Whether these are the signs of the emergence or the transformation of a warrior aristocracy into a landowning aristocracy, and the beginnings of an entirely new political institution, the polis, is another matter (Fine 1983, 46–50; Thomas and Conant 1999). If the origins of the city in history fascinated historians, the origins of the polis tantalized them even further, since the glory would be nothing less than an account of the origins of Western civilization. After at least a century of debates over the absolute origins of the polis, however, it is not surprising that we have various dates for its origins, ranging from the tenth century B.C. to the late sixth century B.C. (Fine 1983, 46). Moreover, the date is being increasingly pushed back toward the tenth, eleventh, or even twelfth centuries B.C.

The range of explanations of its "birth" has also expanded. Traditionally, a rapid demographic growth was an adequate explanation; now, ecological theories that emphasize agricultural pressures, military theories that focus on warfare, economic theories that highlight the rise of the peasants, and religious theories that draw attention to sanctuaries all compete for supremacy. General discussions that mention each of these explanations as being among many such "theories" conclude that probably each has some claim to truth. The problem with this state of affairs is that some definition of the polis is already held to be the true or essential polis. It is often defined essentially as an association (or confraternity) of "free" citizens, a sovereign (or self-governing), embryonic state that dominated its hinterland. For Mann, "The polis was a self-governing, territorial state of city and agricultural hinterland, in which every male landowner, aristocrat or peasant, born in the territory possessed freedom and citizenship" (1986, 197). For Finer, "The polis had five basic characteristics: sovereignty, political unity, identification with a cult, a surrounding rural area forming an extension of its identity, and the absence of kingship" (1997a, 331). For Finley, the polis was the integration of the city and the countryside (1981, 15). Once such a definition is held as essential and universal, tracing the moment of its appearance becomes almost impossible. That which we now call "polis" was never defined with the transparency and consistency we demand of it from the Greeks themselves. Let us recall here the qualifications with which we used the term "Greek citizenship." Similarly, if not even more urgently, we also ought to introduce these qualifications regarding "polis." As Davies warned, its usage represents a compound of different chronological layers denoting a variety of settlements and polities (1997). Also, its usage ignores what is left out: what polities were not defined as polis and why (Whittaker 1995)? Yet, the point of such qualifications is not to lament that we lack evidence, though lamentable it is, nor that the Greeks were never clear about their use. On the contrary, that the meaning, usage, and function of these words changed constantly and often surprisingly attests to the fact that they were themselves stakes in prevailing social struggles and their particular definitions were used to assemble solidaristic, agonistic, or alienating strategies. Against romancing the polis, the task is to focus on moments of the problematizations of both "polis" and "citizen" to get a glimpse of how and against whom they were defined, what authorities (gods, rituals, sacrileges) were invoked in their definitions, and how they were assembled as strategies of solidarity, agon, or alienation.

There are three moments of reversals or problematizations of the city and citizenship relationship in ancient Greece that a genealogy ought to investigate. First is the moment when a tradition invented the polis as the settling together of tribes (synoecism). This tradition would have us believe that synoecism was the drive behind the occidental dethroning of oriental kingship and the invention of warrior-citizenship. Second is the moment of democracy as the government of demos and the invention of peasant-citizenship. The third moment is the ostensible "decline" of the polis as a space of government and citizenship.

Making Greek Citizens

As we have seen above, fortified cities centered on a citadel were known to Mycenaean culture. From the tenth to the eighth centuries, the regional settlements that made up the demos and their inhabitants were organized into chiefdoms that appear similar to centrally organized Mycenaean kingdoms dominated by a chariot aristocracy and *wanax* (Mann 1986, 183). But they were very different. Each emergent polis was ruled by a hereditary leader, *basileis* (Donlan 1997). While the *basileus* differentiated themselves from the rest of the demos as their hegemon, they did not have unqualified dominating power (Drews 1983, 129–30). Moreover, during the eighth century the *basileis* gradually lost its power to landowning demos, which became the hegemonic aristocracy in Greek poleis. The rise of the polis aristocracy, which shared power more or less equally among its members and was unified in protecting its privileges, altered the traditional power relationships. The system of officials and boards joined the traditional institutions of *boule* (council) and the agora (assembly) and were effective means of control used by the aristocracy.

The "polis" before the seventh century, however, stands more for a decentralized and fragmented series of villages that gravitated around a citadel or an acropolis than for a unified spatial settlement. Often, the citadel or acropolis was the residence and stronghold of the *basileis*. The polis, therefore, unlike Mycenaean cities, was typically not walled and was surrounded by households (*oikos* or *oikoi* in plural) in control of some arable and pasture land (Fine 1983, 48). As Fustel puts it, "We must not picture to ourselves the city of these ancient ages as an agglomeration of men living mingled together within the enclosure of the same walls. In the earliest times the city was hardly the place of habitation; it was the sanctuary where the gods of the community were; it was the fortress which defended them, and which their presence sanctified; it was the centre of the association, the residence of the king and the priests, the place where justice was administered; but the people did not live there. For generations yet men continued to live outside the city, in isolated families, that divided the soil among them" (Fustel de Coulanges 1864, 221). "[I]f the territory occupied by a tribal group was small, the various *oikoi* lived close to the place of refuge and . . . the men walked to their fields or pastures each morning and returned to their homes in the evening. If the territory was of considerable size, it is likely that, as conditions became more secure, many *oikoi* took up residence on their own lands" (Fine 1983, 49). According to tradition, however, sometime in the seventh century these tribes were synoecized or settled together to form the better known polis. This is the narrative of the birth of the polis as a unified space. With the increasing numbers of *oikoi*, villages were formed around the acropolis, eventually uniting into the polis. Aristotle in *Politics* speaks of the village being formed from a union of *oikoi* and the polis arising from a union of villages (1995, 1.1.6–11). As Lefebvre claims, "The Greek polis, with its acropolis and agora, came into being through a synoecism, a unification of villages, upon a hilltop. Its birth was attended by the clear light of day" (1974, 247). Or from his analytic perspective, "For the citizen and city-dweller, representational space and the representation of space, though they did not coincide, were harmonious and congruent" (247). As a result, Lefebvre says, "The Greek city, as a spatial and social hierarchy, utilized its meticulously defined space to bring demes, aristocratic clans, villages, and groups of craftsmen and traders together into the unity of the polis" (249). This uncritical acceptance and reproduction of ancient synoecism must be subjected to a critique.

Critique of Synoecism

That synoecism, while it may capture some elements of how some poleis were established in later centuries, notably in the sixth and fifth, does not adequately describe the manifold appearance of poleis in earlier periods has important consequences for investigating citizenship. Both ancient and modern theories of the origins of the polis in terms of synoecism often assume a homology between space as a container in which a group exercises sovereignty and the political space (polis) that gives such a group its name and institutions. (Synoecism, therefore, can be considered as a progenitor of "sovereignty.") While in archaic and classical periods such homology existed to an extent, it would be inaccurate to assume it for any earlier period in which the polis emerged. In the ninth and eighth centuries b.c., the establishment of strict boundaries in which a space of citizenship was defined was not always as definite. The formulation of relations between various poleis strictly in terms of confrontation, or submission of citizens and foreigners or insiders and outsiders was not as definite as in later periods. "The birth of the city has thus been presented as resulting from the disintegration of a society based upon private solidarity, dominated by noble clans organized into phratries and tribes, and placed under the authority of a monarchical institution that was progressively dismantled as, within the confines of the territory, a community based on public law developed" (de Polignac 1995, 1). "The city was thus believed to have developed in a concentric fashion, with the city territory spreading out around the town, which was the seat of the city, and the prestigious acropolis and temple where the city cult ensured and expressed the unity of the group" (de Polignac 1995, 2). De Polignac argues that that model may conform to the model of how Athens developed, but many other Greek poleis do not follow the same pattern. By questioning the accounts given by Greek philosophers as accurate authorities, he instead suggests a model of the Greek polis in which centers and peripheries of the city form an intricate fabric of agon, fear, and solidarity all at once. The concept of synoecism as spatial agglomeration or unification, therefore, conceals the polycentric political and spatial order of the polis.

The argument is that the struggles over sanctuaries, temples, and other sacred places that began emerging in the ninth century defined a polycentric space. De Polignac argues that the sanctuary was often situated right on the threshold of the polis territory (1995, 33). In areas with various scattered tribes and communities, sanctuaries situated at equal distance from them all continued to be shared. The organization of space was therefore more complex than a bounded territory; instead space was arranged vis-à-vis manifold relationships of different groups (de Polignac 1995, 36). How did struggles over the liminal space of the sanctuary crystallize into the polis in the eighth century? De Polignac answers that question by following traditional theories of hoplitic warfare. As is well known, Homeric warfare in the form of raids by heroic warriors with chariots belonged to the world of chiefdoms that were independent in a pastoral economy. With the increase of population, land was increasingly used for agricultural purposes, prompting a new concept of space. This led to a change in the objective of warfare, from heroic raids to protecting arable land against invasion. This took the form of group tactics, by means of which the enemy could be repulsed in a battle on the plain. The space can be claimed only with a permanent appropriation, rather than with a temporary chance for pillage. Thus, "the basic elements of archaic and classical warfare were elaborated: two armies drawn up in serried ranks would confront each other within a defined area, a plain, from which each would attempt to eject the other so as to remain in occupation of the terrain" (de Polignac 1995, 49).

This was related to the development of hoplitic warfare (Mann 1986, 199–201; Robertson 1997, 151; Vidal-Naquet 1986, 256). The shift from heroic warfare to hoplitic warfare coincided with the appearance of pieces of weaponry in the archaic sanctuaries (de Polignac 1995, 48). To put it in other words, the objectified form of martial capital underwent change: breastplates and helmets were redesigned and the shield became the most important piece of defensive equipment (Snodgrass 1964). The round shield held by means of a double handle on the inner side, through which the left forearm and the hand passed, was the essential item in the cohesion of the hoplite phalanx. The wall of shields, each one overlapping the next, ensured the protection of the whole line of men, instead of each separate shield protecting a single individual (de Polignac 1995, 48–49). This was closely associated with a transformation in the embodied form of martial capital: hoplitic warfare required different skills and prowess than heroic warfare. The countless drills for coordination, assemblage, and movement of the phalanx demanded a different citizen-body. This, in turn, resulted in institutional forms of martial capital: the gymnasium, the symposium, and the sanctuary. All this combined to articulate a new warrior ethic, an ethic that valued fraternization over heroization. The consecration of pieces of weaponry in a sanctuary did not necessarily confer a warrior stature upon the deity concerned, but rather underlined the protection expected from her. The sanctuary thus became the stake in the struggles for influence and the formation of a warrior-citizen identity. More importantly, sovereignty meant not only the appropriation of space, but claiming the foundation myths, the deities, the sanctuary, and the rites of a territory (de Polignac 1995, 53). By using traditional theories of hoplitic warfare, de Polignac arrives at a somewhat original position, where synoecism simultaneously emerges from struggles over citizenship, rather than being reduced to an epiphenomenon. As well, synoecism does not necessarily imply a spatial agglomeration or unification, but a configuration or order with both spatial and political meanings (Snodgrass 1980, 34).

The double consequence of an essential transformation in martial capital was the articulation of the polis as a polycentric and dispersed space that warrior-citizens both identified themselves with and laid claims to. When heroic warfare gave way to hoplitic warfare, a new aristocratic warrior-citizen ethos appropriate to it was articulated, which began to assemble various solidaristic, agonistic, and alienating strategies for defining itself and its otherness. De Polignac, however, overemphasizes the centrality and unification of the new polis, essentially following the accounts he sought to supplant: "This signalled the emergence of a new type of social organization and the birth of territorially-based community known as the polis, which gathered into a single decision-taking body all the local *basileis* who had previously been more or less independent of one another" (1995, 58). As we shall see, the unity that was attributed to the archaic and classic polis can also be called into question. Moreover, von Reden argues that the skepticism toward synoecism can be extended to Athens as well. Von Reden illustrates that there is enough archeological and textual evidence to show that the narrative of synoecism was a creation of the dominant citizens in the city. Athens in the fifth century was an imagined place of unity. Underneath this imagined unity there was difference, strife, and agon. "The territorial construction of Athens as one place, civic unity and hegemony, then, were related themes" (von Reden 1998, 177). In sum, synoecism can be seen as a narrative strategy used by the dominant groups of the polis, first by warrior-citizens and later by aristocrat-warrior-citizens, to construct a harmonious and congruent space in order to impose a vision of their own hegemony as the vision of the polis, and hence its polymorphic usage (Snodgrass 1980, 34). Their identification with the polis was not only represented by their claims to the city, but also its representation as a unified and harmonious entity. But the narrative is too rational and rationalized to account for the messy realities of the emergence of the polis as both a political and spatial order. As we have seen earlier, it becomes even more problematic when it is further generalized to the founding of the occidental city in history.

Kingship Never Dies

Along with synoecism, the other narrative that sustains orientalism and its emphasis on a sharp distinction between the occidental and oriental forms of government is the dethroning of the kings with the emergence of the polis in the eighth and seventh centuries B.C. (Fine 1983, 53; Starr 1961). The crux of the matter is that while the Near Eastern kingship developed into a royal army that was equipped, fed, and led by a royal bureaucracy, Greek kingship was dethroned by the association of warrior-citizens (Weber 1909, 157). This is the contrast Weber wanted to establish between the oriental civilizations, where the kingship was a central and centralizing power that persisted down to their disappearance, and Greece, where the polis developed. For two main reasons, however, it is doubtful that such a sharp distinction can be drawn.

First, there is considerably more continuity and emulation between the Greek aristocracy and the oriental bureaucracy. As Burkert put it, "Emanating from the Near East, in connection with military expansion and growing economic activities, a cultural continuum including literacy was created by the eighth century extending over the entire Mediterranean; it involved groups of Greeks who entered into intensive exchange with the high cultures of the Semitic East. Cultural predominance remained for a while with the Orient; but Greeks immediately began to develop their own distinctive forms of culture through an astonishing ability both to adopt and to transform what they had received" (1984, 128). He thus concludes that "[t]he 'miracle of Greece' is not merely the result of unique talent. It also owes its existence to the simple phenomenon that the Greeks are the most easterly of Westerners" (Burkert 1984, 129). Whereas the warrior aristocracy had enjoyed collecting gold and treasure, hunting, and owning fine armor, the new landowning aristocracy left to others the job of looking after their lands, preferring to live in the city, where they resembled the wealthy classes of the oriental city in their passion for the arts and for cultured life. As Morris puts it vividly, "Reclining on couches of Near Eastern type and using vessels with Lydian prototypes, aristocrats sang about Lydian dress, women and military might, judging Greek life against these standards. The new symbols justified their users' claims to superiority—they virtually mixed with the gods themselves, just like the ancient heroes on whom society had depended for its very existence; and they felt like the kings of the East, whose power and elegance vastly exceeded those of the Greeks" (1997, 13). While the new polis no longer displayed the characteristics of the oriental model of a fortified city dominated by a palace or citadel, the aristocracy certainly displayed affinities with the oriental ruling elite. (The irony of this is that these aristocrats probably felt much closer to the oriental kings in their aspirations than the nineteenth-century historians concerned with establishing the racial superiority of the Europeans did.) Also, wars were still waged by warriors in their chariots, cavalry as well as the new hoplite infantry. While the ethos of warrior-aristocrats was blended into aristocrat-citizens, the latter still obligated itself with the burden and privilege of warrior duty to protect the polis. Hence, the orientalization of aristocrat-citizens in valuing beauty, eroticism, wine, arcane mythical knowledge, and athletic skills made them closer to Near Eastern warriors than imagined.

Second, kingship never disappeared from ancient Greece. While it is obvious that their powers were curtailed and circumscribed by warrior- and aristocrat-citizens, the persistent and stubborn emergence of tyrants throughout Greek poleis time and again should be seen in connection with the institution of kingship, albeit a transformed one (Ogden 1997, 148).

To say that the ancient Greek kings were dethroned by warrior- and aristocrat-citizens who then became the "ruling class" for several generations is too sharp a distinction and leads to claims about an essential distinction between the oriental and occidental forms of kingship, which are still held in esteem. As Finer puts it, "From the beginning of recorded history in Sumeria and Egypt—for some two-and-a-half thousands of years—every constituted state had been a monarchy: not only in the known world of the Middle East and eastern Mediterranean, but also in the worlds of India and distant China too. These monarchs had all been absolute, and godlike too, except for the Jewish kingdom where God ruled the kings. Suddenly there was government without kings or god. Instead there were man-made, custom-built republics of citizens" (1997a, 316). Similarly, Finley credited the Greek polis with departing radically from the religious doctrines of the Near East in which "man was created for the sole and specific purposes of serving the gods" (1983, 129). Cartledge also draws a sharp distinction between the conception of Greek kingship and the oriental conception of kingship: "The Greek conception was closer to the later deployment of tyrant or despot as someone who rules with the consent of the ruled with virtue and wisdom and is somehow above the common herd of his subjects" (1993, 105). Or, as Mann states it, with the production of weaponry, "the balance of power gradually shifted from aristocracies to peasantries, from pastoralists to agriculturalists, from mobile chariots to infantries, from the steppes to fields, and from the Middle and Near East to the West" (1986, 185).

To question these sharp distinctions between the occidental and oriental forms of kingship is not to refuse the importance of the emergence of a warrior ethic and its articulation of citizenship as its identity. Rather, it is to refuse to make it an immutable and essential discovery, revolution, or the dawn of a new era. Instead, an emphasis on how this ethic was assembled from various sources, how it constituted an art of governing oneself and others, and how various solidaristic and agonistic strategies were assembled with various technologies of citizenship begins to reveal a different story.

Governing the Polis

When the discussion shifts from grand themes of synoecism and revolutions to governing the polis, attention gets focused on a few institutions such as boule (council), assembly, and elections, and places such as the pnyx and agora. Although little is known about the government and politics of the early poleis, the most important governing body was already the council, which, with variations, had evolved from the council of the elders of Mycenaean kings (Fine 1983, 57). The most prestigious and wealthy aristocrats undoubtedly controlled the relatively small council. Although there is no direct evidence, there are traces of the continuance of assemblies from the era of the kings, bringing together warriors and elder warriors. Any general assembly of the people other than warriors, such as farmers or artisans, is not known. Under these conditions it may be considered inappropriate to argue for the emergence of citizenship in the early poleis, but the warriors, who could be members of both the council and the assembly, had to be well aware of who was and was not entitled to full privileges in the polis (Fine 1983, 58). Being a citizen in an archaic (750 B.C.–500 B.C.) polis meant being born into an aristocratic family, which qualified the citizen to be a member of the polis as an association of tribes or clans known as phratries. Much attention is focused on the development of the council and assembly and changing qualifications for participating in them and the legislation they enacted. While undoubtedly important for matters concerning government, the exercise of power and government of conduct of both oneself and others were by no means limited to these institutions. Moreover, those who established themselves as the qualified members of the council and assembly, even in earlier poleis when such privilege was hereditary, had to establish the legitimacy of their government and regularly prove their capacity to govern.

It is in this pursuit to continuously establish their legitimacy that citizens invented a series of solidaristic and agonistic strategies and assembled corresponding technologies of citizenship, differentiated themselves from others, defined and redefined virtue and vice, and constituted themselves with and against other strangers and outsiders immanent in the polis. Cultivating an image of themselves as superior beings in the eyes and minds of peasants, slaves, artisans, craftsmen, and women was of considerable importance. The warrior ethos and aristocratic citizenship was predicated on heroization and eponymization, where human beings had special virtues that made them closer to the gods than other men, whose beauty, power, influence, and cultivation made them godlike. Thus, religion was a solidaristic strategy for the aristocrats, as it had been for the Homeric kings. But it also limited their power, for they were bound by it to observe the traditional principles of rights and obligations. Warrior- and aristocrat-citizens claimed to have origins in the union of *oikoi*. To justify their status, they placed emphasis on their high birth and ancestry and the unified nature of the polis and its origins as settling together (von Reden 1998). Because of their inherited wealth and status, they often claimed ancestry based on a hero or god, and called themselves the best—the aristoi (Fine 1983, 56).

The citizenry as an association of aristocrats sought to establish and maintain a distinct identity for itself via assembling various solidaristic and agonistic strategies in the polis. Among solidaristic strategies were gift giving, councils and feasts, heroization through cults, and warrior burials (Tandy 1997, 141). Gift giving as a ritualized performance allowed the separation of participants in the rituals from nonparticipants, which brought coherence to the citizenry and distinguished it from others. To be a citizen was to be recognized by another citizen in the ritual of gift giving. In the eighth century, symposia and feasts were powerful forces in the maintenance of aristocratic authority; ritualized performances included forms of conduct transplanted from war rituals and translated into mutual recognition and aid (Tandy 1997, 142). Similarly, participating in burials of the fallen warriors and the exaltation of heroes into cult status with symbols and markers reinforced the formation of warrior and aristocrat citizenry into a group that literally made citizens.

Following the footsteps of Fustel, de Polignac argues that these transformations led to citizenship as an institution that fused religion and politics. In fact, at a certain level, citizenship was religious in the sense that its definition and rituals were closely bound up with founding myths, rituals, and sanctuaries of the city. The case of women is instructive. While they were constituted as noncitizens, they nonetheless acquired a prominent religious space. The sanctuary of the Thesmophorion was set up in virtually every city as the sacred space belonging to women. The cult of Demeter and ceremonies associated with it were acted out in this space, which was at the threshold of the city. The relative isolation of the sanctuary, the secret nature of its rites, and the public nature of the procession symbolized the crucial responsibility of women protecting the city. "That responsibility conferred upon the women a latent citizenship of a religious nature, without which there could never have been any citizenship of the other, political, kind" (de Polignac 1995, 73). But by granting men's citizenship the title "political" and designating women's citizenship as "religious," de Polignac reproduces the same orientation toward women as strangers. Were women any less political than men by virtue of enacting citizenship in other, perhaps illegitimate, spaces? Quite the contrary. The integration of women was not a passive (e.g., religious, spiritual) form of belonging, but a necessary and immanent element for the constitution of the city.

A similar argument can be made about other strangers and outsiders who were nevertheless integrated into the polis. Organizing a cult involving various groups and others was a way of founding a city. The sanctuary of Artemis at Ephesus is an example of a sanctuary that provided a space for strangers and was located on the edge of the city. De Polignac argues that while the polis is frequently conceived of in strictly institutional terms as a community of citizens with full rights, embodied by its sovereign assembly, how this community was delicately defined against its various others is equally important (77). The early polis was extremely heterogeneous and the positions of its inhabitants were much more varied than their statuses. These distinctions were less defined than the distinctions that separated the citizens of the classical polis from its women, children, foreigners, and slaves (78). The polis was thus based on a religious citizenship shared in varying degrees and forms by their kings, warriors, women, and others in an intricate balance of trust, fear, and solidarity expressed in its space.

Much of the conflict among Greek poleis that resulted in hostilities and war was not among poleis as such, but among and between groups that were predominant in them. And for much of the era from the eighth to the sixth centuries B.C., the conflict was among aristocrats for hegemony. Owning martial capital as well as being involved in agriculture and trade situated the aristocrats powerfully vis-à-vis the peasants, slaves, artisans, and other workers. Many peasants, not being able to meet production requirements, fell into debt slavery. Debt slaves were freemen who had lost status, and as such they were different from political subjects or slaves (Weber 1909, 171). For these groups, there was not much they could do to encounter or threaten the aristocratic class, whose opulent display of wealth, power, and status must have seemed impregnable.

Beyond Revolutions

If we have reasons to be skeptical about a revolution in warfare that dethroned kings and established synoecism, we also have reasons to doubt that a hoplite revolution gave birth to democracy as the rule of the demos. The story is well known. By the end of the sixth century, just as the days of the kings with their armor and their chariots had passed centuries ago, the age of cavalry, too, was said to be coming to an end. The hoplitic warfare increasingly incorporated wealthier peasants and other groups who were gradually becoming political, that is, making claims for becoming citizens (Fine 1983, 58; Thomas 1982, 102–3). With the beginning of the money economy, a change in the production techniques of weaponry, the introduction of slavery, and the consequent increase in agricultural production and trade, there were more opportunities for wealth and access to the means of warfare. While the early hoplites came from the wealthy clans and tribes, more people could now afford to equip themselves and become hoplites. Meanwhile, warships also became significant in warfare, resulting in wealth generated from shipbuilding and trade. As well, the growing debt-bondage suffered by peasants led to the challenging of the almost hero-like superiority of the aristocrats. For Weber the debt-bondage of the peasantry was the crux of a bitter strife that came to define the classical polis (1909, 172).

There is a tradition of scholarship that attributes revolutionary character to hoplitic warfare. This tradition, primarily articulated by Eduard Meyer (but already present in Fustel de Coulanges) and elaborated by Weber, drew a sharp distinction between the age of Homeric heroes, when wars were fought by leaders on horseback, and a later age, when the hoplite phalanx formation introduced the peasants into the political field by virtue of their martial involvement. The underpinnings of this tradition were strengthened by Snodgrass (1964), whose study on the evolution of early Greek martial equipment supported the argument that new weaponry had political consequences. But as Raaflaub argued, hoplitic warfare was prevalent in Homeric battles as well, and hoplites were not new in the seventh century (1997, 53). As we have seen, de Polignac also argued the importance of the incipient hoplite in the origins of the early polis. Or as Raaflaub puts it, "The hoplite-farmers were *the* essential group among the citizens" in the original polis (1997, 53). So there must have been other factors explaining the increasing power of hoplite-peasants in the polis. This is not to argue that changing techniques of warfare did not have any effect on the formation of groups and identities, but that the singular, revolutionary changes attributed to them ought to be questioned. It is important to note, as Robertson does, for example, that "[w]ith the development of hoplite warfare, the 'warrior class' be-came wider to the point where, particularly at Sparta, it was identified with the citizen body itself; military elegy is public poetry, strengthening the bonds that keep the warrior class (and, therefore, the state as a whole) together. Despite its prominence in the literary tradition, this aspect of martial endeavour is, as has been shown, absent from verse epitaphs of the Archaic period; instead prominence appears to be given to the war-rior as an individual" (1997, 151). However, while the transformations in hoplitic warfare must have been crucial in allowing the peasants to make claims to the city and demand presence and representation in its institu-tions, to attribute singular, let alone revolutionary, character to them in the "birth of democracy" diverts attention from less conspicuous, though no less significant, transformations occurring almost imperceptibly in various rituals and strategies that allowed more strangers and outsiders to become citizens. In addition, the incessant focus on bitter class con-flicts diverts attention away from various solidaristic (symposia, gymna-sia), agonistic (Olympic, tragic), and alienating (ostracism, exile) strategies and technologies that mobilized peasants, slaves, merchants, craftsmen, women, and metics to confront, challenge, and contest the games of citi-zenship, thereby taking risks of being estranged and alienated.

For de Ste. Croix, for example, in the fifth and fourth centuries B.C. the class struggle for peasants, laborers, and craftsmen was essentially about the control of the state. But the state here refers to the *politeia*, which meant both citizenship and the constitution. In some instances it also meant "a way of life" (de Ste. Croix 1981, 286). De Ste. Croix believed that only adult male citizens could participate effectively in "class strug-gle," except in special circumstances, such as the democratic restoration at Athens in 403 B.C. after the rule of tyrants, when metics and other for-eigners (even some slaves) participated and some were rewarded with citizenship (288). The peasantry demanded as its first concession secure legislation on the matters that chiefly concerned it, but legislation contained no constitutional reforms or a radical departure from the definition of citizenship or politics. For de Ste. Croix, this was a clear indication that the peasants were not interested in their political status, but only in their economic situation. So the ruling aristocracy was able to maintain its political supremacy, only making concessions on matters concerning the economic situation of the peasants. Where aristocratic resistance was more bitter and tenacious, one finds that the new groups had begun to have political consciousness and aspirations; on other occasions the very resistance of the aristocracy provoked revolt, which they had to put down through force, leading inevitably to tyranny. The tyrannies spread throughout the seventh and sixth centuries B.C.

But as Wood (1988) has effectively shown, the peasants were able to acquire much more substantive rights than mere concessions and were not just interested in "economic" gains. In fact, a clear difference between the political and economic, especially in classical Athens, is not easy to maintain. Schmitt-Pantel (1990) also argued that the Greeks did not separate the sacred and profane or the political and economic. In the aristocratic city, participation in collective activities such as sacrifices, banquets, hunting expeditions, practicing with ephebes or hoplites, choruses, funerals, assemblies, and festivals was already a sign of belonging to the group of citizens. These practices formed a chain in the sense that they were continually interwoven and were not separated by sacred and profane, political and religious divisions (Schmitt-Pantel 1990, 200–201). Veyne (1976), Vidal-Naquet (1986), Meier (1990), and many other scholars assume that with the appearance of the classical polis, these practices were merely confined to the assembly and others to the private life of the citizen. Thus, the agora, the assembly, and the pnyx have been valorized as spaces of being political. To be sure, the elaboration of being political in Athens coexisted with a whole discourse on democracy dealing only with matters revolving around the assembly and equality, but "archaic" practices still maintained their strategic significance (Schmitt-Pantel 1990, 204). As Schmitt-Pantel argues, collective practices "were the expression of the civic community as a whole in archaic cities. Later in classical Athens they became visible within particular groups" (1990, 205). Therefore Schmitt-Pantel sees less a rupture between the political and the social, and more a reconfiguration in the "rituals of conviviality." The usefulness of this analysis is that it recovers moments of becoming political from instances of being social (without conflating the two), which citizens who constituted themselves in the assembly and agora would rather not recognize. Similarly, as Ober (1996) argues, there is much to gain from the views of noncitizens in classical Athens that the critics of democracy such as Thucydides, Aristotle, and Plato held in contempt. It is worthy, then, to briefly discuss a few solidaristic, agonistic, and alienating strategies that existed in the polis in tenuous and blurred forms of sociability but became assembled and codified in the classical polis and that distributed, allocated, and differentiated citizens, strangers, outsiders, aliens, and barbarians in the social and spatial order of the polis.

Breeding Difference

To claim that the polis was a difference machine is to refuse to consider it as a unity. For centuries classification struggles raged over categories and classes of citizens and their strangers, outsiders and aliens. That the body of citizens itself was a differentiated group and that there was a difference among its ranks was mostly obvious to the Greeks themselves though it seems much less so to the moderns, given our insistence on referring to "Greek citizenship" as a unified concept. Even Aristotle, who sought the happiness and good order of the city in its unification, recognized that "[n]ot only is the city composed of a *number* of people: it is also composed of different *kinds* of people, for a city cannot be composed of those who are like one another," concluding that "[a] city, by its nature, is some sort of plurality. If it becomes more of a unit, it will first become a household instead of a city, and the individual more of a unit than the household. It follows that, even if we could, we ought not to achieve this object: it would be the destruction of the city" (1995, 1261a10). Thus, when Aristotle declared man as a being of the polis, did he mean that all who belonged to the polis were citizens (1253a2)? Hardly. In fact, only gods and barbarians are beings who do not belong to the polis, but citizens, strangers, and outsiders make up its space. As Saxonhouse observes, Aristotle recognized the essence of the polis as a unity embodying multiplicity (1992). She argues that Aristotle was able to shake off a fear his predecessors displayed toward diversity and embrace the richness of the polis as a space of multiplicity: "The political art is to understand the need for diversity within the city and not to fear it, to acknowledge that it is the diversity that, while building the city, can never bring about a city that has escaped the conflicts of political claims" (1992, 232).

A complex array of categories within citizens and between citizens and strangers and outsiders was generated from within the polis. Slaves, women, peasants, merchants, and artisans were crystallized through the polis and formed by being implicated in the tangled web of strategies and

technologies of citizenship. The formation of the polis was simultaneously the formation of citizens, their virtues, strategies, and technologies
of citizenship that gave them their identity qua others, distributed themselves spatially, and constituted themselves socially and politically. These
city-citizen games were a religious devotion in the sense that it was at the
foundation of the polis. Fustel de Coulanges was not exaggerating when
he claimed that "[t]he citizen was recognized by the fact that he had a
part in the religion of the city, and it was from this participation that he
derived all his civil and political rights. If he renounced the worship, he
renounced the rights" (1864, 185). "If we wished to give an exact definition of a citizen, we should say that it was a man who had the religion of
the city. The stranger, on the contrary, is one who has not access to worship, one whom the gods of the city did not protect, and who has not
even the right to invoke them" (186). "Thus religion established between
the citizen and the stranger a profound and ineffaceable distinction. This
same religion, so long as it held its sway over the minds of men, forbade
the right of citizenship to be granted to the stranger" (186–87). Accordingly, Fustel argues that granting citizenship to strangers was taken so seriously that the formalities to go through it were more complicated than
declaring war against another city (187). Fustel argues that strangers and
outsiders were denied the protection of law and religion, but slaves were
better off because they shared in the institutions of the city, at least via
their masters (189). But the same could not be said about the *helots*,
Spartan slaves who were owned by and worked for the polis and whose
access to the polis was even more restricted than metics (foreigners). The
helots outnumbered Spartan citizens and their movement was controlled
(Powell 1988, 250). By contrast, women everywhere, while considered as
noncitizens, had access to religious and legal resources of the polis and its
protection. Government by women, *gynaikokratia*, in Sparta was lamented in other poleis. Their position in the social and spatial order of the
polis was very different from that of the varieties of metics (foreigners),
whose entry into citizenship was extremely rare and arduous. Then there
were categories such as the *perioikoi*, free noncitizens in Sparta, whose
name literally meant "those who live around"; their numbers may have
been larger than those of the Spartan citizens. The *perioikoi* were integrated into Sparta's hoplites, some of whom rose to influential positions (Powell 1988, 247–48). Metics were resident foreigners but citizens
distinguished several (at least seven in Athens) categories of metics
(MacDowell 1978, 76–77). In Athens, there were metics who were given
property ownership rights *(enktesis)*, who were given rights to pay the

same taxes as citizens instead of the higher taxes paid by metics *(isotelia)*, who were given the privilege of fighting alongside citizens rather than in special units, who were granted immunity from being harmed abroad by other Athenians *(asylia)*, and so on. A general category of otherness was *banausia*, a sort of contemptible recognition of strangers and outsiders. Aristotle, for example, claims that "the best polis should not have *banausoi* among its citizens" (1995, 1278a8). He claimed that *banausic* occupations in the polis should be fulfilled by metics and slaves.

Obviously, these categories were negotiated and allowed strangers and outsiders of the polis to make claims to certain rights of citizenship by using their social, symbolic, economic, and martial forms of capital. Metics, helots, *gynaikokratia, perioikoi,* artisans, merchants, and *banausoi* were only some of the bewildering forms of otherness with which citizens delineated noncitizens and devised various agonistic and alienating strategies, which we shall see below. But citizens were also differentiated within themselves and assembled various solidaristic and agonistic strategies to maintain these differentiations.

The differentiations within citizens was as serious as their differentiation from others. Throughout centuries, whether codified by legislators such as Draco, Solon, and Cleisthenes in Athens, or remaining latent in many other poleis, or becoming deeply entrenched as in Sparta, various classes and categories were devised and contested that differentiated citizens according to their wealth, status, descent, or some combination. In seventh-century B.C. Athens, for example, *geomoroi* were freemen, generally peasant farm holders, lower on the social and political scale than the *eupatridae,* the aristocracy, but above the *demiourgoi,* the artisans. The *geomoroi* were ineligible for any major political or religious post but had the right to attend sessions of the assembly. In 580 B.C., three *geomoroi* shared the archonship (magistracy) with five *eupatridae* and two *demiourgoi.* At the beginning of the sixth century, the introduction of four classes of citizens by Solon is an example of this differentiated polis. The four classes were the wealthiest class or *pentakosiomedimnoi;* the *hippeis,* or cavalry class; the *zeugitai,* or hoplites; and the *thetes,* the class that later provided most of the rowers for the fleet. For each class there were elaborate rules of conduct as citizens. A legislator such as Solon, who is widely credited with making a gesture toward "democracy," "equality," and "justice," obviously saw no contradiction in introducing very well-defined classes of citizens. In Syracuse and in Samos, where the polis was divided into only two classes, the *geomoroi* were the oligarchs, in contrast to the demos. At Corinth, citizenship was confined to the adult males of a single clan, the *Bacchiadae*, but its unity was challenged very early.

When, therefore, the term *polis* or *citizen* is used in Greek thought, it never seems to have, and could not possibly have, meant a unity or harmony. When such things as unity and harmony are praised, as in the funeral oration tradition, and especially that of Perikles, they were solidaristic strategies that expressed the will of the dominant citizens rather than an achieved reality (Loraux 1986). Similarly, synoecism was an invented tradition of ancient Greek citizens that has been uncritically accepted by nineteenth- and twentieth-century historians. Also, the association of being political with being a citizen and the perception that the activities of noncitizens were outside the political realm was an interpretation from the perspective of citizens, rather than that of strangers and outsiders.

The two well-known institutions of symposia and gymnasia can be interpreted as solidaristic and agonistic strategies devised for transmitting and inculcating virtues of citizenship. The symposium, or feast, for which (many literary scholars now believe) much surviving poetry was originally written, was an eating and dining occasion with a strong ritual element. Its existence is reflected in the marked emphasis, beginning with the Homeric poems, on ostentatious feasting and formal banqueting as assertions of status (what have been called "feasts of merit"). The gymnasium was the venue where the body of the citizen was habituated into conducting oneself both as a warrior and a citizen. That the love of boys is notoriously absent from the Homeric poems and that it becomes explicit with the rise of the polis illustrates the importance of inculcating virtues of citizenship from the older citizen (the *erastes*) to the younger *eromenos*. The gymnasium was the venue in which such relationships typically developed (Sennett 1994, 44–46, 50). Both symposia and gymnasia in different ways mirrored a warrior ethic. By contrast, another well-known institution, the Olympic Games, can be interpreted as an agonistic strategy of group formation that allowed citizens to both inculcate and display their embodied virtues.

Lesser known but no less significant strategies can also be found in the polis. Two such institutions are *xenia* and *epigamia*. Both were ritualized forms institutionalizing relationships among cities across poleis. *Xenia* was "ritualized friendship" in the sense that citizens who drank and heard poetry together inside their own poleis established comparable groups across other poleis. They cemented their ties, which had perhaps been formed on casual or trading visits, with formal relationships of *xenia.* At some point quite early in the archaic polis this technology developed into something still more definite, the *proxenia. Proxenoi* were citizens of a polis who looked after the interests of citizens of another. Another way of institutionalizing relationships between citizens across poleis was *epigamia,* an arrangement by which the offspring and husband of marriage were treated as citizens of the wife's polis if the husband settled there. Athens, for example, granted epigamia to Euboea as late as the fifth century, a time when Athenian citizenship was fiercely protected. There are still earlier instances where one encounters epigamia when for one reason or another it was being suspended or denied.

Another much less known and understood practice that began as an alienating practice and evolved into an agonistic practice was *atimia.* In the sixth and early fifth centuries Athens, *atimia* was outlawry, which was imposed as a penalty for various offenses. This meant that a man designated as *atimos* forfeited rights and privileges, but it is hard to know what exactly that meant in practice. However, we know that if a man became *atimos,* anyone could kill or otherwise maltreat him without becoming liable to penalty. Thus, such *atimia* was roughly equivalent to expulsion from Attika, and it could be imposed on aliens as well as Athenian citizens (MacDowell 1978, 73). By the late fifth century *atimia* became more like "disfranchisement," but it still involved losses more than just the right to vote. Also an *atimos* was still better off than an alien. "*Atimia* remains one of the most difficult topics in the study of Athenian law" (MacDowell 1978, 75). Associated with *atimia* was the practice of outing, *endeixis.* Since among the penalties was being barred from public spaces and offices, another citizen could point out an *atimos* if he was present in those spaces. That way *atimia* became an agonistic rather than an alienating strategy, such as ostracism and exile.

Perhaps more controversially, warfare can be interpreted as a ritualized strategy of citizenship formation. As has been noted earlier, symposia and gymnasia were mirrors of warfare, but we can equally claim that, in fact, symposia and gymnasia were causes of warfare in the sense that the solidaristic strategies developed there among citizens had to crystallize into agonistic strategies that confirmed them against other citizens. At a certain level, warfare illustrates well the need for strangers and outsiders, not as objects of elimination, but of self-formation— alterity as a condition of citizenship. It is in this sense that Plato's belief that war against other citizens of a polis should be pursued until victory, but against barbarians to the death makes sense. Other well-known alienating strategies, such as ostracism or exile, ought to be interpreted against this differentiation between strangers, outsiders, and aliens. While being engaged in solidaristic or agonistic strategies meant that whether or not one was a citizen, one could constitute oneself as being political, being excluded (ostracized or exiled) meant being banished from political space.

All of these strategies could only be materialized in space, hence the enormous attention given over time to the organization and arrangement of the space of the polis. All the poleis during the archaic era maintained a spatial system of dividing citizens into clans based on common descent, an arrangement that survived as a means of determining and dividing among the citizens their duties and debts to the polis, in such matters as martial obligation, public offices, and tribute. But during the sixth and especially the fifth century, the transformation of the polis from phratries to demes must be understood against the background of the various strategies we mentioned. The birth of the demes as domains in which citizens were registered and from which election lists were drawn was no doubt itself a strategy for breaking the hold of descent, but also a condition that made new strategies of citizenship possible (Weber 1909, 181–82). While democracy has been interpreted as a new mode of being political, where a citizen was no longer a member of a clan or tribe by birth and descent, but a member of a deme (Lévêque, Vidal-Naquet, and Curtis 1996), as Osborne (1985, 151) demonstrates, kinship ties were still important.

Focusing on these strategies of citizenship, exploring how various technologies were assembled and how virtues were defined, inculcated, and bred draws our attention away from revolutionary changes to piecemeal, fitful, but effective thoughts and practices from which perhaps larger revolutions issue. While so much has been said about the epic struggles between warriors and kings and peasants and warriors, finer struggles that were waged over the rights to the polis and the right to being political via minor categories and events have been overlooked. Yet, being political was a matter of life and death. Take, for example, the struggle over the grand inquisition, *diapsephismos*, conducted in Athens three times, in 510, 445, and 346 b.c. (Manville 1990, 175). The first inquisition was held immediately following a tyranny at Athens; registration lists by tribal descent were investigated to differentiate citizens, strangers, and outsiders. While these categories were not yet codified, obviously the inquisition relied on some definition. Some five thousand individuals were struck from the citizenship lists. Aristotle says almost nothing about these inquisitions (1984, 13.5, 21.2, 4). But Manville quotes Andocides saying, "Some they put to death, some they exiled, some they allowed to live in Attika deprived of their rights" (1990, 183). Those who were struck from the list but still remained in Athens were *atimoi*. Being deprived of their rights as citizens, they had no recourse to the protection of justice or courts of appeal. Manville says, "The men who were killed or exiled obviously suffered more, though the *atimoi* might have feared that the same fate would soon befall them. All of these victims of revenge in the aftermath of the tyranny were in fact victims of their citizenship undone; and herein lies the story of the *diapsephismos*" (1990, 183–84). This is how, by the second inquisition, *atimoi* as an alienating strategy evolves into a more general but better defined agonistic strategy, *metoikia* or metics.

Citizens Becoming Strangers and Outsiders

That the Macedonian conquest of the Greek poleis in the fourth century reintroduced divine law and subordinated them to a centralized rule not based on an oracular tradition but on theocratic kingship presents major problems for anyone who wishes to establish a continuity between the polis and Christianopolis. We shall deal with these difficulties later. What we shall deal with here is the nostalgia and lamentation that goes with the "decline of polis." That the center of the Mediterranean culture shifted to the poleis of Asia Minor and the Levant, and that the Greek poleis under Macedonian rule as well as the new Hellenistic poleis in Asia Minor displayed markedly different political character, have been interpreted as representing the decline of citizenship. In the new polis, maritime capitalists, merchants, and agricultural capitalists became the dominant groups. As the nostalgic narrative went, to run the increasingly complex and widespread Macedonian Empire, the kings had to rely on merchants and capitalists for the necessary revenue, and a growing class of diplomats, administrators, and officials capable of organizing and governing this complex empire. Thus, the Macedonian kingdom ultimately showed the same tendencies that Near Eastern kingships embodied: the emergence of large bureaucracies, which eventually hindered their vitality and energies. The bureaucratic state and empire invaded the sphere of "civic freedoms" and the citizen was transformed into a subject.

With the decline of the polis, the active civic life of the citizen that had characterized the classical Greek polis came to an effective end. But did it? The narrative of decline suspiciously invokes the voice of the dominant Greek aristocrat and peasant citizens. We can argue that in the Hellenistic and Roman era, the Greek citizens did not simply withdraw from the public sphere and become "inactive." But there were different modes and orientations of being political and there were new experiments and new practices, made possible by the emergence of the question of what it meant to be a citizen. Ober (1996, 147), for example, effectively argues in the case of Athens that "[t]he hypothesis that fourth-century Athens was characterized by a pervasive malaise is much harder to sustain if we look beyond the opinions of the literary elite to the social and political conditions of Athenian citizen society as a whole." Similarly, Foucault's observations about the ostensible decline of "politics" in the fourth and third centuries B.C. are relevant here. Foucault suggested that we should think in terms of the organization of a complex space in which the centers of power were multiple, and the activities, tensions, and conflicts were numerous (1984, 82–83). He argues that being political in this era cannot be "reduced to a decline of civic life and a confiscation of power by state authorities operating from further and further away." For Foucault the formation of oneself as the ethical subject of one's own actions became more problematic under these circumstances. In this rapidly changed context, the political actors, citizens, did not simply fall back into "decadence, frustration and sullen retreat." Rather there was a "search for a new way of conceiving the relationship one ought to have with one's own status, one's functions, one's activities, and one's obligations." In other words, "the new rules of the political game made it more difficult to define the relations between what one was, what one could do, and what one was expected to accomplish." The political practice, of acting upon others and acting upon oneself, became problematic (Foucault 1984, 81–86). The Hellenistic world may have induced some form of withdrawal from political activity, but this should be seen as a new problematization, which had two aspects. First, there is a certain reversal in the relationship between status and politics, where the former no longer determines the latter in an unproblematic manner. Second, being political is associated less with being virtuous than being logical: "In a political space where the political structure of the city and the laws with which it is endowed have unquestionably lost some of their importance . . . it appears that the art of governing oneself becomes a crucial political factor" (Foucault 1984, 89). Thus, it is the modality of a rational being and not the qualification of status that establishes relations between the governors and the governed. While some were drawn to cults and withdrawal from the formal public sphere, others were engaged in new experiments and practices such as new religions, associations, and fraternities (Mumford 1961, 201–3).

Thus, we can interpret the "decline of the polis" in a different manner. Instead of searching for the "classical polis," we may, once again, ask how the social space was organized, what groups struggled for dominance, and what forms of capital became available in their struggles. Without lamenting we can see that one of the reasons for the decline of the polis in the fourth century was that a large number of people were no longer living as settled inhabitants of the polis. The polis ceased to be a space to which it was worthy to seek rights and lay claims. The kings found that Greek armies and servants without strong city loyalties could easily be directed for the purpose of establishing imperial governments over territorial areas in Greece as well as in Asia and Egypt (McKechnie 1989, 3).

Once again, it is important to remember that the description and analysis of Greek citizenship as an aggregation of poleis is in essence and origin the Greek citizens' own. It comes from the ancient texts written mostly by citizens. But this was essentially the representation of the aristocracy and peasantry who had the symbolic and cultural capital to define their own conditions of life. Just as they articulated the glorious civic virtue, so too did they lament its decline. There were many strangers and outsiders mentioned only in passing, sometimes with curiosity, occasionally with disapproval. "They were the exiles, who used to have a city to live in but (at a given time) had one no longer; the mercenaries, who might stay in a place as long as a war, or an employer's money, lasted; the raiders who could live a short time on the loot of one place; the traders, actors and others whose movements would depend on local demand and professional success" (McKechnie 1989, 4). In the fourth century there were more such strangers and outsiders than there had been before. But the new outsiders were not only those who had no rights to the city, but also those who were outside the city. In other words, we shall instead investigate how, at the moment when strangers and outsiders lost their immanent relationship to the polis, citizenship ceased to be a valorized identity.

Thus, McKechnie resists the temptation to interpret the fourth century as the breakdown of unity or the ascendance of Macedonian kings as a drive toward unity; instead he sees a shift in power relations (1989, 8). "The increasing size, and economic and strategic importance, of the community of Greeks living outside the cities created during the fourth century a mass of economically active people who had nothing to gain from the continuance of the system of making political decisions by a majority vote of citizens" (10). In the fourth century, for the most part texts represent the aristocratic city-dwelling point of view (17). Isocrates, for example, represents wanderers as a threat to property-owning citizens. But these wanderers were ironically created by the citizens themselves, or by the transformation of their immanent relationship to strangers and outsiders into a fear of difference: after the Peloponnesian War mass exilings in Athens had led to increasing numbers of outsiders. The tyranny of the Thirty at Athens had deployed alienating technologies, such as exile and expulsion, to limit citizens to three thousand men (23). As a result, McKechnie estimates that by 324 B.C., there might have been as many as twenty thousand exiled men and women, searching for settlement in various areas of mainland Greece as "refugees" (27).

In addition to these exiled wanderers, in the fields of building, medicine, education, and "entertainment" there were also traveling skilled workers who could expect to stay in one city for several months or even years. These traveling workers were different from metics in that they never became permanent residents in cities (McKechnie 1989, 142). There were sculptors, builders, and stoneworkers (144). Hippocrates, who first began charging fees for teaching pupils, gives a glimpse of the traveling way of life shared by doctors. His *Law* is a manifesto for young doctors on how to practice traveling from city to city (148). There were traveling philosophers and traveling entertainers, *hetaerae*. "It can be said with some confidence that in the fourth century B.C. more Greeks than ever before were receiving the technical training that would enable them to live from skills whose exercise normally involved enough travelling to make their practitioners effectively persons whose lives were lived outside the cities" (157). Appropriately, a new concept emerges at this time, *technai*, that is almost equivalent to the professions (158). Passages in Plato seeking to limit the application of the term *techne* or to incorporate features of the life of mobile skilled workers into regular city life can be seen as responses to the challenges to thought implicit in the recruitment of young men with means to pay for training into skilled traveling "professions" (Burford 1972; McKechnie 1989, 158). Vidal-Naquet's (1986, 230–31) perceptive analysis of Plato's ideal city provides a glimpse of the difficulties he experienced in placing these traveling professions in the city. For Vidal-Naquet, in the Platonic idea of the city, while seemingly presenting a classical division of labor, artisans actually play a prominent role. In fact, the role of citizen-warriors is conceived as protecting the artisans and their production. He goes as far as to declare the artisan a hero, albeit a hidden hero of the "new" Greek polis (Vidal-Naquet 1986, 236). Vidal-Naquet argues that while the classical Greek polis was ambiguous about the artisan, the value of Plato's work is that it brings this ambiguity into sharp focus by trying to resolve it. This is consistent with McKechnie, who notes that the kings needed support from philosophers and other professionals. So their moves toward gaining the allegiance of the professionals at the highest level were as much part of their drive to dominate the world of the Greek cities by controlling the Greeks outside the cities as were their moves to recruit mercenaries to drive the raiders off the seas and thereby bring cities under their control (McKechnie 1989, 159–60).

McKechnie agrees with de Ste. Croix that the merchants formed an "international" class. Athenian merchants, for example, were obliged to behave as temporary and alien visitors while abroad, and to come home in order to act as respectable Greek citizens (1989, 181). In the mid-350s B.C., Isocrates expressed the hope that making peace would enhance the revenues of the city and would cause it to be full again of "merchants, foreigners and metics of whom the city is now empty" (quoted in McKechnie 1989, 185). At times statesmen and philosophers also acted as merchants by taking goods with them in their travels in exchange for local currency.

It would be mistaken to assume that all mercenaries were destitute and unable to invest in becoming professional soldiers, or that all who could spend money on starting up as mercenaries would resume city life when the opportunity arose. What is decisive in terms of the choice available to mercenaries was the cost of armor and weapons. If the outsiders could afford warfare equipment, they could become mercenaries at least in the hoplite role. If the king supplied the equipment, they could become dependent on his warfare. The standard equipment included helmet, shield, greaves, and red tunic. Some hoplites also had thoraxes (McKechnie 1989, 81). McKechnie reaches two conclusions. First, Isocrates was right in saying that the wanderers were banding together, and the units of wandering mercenaries, recruited into large armies, in some cases had an important influence on events. Second, the rate of pay was consistently low and employment was not certain (93). There were also *leistai* or raiders, who were independent of the control of any polis and maintained themselves by raiding poleis from the sea. The *leistai* were, however, not outlaws or outcasts (104). Rather, the growth of piracy in the later fourth century was aided by the weakness of the cities, enabling the *leistai* to enter into negotiations with citizens (122).

The fourth century then witnessed the emergence of a whole new cast of strangers and outsiders, giving new meaning to the old ones. The Hellenistic period was an age of immense, cosmopolitan cities, such as Alexandria, Antioch, and Pergamon, crowded with immigrants, citizens, natives, itinerants, and slaves, representing a multiplicity of races, ethnicities, and languages. Although big cities had a long history elsewhere, such as in Babylon, for most Greeks the dominance of such cities was a new phenomenon. One of Theocritus's three urban mimes, *Idyll* 15, offers a vivid portrait of the huge, diverse city of Ptolemaic Alexandria. In the course of the poem, two fictive Syracusan women go on an excursion through the congested streets of Alexandria. The poem reveals a cosmopolitan Alexandria where various groups, including Syracusans, native Egyptians, and various non-Dorian Greeks, intermingle (Burton 1995, 10). To describe this multiplicity as the decline of the polis is to agree with the "old" characters, who watched with frightfulness the formation of new groups and their claims to the city. If Plato's ideal city in which philosopher kings rule is one response to such frightfulness, the Stoic idea of the city as cosmos is another. In a sense Stoicism is a philosophy of outsiders, reflecting on their condition and creating a sense of identity that was only marginally associated with the city but was of a broader order. The Stoics problematized the citizens' assumption of their own racial and linguistic superiority and considered the new cosmopolitanism on a philosophical basis. The earlier citizens had articulated that it was a dictate of nature itself (or the providence of Zeus) that humanity had been divided into Greeks and barbarians and that Greeks had been divided into citizens and strangers and outsiders. The Stoics articulated, on the contrary, that all people share one common reason and are subject to the one divine logos; therefore, the true Stoic sage is not a citizen of any one polis, but of the cosmos. The later Stoics transformed this idea by stressing acts of recognition toward defeated enemies, slaves, women, and girls. (As we shall see, many historians have argued that this Stoic principle helped prepare for the acceptance of Christianity, in which, according to the Apostle Paul, there is neither Jew nor Gentile, neither freeman nor slave.) It is one thing to make the universe a city of gods. It is another to conceive of it as a city of man. The Stoic idea of the cosmic city embodied both senses as an analogy between city and cosmos (Schofield 1991, 84). Thus, articulating the Stoic conception of the citizen as a being of the cosmos was possible only at a moment when strangers and outsiders had lost their immanent relationship to the polis, a moment when the polis ceased to be that space to which it was worthy to lay claims.

Poetics, Politics, Polis

It is appropriate to "provisionally" conclude this chapter (for we shall revisit it at the end of the next chapter) with a discussion of poetics and politics. We noted above how important symposia and gymnasia were as institutions of solidaristic strategies in the constitution of citizenship. Poetics (practices of creating, performing, and transmitting poetry) were instrumental in coalescing the aristocracy into a group. Such strategies as gift giving, poetics, and burials helped the aristocracy forge a specific identity and distinguish itself from groups that it constituted as its other; poetry and epics helped to attain a symbolic endurance that was transmitted from generation to generation and from polis to polis. While Tandy (1997) considers poetics as strategies of exclusion, they were in fact not geared toward exclusion, but toward forming themselves, strangers, and outsiders. The act of remembering and its consecration of particular aristocrats in each city made reconstituting these epics and the events they depicted a form of symbolic capital of citizenship that sustained its definition against others who were immanent in the polis. As Tandy himself argues, "When the fifth century historians of Greece began their inquiries into the past and started to compile their lists of kings, leaders, and victors, their sources were often local lists, some perhaps kept in written form, mostly kept in the memories of those assigned the task" (1997, 181). Those aristocrats who retained this information on behalf of their cities were called "rememberers" or "knowers." The rememberer in early Greece was probably often a *basileus*, his follower, or one of his kin (184). Ultimately, the *basileus* was the controller of what the rememberer remembers or the collective memory of the citizen body (190). It is in this sense that poetic practices of citizens constructed narratives that helped them establish their own superiority to and distinction from strangers and outsiders. Yet, with the introduction of peasants into citizenship, the delicate relationships between a warrior ethos, memory, and poetics were transversed and transformed. In other words, poetic strategies remained essential for governing conduct in and out of the symposia and making claims to the polis or becoming political. As Sennett (1994) emphasized, *King Oedipus* is essentially a tragedy of the stranger. Oedipus is a stranger in Colonus. The same is true of many other Greek tragedies: Orestes is an alien, Electra is a stranger in her own city, Iphigenia is a stranger both in Aulis and Tauris, Prometheus is an outsider, Dionysus is an outsider in Bacchae (Heller 2000, 148). Similarly, there were significant differences between *Iliad* (Homer), *Odyssey* (Homer), and *Theogony* (Hesiod), on the one hand, and *Works and Days* (Hesiod) on the other, which is important for seeing the relationships among polis, poetics, and politics.

Homer, Theognis, and Hesiod represent some fundamental aspects of the politics of the polis (Starr 1986, 16–17). As we have seen above, while

Homeric poems reveal a world of warriors, Hesiodic poems give a glimpse of the polis in the late eighth or seventh century B.C. from the perspective of a peasant. But Hesiod is not a miserable poor peasant. Rather, "it" represents reasonably wealthy peasants, who are assumed to have a number of slaves, as well as occasional labor (de Ste. Croix 1981, 278–79). That is why the voice of Hesiod is not one who is excluded or estranged, but one who is an immanent stranger (Morris 1997, 16). It becomes obvious that hereditary aristocracy rules Hesiod's polis, but he considers aristocracy made up of "gift-devouring kings" who scorn justice and give crooked judgments. The outlook of this aristocracy is, in turn, revealed in Theognis of Megara, who is an elusive figure. Known through a large collection of poems called the *Theognidea,* (about fourteen hundred verses in all) and cited by Nietzsche as the spokesman for Hellenic nobility, he is nonetheless an opaque historical personage. Ancient tradition dated Theognis to the mid-sixth century B.C. *Theognidea* is now dated to the period 640–479 B.C. The poetry is therefore situated between the heroic age, depicted by Homer, and the classical age, which attained its apex in the second half of the fifth century. The *Theognidea* is probably the work of more than one poet (Cobb-Stevens, Figueira, and Nagy 1985, 1). The world of Theognis is radically different from that of Hesiod. The secure and powerful world of aristocrat citizens is questioned and has become questionable. As a class-conscious aristocrat, Theognis laments the confiscation of lands and cries bitterly for vengeance. Theognis divides the polis into two groups: the bad *(kakoi)* and the well-born *(agathoi).* *Agathos* and *kakos* originally had the genetic connotation of high-born and low-born, but are used in the diction of Theognis to designate one who is intrinsically noble or base, regardless of birth (Nagy 1985, 54). Theognis is mostly concerned with the breeding of the good and avoiding the mixing of the good and the bad. He is also convinced that the bad can only be governed by making them love their master, and that that can only be accomplished with force. Theognis displays a bitter resentment toward injustice done by *kakos.* Theognis presents a prime example of a familiar traditional theme in Greek poetry: the polis is afflicted with conflict (stasis) and this affliction is here envisaged as a violent seastorm that threatens the ship of state (Nagy 1985, 23–24). The sentiments of the aristocracy were so congenial to the poetry of Theognis that his poetry merged into a collection of elegiac couplets, which were sung at *symposia* throughout the fifth and fourth centuries B.C. In other words, "the poet of a class who became a class of poetry" (Murray 1993, 221).

Although we speak about "Homer," "Hesiod," and "Theognis," it is doubtful that these "poets" were singular bodies. As Osborne notes, "Hesiod" means "he who emits voice" (1996, 140). This is a clue that Hesiod was likely to have been a persona rather than a person. What did the persona of the poet signify? Again, for Osborne the persona of the poet is a composite of "successive poets [who] have drawn on the tradition within which they work to create poems which use the past to think about, and to engage, the present" (1996, 152). This is also a wonderful image with which to describe "authors" assembling genealogical investigations. At any rate, as poetic practices used the past to engage the present, they did so from a perspective and created a way of seeing the world from the eyes of their group, or class, as Murray would have it. The fundamental question about poetics is not that it was "political" in the simple sense of serving particular interests, but in the sense of creating, embodying, and transmitting a perspective from which good from evil, noble from base, virtue from vice, honor from dishonor, greatness from pettiness, and magnificence from poverty were made distinguishable, and by virtue of that fact, were also made questionable and contestable. These forms of otherness were created in tandem and were open to reversals, reinterpretations, and contestation. It is through these complex and open solidaristic and agonistic strategies that poetics became political and it is these frightful possibilities that led Plato to expel poets from the polis (Schofield, 1999). It is then possible to undertake genealogical investigations that produce different narratives when we abandon the perspectives of orientalism and synoecism, questioning the narratives of "Greek citizens" who orginally constructed them and of those later citizens who inherited them as theirs or invented them as given. When we recover those moments of becoming political amongst ancient Greek strangers, outsiders, and aliens and strategies and technologies through which they claimed rights to the city, we are making ourselves strangers to Greek citizens. This is different from arguing for or against the continuity or discontinuity between "us" and "them." Rather, it is about recovering spaces where being and becoming political were previously thought not to have existed.

Civitas

Plebeians
Slaves
Clients
Freedmen

But thou, Roman, learn with sovereign sway
To rule the nations. Thy great art shall be
To keep the world in lasting peace, to spare
humbled foe, and crush to earth the proud.
—Vergil, *Aeneid*

That in *our* imagination the polis and civitas are almost equivalent, represented principally by Athens and Rome, is a testimony to the power of an occidentalizing discourse. For one thing, neither Greeks nor Romans thought of their cultures or institutions as equivalent and both were more aware of differences. For another, both were right. That it appears otherwise to moderns owes its power to the will to invent an occidental "Gracco-Roman" tradition that can be traced to the thirteenth and fourteenth centuries in Europe. We shall see the conditions under which that will was mobilized when we explore Christianopolis. Here we are concerned with how different the civitas was from the polis.

The Roman civitas became a starkly differentiated social and spatial order, where the social position of its citizens, the landowning aristocracy, and their privileges were not only marked out by a distinct style of life, manifest in special dress, rituals, festivals, and feasts, but were also formally recognized and codified in law. That Roman law gradually developed a remarkably precise and complex system of differentiations that designated citizenship as alterity was both an embodiment and an expression of the dominance of the Roman citizens. Throughout the Roman era, the public subordination and humiliation of the poor, the plebeian, the peasant, the weak, the unpropertied, the artisan, the merchant, and the slave was prevalent, ritualized, and routinized to an extent that was unimaginable and inconceivable in the polis (Saller 1988, 549). This is the source of a modern ambivalence toward the Romans. While praising their achievements, for example, Brunt also moralizes that "[t]he Roman class practiced [robbery] on the largest scale yet known; they robbed their subjects abroad, so that they could better rob their fellow-countrymen (1971, 40). For Thébert this ambivalence toward the Romans as both civilized and violent citizens is not a contradiction, but has its roots in Romans themselves. If the freedom of the citizen was intimately linked with the city, so was slavery. The constitution of citizenship made it necessary to exploit foreigners who were reduced to slavery. But did the image of the slave really remain "a negative image of the citizen" (Thébert 1993, 139)? Again, this is to invoke a logic of exclusion. For Romans the antithesis of the citizen was the barbarian and they developed a much more complex and nuanced relationship to slavery. As we shall see, the omnipresent Roman usage of clientage, a system of personal bondage that worked as a solidaristic strategy, attests to the fact that slaves were immanent, needed, and functional in the civitas.

Roman citizens constructed various strategies of otherness, codified these strategies in law, and developed a variety of technologies in which these categories were problematized as sources of conduct and questions of government. Among these technologies, perhaps the most remarkable was the census: every five years, the Romans enumerated citizens and their property to determine their liabilities, obligations, rights, and privileges in what must have been one of the most elaborate devices of classification ever invented. Taking the census was itself an elaborate ritual occurring in Rome, requiring all those with claims to citizenship and their entourage to arrive there and participate in its routines, norms, and practices. The status of a citizen depended largely on his being assigned a precise place in a vast system of orders, classes, tribes, and centuries that the census determined and codified.

Roman Citizens and Their Others

The identity of the Roman citizen was formed not only against strangers and outsiders, but against aliens. Unlike the Greeks, however, Romans increasingly thought of themselves as the natural rulers of aliens or barbarians—an outlook that dominated their attitude toward strangers and outsiders as well (de Ste. Croix 1981, 329–30). As Vergil expressed it: "Let it be your work, Roman, to rule the peoples with your sway—these shall be your arts: to impose the habit of peace, to spare the conquered and put down the proud (*Aeneid*, 6.847–53). Of course, the proud meant all those who resisted Roman rule. As de Ste. Croix illustrates, on several occasions Cicero shows real awareness of the hatred Rome had aroused among many subject peoples by the oppression and exploitation to which it exposed them (1981, 331). While the way this dominant Roman identity stood against aliens and barbarians has occupied much attention, the way it was defined against immanent strangers and outsiders has attracted less.

When founded by Romans who were ethnically Latin (traditionally in 753 B.C.), Rome was originally quite small. By 509, its territory would still be about four hundred square kilometers (Finer 1997a, 389). Although its territory expanded greatly in the next three centuries as it incorporated conquered cities, the direction of the civitas was always vested in its aristocratic citizens, made up of patricians and wealthy plebeians. As Rome expanded, "Roman" ceased to be an ethnic designation and became more a symbol of status and outlook. It "became dissociated from a specific ethnic group and came to connote citizens of the *civitas* irrespective of their ethnic origin and, at the same time, a specific way of life" (389–90). As Rome expanded, the spatial organization of Italy was quite unlike any of the Greek leagues. It comprised a network of cities, all politically isolated from each other but each in a subordinate relation to Rome. Rome did not grant what the Greeks called *isopoliteia*, but granted differentiated citizenship rights on a graded scale: full-citizen, citizen without vote, or just ally (Sherwin-White 1973).

Like the very early Greek settlers, the Etruscans who founded Rome lived in independent cities that formed the center of trade and politics. From the eighth century B.C. until the sixth, each Etruscan city was ruled by a king and administered under his rulership. The same pattern also persisted in Rome from its founding until the sixth century B.C. (753–510 B.C.), when, according to "tradition," the king was overthrown and driven out of the city. This "revolution" was apparently related to the rise of a patrician class with the ownership of martial capital. The early Roman citizenship originated about the same time the kingship was dissolved. It was a distinct status for the patricians and meant that their association with each other was based on sociation and place, as opposed to clan or kinship. But soon after the rise of citizenship as a special status for the inhabitants of Rome, an internal differentiation of patrician citizens from that of plebeian citizens arose (Tellegen-Couperus 1990, 4). This narrative obviously parallels the origins of the polis. But given that it owes much of its coherence to later Roman historians who invented traditions, it should be viewed skeptically, especially the accounts of a revolutionary overthrow of kingship (Mitchell 1990, 254).

Nonetheless, a group defining itself as the "patricians" formed a kind of nobility, acquired considerable amounts of land, and began keeping cattle and chattel slaves. They were entitled to serve as magistrates and priests, which meant they were effectively governors of the city. The plebeians, on the other hand, were mainly artisans and small farmers. Their struggles for recognition and claims to citizenship occupy the traditional history of the civitas as the "struggle of orders." While the plebeians were not allowed to hold any public office or participate in the assembly, they were called upon to dispose their obligations in times of war (Tellegen-Couperus 1990, 6). And since they had no slaves to maintain work while away at war, they were often reduced to debt bondage or slavery. So the boundaries between plebeians and slavery were fluid and these categories were occupied mostly by peasants. Aristocrats, peasants, plebeians, and slaves were therefore immanent categories of the civitas. Roman citizenship was defined, on the one hand, against and with, plebeians, and, on the other, against and with slaves (Tellegen-Couperus 1990, 7–8). Although the struggle of the orders shaped the civitas in the early republic, gradually the distinction between patricians and plebeians, and hence the struggle, disappeared (Brunt 1971). By the fifth century, after violent wars and battles, the plebeians gained the right to hold their own assemblies and choose their officers, though the patricians were still not directly bound by the decisions of these assemblies (Nicolet 1980, ch. 1).

While in the early republic (510–367 B.C.) citizenship was a special status for the patricians defined with and against plebeians and slaves, in the late republic (367–27 B.C.) citizenship came to represent the status of a Roman within the general territorial order of law and his difference from the clients, slaves, serfs, aliens, and debt servants. With the expansion of Rome, some cities were directly annexed to the republic, while alliances and treaties controlled others. Yet some others, and by far the largest group, were founded as new *municipia* and *coloniae*. The administration of these new cities was left to the cities themselves, but their autonomy was restricted and evolved within the context of Roman law and territory. Some of these cities were granted complete Roman citizenship, some were granted citizenship without voting rights, and others were not granted any citizenship rights at all. It was not until 89 B.C. that Roman citizenship was granted to all Italian cities, after a bitter and bloody Social War of citizenship (Keaveney 1987). Still, the grant of citizenship to a city did not mean that all its residents were declared citizens, but only those who were qualified by property or wealth. As a result, a complex system of group differentiation based on a gradation of citizenship arose. Even throughout the period known as the principate (27 B.C.–A.D. 274) of the Roman Empire, group differentiation based on a gradation of citizenship, or more precisely territorial citizenship, was a decisive aspect of the civitas.

The Romans then invented a citizenship that was very different from the Greek conception by virtue of its territorial principle and categories of otherness: it was not exactly a dual citizenship, but it was certainly a graded citizenship. A Roman citizen's precise obligations, privileges, and rights were a combination of his territorial identities: as Roman, as a citizen of the kind of a province, and as a citizen of the kind of a city. While in its origins the Roman practice of citizenship may appear similar to Greek citizenship, it was fundamentally different. It is this difference that requires further discussion.

Governing Rome, Patronizing Clients

Etruscan culture was centered on the polis (Weber 1909, 260). It appears that the Etruscans had a sort of federation of cities, rather like the early Greek poleis, with each city enjoying a broad autonomy in a federation held together by religious bonds (Banti 1976, 205–6). Etruscan cities apparently display elements of the Mycenaean-Homeric polis, with the presence of a dominant warrior caste with cultural, martial, and legal functions. Most of the Etruscan cities, however, evolved into aristocratic republics during the sixth and fifth centuries B.C. This development probably weakened the federated character of the system. It probably also provided a model for Rome.

While the influence of Etruscan culture on Rome is broadly accepted, the claim that Greek culture was transmitted to Rome via the back door by Etruscans should be viewed skeptically. Early Rome (753–510 B.C.) was strictly aristocratic and theocratic. It was ruled by a king and a Senate, which was an advisory body appointed by the king from the heads of the principal patrician families who had settled in Rome. These appointed senators were known as the *patres* and they formed themselves as a distinguished group. Originally the Senate seems to have comprised a hundred citizens, though by the end of the sixth century B.C. this number increased considerably to perhaps three hundred. The patricians were drawn from large landowners. Those who did not belong to the ruling aristocracy of patricians were classified as plebeians, largely drawn from peasants, but also from artisans and merchants. Under the Senate there was an assembly called *comitia curiata*. When the people were assembled they were divided into thirty *curiae*. The city was divided according to clan and descent. Originally a *curia* was based on kinship, but later it was also organized on a territorial basis.

Tradition had it that by the late sixth century B.C., the kings were overthrown in Rome. This raises, once again, the thorny question of oriental despotism. As with Mycenaean and early Greek poleis, it is a fair question to ask why, under favorable conditions such as the lack of irrigation and the water problem, kingship did not dissolve or was not overthrown earlier. Why did the classical civitas not develop earlier than the very late sixth century? Moreover, was kingship overthrown by a revolution, as citizens would have us believe, or did it gradually dissolve into new strategies and technologies of citizenship? It seems plausible to assume that kingship was not overthrown in a revolution and that it continued its existence and was in fact behind the development of the Roman civitas as an extremely centralized polity, a trait that always characterized it.

For more than two centuries, the early Republic (510–367 B.C.) was dominated by the struggle of the orders and the rise of plebeians into power. But this narrative of the division of the Roman civitas into patricians and plebeians locked in an epic battle raises another thorny problem for citizenship and its categories of otherness. The difficulty arises from a uniquely Roman solidaristic strategy that was institutionalized in a technology: clientage (de Ste. Croix 1981, 340–41). The origins of clientage are obscure, but the fragmentary law code known as the Twelve Tables in 451–450 B.C., which is considered by historians as the most extensive and dependable document on early Roman history, designates the patron-client relationship as protected and sacred (Saller 1988, 550–51). This technology must have had deep roots in the Roman civitas. Whatever its origins, the patron-client relationship is very important in investigating the early Roman civitas. There was a difference between clientage and slavery. Clientage arose when a person without property put himself under the protection of a citizen, while bondage was a result of indebtedness secured by liability (Weber 1909, 266). Until the plebeians accumulated some wealth, most of the clients of the patricians were drawn from the plebeian order. Since the clientage was a "voluntary" relationship based on trust and loyalty, the plebeians were never able to realize themselves as a group for political struggle against the patricians. This was likely one of the most important reasons why the landowning aristocracy maintained its power until the decline of the Roman Empire (Brunt 1971, 57; Saller 1988, 552; de Ste. Croix 1981, 340–41).

Nevertheless, the plebs were increasingly involved in governing the city, which rested on their claims as warriors (Weber 1909, 264). As long as warfare was centered on close combat between knights, the Roman patrician advanced to battle at the head of his clients, who were equipped by their patron (280). However, when warfare came to depend on hoplites, clientage began losing its martial and later political importance. Other forms of clientage, however, continued their importance. Being called upon as warriors to dispose their obligations to the city but not being able to constitute themselves as political agents in the assembly and other public offices was the crux of the plebeian struggle for recognition until they acquired their own assembly. The plebeian order was not a homogeneous class and it included peasants, artisans, and merchants, some of whom acquired wealth while others remained poor (287). The distinction between the patricians and the plebeians was one of a mixture of birth and wealth (Mitchell 1990, 19). The conflict of the orders was possible only because there were plebeians rich enough to engage in it, and they had acquired this wealth by participating in war alongside citizens (Brunt 1971, 47). For plebeians, war, therefore, could bring misery, followed by debt bondage and slavery, or wealth, and hence the ability to conduct oneself as political and claim rights to the city. Either way, the plebeians remained entirely within the social and political order of the city. But as Weber recognized, "it was not because they were plebeians that they had no clan, but rather it was because in earliest times they had not entered the circle of wealthy and powerful clans that they became plebeians" (1909, 287). This distinction is significant in that plebeians were not excluded, but were immanent in the civitas. When the patricians and the plebeians reached a settlement, the latter gained the right to form clans and to establish their own clientages.

Struggling for Recognition

An effective agonistic strategy developed by the plebeians in their struggle for recognition between 509 and 287 b.c. is worthy of consideration for it illustrates how the plebeians were immanent in the civitas. This strategy was secession or withdrawal from the city or resistance to martial obligation (Brunt 1971, 57; Saller 1988, 552). That the withdrawal from the political game was a serious threat to Roman citizens illustrates that strangers and outsiders were necessary for the constitution of citizenship.

The struggle between patricians and plebeians revolved primarily around the issue of debt and representation (Ferenczy 1976). Throughout this era the debt burden for the plebeians remained heavy. Roman citizens had managed to codify their agonistic strategies with very harsh debt laws and the plebeians struggled to gain power and representation to change those laws. There were essentially two technologies that regulated debt laws. The first *(nexum)* was a procedure of default, where a plebe taking a loan could put himself into debt bondage under his creditor. This was essentially the result of taking a loan and involved bondage in Rome. A second technology *(manus iniectio)* entitled the creditor to seize the debtor and sell him into slavery abroad or inflict capital punishment. Default on debt, therefore, was a crime with grave consequences for the plebeians. Although *nexum* was abolished in c. 326 B.C., default on debt remained a powerful instrument of rule for the aristocracy (Lintott 1999). On several occasions, the plebeians refused to enlist as warriors and refused to dispose their obligations. On others, they withdrew from the city temporarily, threatening citizens by withdrawing their services and presence. To these actions Roman citizens reacted reluctantly but positively by eventually recognizing, at least for the wealthier plebs, plebeian representative councils.

Thus, the year 287 B.C. is traditionally seen as the end of the struggle between the patrician and the plebeian orders. By a final secession the plebs forced the patricians to acknowledge that the decisions of the plebeian assembly *(plebiscita)* had the force of law for the entire republic. In a sense, the technologies of debt bondage in the "Orient" were not very different in their results from Roman *nexum*. Similarly, the principal objects of struggle in Solonian Athens were more or less the same as those in Rome: codification of the law, abolition of debt bondage, and breaking the monopoly of office held by a limited circle of aristocratic families. Nevertheless, "[t]he vital difference between archaic Athens and Rome is that the Solonian and later reforms produced an independent Athenian peasantry able to achieve thoroughgoing democracy, whereas at Rome the citizen masses never gained control of the state despite the legal validity of *(plebiscita)*" (Saller 1988, 553).

Romanizing Others

If an effective strategy for the continuing domination of the plebs by the patricians was clientage, another was undoubtedly the territorial expansion of Rome in Italy and colonization in the Mediterranean, which helped ease tensions between the orders since more land became available, and hence more opportunities for wealth. As a result, some plebeians had accumulated some wealth and become quite influential in certain ways. The wealthier plebeians may have had less interest in pursuing the "old" politics.

As Rome continued its territorial expansion, some cities were directly annexed to the republic *(civitates liberae)*, while alliances and treaties controlled others *(civitas foederata)*. Yet some others, and by far the largest group, were founded as new *municipia* and *coloniae*. The administration of these new cities was left to the cities themselves, but their autonomy was restricted and evolved within the context of Roman law and territory. Some of these cities were granted complete Roman citizenship, some were granted citizenship without voting rights, and others were not granted any citizenship rights at all (Weber 1909, 306–7). Latin cities were among the former group, while Italian cities occupied the latter group (Saller 1988, 558–59). Thus, "[t]he Romans gradually stumbled on the invention of extensive territorial citizenship. Citizenship was granted to loyal allies and added to the intensive, Greek-style citizenship of Rome itself to produce what was probably the widest extent of collective commitment yet mobilized" (Mann 1986, 254). But this assumes a continuous isotropy in this extension, while it was highly differentiated and very different from modern territorial citizenship. Sherwin-White, for example, shows that *civitas libera* became more important in the later republic and early empire than *civitas foederata* (1973, 176). Since Rome could not enter into a treaty with a subject civitas to incorporate it into its realm of government, it declared it free first and then entered into a treaty: "The Roman adaptation of the declaration of freedom thus preserved the right of conquest, without involving Rome in the encumbrance of provincial government" (177). For Sherwin-White, "To speak of 'client states' is to use a metaphor. It is not a term of international law for the Romans. There are in fact no client states. The term is one that belongs to personal law and custom; but the *clientela* was the obvious expression for the relation between the strong and the weak, and . . . clientship and patronage came to form the background of the Roman attitude toward them" (1973, 188).

Thus, we can argue that urbanization was simultaneously a solidaristic and agonistic strategy of Romanization. Conquest was pursued by either direct agonistic challenge or solidaristic encouragement, which were always simultaneous with acculturation and urbanization as integral components of territorial expansion. This complex process is best seen in the expansion of Rome in Italy. By the middle of the third century B.C.,

Roman civitas had expanded to the whole of Italy. In these areas there were a variety of distinct urban types: Etrurian and Campanian cities, Greek poleis, and nonurbanized areas, such as Calabria and the Apennines. By the end of the first century B.C., many of these regional differences had disappeared and civitates were governed with differentiated rights, but within a Roman legal and political framework (Lomas 1998, 65–66).

Yet, behind the strong will to Romanize there lay complex and contradictory tendencies that eventually led to the formation of new groups and new problematizations of being a Roman citizen (Saller 1988, 553–54; Weber 1909, 307). The first was the rise of slavery plantations. In newly acquired territories, a form of squatter's right developed in which uncultivated land could be occupied and improved by soldiers, in return for part of the harvest as taxes (Weber 1909, 311). It was this type of citizen right that led to the formation of enormous landed estates, where an "agrarian capitalism" began developing (Weber 1909, 312). That such rights developed intensified the pressure for further colonization: "Throughout the period when Rome was expanding within Italy, the masses frequently pressed for division of the *ager publicus,* and the propertied classes regularly responded with suggestions for conquering new lands to be divided or for sending out new colonies" (Weber 1909, 312–13). These public domains were increasingly transformed into land estates run as slave plantations (Weber 1909, 315). The large slave plantation began displacing the peasant-warriors since it became almost impossible for peasant-warriors on small farms to compete with large plantations and at the same time serve in long, drawn-out wars of conquest (Saller 1988, 554). As a result, the slave trade became even more significant since it was apparent that continuing expansion required a standing army that could no longer be equipped only with citizens (Weber 1909, 318). This radically transformed the meaning of being a citizen, which was, of course, predicated upon being a warrior. Thus, a second problem emerged. New struggles among the propertied groups were added to the old conflicts between peasants and aristocrats. On one side was the aristocracy of office (senators), excluded by law and custom from industry and finance and centered on the Senate. On the other side was the "capitalist class," which was excluded from the Senate, whose political base was the group of voting units reserved for those with the highest *census* in the centuriate assembly (equestrians) (Weber 1909, 317–18). The third problem was the concentration of wealth in the hands of few. As Romanization via urbanization continued, it afforded enormous opportunities for profit for the owners of slave plantations (or agrarian capitalists) and aristocrats. It was in this context that sumptuary laws were passed to control lavish expenditures by citizens, especially in extravagant banquets (Saller 1988, 554).

These problems and the new group struggles they engendered were most obvious at a moment when the established political and spatial order was destabilized. The moment is revealing for the kinds of struggles that peasants, artisans, merchants, and slaves waged to gain recognition and seek justice as citizens. The first was the regime of two brothers, Tiberius Gracchus and Gaius Gracchus, known as the Gracchi regime, which unleashed a struggle between various groups and also resulted in a conflict between the Roman citizenry and the allies (Weber 1909, 320). In 131 B.C., Tiberius Gracchus introduced a bill in the assembly proposing to reinstate land to small proprietors, which would have restored the peasant-soldier to the Roman army (Tellegen-Couperus 1990, 45). As argued above, by this time most of the public lands were in the hands of large landowners, who regarded them as their own property. The bill proposed that if citizens had more than the permitted amount of land, the extra would have to be divided into small lots and allocated to other citizens without land. Although the bill was accepted after considerable resistance, Tiberius Gracchus was assassinated by a number of senators. Whether he led to his own assassination by his clumsy maneuvering and ambitions is not important. What is important is that the agrarian reform proposed by his bill encroached too far into the established interests of the senatorial and other aristocratic groups. Later, Gaius Gracchus proposed to give citizenship to the Italian allies and so incorporate them into Rome. But the proposal did not prevail in the Roman Senate because citizenship not only conferred a claim to distributed land, but also gave the popular assemblies their power and the opportunities for sharing wealth (Weber 1909, 320–21). In 121 B.C., Gaius, like his brother, had to pay for his reforms with his life. These reforms would have alleviated to some extent the deepening cleavage between social groups and could have widened participation in Roman politics by extending citizenship.

Although some reforms of the Gracchi were carried out in altered form, they did not amount to any significant change (Tellegen-Couperus 1990, 45). The occupied lands on the public domains were declared private properties by the agrarian law of 111 B.C. This was then followed by the military reform of 104 B.C., which replaced the self-equipped citizen army with an army equipped by the state and recruited from the unpropertied classes. The whole of Italy was now in the hands of estate owners (Weber 1909, 321–22). For Weber, "Rational exploitation of slave labour was one of the basic problems of Roman plantations, because their need for labour fluctuated. Just as today we say that idle machines 'eat up' profits, so in antiquity slave capital literally ate up a plantation's profits" (324). As a result, "The Roman army was recruited from the younger sons of Roman peasants; having no hope of an inheritance, they fought to win land for themselves and so gain the status of a full citizen. This was the secret of Rome's conquering power" (394–95).

Now with the decline of the peasant-soldier, Rome's conquering power dwindled, and with it arose a steady inflow of slaves. Widespread urban and rural rebellions made the functioning of the constitutional machinery and political game impossible. The revolts in Rome in 88, 67, and 52 B.C. were decisive in bringing down the republican political order (Saller 1988, 562). While corruption had become increasingly prominent, the emergence of organized violence between 101 and 19 B.C. was perhaps even a more serious threat. In addition, the age of civil wars, which began in 88 B.C. and continued for more than half a century, pitted one citizen army against another to settle quarrels between their generals (Nicolet 1993, 42–43). Throughout these upheavals, the dominated groups focused broadly on three major agonistic strategies in their struggles for recognition and justice, especially between 133 and 44 B.C.: the agrarian laws such as the grain laws (the distribution, at first at a reduced price and then free); the suppression or suspension of taxes; and, finally, the laws concerning debts and interest rates (Nicolet 1993, 45). While some gains were made, by and large those without landed property had a precarious and isolated situation in the social space and could not raise any significant claims of citizenship.

To say that throughout the republic and at the beginning of the empire the basis of Roman imperial administration was the city is to overlook that the republic and the empire were *the* city. Without Rome both as an ideal civitas and a center of government and administration, the expansion to and incorporation of new territories, systematically organized into municipalities, in a wide range of gradations of citizenship, would not have been possible. That is why the emergence of slave plantations and estates brought about radical changes to the political administration: the estates successfully sought to escape incorporation into the system of municipal administration and remained outside the orbit of cities. As the demographic center of the empire moved inland, the estates became the center of soldier recruitment. As a result, as Weber (1909, 401) emphasized, more and more influence on imperial policies was exercised by the great estate owners. Moreover, as relatively self-sufficient economic enterprises, the great estates produced for the long-distance market rather than the local market, which dramatically undermined urban economies and resulted in an overall urban decline and a flight to the countryside (Thébert 1993; Weber 1909, 406). For Weber the decline of cities was the beginning of the decline of the Roman Empire. While the groups in provincial cities had never enjoyed the full privileges and rights of citizenship, they received universal citizenship in A.D. 212, though ironically after citizenship had lost its meaning and status (Finer 1997a, 385–86; Saller 1988, 567).

Citizens, Slaves, Freedmen

As we have seen above, these grand themes have dominated both the views of the Romans themselves and ancient and modern historians of the Romans: the epic struggle between the orders (patricians and plebeians), struggles for citizenship during the expansion of Rome in Italy, and the rise of agrarian capitalism based on slave plantations and the consequent transformations of the republican and imperial systems of government from being based on the city to being based on the plantation. These themes are obviously important for citizenship as alterity: that plebeians struggled with such persistence and determination for centuries to acquire at least some citizenship rights and achieved a limited success without being able to ever reach the status of the Athenian peasant, and that the transformation of the republic into an empire and into an estate-based polity dramatically changed the meaning of being political. Yet, somehow, these grand themes overlook strategies and technologies of citizenship that were assembled to establish the identity of the Roman citizen and construct its others, including merchants, traders, mercenaries, builders, and slaves. That Roman citizenship was articulated as a juridical status as opposed to an immutable identity of birth or descent is built upon these rather minute technologies of citizenship that made such a citizenship status possible. The solidaristic and agonistic strategies that Roman citizens developed were fundamentally different from the strategies of Greek citizens. The technologies that they assembled via these strategies and the different forms of capital they accumulated stand in sharp contrast to the Greeks. Three such strategies and technologies of citizenship will be singled out for further discussion: census, manumission, and *collegia*.

Making up Citizens: Census

While theoretically Roman citizens enjoyed an equal juridical status, there were vast differences among various groups within the citizenry, depending on their situation in the vast socio-spatial space of the Roman system of government (Finer 1997a, 387). There were also vast differences between the citizenry and other groups. No other institution gave a more telling expression to these differences than the Roman invention of the census, which divided the citizen body into classes according to their property. All rights and obligations flowed from this classification and the stability of both the republic and the empire became dependent on it. The census was a system of periodically counting and categorizing citizens. The status of a citizen depended largely on his being assigned a precise place in a vast system of orders, classes, tribes, and centuries (Nicolet 1993, 26).

That the origins of the Roman census were associated with military organization and that it was devised to recruit, assemble, and mobilize military legions is well known. However, that its invention coincided with the transformation of locally recruited martial forces (hoplites and clients) into an army of soldiers recruited from a considerably expanded body of citizens is less emphasized (Mitchell 1990, 253). In other words, while the census may have originated as a method of martial obligation, its systematization is a consequence of its transformation from a martial into a social and political strategy of classification.

Two technologies were the bedrock of the census: centuriate and curiate. They were distinguished by the martial character of the former and the urban nature of the latter. They increasingly became mirror images of each other in the sense that martial obligations were enmeshed with political obligations. Before 225 B.C., Roman census information was imprecise and unreliable, but as a result of the shift to new territorial tribal districts, precise census records were developed that recorded the names and properties of those with martial and financial obligations (Mitchell 1990, 236). However, by 179 B.C. the territorial system was reformed and the well-known five census classes were introduced. Mitchell argues that "classification was done for political and economic reasons and had nothing to do with military service" (1990, 248). First, tribal census records obviously included more than actual or potential personnel for martial obligations. Listed were senior men over sixty, minors, wards, women, and slaves, among others. Second, there were obligations of being physically present in Rome and declaring obligations. A father who withheld the name of a son from the census, and thus kept him from fulfilling his hereditary obligations, was subject to severe punishment. Wives, widows, daughters, minor children, and orphans were registered because they were also obligated. Obviously, the census had become a method of social and political classification and, judging by penalties associated with it, both a system of classification and an object of classification contested by citizens.

It is in this sense that while the complex system of classification was piously defended as a symbol of the civic unity of the city, in reality it was both a strategy and a technology to conceal its disunity (Nicolet 1993, 36). First, the number and the frequency of times that citizens were required to be present in Rome were extraordinary. Every five years citizens were obliged to take part in the census, which took about eighteen months to complete. (After the Social War in 89 B.C. some counting may have been completed locally.) Every year, at least for ten days, numerous offices were filled via elaborate elections. There were also occasions when laws and trials brought before the *comitia* required a vote. Second, these practices of presence, declarations of property, rank and order, claims and counterclaims were solidaristic and agonistic strategies that embodied ways of being political. While Nicolet concludes that citizenship was indeed a full-time job, it can also be concluded that claiming to be a citizen occupied the energies of at least some strangers and outsiders (Nicolet 1993, 36–37). The census was not a game just played by citizens, but a game that distributed citizens, strangers, and outsiders in the social and spatial order of the civitas. This is important to recognize because the images of being political given to us by the austere Roman citizen conducting himself in the senate sharply contrast with the images of being political given here by mothers contesting census classification to protect their sons, widows contesting property qualifications, and clients and slaves claiming rank and order in the streets of Rome. To be sure, these acts of being political were just as constitutive of Roman political life as the actions of citizens in the senate.

Making Citizens Ex Nihilo: Manumission

A remarkable feature of Roman citizenship was, unlike Greek citizenship, its automatic grant to slaves who were freed with the proper formalities (Balsdon 1979, 86). This meant the introduction of a fluid conception of identity into and out of which individuals could slip. Its exercise, however, became itself an object of political struggle depending on the need for slaves for production or war. So by a complex law of 2 B.C., a citizen was forbidden to emancipate more than half his slaves by will if he possessed between two and ten, more than a third if he had between ten and thirty, more than a quarter if he had between thirty and a hundred, a fifth if between a hundred and five hundred, and in no circumstances whatever more than a hundred, a limitation that could affect only the very rich (Balsdon 1979, 87). While the origins of Roman slavery are similar to those of Greek slavery, it never disappeared in Rome. Both Rome and Greek poleis had chattel slavery right from the beginning, usually from conquered aliens. Neither had any tradition of free citizen working for free citizen. Both experienced labor shortages because of demands made by the political and martial obligations of citizens. Both suddenly acquired large quantities of slaves, although Rome, unlike Greek poleis, acquired its slaves through conquest (Mann 1986, 260). While slavery was widespread and was a very significant factor of production, it eventually declined in the Roman Empire. Neither humanism nor slave revolts explain this. The effacement of the distinction between the freemen and slaves is primarily due to free labor becoming more available for exploitation, which was, in turn, caused by the declining fortunes of free peasants. However, it is problematic to talk, as Mann does, "of the people within the Roman imperial domains as *massified,* sharing a common experience and destiny. Gradations of nationality, citizenship, and tenure types became to a degree eroded" (1986, 262). As we shall see below, just because certain gradations disappeared based on economic capital does not mean that certain differentiations did not persist because of social, symbolic, and cultural capital.

Roman technologies of citizenship, such as consecration, were legal and formal, rather than symbolic and informal. Nevertheless, such technologies allowing the slaves to become freedmen are indicative of both the values given to citizenship and the rules of conduct required for its practice. Social capital in its objectified form was never adequate to constitute oneself as a citizen. For the freedman, the first moment of celebration was perhaps the best aspect of his citizenship. The new citizen had to buy a toga and learn how to wear it. He had to get used to the strange possession of three names, perhaps all new. "The new citizen must often have felt very lonely, a stranger in a new world. He was formally estranged from his parents and, unless they had been included in this grant, from his wife and children. The men who acquired citizenship through the tenure of magistracies in Latin towns or colonies came off best, for their parents, children and sons' children shared in the grant" (Balsdon 1979, 91). In every respect the emancipated slave came off worse, for though his sons and grandsons would fare better, he would never be more than a second-class citizen. Various opportunities open to the freeborn Roman were unavailable to him (Balsdon 1979). The freedmen formed essentially an urban milieu, though there were freedmen in the countryside. The freedman was an immanent outsider. He did not have the coherence of the aristocrat, who was sure of his superiority; nor did he have the rustic simplicity of the peasant (the penultimate stranger) or the irreverence of the domestic slave. The freedman stood where several divergent and even opposing forces intersected. While he was free, he could not efface the signs and symbols of his slavery, nor could he avoid numerous new regulations that now conditioned his existence. "The freedman ceaselessly swung back and forth in pendular fashion between the past and the future, citizenship and slavery, assimilation and rejection, and he was a channel for the greater part of the heterogeneities and contradictions of the society that surrounded him" (Andreau 1993, 179). The legally free but socially enslaved image of the citizen as outsider is perhaps the ambiguous and paradoxical symbol of the way in which Romans transformed ways of being political into highly legalistic games.

Becoming Citizens: Collegia

The private associations *(collegia)* of craftsmen, traders, and other itinerant professionals played a significant role in the formation of group identities and were closely associated with citizenship fraternities. In other words, throughout the ancient poleis and civitates, being constituted by citizens as their others did not mean that craftsmen and traders were isolated and fragmented. Moreover, the relationships between *collegia* and citizens were regulated through a variety of practices that allowed certain members of *collegia* to claim citizenship rights or at least some social, legal, or political privileges of citizenship. There were several practices that allowed the formation of *collegia*, benefited their members, and created a group identity: funerary and mortuary practices, honorific practices, festivals, commensalism, processions, and gathering together in stadia. As solidaristic and agonistic strategies, unlike what Weber thought about commensalism as the origins of fraternity (1917, 37–38), these practices distributed individuals across a social space, ritualized distinctions of rank and order, and routinized difference and identity by embodying them in spatial configurations.

Mortuary spaces, for example, were integral parts of the city, so much so that "the city of the dead was an extension of the city of the living" (van Nijf 1997, 35). The builders of the streets of tombs were inspired not so much by the gaze of the outsider, as by that of insiders. They were crossed by the main roads leading into the city and alternated with farm plots, different types of habitation, and workshops of craftsmen. Various studies constitute epitaphs as records of claim to privileged status in the order of the polis or civitas and interpret mortuary ostentation as symbolic capital in its objectified form (Meyer 1990, 1993). While prominent among them, the use of ostentatious funerary style was not restricted to only the citizens. Rather, and more importantly, craftsmen, traders, and other wealthier plebs imitated and aspired to these ostentatious displays in material space to claim a status in and belonging to the privileged space of the polis or civitas. It was in this sense that *collegia* formed by craftsmen and traders provided economic and symbolic capital to enact funerary practices as solidaristic strategies.

It is well known that the poleis and civitates were marked by the omnipresence of statues, statue bases bearing inscriptions, and other honorific plaques on monuments, commending the names and faces of the members of the leading families, tribes, and demos to the collective memory of citizens, strangers, and outsiders. While the majority of these artifacts were built by the public institutions of the city, the *collegia* also developed honorific practices through which they contributed to the production of these artifacts to honor the leading citizens and through which they made themselves present and recognizable in urban and social space simultaneously. Yet, the range of available solidaristic strategies associated with honorific practices was not limited to building these artifacts: exchanging gifts and adopting patrons were also among these strategies (van Nijf 1997, 81). To establish a recognized collegium, it became necessary to engage in honorific practices.

With the "oligarchization" of citizenship (de Ste. Croix 1981, 518–37) and its shift from civitas to estates, the significance of public festivals, ceremonies, rituals, banquets of redistribution, and agonistic gatherings acquired a new urgency and significance in the late Roman Empire. While all these practices and strategies of group formation were present in the poleis as well as in the civitates, the civitas in late antiquity is marked by an increase in these practices and their urgency to establish authority and hierarchy. Yet, technologies to establish strict hierarchical norms through the distribution of various groups in material space (whether in seating arrangements in stadia, auditoria, and banquet tables, or their place in processions, ceremonies, and rituals) according to their rank in social space also opened up possibilities for contesting, questioning, and altering these norms. The solidaristic strategies used by citizens to reinforce their declining authority through the inscription of hierarchical norms in civic rituals shifted the locus of politics from the boule, demos, and agora to the street, stadia, auditoria, and banquet halls, and as such could also be reversed and used as agonistic strategies by strangers and outsiders (van Nijf 1997, 131–37). Again, these images of being political in less conspicuous spaces of civitas contrast sharply with citizenship associated with the senate.

Conclusion: New Images of Polis and Civitas?

Solidaristic and agonistic strategies such as manumission, funerary practices, honorific habits, commensalism, processions, and gathering together can be interpreted as strategies that allowed strangers and outsiders, including slaves, clients, artisans, traders, and itinerant professionals, to make claims to becoming political, to move in and out of subject positions with various privileges, and to use and transform various forms of capital in engaging in strategies that became available to them. Time and again, the presence of strategies shows that being political was not a restricted or exclusive space of citizens, but a contested space that was configured by various groups and forms of otherness and was negotiated by invoking various forms of capital and strategies that assembled specific technologies of citizenship. The omnipresent problematizations about who was the citizen, in turn, attest to the contested character of the space of being political. The logics of exclusion and closure appear poorest in accounting for these various strategies and forms of capital available to agents in their pursuit of becoming political (Patterson 1991, 207). Being political was not an exclusive domain of being a citizen, as Giardina claims: "Whereas Greek *politeia* meant integration into a sovereign political community in whose decisions the new member took a part, Roman citizenship meant, above all, civil rights, since the normal single citizen, outside clientage networks, counted for nothing" (1993, 13). This association of being political with being a citizen and conducting oneself in the council and assembly is precisely the image of citizenship that the ancient citizens themselves would have strangers and outsiders believe. As has been noted earlier, this valorization of citizenship as the sole and exclusive space of being political is prevalent in Finley (1983) as well as in Nicolet: "There is no word in Latin for the 'political man' except for the bare term *civis*, which also designates the citizen" (Nicolet 1993, 48). Nicolet concludes from this that the only way open to being political was by being a citizen, which overlooks that being a citizen was always defined against those strangers and outsiders it needed to become political.

Christianopolis

For the Christians are distinguished from other men neither by country, nor language, nor the customs which they observe. For they neither inhabit cities of their own, nor employ a peculiar form of speech, nor lead a life which is marked out by any singularity. The course of conduct which they follow has not been devised by any speculation or deliberation of inquisitive men; nor do they, like some, proclaim themselves the advocates of any merely human doctrines. But, inhabiting Greek as well as barbarian cities, according as the lot of each of them has determined, and following the customs of the natives in respect to clothing, food, and the rest of their ordinary conduct, they display to us their amazing and remarkably different condition of citizenship. They dwell in their own countries, but simply as strangers. As citizens, they share in all things with others, and yet endure all things as if outsiders. Every foreign land is to them as their homeland, and every land of their birth as a land of strangers.

—*Epistle to Diognetus,* **Chapter V**

To me, however, the whole world is homeland, like the sea to fish—though I drank from the Arno before cutting my teeth, and love Florence so much that, because I loved her, I suffer exile unjustly—and I will weight the balance of my judgement more with reason than with sentiment.

—**Dante Alighieri,** *De Vulgari Eloquentia*

Somewhat resembling the narratives of decline concerning the third and second centuries B.C. of the Greek polis, the civitas between the third and fifth centuries A.D. also appears to decline in the modern imagination (Christie and Loseby 1996; Liebeschuetz 1992). Against the background of the mighty Roman Empire, the cities appear to be in a condition of stagnation, malaise, and desperation. It is as if the worst fears of Tacitus (55–120 A.D.) were now being realized and the barbarians were destroying the empire both from within and without. The origins of Christianity are located within this context of the malaise and stagnation of cities in late antiquity. Christianity originates almost against and despite cities. Yet, as Peter Brown has so recently illustrated, if it is simplistic to interpret the history of late antiquity in terms of a malaise that gripped the cities, it is even more questionable to locate the origins of Christianity against and as a direct response to this background of decline and decay (1978, 2). Brown warned that "[t]here is a danger that we may draw the nets of explanation too tightly around the average inhabitant of the Roman world. A period of military defeat and undeniable insecurity among the governing classes of the Roman Empire may not have had repercussions in Roman society at large sufficiently drastic to produce, by way of immediate reaction, the religious changes we ascribe to this period" (4). Brown is thus skeptical about whether a general crisis of Roman society can explain the rise of Christianity in late antiquity. It is true that in that period, Mediterranean men came to accept that divine power did not manifest itself directly in the average individual or through institutions, but through exceptional human agents, who had been empowered to bring it to bear among their fellows. Hence the importance of the rise of the Christian church in this period (12). But behind the rise of this orientation lay a change in ways of being. Brown argues that rather than succumbing to a crisis, the Roman nobility displayed an ambition of power and consolidated its wealth. This became especially prevalent in Greek cities in the East (32–34). Throughout the empire urban notables mobilized their traditional cultural and religious resources to establish new solidaristic, agonistic, and alienating strategies (33). Just as "in every age a governing class thinks of itself as suffering from besetting weaknesses that are the antithesis and, maybe, the unwitting product of its dominant virtues, the Roman governing class in the third, fourth and fifth centuries displayed acts of ruthlessness and anger" (40). Moreover, the city in late antiquity was neither impoverished, nor devoid of ceremony. The display of wealth in ceremonial life shifted from public buildings and public cults to "private" palaces. The glory of the city in late antiquity lay in its private palaces (49). The pagan festival and ceremonies that were limited to Rome, such as the feast of the Kalends in

January, spread across the empire (50). That the spaces of the appearance of new groups, their virtualization and realization, shifted from forum to palace should not be interpreted as decline, but as change. Brown, for example, sees the rise of Christian identity in the rise of martyrs as the friends of God, who constituted themselves with the aspirations of a group distinguished from, and far superior to, their fellow men by reason of a special intimacy with the divine (56). Friendship with God raised the Christian above the identity he shared with his fellows. "He resisted [strangers and outsiders] with such determination that he would not even tell them his own name, his race, or the city he was from, whether he was a slave or a freedman. To all their questions he answered in Latin: 'I am a Christian!'" (56). But to understand the emergence of this identity as a viable conduct of oneself, we ought not only to focus on the relationship between the Christian men and women and their God, or their citizenship in the heavenly city, but also how they constituted themselves with and against other groups, especially that of citizens, in the earthly city in which they were strangers and outsiders. In other words, we ought to understand the crystallization of Christianopolis as the earthly city in which Christians constituted themselves as citizens.

Christian Cosmopolis

A significant aspect of the rise of Christianity as a cosmopolitan identity was that it was also intensely and inextricably local, based on dense networks of associations, alliances, solidarities, and mutual aid. This aspect of the rise of Christianity comes out clearly in the tightly knit world of the first urban Christians explored by Meeks (1983) and Winter (1994). By focusing on letters written by Paul of Tarsus in his missionary activities in cities across the northeastern quadrant of the Mediterranean basin, Meeks draws a vivid picture of the formation of early Christians as members not of a universal church, but of local groups and congregations. Meeks shows how the formation of these early Christian groups, like the formation of any other social group, involved developing a specific language of insiders and outsiders, using space to mark themselves out qua others, establishing a symbolic presence to differentiate themselves, and developing means to resolve internal conflicts and to reproduce and expand their membership. Of particular interest is the formation of *ekklēsia*, modeled after the assembly in Greek poleis (Meeks 1983, 79). By adapting household assemblies, the Pauline Christians were superimposed upon or inserted into an existing network of relationships, both internal (kinship and clientship) and external (friendship and occupation).

They also incorporated the existing practices of voluntary associations, in which membership was established by the free decision to associate, rather than by birth (Meeks 1983, 77–78). While early Christians of all sorts seem to have called each other brothers and sisters, these terms occur more consistently and systematically in the Pauline letters, indicating that the group was conceived as a brotherhood. The Pauline groups seem also to have developed institutions outside the framework of municipal and other organizations of the city (Meeks 1993, 37–51). Yet, despite the strong and intimate sense of identity formed by the Pauline groups, their strong beliefs and norms, and their perception of their own discreteness from the world did not lead them to withdraw into the desert. As Meeks says, "They remained in the cities, and their members continued to go about their ordinary lives in the streets and neighbourhoods, the shops and agora" (1983, 105). But this is scarcely unexpected since these groups, like any other group, needed the city to form their identity against others or, rather, in the presence of others. In other words, that the Christians sought rights to the city was among the most important factors for the articulation, maintenance, and transmission of technologies of citizenship that were eventually codified and institutionalized. How did the Christians claim rights to the city and articulate "their amazing and remarkably different condition of citizenship"?

To explore that question, we need to make some connections between earlier associations that emerged in the Roman Empire, such as *collegia,* cults, and clubs, and the practices of the Jewish Diaspora in the earthly city, and how the Pauline Christians later inherited, appropriated, and transformed these associations and practices to assemble new strategies and technologies of citizenship (Wilson 1995).

The Jewish Diaspora was scattered throughout the Hellenistic and Eastern Roman cities, with varying degrees of local organization, solidarity, and size. "Whatever the details of local organization, which probably varied somewhat from one town to the next, the Jews in those cities where their numbers constituted a large segment of the population formed a virtual city within the city, for which one Greek term was *politeuma* (Meeks 1983, 35). Obviously derived from *politeia,* a body of citizens, "This was a recognized, semiautonomous body of residents in a city who, though not citizens, shared some specified rights with citizens" (Meeks 1983, 36). As we have seen, while such an arrangement was not unusual in the civitas to accommodate significant groups of strangers and outsiders, it was unique that the Jews had a parallel institution that they invested with the term citizenship (Elliott 1990, 24–49). The origins of this strategy can be seen in the conduct of Jews as exilic people of God in Babylon who were instructed by their prophets to continue to "seek the welfare of their [earthly] city for seventy years, and then their return to the promised . . . [heavenly city] would be realized" (Winter 1994, 16). While other exilic groups were also treated as aliens in Babylon, the Jews were unique in seeking accommodation in the city via solidaristic strategies, rather than developing agonistic or alienating strategies like other groups (Eph'al 1978). Nonetheless, and perhaps expectedly, the relations between the *politeuma* and *politeia* were subject to various interpretations and often focal points of controversy. The Jews sought at every opportunity to acquire rights identical with those of citizens, but at the same time they insisted on guarantees that they would not have to violate their religious laws, notably Sabbath observance, dietary rules, and avoidance of "idolatry." It is in this sense that perhaps they would bequeath an "amazing and remarkably different conduct of citizenship" to the Pauline Christians (Winter 1994, 15–17). They could not participate in the civic cults and still remain Jews. As a result, a competition inevitably developed among the various *polituemata* and other groups in the city, which entailed for the Jews some peculiar ambivalences. While they showed themselves adept and vigorous in pursuing the opportunities that Hellenistic and Roman urbanization created for diasporic people, this provoked resentment and jealousy among other groups and hence the emergence of various agonistic strategies within both (Meeks 1983, 36).

The Pauline Christians found themselves already in the context of a culture of associations, cults, and clubs that developed in the Hellenistic polis and the later Roman civitas; these practices had then been appropriated by diasporic Jews, who established their own *politeuma*. While to a significant extent the Christians inherited their jargon from Judaism, the Pauline Christians very quickly developed their own slogans, which distinguished them from other Jewish groups (Meeks 1983, 94). Similarly, while there were affinities between *collegia* and the Pauline Christian groups, fundamental differences were articulated. Both *collegia* and Pauline groups were relatively small, and their membership was established by the free decision to associate, rather than by birth. But this does not mean that there were no attributes of differentiation: there were other factors such as "ethnicity," rank, office, and profession. In fact, both Meeks (1983, 73) and Winter (1994, 203) insist that the Pauline Christians were typically drawn from artisans and traders and constituted a "middle" stratum in the social register of the Roman Empire. Both groups incorporated persons sharing a common craft or trade. Both also depended on the beneficence of wealthier persons who acted as patrons (Meeks 1983, 78; Winter 1994, 41–60). But differences were significant. The Christian groups were exclusive and totalistic in a way that no club or any pagan cultic association could contemplate. While the Pauline groups were more open than earlier Christian groups, to be baptized nevertheless signaled for Pauline converts a thoroughgoing socialization, supplanting all other loyalties (Meeks 1983, 78). It was also of major significance that while the goals of associations, cults, and clubs were fellowship and conviviality, it was salvation for the Christian groups (79). Yet the Christian groups were much more open to other groups than were associations. It was precisely the heterogeneity of status that characterized the Pauline Christian groups (79).

The Pauline Christian groups assembled various strategies and technologies of citizenship that eventually distinguished them from other groups and gave them their unique ways of being political. In terms of solidaristic strategies, the constitution of the group as a brotherhood and the insistence on baptism ritualized a distinct belief that revelation was available only to its members. Of specific importance was the appropriation of the honorific practices of benefactions from *collegia* and transforming them simultaneously into strategies for seeking the approval of the leading citizens of the city and for developing a distinct identity through civic rights and obligations (Winter 1994). They also developed agonistic strategies by establishing their superiority by virtue of their privileged relationship to God and stigmatizing other groups for being estranged from God. While these strategies enabled them to distinguish themselves from both the Jewish groups and the *collegia* and *politeia*, it also allowed them to sharpen over time various strategies and technologies of citizenship by which their members governed themselves and others within the group. And those who failed to govern themselves were subjected to alienating strategies, which included excommunication as punishment by depriving the offender of the right to participate in the sacraments, or excommunication as expulsion by cutting off the offender from all communication with the group or its members.

While it evokes the Greek assembly, the Pauline use of *ekklēsia* ought therefore to be interpreted as a unique invention. Unlike the Greek polis, the *ekklēsia* of Christianopolis represented and embodied both the political and the cosmic order (Winter 1994, 204–5). While Christians formed a strong sense of group identity in various cities through *ekklēsia*, they were also made aware that they belonged to a larger movement of Christianity.

The disciplined and tightly knit local groups and the networks they established in an ever-expanding circuit or sphere of influence that was eventually institutionalized by a supralocal organization was no doubt a major factor in the social and political success of Christianity at the end of the Roman Empire (Meeks 1983, 107).

The ambivalence of the early Christians toward the city, both as an earthly strategy of survival and a heavenly strategy of salvation, permeates the later Christian attitude toward the city. The image of the Christian as a wayfarer—*homo viator*—who is at once a habitant and a wayfarer of the city engendered two meanings of estrangement that are at the root of this ambivalence: estrangement from God and estrangement from the world. While the former was associated with evil because it resulted from the failure to observe the cosmic order ordained by God, the latter was considered good because the just man never sought comfort and refused to dwell (Ladner 1967, 235). But herein lies the paradox of the Christian man: if following God entailed estrangement from this world, how could he search for justice in this world? The Jews and the Pauline Christians responded to the paradox by being viators within the city as the *Epistle to Diognetus* so poignantly captured: that the Christians engage with the city as if they were citizens, but endure it as if they were strangers. While the motifs of homelessness, estrangement, and alienation are among the most widespread in early Christian ascetic thought, they are, therefore, always coupled with their opposites: stability, belonging, and citizenship. From these sources, throughout the seventh, eighth, and ninth centuries, the Christians assembled new strategies and technologies of citizenship, governing themselves via monasticism, knightly orders, and eventually guilds.

Thus, rather than stagnation and decline, late antiquity is marked by a reconfiguration and crystallization of new citizens, strangers, and outsiders, new solidaristic, agonistic, and alienating strategies and technologies, and new spaces of being political, all generated within the city. It was this reconfiguration that bequeathed certain ways of being political that led to the birth of Christianopolis, whose main trajectories are well known. By the end of the Roman Empire cities were increasingly fortified. As the cities became citadels, the Christian church, legalized in 313 A.D., became an important element of the city, for most of the citadels were inhabited by bishops and their entourages, sometimes with smaller parishes as well. Some lay counts or dukes also centered their authority in the urban citadel and claimed authority over the city, thereby disputing ecclesiastical authority. Both ecclesiastical and lay lords generally controlled substantial lands within and outside the walls. Monasteries, usually but not always outside the walls, became focal points of settlement. The Jews and Syrians, with their linkages to long-distance markets in the East, were part of these early cities from the beginning. Throughout the sixth, seventh, eighth, and ninth centuries, the distribution and arrangement of cities were essentially determined by their defensive and religious functions. So the cities before and until the late tenth and eleventh centuries remained principally administrative (lay and ecclesiastical) and military centers. The earliest Christianopolis then was already occupied by the nobles, princes, wealthy churchmen, monks, and a few artisans and merchants (Martines 1979, 7–12; Nicholas 1997a, 81–84; Reynolds 1997, 156–57).

Although typically the city was walled, its groups were not contained within the wall. Rather, each had some connection and claims to the immediate as well as the wider vicinity of the city; even the earliest cities were more polynucleated than their cloistered images suggest (Nicholas 1997a, 29, 93). Similarly, while quite imprecise, the words designating the city (*burgus, burh,* burgh, bourg, or burg) could refer to this polynucleated space as well as its fortified nucleus, and, by extension, words designating its members, such as burgess, did not necessarily apply to its residents but to those who had claims to the city via either property or office (Hilton 1992, 9). That landowning lords, whether ecclesiastical or lay, dominated the early Christianopolis and that most of its inhabitants were their serfs explains how they were able to claim ground rents in perpetuity from tenants in return for the status of "free unfreedom" (Nicholas 1997a, 116). This peculiar status allowed the serfs to rise from mere "city dwellers" to "citizens" and eventually to "burgesses" in the twelfth century.

Becoming Citizens: Images of Revolution

Two images of revolution dominate our perceptions of the European city as narrated by the "revolutionary" citizens themselves in the eighteenth and nineteenth centuries. That merchants, organized in guilds, constituted themselves as citizens and usurped powers from the landowning nobility in the eleventh and twelfth centuries was the first image of the revolution as the communal movement. That in the mid-thirteenth century many artisans, also organized in guilds, challenged the patriciate, as the dominant merchants were designated, and gained access to power and participation in the city was the second image of revolution. So, according to the eighteenth- and nineteenth-century narratives, the European city, a species belonging to the genus of the occidental city, went through the stages of "evolution" that culminated in "democratic" government, its true differentia. If these narratives suspiciously parallel the narratives of revolution from the aristocracy to the demos in the polis and from the patricians to the plebeians in the civitas, it is not because cities go through inherent and natural stages. Rather, it is because later "revolutionaries" drew such parallels by appropriating the images of citizenship from the polis and civitas and because modern historians reproduced these narratives (Springborg 1992, 4–6). We have every reason to doubt these narratives, not because they give us false or implausible images, but because we must understand for what purposes or uses these images were mobilized.

The trajectories of the city from the twelfth century until its incorporation into the state in the fourteenth and fifteenth centuries is a complex and involved history in which two moments were most apposite for the crystallization of citizenship and its others. The first moment was defined by struggles of the various factions of the nobility to claim rights *of* the city (the first image of revolution). Various solidaristic, agonistic, and alienating strategies and technologies of citizenship were developed by the nobility to lay claims to the city and to constitute themselves as citizens. The second moment occurred throughout the thirteenth and fourteenth centuries once various factions and segments of the nobility had coalesced into a dominant recombinant group. It involved the development of various strategies and technologies of citizenship to maintain, enhance, and consolidate rights *to* the city, representing a shift in focus from associational struggles to municipal consular struggles (the second image of revolution).

Struggling for the Rights of the City

Across Europe, beginning in the eleventh century, the struggles within the feudal nobility led to the formation of two distinct groups and styles of life (Hilton 1992; Martines 1979). The struggle can be interpreted as essentially one over the rights of the city in the sense that each group wanted to have the exclusive rights to hold property in the city, and extend these rights into the countryside, and in so doing, contributed to making the city an object of desire and aspiration (Lansing 1991, 5). The nobles who owned land in the countryside came up against those who acquired property exclusively in the city. The former began differentiating itself from the latter by excluding the members of the nobility in cities from participating in warfare and politics. The urban nobility gradually but persistently began declaring itself as the citizenry, distinct from rural nobility as well as from the peasants and slaves whom the feudal nobility ruled. Of course, this description does not fit all European cities, but the traditional distinction between Roman (Italian) and German (English, French, German) types is misleading (Rörig 1932). The differences between Italian and northern European cities is perhaps quite dramatic, but when we take into account all variations in England, France, Flanders, Germany, and Italy, differences are of degree rather than kind (Nicholas 1997a, 246).

At any rate, across Europe, nobles including lords, knights, and bishops (who were large landowners by virtue of their office) began founding cities either as bastides (defensive) or "planned" cities, or they staked claims to existing ones. Their urban properties included buildings as well as strategic possessions such as gates, bridges, and towers (Nicholas 1997a, 121). As a result, although commerce was gradually expanding, the nobility was the dominant group in medieval cities well into the twelfth century (Nicholas 1997a, 115). In differentiating itself from other urban and feudal groups, the nobles typically formed a sworn association, a brotherhood, or a "warrior guild," which included bishops, some feudal magnates, episcopal clergy, knights, and their surrounding kinsmen, as well as the thriving propertied groups engaged in trade and finance—notaries, merchants, and artisans. Since the urban nobility led the warrior guild, it dominated its early assemblies, in which decisions concerning the city were made. While the assembly was considered to be the highest and sovereign organ of the guild, its power over the city was by no means sovereign or even effective, but rather tenuous and contestable by other lesser groups such as merchants and artisans, who were also beginning to organize in guilds. By the twelfth century, many cities either formally or informally understood that the noble clans were in control of "offices" of the city government. But Weber downplayed the importance of clans: "The *direction* of affairs quite naturally fell to men who were respected because of their wealth and, not to be forgotten, their military power, which in turn rested upon wealth" (1921, 1266). However, although the dominant notables who monopolized urban government were called the "patriciate," this is a modern construct rather than a contemporary term. The contemporaries called the dominant groups in the city, especially in northern Europe, "lineages." Lineages included both blood relations and persons who were adopted into the group (Nicholas 1997a, 213). While economic capital, either accumulated in real estate or commerce, was important, lineage was just as important and constituted a significant solidaristic strategy whose importance never diminished. That modern historians insist on calling these groups patricians probably has much to do with establishing affinities with the civitas and the medieval city and the importance of downplaying kinship as a solidaristic strategy of citizenship in the occidental city.

Moreover, the patrician groups were neither homogeneous, nor impermeable. While they originally excluded merchants, increasingly not only merchants but also wealthier artisans constituted themselves as patricians of the city. In some cities such as Venice, the patrician domination led to the formation of a powerful urban nobility. In some other cities, such as Lübeck, Cologne, Metz, and Florence, the patricians included merchants and even some artisans. With the rise of the communal movement in the twelfth century, the struggles of the rights of the city revolved around definition and membership of the "commune," which was originally by no means the entire city.

Much has been written about the communal movement in the twelfth century, both by historians and political scientists. The dominating image has been one of "citizens" revolting against the lords and usurping power from them for their "freedom" (Barber 1974). As Jones says, with priority in trade, Italy seemed to be leading Europe in the transformation of cities from patrician *civitates,* "warrior guilds," into mercantile communes and merchants were neither "burgesses" nor "guildsmen," but citizens (1997, 104). That many cities in France, Germany, England, Italy, and the Low Countries received charters by lords, kings, princes, and bishops granting them rights to govern themselves is beyond doubt. But this process was much more complicated and diverse than that image suggests. First, before some cities declared themselves communes, they already had some form of council or municipal government, and practiced certain liberties such as holding courts. Therefore, charters were complicated technologies that simultaneously legitimated existing political arrangements in the eyes of *all* dwellers and inhabitants of the city and won the recognition of such arrangements by higher authorities. To interpret a charter as a revolutionary usurpation gives us, therefore, a doubtable image. Rather, it was a technology of citizenship that was suitable for both the granting authorities, formalizing their expectations and ensuring acquiescence toward them, and urban notables, legalizing their status of citizenship by enabling them to exercise power within their jurisdiction. Second, the communes never included *all* their dwellers and inhabitants, but only certain segments, mostly wealthier landowners and merchants. The commune was, therefore, about a claim by the patriciate to represent the entire city as it constituted itself as the legitimate dominant group in the city, capable of governing the conduct of itself and others.

As such, the commune was not always against the lords or kings but was, in fact, recognized by them as an appropriate agonistic strategy for negotiating with the commune leaders on mutually agreeable terms. The charter as a technology of citizenship was the symbol of this negotiated aspect of domination. For the charter never meant the independence or sovereignty of the city, but rather recognized certain liberties of commune leaders governing themselves and others within the broader rule or even sovereignty of the king, the prince, the lord, or the bishop. That the commune was a solidaristic strategy that used technologies, such as the swearing of oaths of allegiance and mutual aid, the creation of corporate insignia, and the articulation of norms of conduct, does not necessarily make it the direct descendant or natural outcome of the Christian *ekklēsia* or Roman *collegia*. Rather, it is plausible that these technologies were consciously appropriated for both their symbolic and their real effects, yet were unrecognizably transformed under new conditions.

For these reasons it is questionable to refer to "city" in the singular as though it was a unified political, social, or spatial order. Even after the granting of charters, the city would contain multiple and overlapping networks of power and jurisdiction within itself. Before even the rise of the craft guilds, there were various lesser associations, bishoprics, and parishes, as well as other groups in the city, scattered across space but claiming certain liberties of governing themselves (Nicholas 1997a, 153). That artisans, lesser merchants, and workers were constituted as the strangers of the commune was evident in the fact that while they were not members of the commune, as inhabitants of the city they were obligated to pay taxes to the commune and serve in its militia. That merchants, artisans, and other groups struggled to speak for the whole city as a unified order, claiming to represent its interests, was a reasonable agonistic strategy (Reynolds 1995b, 8). What is not reasonable is to interpret this strategy as evidence of the unity of the city. The use of the term *citizenship* in charters, implying that higher authorities recognized citizens as a unity, was not accidental either, for the patriciate of the commune constituted themselves, though not with a clear and consistent language, as the citizens of the city and as distinct from strangers and outsiders. Though the city air may have made men free, as the famous German adage expressed, the patriciate was, as we shall see, obviously was much freer than strangers and outsiders, whose conduct was subject to technologies invented by the patriciate (Mitteis 1972).

The factional struggles within the patricians were no less significant than their struggles to establish the rights of the city. Throughout the twelfth and the early thirteenth centuries, the factional struggles of the patricians took three forms: a struggle *between* cities over control of roads, tolls, customs, seaways, and traffic, such as that between Pisa and Genoa (1067), Siena and Florence (1082), or Milan and Lodi (1111); a struggle *within* cities between various clans and lineages; and a struggle *between* cities and their countryside (Martines 1979, 22–23; Waley 1988, 97–101). As Martines notes, many historians have typically interpreted these struggles, especially in Italian cities, as expressions of jealousy, petty politics, clan rivalry, or noble ambition. But with the appearance of the success of the commune against imperial powers, especially in Italy, various patrician factions struggled over control of the commune to consolidate their lineages (Martines 1968b). By contrast, these factional struggles were checked in French and English communes, where strong states surrounded them (Reynolds 1997). In Italy, to protect and reorient themselves, the patriciate began forming smaller and more defined corporate groups composed of clan lineages.

The early history of Florence illustrates how each faction used spatial technologies to reinforce their solidaristic and agonistic strategies. The familiar image of Florence as a city structured by public buildings extolling the virtues of a republic, such as the monastic churches, the palaces of the guilds, and the city hall, dates from the end of the thirteenth century. Until that time, however, the city was largely shaped by fortifications and towers of the patriciate (Lansing 1991). Most north Italian cities by the late twelfth century included striking narrow stone towers (Martines 1979, 32–34). The dominance of towers was a dramatic expression of the power of the patriciate, who distinguished themselves from the feudal nobility. The noble clans began building small fortified villages *(castelli)* in the twelfth and early thirteenth centuries and expanding the city to its countryside *(contado)*. The space of the city was therefore defined from the outside, and not by moving to an already existing "inside." The noble clans who resided in these fortified villages began making claims to the city by acquiring property in the city. Their identity was being transformed on the basis of their urban properties, rather than the rural properties that the feudal nobility held in the countryside. The conflict between the city and the countryside was neither a class conflict, nor a conflict of ideals. Rather, it was a conflict between various factions of the nobility. With the beginnings of city government and its corporate identity, which was dominated by the urban nobility, the city began expanding into the countryside and dominating the properties of the rural nobility. This resulted in a dilemma that was never resolved. The city dominated by the urban nobility needed the rural nobility because they provided the cavalry of the city. But for the new sensibilities of the urban patriciate, their arrogance and violence were "intolerable." The urban patriciate could never decide definitively whether to leave the nobles outside the city or compel them to live inside. If left outside, they levied war on the city. If forced to live inside, they fought one another or tried to take over the city government (Finer 1997b, 960). The intense hostilities among various corporate groups were inscribed in the spaces of the city itself. Marked by very tall towers, the city was also quite densely settled, each neighborhood representing the identity and power of clans. Those who counted themselves as citizens were attached tenaciously not merely to the city, but to a street, a parish, and an ambience. These local neighborhood associations and their spatial presence was so strong that Dante detected neighborhood differences in speech and language in Bologna (Martines 1979, 37).

The early thirteenth-century patriciate in Florence was therefore a hybrid, including a full range of interests, principally those who had rural and those who had urban properties, each maintaining connections with the countryside *(contado)*. The lineages that dominated the city government were marked by fragmentation and atomization: the units of the city government consisted of warring neighborhood and tower associations. The confederation of these associations was, practically but unstably, the city government. Ambitious patrician clans built towers not only for defense, but in hopes of dominating neighborhoods and controlling consular offices. The original consuls, first documented in 1138, are somewhat representative of the neighborhood associations (Lansing 1991, 9). Florence was therefore an intense spatial configuration, generated by hundreds of family nuclei, each constituting a locus of power and influence within its own neighborhood.

Alternatively, Venice was and is seen as a harmonious and unified city, where the patrician guild was able to achieve closure against all outsiders (Boholm 1990). Ostensibly, the patriciate in Venice was also able to mediate many conflicts within its own ranks via solidaristic and agonistic strategies without lapsing into violence. The boundaries between landowning and merchant groups were more permeable and thus the patriciate developed some stability and coherence (Robbert 1999, 40). Throughout history, beginning with the Venetians themselves, explanations varied to account for this supposed stability, ranging from its geographic structure to the domination of the patriciate. Its geographic location, isolated by mountains from its hinterland, meant that Venice did not have to contend with a strong landowning nobility. Also, Venetians did not have to expend vast sums on the erection of city walls. The watery environs contributed to a sense of security and stability (Tenenti 1973). Within the city itself, the canals served a double purpose, both uniting and separating Venetians from one another. Most eminently, the sixteenth-century writer Botero saw in the canals a partial explanation for the city's internal stability. According to Botero, the canals prevented the rapid assembly of crowds and so hindered mass demonstrations of discontent with the regime (cf. Romano 1987, 66–67; Tenenti 1973).

Nevertheless, the alleged harmony of Venice is as much a construction of the Venetian citizens themselves as a solidaristic strategy. While undoubtedly more stable than other Italian cities, Venice was rife with conflict, strife, and clashing interests, which occasionally broke out into violence, conflict, or vendettas (Romano 1987, 6). Still, the Venetian patriciate successfully generated a believable image of itself as the vanguard of harmony by investing in memorializing strategies, such as the translation of relics of Saint Mark in the facade of the basilica in the Piazza San Marco, or in monumentalizing strategies of commissioning buildings to encourage accord and harmony.

While Florence and Venice may be contrasting cases, not only with each other but with other cities in southern as well as northern Europe, behind the ostensible revolutions of the communal movement were long histories of struggles within and among various noble clans across European cities. In securing the rights of the city in the sense of acquiring privileges of representation, jurisdiction, and a corporate status, these noble clans were able to constitute themselves as a distinct group, consciously appropriating the images and symbols of citizenship bequeathed from the polis and civitas, maintained and transmitted by Christianopolis, and appropriated and transformed by that illustrious technology, the guild.

Guilds as Protean Technologies of Citizenship

In all these struggles within the nobility to secure their rights of the city and constitute themselves as citizens, guilds were effective technologies of citizenship that enabled various groups to develop solidaristic and agonistic strategies. While the word is not used in southern European cities, both northern and southern cities had similar associations as brotherhoods. The word itself is Germanic and the institution has definite affinities with the Christian *ekklēsia*, as well as the Roman *collegia*. But its origins are also traced to the period before the adoption of Christianity by the Germanic tribes. Nonetheless, as argued above, these affinities ought to be interpreted as conscious appropriations of citizens, rather than signs of a natural evolution. Nor was there a uniform model: guilds assumed many forms.

The guild with its principle of voluntary mutual obligation, reinforced by oaths, ceremonies, and sociable feasting, was an effective technology of citizenship, enabling a group to form itself and its others and to govern conduct, both of the self and others and of markets and exchange (Sennett 1994, 201–4). The guild was a flexible technology. A guild formed for one purpose could be fairly easily changed by its members to serve another or could serve different purposes for different members. As a protean and flexible technology, it could be defined as being either useful or dangerous by various authorities. Secular authorities such as kings, lords, and magnates invariably considered guilds as seditious entities. When banning them proved impractical, they requested licensing or fees. Religious authorities, too, considered the guilds dangerous and, wherever possible, attempted to curtail their formation (Reynolds 1997, 67–68). As Reynolds argues, for example, "In the twelfth century guilds renewed their originally bad reputation with the clergy when town or merchant guilds led campaigns for self-government in episcopal or abbey towns, while the heretical nature of some fraternities widened the area of suspicion" (73). Eventually, an entire branch of law would emerge, dedicated to determining the lawfulness of various guilds (Ullmann 1988). As early as the ninth century there were instances where the formation of any guild was forbidden. In the eleventh, twelfth, and thirteenth centuries, the guilds appeared in various forms, the merchant and craft guilds being the most common forms, but also including religious fraternities and brotherhoods, scholarly and professional associations, and manifold social and ceremonial groups (Black 1984). Beyond doubt, the guilds were the most important technology of citizenship in the struggle of various groups for dominance in the city. As the nobles established their domination and created municipal governments, the conflicts among various guilds over their rights became the main battlefield. Eventually, the guild was a crucial object of struggles waged by dominated groups of lesser merchants and craftsmen against the dominant patriciate of municipal governments (Martines 1979, 77).

That there were so many varieties of guilds and that their membership varied from city to city and through time illustrates that it was a technology of citizenship whose boundaries were often contested. The early guilds were formed by landowners and merchants. "Initially all citizens were in the merchant guild, though some guilds included outsiders. In excluding some groups of inhabitants from membership the guilds were in effect barring them from citizenship. This was the case with artisans in many places in the twelfth century" (Nicholas 1997a, 130). But it can be argued that the guild was not merely, let alone principally, a technology of exclusion but of citizenship in the sense that it was able to resolve quarrels among members, provide charity and burials for indigent members, and engage in a variety of practices that provided models of conducting oneself and others through rendering membership as an object of desire. The rights of the city were not restricted to guildsmen. However, inhabitants who enjoyed these rights but were not in the guild were often punished by the guilds by imprisonment or debarment for "causing injury to a guild brother." The guilds often attempted to impose membership on privileged inhabitants of the city, ensuring that they would not be snatched up by another guild. There was, therefore, an unceasing competition among guilds to build their membership, as well as to claim rights of the city. Guild membership usually descended to the eldest son and while it could be purchased, it could not be obtained by marriage. The majority of inhabitants of most English towns were thus not free, for freedom of the borough had to be bought or gained through membership in the guild (Ballard 1913, lxx; Hilton 1992, 92; Nicholas 1997a, 132). In England, royal authorities were most wary of craft guilds. In London, for example, nineteen illegal guilds were fined in 1179. Many guilds were also declared illegal in other cities (Hilton 1992, 70). Beyond doubt, the wariness was a consequence of the ability of many craftsmen to declare themselves as guilds and swear an oath of allegiance. The guilds also enabled strangers and outsiders to form themselves into a group and claim certain rights. Foreign merchants living in London, for example, formed themselves into a guild (Nicholas 1997a, 136). By 1200 virtually all cities of northern Italy had several artisan guilds that were clearly organizations of masters without showing signs of a devotional fraternity, in a form resembling the ancient *collegia* (Nicholas 1997a, 137). The emperors and municipal authorities became intensely suspicious of the craft guilds and their claims. As we shall see, when formed later in the twelfth century, the artisan guilds involved craftsmen, such as clothmakers, goldsmiths, butchers, tanners, cordwainers, shoemakers, skinners, saddlers, cobblers, leatherworkers, and harnessmakers. Being immanent strangers of the city, craft and artisan guilds became political in claiming rights to the city in the sense that, if the communal movements, by successfully establishing their rights of the city, had made the city into a de facto object of desire and aspiration with an identifiable corporate status, charters, and declared liberties, artisans and craftsmen became political by demanding representation and involvement in its workings, securing rights to become citizens.

Struggling for the Rights to the City

The most striking images of a revolution against the patriciate were provided by the Italian cities, especially with that illustrious group, the *popolo*, whose members were called *popolani*, which modern historical sociologists, beginning with Weber, preferred to translate as the plebs.

The *popolo* was a broad-based association of strangers of the commune: lesser merchants, craftsmen, notaries, tradesmen, and workers. Their guilds were organized together into a federation, enabling them to act as a block. Throughout the thirteenth century, the solidaristic and agonistic strategies of the *popolo* came to clash with the established patrician lineages. While the new group came to be called the *popolo*, indicating its origins in broader segments of the city, it certainly did not include everyone but primarily the groups who were making claims to the city and its government. By the mid-thirteenth century, the *popolo* gained power in many cities, marking the rise of artisanal groups in the city. The *popolo* passed laws restraining the nobles and providing new rights for the guilds in the city. Lansing (1991) argues that the guildsmen who drafted these laws knew exactly whom they wanted to exclude from the city and its government. A Florentine law of 1286, for example, excluded all those who lived in houses that included a knight within the past twenty years (Lansing 1991, 13). Yet the *popolo* also included some noblemen as long as they accepted its political aims and perhaps betrayed the aims of those who once held their loyalties. The *popolo* challenged the entrenched privileges of the nobility by an order of resolute men. The possibilities of being political were opened up to new groups to enact their will and make claims to the city. As early as 1218, for example, the *popolo* of Florence was able to secure the appointment of a commission to inquire into the fiscal administration of the past twenty years (Martines 1979, 49). The mandate of the commission included an order to audit the variety of communal rights and properties that had strangely ended in private hands.

The *popolo* was organized via armed societies or companies whose membership was drawn from mainly the ranks of guildsmen. The organization of armed companies at Florence paralleled arrangements in other cities with a militant *popolo*, such as Bologna, Cremona, Piacenza,

Siena, Lucca, Perugia, and Milan (Bowsky 1967; Martines 1979, 51–52). The *popolo* had its own statutes and its own tax system. The *popolo* was diverse. Two broad groups dominated it. The first included wealthy merchants, bankers, moneylenders, and professional people, such as physicians and lawyers, who held land and were even wealthier than some magnates but were denied admission to the councils on grounds of lineage. A second group included prosperous artisans and shopkeepers, who did not want the offices themselves, but demanded equitable taxation, an accountable financial administration, and an end to favoritism toward the magnates in the judicial system (Nicholas 1997a, 263).

In the 1250s the geographic distribution of the Florentine companies followed that of the commune citizen militia, although the new companies often included men from more than one parish. With the liquidation of the Florentine knights, the twenty new companies absorbed the remnants of the moribund militia. Florence had six administrative districts. Every company had its distinctive banner and every house in the city was administratively under the sign of a company. Rigorous regulations required guildsmen to keep their arms near at hand, above all in troubled times. Long before the tocsin of the Parisian sansculottes, as we shall see in the metropolis, there was the call to arms with the ringing of a special bell, posted near the public square (Martines 1979, 52). These neighborhood organizations were solidaristic strategies that played a significant role during the early fourteenth-century struggles (Trexler 1993b, 63–64). This image of Florence, which approximated a warrior encampment, was paralleled in other Italian cities dominated by the *popolo* in the mid-thirteenth century and stands in sharp contrast to the distinction Weber drew between the ancient polis as a warrior encampment and the medieval city as a peaceful space of acquisition and accumulation. We shall return to this issue at the end of this chapter.

The patriciate recognized the challenge of the *popolo* and developed new agonistic strategies and technologies. The result was continuous battles *on* and *for* the streets of Florence and other Italian cities (Martines 1972; Petit-Dutaillis 1947; Reynolds 1997; Rotz 1976). Whenever possible, the patriciate sought to overwhelm the *popolo* and outlaw its neighborhood associations and even sometimes the guilds. Nonetheless, the patriciate also had to reckon with the *popolo*, whose organizing capacities and command of warfare constituted a powerful force. The invention of an agonistic technology was a solution to the warfare over consular offices: the *podestà*, who was a salaried executive, chosen by the council to serve for a fixed term. Originally, the *podestà* was an imperial appointee.

Regardless of whether the *podestà* was formed by inviting an insider (Nicholas 1997a, 249), outsider (Hyde 1973, 101–2), or an insider in the twelfth and an outsider in the thirteenth centuries (Jones 1997, 412), the essence of the office was that the *podestà* was the head of the commune, the guardian of law and the highest judge, the master of bureaucracy and the chairman of the various consuls, the defender of consensus and the commander-in-chief in time of war (Hyde 1973, 101–2). Obviously, the establishment of the office of *podestà* represented a widening of the basis of municipal government and a concession by the patriciate, which had monopolized the consulate. Often it was factional strife that provided the occasion for the change of regime, the *podestà* being called in for the immediate purpose of mediating between factions (Hyde 1973, 103).

The *podestà* was transformed into an elected office in almost all Italian cities, and was charged with resolving conflicts among the neighborhood, merchant, and craft associations. In fact, according to Jones (1997, 413–14), the offices and incumbents of *podestà*-ships and the rest began to be professionalized. The shift from consular to podesterate technology of citizenship with multiple councils was connected with the advent of the *popolo*. The *podestà* had his own staff—knights, judges, notaries, clerks, and police—but he was attended in all political matters by a formal body of advisers, all eminent members of the commune with considerable experience in communal political matters. What can be considered as an aristocratic-professional officialdom, the *podestà* exercised its functions in traveling the rounds. The *podestà* was elected from within the city, and if there was no eligible candidate in the city, he was called in from another city, appointed for a short term of office, equipped with the highest judicial power, and normally paid a fixed salary. He was a nobleman with a university education in law (Martines 1963; Weber 1921, 1274). Obviously, the alienating strategies and technologies reached their limits within the context of the warring lineages, and facing dangers from the increasing demands of strangers for becoming political, the lineages consented to resolving differences by agonistic strategies and technologies. These fractures within the nobility explain the development of the *podestà* as a new agonistic technology to contain the rising power of the *popolo* (Nicholas 1997a, 248–52; Reynolds 1997, 189). The technology was by no means restricted to the Mediterranean cities; it was also found in the north, for example, in Regensburg or in the circuit of mayors in French cities (Nicholas 1997b, 232).

The relations between the commune, the *podestà*, and the *popolo* generally followed three stages. At first the *popolo* was a new group alongside the commune, mainly concerned with adopting solidaristic strategies, such as representing the interests of its members to the *podestà*. During the second stage, the *popolo* formed into a corporate body and followed agonistic strategies, making claims to share power and offices with the governing class of the commune. After this phase, which was often accompanied by instability, confrontation, and violence, the *popolo* would succeed in securing the main centers of power, thereby establishing its ascendancy over the commune without, however, entirely transforming its constitution or, in practice, eliminating the influence of the patriciate. Although the rights of the patriciate were not abolished, members of the *popolo* enjoyed greater rights than other strangers and outsiders. Also, where possible, the *popolo* would engage in alienating practices, such as the exclusion and debarment of the patrician members of offices. In Florence, for example, in the late thirteenth century, the *podestà* and the *capitano* each had their own greater and lesser councils, those of the *podestà* alone being open to non-*popolani* (Hyde 1973, 114).

Thus, the *popolo* did not mean, any more than the entry of the peasants into the ancient polis, that it included all strangers and outsiders of the city (Waley 1988). Rather, being included in the *popolo* still required property qualifications or minimum tax assessments; five to thirty years of residence; membership in a guild, which meant social connections and standing; and continuous tax disbursements for periods up to twenty-five years (Martines 1979, 67). In other words, without economic and social capital, citizenship was still unobtainable by many artisans, laborers, urban peasants, and other groups. The *popolo* changed the qualifications for citizenship with the intention of breaking the control of the patriciate and richest citizens, but without demanding "universal" rights to the city. When the *popolo* was succeeding, it drew richer merchants, artisans, and financiers into its circles, but once in power, these groups were not interested in any of the causes of the *popolo* against the entrenched patriciate, except for their own specific rights (Waley 1988). As Martines argued, "[A]side from its short-lived campaign against serfdom, the *popolo* offered nothing tangible inside the city to the crowds of poorer men who were not in its organized ranks" (1979, 69).

The *popolo* left an indelible mark on the city, perhaps more so than the patriciate, using a "revolutionary" rhetoric as a solidaristic and agonistic strategy and inscribing itself in the spatial order of the city. The transformation of the city of Florence in the thirteenth century was, for example, expressed in the radical alteration of its spatial order. By 1250, it had almost created a new city. By that time, when the Florentine *popolo* seized power from the nobility, the *popolo* leaders quickly removed their headquarters from the church of San Firenze—located in the old city and too near the towers of the fierce Uberti clan—to the church of Santa Croce, the Franciscan stronghold (Martines 1979, 54). There, just outside the new walls, the *popolo* could rely on the martial support of the new neighborhoods lying just inside the city walls. By 1300, the old city within the ancient walls was almost completely gone. So, too, were most of the towers that symbolized the power of the nobility, and those towers that did survive were dwarfed by huge public buildings that now gave a new image to the city. These included large guild palaces, a city hall, and a new cathedral (Becker 1965). The old city dominated by the towers of the nobles was replaced by a new corporate order, expressed in new spaces that were defined by new monumental buildings of the *popolo*. By the late fourteenth century, the guildhalls, courts, municipal buildings, and cathedrals dominated the city.

While in northern cities the formation of the patriciate and its struggles with lesser merchants, artisans, and workers proceeded within the context of the higher authorities of kings, princes, and lords, they also followed similar trajectories (Reynolds 1997). The English city is a case in point (Reynolds 1977). The decisive element in shaping the development of the English city was the power of the state. After the Norman Conquest, the English feudal nobility was largely formed outside the cities, and the city was sharply marked against its countryside. While both lay and ecclesiastical lords founded cities, their objectives were invariably broader than merely creating economic machines for tax farming. That the English cities were rather acquiescent toward the state, in contrast with their Italian, French, and German counterparts, did not mean that their citizens were purely dedicated to economic pursuits, but that both the landowners and the merchants found solidaristic strategies waged against the broader authorities to be more effective for constituting themselves as citizens. Such events as the violent uprisings, the creation of a citizen militia to fight lords, and the usurpation of a royal or feudal castle, which were characteristic of southern and some northern cities, were not common but certainly existed in English cities. But Weber's claim that the English city became a corporation exclusively dedicated to economic pursuits is questionable (1921, 1276). As well, contrary to what Weber implied, there was not one but multiple and overlapping guilds in the city (1277). We can certainly doubt Weber's assumption that "[t]he special legal status of the English citizens thus was composed of a bundle of privileges obtained within the partly feudal, partly patrimonial overall association of the kingdom; it did not derive from membership in an autonomous association which had organized its own system of political domination" (1278). By contrast, as Reynolds (1995a; 1995b) has argued, the guilds in English cities had also developed de facto liberties and privileges, constituting themselves as citizens (see also Swanson 1989). The royal charters often recognized and consented to these, rather than having invented them (see also Isin 1992; Skinner 1978, i, 1–22).

Citizens qua Jews, Prostitutes, Scholars, and Vagabonds

So far, we have critically investigated two moments of struggle in Christianopolis and argued that the focus on their revolutionary character by the eighteenth- and nineteenth-century revolutionary citizens— bourgeoisie, as in city-dwelling citizens—has concealed specific strategies and technologies that were invented and the complex ways in which they were deployed by various groups. That this focus is inherited from the dominant citizens themselves is beyond doubt: the chronicles, histories, poetry, and accounts of medieval cities, as in the ancient polis, are by and large the accounts of the victorious citizens, who were typically wealthy men with some combination of property, lineage, or profession, even at the times of the *popolo*. The views of strangers, such as artisans and traders, let alone outsiders, such as urban peasants, seasonal workers, the Jews, prostitutes, and vagabonds, did not necessarily make it into the majestic accounts of the chroniclers and historians. Yet, they were not incidental, but an immanent aspect of the formation of dominant groups and their identity, and their ways of being political. As we emphasized earlier, when modern historians typically give an account of the rise of citizenship, they give it from the point of view of the dominant but not the dominated groups against and at the expense of whom such an identity was articulated.

Thus, the very few accounts of the formation of medieval citizenship typically fall into this pattern. Ullmann (1966; 1967; 1975), for example, sees medieval citizenship as a conflict between two conceptions. The descending conception comes from theocratic theory of kingship and Christian cosmology. The ascending conception is articulated in practice. The humanistic tradition elaborates upon the ascending conception of power and invents the citizen as a political "man." The appropriation of Aristotle becomes possible only at the moment of this articulation (see also Luscombe 1992). "By distinguishing between the individual as man and the individual as citizen, Aristotle bequeathed to the later medieval world and subsequent generations one of the most fruitful distinctions:

the distinction concerned nothing less than the difference between ethics and politics—the individual as man answering the description postulated by ethics and the individual as citizen answering the description postulated by politics" (Ullmann 1966, 119). This conception was not only elaborated upon in the Italian city republics, but also in other medieval cities: "A glance at the charters of any northern medieval king demonstrates that when he addressed them to cities, he addressed them to the citizens of London, York, Rheims, et cetera" (121). For Ullmann, "The city reinvented the natural man with his rights and the rebirth of natural man, of the mere *homo* who had been hibernating under the surface for so many centuries, entailed the rebirth of the citizen in the public sphere" (123). While reinvented in cities, the citizen was becoming the judge and master of his own social and political life because he was the bearer of the idea of the state. The idea of the mere subject individual as a recipient of orders, decrees, and laws was receding into the background (Ullmann 1967). The government was no longer the superior that laid down and gave the law to a subjected mankind, but liberated man himself was to see in the government his servant and the protector of his own interests (Ullmann 1966, 135).

This account by Ullmann typically illustrates the valorization of the unified city. Such accounts fail to recognize that the city was a fissiparous, fragmented, and pluralized social and political space, always embodying struggles of the nobility against the merchants, the merchants against the craftsmen, the craftsmen against the peasants, the peasants against the Jews or immigrants or aliens, and various struggles within and among these groups. Moreover, the city never invented "man" as the universal bearer of rights, but *particular* "men" as bearers of *particular* rights against *particular* groups. When we investigate these charters genealogically, it becomes obvious that they were not granted to all dwellers of the city, but constituted only a particular group as the legitimate body politic (Tait 1936; Weinbaum 1937). Ullmann clearly exposes the limits of thinking about being political on the basis of the narratives given to us by those who constituted themselves as citizens. The formation of "medieval citizenship," however, cannot be understood without exploring the formation of its alterity, its strangers and outsiders and the strategies and technologies of citizenship that constituted them. Earlier we focused on some strategies of citizenship, such as claiming rights to the city by acquiring properties and technologies of citizenship including the guild and the charter. Quite similar to the position of merchants and mercenaries in the ancient polis, the medieval city also constructed outsiders, such as the Jews, scholars, and immigrants. How were they constructed as strangers and outsiders within their own cities? To answer that question, we need to focus on a few social practices by which the citizens constituted themselves as distinct from others, through ways of conducting themselves as virtuous selves. Then, we need to focus on how they constituted immanent strangers and outsiders as those who not only lacked these virtues, but were incapable of acquiring them, and yet who were definitely needed in the city to enable the articulation of citizenship virtues.

Ritualization of Conduct

The ritualization of the ceremonial life of the Italian commune was clearly a major preoccupation of city governments, corporations, and groups. As Trexler (1980) articulated, the amount of money spent by families, confraternities, religious bodies, and governments was nothing short of astounding. The time that merchants, bureaucrats, workers, and governors expended in almost endless rounds of procession and pageantry was enormous. The cost to the productive process in the city was formidable, especially to the poorer merchants, traders, and artisans. Why, then, did chronicles consider these events as being so crucial, and why did citizens expend such energy in a formal ritualization that moderns dismiss as spectacle? For Trexler (1980, 213), the answer is that the contemporaries believed that in these rites they witnessed the political process at work. But this answer evades the question. The ceremonial ritualization of public life was crucial to the construction of a citizen identity and to projecting onto lesser groups the virtues of citizens. In addition, while these ceremonies focused on unity (which meant the representational capacity of the dominant citizens), they subtly but powerfully projected the rank and order within the city (Trexler 1980, 214). All ceremonial rituals, such as calendrical and unscheduled celebrations during stable times, were intended for visiting foreign dignitaries. Rituals of danger, in which inhabitants, through formal congregations, sought to guard against threats to the political and social fabric of the city, were simultaneously ritualizations that both united and divided the city: united in the sense that they projected onto the othered groups that the virtues of citizens guarded and protected the city, and divided in the sense that they projected everyone's position in the social and political order onto the spatial order of the ceremony in question (McRee 1994). Technologies of citizenship, such as the ranks assigned to people in processions, cavalcades, festivities, meals, and public events; the quantity and quality of gifts offered by city governments to their guests and visitors, from princes and noblemen to craftsmen and even beggars; the travel expenses granted to official delegations to meetings of the provincial estates; and the clothing ordinances specifying the quality and quantity of precious textiles and jewelry a person was allowed to wear according to his rank and position, all combined to achieve this twofold projection of the political onto the spatial order (van Uytven 1999, 20). But these ceremonies also embodied and cultivated certain habits of consumption that were closely linked with status. The social contempt for certain kinds of food was connected to the belief that the food one ate determined one's nature (27). Also, the way one ate and the company with whom one ate were even more revealing about the mentalities concerning virtue than the food itself (28). Clothing appropriate to the occasion also reflected social position, or at least ideally ought to have in the view of sovereigns, urban governors, and moralists (29). That sumptuary regulation mostly pertained to clothing, designating either values or types (velvet, silk) appropriate for each social group, both inscribed and reflected its standing as a significant technology of citizenship (Hunt 1996a). As we shall see below when discussing how the Jews and prostitutes were constituted in the city, the mirror image of sumptuary regulation was vestiary regulation, a strategy of making people wear certain types of clothing or markers, such as earrings. At any rate, it is important to note that while citizens regulated their consumptive habits, they also established charities to avoid letting their members fall into poverty, as it would shame the entire citizenry and hence the term the *shamed poor* (Trexler 1994).

The ritualization of ceremony and the conduct of public selves were crucial in establishing the virtues of the dominant citizens in the city, so much so that the groups that demanded rights to the city by attempting to constitute themselves as political agents and articulate their claims to becoming political often did so by emulating and reproducing the virtues of the dominant citizens. The *popolo*, for example, despite all its revolutionary rhetoric, was intent on incorporating virtues of citizenship, rather than articulating a new synthesis. As Jones (1997, 328) says, "With parvenu avidity *popolani* of varied rank turned as well to imitating in all its forms, worthy and unworthy, the noble way of life." They pursued and cherished the dignity of knighthood; they began to elevate kin and family by establishing family tombs and taking aristocratic names and using money in aristocratic style. With no regard for sumptuary laws and the maxim "prodigality does not make gentility," they spent money on conspicuous banquets, distributing horses, goods, and money, and family ceremonials of weddings, dowries, christenings, funerals, and knightings

(328). For the *popolani,* becoming political meant becoming like citizens and emulating the virtues they established.

Technologies of Otherness at Work

By contrast, the constitution of Jews in Italian cities illuminates their immanent stranger status. On the one hand, the Jews were among the most socially and economically successful groups in the Christianopolis. On the other, they suffered political marginalization and cultural stigmatization. For Hughes, the success of the Jews was built on the chronic financial needs of urban governments, which encouraged cities to ignore ecclesiastical hostility to the Jews and their usury. They were welcome both for the forced loans extracted as the price of their admission and for the good of the urban poor, who could often find no other creditors (Hughes 1985, 157). But throughout the European Christianopolis, the Jews always feared strategies of outcasting. The Jews in France, for example, were expulsed in the fourteenth century, only to be readmitted on the condition that they made substantial annual payments (Jordan 1998). The decades following the Black Death saw the formation of Jewish groups throughout northern Italy around a nucleus of banking families who signed charter privileges with cities. The Jews always insisted on their right to stand apart and always remained visible and vulnerable. "Yet Jews often became full members of Italian cities, which not only recognized their rights to citizenship but also occasionally appointed them to public office" (Hughes 1985, 158). Throughout Italy the Jews were scattered in cities and their houses were side-by-side with Christian citizens. This led Louis Wirth to believe that it remained always so (1927). It is true that by the fifteenth century, it had become extremely difficult to distinguish Jews from Christians who spoke the same language, lived in similar houses, and dressed alike. Nonetheless, social assimilation without religious conversion troubled the church, which in 1215 had advocated with a conciliar legislation an alienating technology of "branding," whereby Jews were to be marked with a special sign (Goodich 1998; Hughes 1985, 158). While city governments never enforced this legislation, in the fifteenth century the Jews were increasingly "branded" and sequestered. Padua (1430), Perugia (1432), and Florence and Siena (1439) instituted the Jewish signs, either the infamous circle cut out of red or more commonly in northern cities, yellow cloth displayed on the chest. Throughout the fifteenth century, as aristocracies consolidated their power, many Italian cities also introduced the earring as a sign for Jewish women (Hughes 1985, 161–65).

Similarly, in Venice, while the government, motivated by utilitarian economic considerations, was willing to adopt agonistic strategies by granting the Jews charters allowing them to live in Venice, it still required that as strangers they be sequestered, both to demonstrate their inferiority for theological reasons and, more practically, to restrict as much as possible social contact between them and the Christian citizens. Accordingly, legally Jews could pursue only a very strictly limited range of economic activities and, among other restrictions, they were not allowed to own real estate or to employ Christian servants on a regular basis. Additionally, in order to be immediately recognizable as Jews, they were required to wear a special colored head-covering. But the most basic and visible manifestation of the Venetian alienating strategy was ghettoization, keeping the Jews in place by the establishment of the segregated and compulsory Jewish quarter (Ravid 1999, 237; Sennett 1994, 231–37). Finally, in many medieval cities, an association was made between the Jews and prostitutes, and Jewish women were automatically considered prostitutes. In some cities Jewish women were required to wear the same signs as prostitutes. While the Turks and Greeks were subjected to similar agonistic strategies of citizenship, the Jews and prostitutes occupied a uniquely ambiguous position in the social space of the city. As Sennett says, their impurities of "difference haunted the Venetians, yet exerted a seductive power" (1994, 215).

The way in which prostitutes in medieval cities were regarded is structurally similar to the relationship that strangers and outsiders had to the city. It is well known that prostitution was seen as a practical means of allowing young men from various groups to practice and assert their masculinity and relieve their sexual needs *without* becoming a threat to the established sexual order and as a check on rape, homosexuality, and extramarital affairs. It is well documented that young men were regularly given money to attend brothels that were quite conspicuous in medieval cities (Richards 1991, 116–17). But what is less known and accepted is that prostitution was a technology of citizenship for governing the passions of citizens and strangers in the medieval city: while its encouragement was justified in deterring citizens from "homosexual" passions, it was also keeping the wives and daughters of citizens off-limits by governing the passions of visiting peasants, merchants, pilgrims, migrant workers, soldiers, sojourners, and clerics. There is, therefore, something rather immanent about prostitution in the medieval city, rather than being merely a necessary evil that was found out there and regulated (cf. Hunt 1996a, 184–85). The brothels were regulated and licensed with special rigor and those prostitutes or operators who did not follow the rules were prosecuted with a fierce zeal (Richards 1991, 128). The medieval city was the space of the production of that ambiguous difference that was marked as prostitution and which was intricately woven with citizens, strangers, and outsiders. In April 1403, for example, the government of Florence established the Office of Decency, the first standing magistracy in the city's history exclusively charged with enforcing public moral conduct. Its specific duty was to wean men from homosexuality by fostering female prostitution, and this was to be accomplished by building or acquiring an edifice suitable for a brothel, recruiting foreign prostitutes and pimps to work in it, and assuring them a remuneration and protection, which would induce them to come and stay (Trexler 1993a, 31). Like other Italian cities of the fifteenth century, Florence believed that officially sponsored prostitution combatted male homosexuality and the decline in the legitimate population. Upon the charms of these foreign women, therefore, was vested the welfare of a political and social order (32). "Like so many outsiders the prostitutes of Florence were to mediate insiders' values and institutions" (34).

The rise of the medieval university as a corporation of scholars and their struggles with city governments reveal a remarkable moment of group formation and differentiation qua the city. Throughout the twelfth and thirteenth centuries, universities were established in medieval cities as corporate bodies. "The student universitas, or corporation, or guild, received from the city of Bologna a charter which permitted it to make contracts with the professors, to regulate the rents of student lodgings, to determine the kinds of courses to be taught and the material to be covered in each, to set the length of lectures and the number of holidays, to regulate prices for the rent and sale of books. The professors were paid directly [in Bologna] by the students in their respective classes" (Berman 1983, 124). The student guild was also given wide civil and criminal jurisdiction over its members. Thus students were exempted from the civil disabilities of alienage and acquired, in effect, an artificial citizenship of their own. "The word 'university' has nothing to do with the universality of learning, and it is only by accident that the Latin term *universitas* has given rise to the established nomenclature. For *universitas* was a general word of wide application in the twelfth, thirteenth and fourteenth centuries and was used to denote any kind of aggregate or body of persons with common interests and independent legal status: it indicated a defined group whether a craft guild or a municipal corporation" (Cobban 1975, 22–23). One of the most interesting developments in the medieval university is that of the *nations*. "Being aliens, most of the students were in a precarious legal situation. For example, any alien might be liable for the debts of any of his fellow countrymen. A Bolognese merchant with a claim against a London merchant could exact damages from any of the English law students at hand. To protect themselves against these and other hazards, the students banded together in 'nations,' on the basis of their ethnic and geographical origin . . . altogether some twenty or more nations" (Berman 1983, 124). At Bologna the nations were organizations of students; at Paris they were societies of masters. At Bologna the nation can best be pictured as a subdivision within the university of out-of-town students who banded together for mutual protection, help, and collective security against local authorities (Daly 1961, 30). In Bologna, "In 1245 the students were finally given the same legal rights as citizens, excepting political rights. Sometimes students who had lived at Bologna for more than ten years were granted actual citizenship, but then they lost their university rights and privileges" (32). "Students who were citizens of Bologna were not allowed in the nations, nor were members of the nations regarded as citizens of the commune" (33). "There were only *four* nations at Paris, and their membership was made up of *masters of arts* and not of students in arts. Furthermore, the nations were confined to the faculty of arts alone. There were no nations in medicine, law, or theology. Unlike Bologna, members not only from foreign lands but also from Paris itself were included in them" (48–49). While the conflicts between universities and city government have been interpreted as "town-gown" conflicts, they reveal intriguing aspects of the city as a difference machine. While the city governments dominated by patrician families were intent on developing their way of life and localism as the dominant vision of the city, the scholars posed a challenge to this by engendering a style of life that was more cosmopolitan than local. The same localism of the city government and its dominant groups was also present in the way immigrants or aliens were treated in the city as strangers and outsiders (Pearsall 1998).

While vagabondage was discursively defined in the eutopolis, which we shall discuss in the next chapter, Christianopolis had already begun defining vagabonds in the fourteenth and fifteenth centuries. This definition was closely associated with the embodiment of social differentiation within the spatial order of the city. Paris was, for example, among the densest cities in Europe where social differentiation was embodied in the height of the buildings. The social position of inhabitants changed from one floor to the next and climbing up the stairs of the houses of citizens meant going downhill in terms of recognition and respectability. The situation was the same in the medieval as well as the early modern period (Braudel 1977, 200; Geremek 1971, 78). To live on the ground floor, and to have a window overlooking the street, made it possible to engage in exchange or craft, which the guilds regulated as public activities. Typically, in the most densely populated districts of Paris, rooms on the upper floors were leased to the poorest residents, and the ground floors were occupied by a workshop, an inn, or the apartment of a citizen (Geremek 1971, 81). But this also meant that citizens increasingly encountered the unemployed, poor, and unrecognizable wanderers of the city, whose numbers were growing. Parisian citizens did not live together as clans in large mansions or compounds, as did the Florentine and Genoese citizens (Robbert 1999, 28). These encounters created both an anxiety and a heightened awareness of otherness in the sense that citizens in such a dense city and spatial arrangement typically were not isolated and sequestered from the wanderers. It was at this moment that unrecognized and unclassified wanderers were constituted as vagabondagers via legislation and proclamation. In September 1367, a royal proclamation was made throughout Paris ordering all able-bodied but unemployed wanderers to report to various sites of public works in return for a standard municipal payment. Those who failed to do so were subject to immediate and severe penalties, including whipping and battering. That similar proclamations and ordinances were repeated throughout the century meant that they were rarely successful. Nonetheless, the growing impatience of the authorities was visible. As far as vagabonds were concerned, however, action was confined to the ritual proclamation of the obligation to work (Geremek 1971, 35). The last decade of the century introduced new agonistic strategies and technologies against vagabonds as criminals. In 1395, the authorities decided to search out the homeless in their hideouts. Those who were sleeping on boats in moats and were not members of the crews were to be arrested. Later in the century vagabonds and those who were not willing to work were flogged and banished from Paris (36). Finally, in 1473 the Parlement passed an ordinance that was the foundation of the repressive early modern legislation on vagabonds. "All this legislation reflected the feeling of social insecurity which was always stronger in the presence of people who were not integrated" (41). But that conclusion assumes that integration was the objective of such legislation. What if it was about constituting them as necessary strangers without whom the citizens were unable to articulate their virtues and distinction?

This discussion of the ritualization of conduct of citizens, in clothing, seating, spectating, eating, gift giving, and ceremonies, as well as the incredible attention given to the Jews, prostitutes, scholars, and vagabonds by stigmatizing, enabling, branding, regulating, and controlling illustrates that becoming political was by no means restricted to the venerable spaces, such as the guildhall, or to the revolutionary and epic struggles between the nobles, merchants, and artisans, but was also prevalent in minute practices, everyday battles, attentive technologies, and less known and visible spaces, such as the streets, ghettos, brothels, cloisters, and universities of the city.

Polis, Civitas, Christianopolis

While it is not implausible to see the two moments of the Christianopolis as "revolutionary" transformations, casting them in a different light by focusing on the transformations of fluid and overlapping groups and the strategies and technologies of citizenship they developed allows us to see rather different aspects of becoming political, not as revolutionary orientations, but as moments of realignment and reorientation within the political, social, and spatial orders of the city.

That the *popolo* became a separate body within the commune with its own finances and its own martial organization led Weber to declare it as the first "deliberately non-legitimate and revolutionary" political association (1921, 1302). Similarly, later historians thought that the ascendance of the artisans was both politically and economically revolutionary, going so far as to claim "democratic" revolutions. For Hyde (1973, 115), for example, "The triumph of the *popolo,* despite many differences of detail, marked everywhere a revolution of the first magnitude in the life of the Italian cities—the only successful 'democratic' revolution in the history of the communes, involving far greater changes in the distribution of power than the rise of the communes themselves a century and a half before." More recently, Jones (1997, 328) claimed that "[i]n their own age and after, the Italian republics above all other communes stood for revolution: the triumph of *libertas,* the subversion of the established order of God-given hierarchy and sacral rulership by a diametrically contrary system of community, collegiality and collective self-government." For Jones, cities signified freedom, a passion for liberty that many established cults and festivities honored in banners, plazas, and other public monuments. But to attribute the "passion" for liberty to a revolutionary munificence or to claim that "cities" stood for "freedom" is to believe too much in the narratives generated by a triumphant group of new citizens who were able to constitute themselves as being political and claim their right to the city. As admirable as this moment of becoming political may be, the *popolo* was not the whole city; it was neither as widespread as it claimed, nor as revolutionary as it appeared.

Moreover, if the focus on the "revolutionary" character of these transformations is pressed into the direction of drawing direct parallels with the polis and civitas, it all gets tangled up in a quasi-evolutionary logic with an emphasis on the differentia of Christianopolis as a species of the occidental city: that Weber eventually wanted to draw strong parallels between the demos and plebs and the *popolo* was not without consequence. Weber was especially impressed by the parallel between the rise of the plebs in Rome, with their own assembly and officials, and the *popolo*. That the plebs were organized as a sworn association and that it was through the veto that the plebs managed to get their resolutions recognized as binding for the entire city was most significant for Weber (1921, 1308). Even more impressive for him was that while the struggle between the patricians and the plebeians eventually disappeared, being replaced by a struggle between the new officeholding nobility and the wealthier plebeians, in the medieval city the plebeians "finally" triumphed. Weber was intent on seeing these similarities, despite the fundamental economic and social differences between the medieval Italian and the ancient Roman cities, which he recognized. This insistence led Weber to make one of his most objectionable historical statements: he believed that "in the struggle of orders the institutional possibilities are quite limited historically and they follow their own development" (1309). That the plebs and the *popolo* followed an ostensibly similar trajectory and had used a similar institutional structure was, for Weber, an indication that the institutional possibilities for becoming political were limited.

This was nowhere more apparent to Weber than in the organization of the city as an ostensibly unified territorial association. Weber was specifically interested in demonstrating that the dissolution of clan and kinship ties was *the* revolutionary aspect of the occidental city. In the rise of the *popolo* he saw this revolutionary dissolution—yet again. As we have seen earlier, for Weber the most characteristic transformation from clan divisions in the city to territorial divisions was apparent in the demos, which became the division of allocating rights and responsibilities. The consequence of this was the treatment of the polis not as a confraternity of tribes for defense, but as a compulsory territorial association. We have also seen earlier that this radical break from clans to demos has been discredited. For Weber, similar transformations occurred in the civitas from gentes and curiae to tribus (1921, 1312–13). That the *popolo* usually had a territorial organization and that its officials were elected by districts within the city was, for Weber, the indication that the medieval city had fulfilled its revolutionary destiny as a species of the occidental city. Another factor for Weber in this development toward the city as a territorial association was the change in the nature of law. It was transformed from charismatic legislation bound by the traditions and customs of the patriciate to the law of the territorial association, which was rationally instituted and mostly written (1313). Another consequence of the revolution was in city administration. The officials of the city were not like modern civil servants with career paths and pathos, but they were modestly compensated for their work and were drawn by lot (1314). The seizure of power in medieval cities by the *popolo* had similar consequences: numerous revisions of urban laws, codification of law, a whole slew of statutes, and a spring tide of officials (1315).

That these Weberian theses cannot be sustained by evidence is important to illustrate, but it is not my main concern here. For considering citizenship as alterity within the context of various strategies and technologies articulated by various groups, it will suffice to say that what eventually led Weber into these cul-de-sacs was the orientalist perspective from which he ordered his evidence. Nevertheless, we still have to assess a few Weberian theses before we leave him behind to explore the eutopolis and the metropolis, which, for reasons beyond our scope here, did not command his attention, and in the case of the cosmopolis, was only dimly emergent in the early twentieth century.

Wayfaring without Weber

At the outset, Weber was more concerned with differences than with ostensible similarities between the polis, civitas, and Christianopolis. He recognized that the diversity of social, political, and spatial orders in medieval cities was much greater than that of the poleis or civitates. The nucleus of the ancient polis was everywhere a warrior aristocracy, whereas in some medieval cities artisans formed the nucleus of the city, in others the artisans forced the aristocrats to join the guilds, and in still others aristocrats were excluded from the city entirely. The source of this diversity was partly a factor of historical geography: southern European cities such as Genoa and Venice, in which commercial capital became dominant, were very close to the polis. But throughout mainland Europe, where early industry was emerging, cities began developing a distinct group differentiation. It was in cities such as Florence and Lübeck that "industrial" capital and a "free" labor emerged (Pirenne 1925, 185–86). Although in antiquity free labor existed, it was stifled by the existence of slavery. Of course, slavery existed in medieval Europe: the craftsmen and merchants who moved into a city were to some extent serfs themselves, only being allowed entry into the city by their masters in return for tribute (Weber 1909, 338). Yet, the fact that the serfs could change their status to free laborers in return for paying rents in perpetuity was consequential for their ability to form themselves into guilds and acquire citizenship rights that were, if not inconceivable in the polis as Weber thought, at least very difficult (Weber 1909, 339). But it was possible in the civitas and Weber never explained why this possibility did not lead to the articulation of rights and the development of such legal technologies as charters, contracts, and corporations in the civitas.

Similarly, Weber argued that the characteristic group differentiation in medieval cities was between aristocrats and merchants and later between merchants and artisans, and in the polis it was between aristocrats and peasants as creditors and debtors. It is doubtful whether, as Weber believed, all struggles in antiquity were essentially based on landownership, whereas in medieval cities struggles were essentially about the ownership of the means of production: "In antiquity the peasant did not want to become a debt bondsman, which meant working the land for an urban rentier. In late medieval cities the artisan did not want to become a cottage industry worker, which meant producing goods for a capitalist entrepreneur" (Weber 1909, 342). These crude Weberian dichotomies are more Marxist than previously thought, as is his attribution of revolutionary character to the dispossessed classes. For Weber, the peasant-citizens who fell into debt slavery, being unable to equip themselves, were the source of a revolutionary instinct, hoping for a redistribution of land, a cancellation of debts, or public support. In that vein, Weber believed that "[t]he class struggles of early antiquity took place between the urban patriciate as *creditors* and the peasants as *debtors* or as dispossessed debt slaves" (Weber 1921, 1341). The interests that dominated the conflict in the ancient polis were the interests of debtors and consumers, whereas the producer interests of the artisans were the objects of class struggles in the city. The typical outsider and stranger in the medieval city was one who could not become a member of an association or a guild. By contrast, in antiquity it was the peasant without land, merchants, slaves, mercenaries, and women. As we have seen, these contrasts are not only crude, but unsustainable.

We can certainly doubt Weber's conclusion that the medieval aristocrats and lords were not, as in antiquity, citizens of cities as such. Weber knew that medieval landowners tried to keep their feudal estates from being incorporated into cities, and they sought to associate themselves with cities as "external citizens" (1909, 350). But this interpretation confuses the "city" with its spatial order in the sense that lacking dwellings in the city somehow disqualified the nobles from citizenship. But strategies available to the nobles to claim rights of the city were more varied than residential property and involved acquiring other forms of capital and assembling matrimonial and sacramental strategies.

As we have seen, *collegia* were guild-like technologies and Weber was mistaken to conclude that the use of slavery as a substitute for free labor impeded the rise of craft guilds in antiquity. Thus his observation that the medieval *popolo,* in contrast to the patriciate, was organized purely on the craft guild principle is questionable. As we have seen, recent scholarship has established that the *popolo* included various groups, rather than being only a confederation of the craft guilds. Weber insisted that while the ancient polis was organized by demes or tribus, according to territorial, primarily rural districts, the typical medieval city was organized around the craft guilds. He argued that the division of the city into territorial communities and their extension into the countryside is a characteristic that was entirely absent from the medieval city. "The historical uniqueness of this type of *city*-constitution, which prevailed especially during the democratic period of the ancient polis, simply cannot be stressed too strongly" (1921, 1344). But Weber was mistaken in seeing a radical difference between the territorial principle of the ancient democratic polis and the medieval democratic city, because the *popolo* was as intensely territorial as the demes in the ancient city. Using neighborhood associations and armed companies, the *popolo* was organized around territorial units.

That Weber saw the revolutionary spirit as quintessentially an occidental spirit was ultimately his guiding principle of interpretation: "The patrician families monopolising the council seats could everywhere maintain this closure easily only as long as no strong contrast of interests arose between them and the excluded part of the citizenry. But once such conflicts emerged, or once the self-esteem of the outsiders, based on growing wealth and education, and their economic dispensability for administrative work had risen to a point where they could no longer tolerate the idea of being excluded from power, the makings of new revolutions were at hand" (1921, 1281). His orientalism was the thread that connected the guilds and the demos across centuries: "The similarity of these democratic 'developments' with that of the ancient city is very striking. Most cities of antiquity experienced a similar early period of growth as 'cities of the nobility', beginning roughly with the seventh century B.C., and later a rapid spurt of political and economic power which was accompanied by the development of democracy or at least a trend in this direction" (1282). This evolutionary logic invoked by Weber, which sees the medieval city as a species belonging to the genus of the occidental city going through the stages of "evolution" that culminate in "democratic" government, its true differentia, is sustained by orientalism.

Homo Politicus, Homo Viator, Homo Economicus

Yet, the most questionable conclusion Weber drew from his comparative typology of the polis and Christianopolis was that while the former bred the homo politicus, the latter was unique in breeding the homo economicus. While being political was an object of desire and aspiration via orienting oneself toward the city in the polis and civitas, Christianopolis evolved in the direction of orienting men and women toward the pursuit of their "economic" interests and made being economic an object of desire and orientation. For Weber, the establishment of a city or the granting of corporate status to an existing city was fundamentally an economic undertaking. The city became autonomous because territorial powers had not yet possessed a trained apparatus of officialdom, specialized knowledge, continuity, and routines able to meet the demands of administering a city. "The more unitary the organization of the larger political association, the less was the development of urban political autonomy. For all feudal powers without exception, beginning with the kings, viewed the development of cities with utter distrust. Only the lack of a bureaucratic apparatus and their money requirements forced . . . the kings to seek support in cities. . . . But as soon as their political and financial resources permitted the royal or provincial patrimonial powers to develop the necessary administrative apparatus, they tried to destroy the autonomy of the cities again" (1921, 1352). By contrast, "The typical ancient city, its ruling strata, its democratic interests—all these were politically and militarily oriented. . . . The downfall of the patriciate and the transition to democracy were caused by a change in military technique. It was the self-equipped disciplined hoplite army which carried the struggle against the nobility, ousting it militarily and then also politically" (1352). "The specifically medieval city type, the artisan inland city, was altogether economically oriented. The feudal powers of the middle ages were not by origin city-kings and city nobles. Unlike the nobility of antiquity, they were not interested in putting into their service specific instruments of military technique offered only by the city. . . . The economic interests of the medieval citizens lay in peaceful gain through commerce and the trades, this was most pronouncedly so for the lower strata of the urban citizenry" (1353). "The political situation of the medieval citizen determined his path, which was that of a *homo economicus,* whereas in antiquity the polis preserved during its heyday its character as the technically most advanced military association: the ancient citizen was a *homo politicus*" (1354).

This led a generation of historians to draw a sharp distinction between being political and being economic, the former being associated with the ancient polis and the latter with the medieval city. It thus became a received view that while the ancient "man" was political, the medieval "man" was economic. The dominant influence in ancient Europe was land and prevailing ideas were those of aristocrats, who were adverse to labor, productive enterprise, trade, and practical knowledge (Jones 1997, 7). For Jones, this distinction became clear in the thirteenth century, when the first explicit praise of profit and the virtues of thrift, in the use of money and time, appeared, along with the forms and formulas of a mercantile religion, adjusted to the exigencies of commerce. Together they marked the birth of a distinct ethic, an ethic replete with its own professional pride and principles, for which commerce was a source of honor and fame, and the name of a merchant a glorious thing (11–12).

Weber and the subsequent scholarship assumed that the difference between the polis and Christianopolis was between war and peace. That the ancient polis was, in its origins and its mutations, a warrior association and that, by contrast, the medieval city was an island of peace in a sea of war is a questionable assumption. That the medieval city was never in pursuit of expansion or colonization and that the ancient polis was always in pursuit of new land and settlements is absurd. What led Weber and the subsequent scholarship astray appears to be orientalism: it became so important to "discover" the origins of modern capitalism in medieval cities and contrast it with the oriental city-states that every fact appeared in that light. But Weber was also implicated in a modern bourgeois strategy of citizenship that depoliticized citizenship as a moral order mobilized by an economic order. To reduce the differences between the ancient and medieval cities and their group configurations into merely a difference between being political and being economic is a specifically modern interpretation. How citizens in the ancient polis and Christianopolis constituted strangers and outsiders was vastly different and these differences will not fit into that simple formula. *Homo viator,* strangers and outsiders of Christianopolis, such as artisans and merchants, could not conceive of themselves or act any less "political" than Greek peasants or Roman plebeians. Conversely, peasants or plebeians could not be any less "economic" than merchants and artisans were. These were nineteenth- and twentieth-century categories that obfuscated the complex workings of citizenship, identity, and difference.

Eutopolis

Humanists
Vagrants
Poor
Colonists

I know that rich and poor,
fools and wisemen, priests and laymen
nobles, peasants, princes and misers,
small and large, fair and ugly,
ladies with upturned collars,
and of any class whatever, wearing
costly hats or simple bonnets.
Death seizes without exception.
—**François Villon, *The Testament***

Eutopolis is the realized utopia as an order that generates happiness as harmony, or, rather, it is the corporeal embodiment of utopia. When dominant groups dream a naturalized, eternalized, and universalized order and when their visions become realized utopias, this is the moment of the birth of the eutopolis. The eutopolis had two moments. The first was the articulation of the city in the fourteenth and fifteenth centuries as a de jure corporation, a legal entity independent from its members and "perceivable only by the intellect." It made the dream of the rational city a legal reality. The second was the articulation of the city as a rational spatial order in the sixteenth and seventeenth centuries. When the two moments overlapped in the New World as well as in the old, the eutopolis was born. In its first moment the eutopolis became a technology of citizenship by which dominant groups encased their position in the social order by fusing the political and economic orders that produced a legal order. In its second moment, law and geometry were fused to create the rational city as a concrete, spatial order.

That the story of the eutopolis is always told as a struggle of the city against the state has obfuscated more than it has revealed. It became even more troublesome when Fernand Braudel elevated such an ostensible battle into a universal history by asserting that history always featured revivals and that such revivals always featured two runners: the city and the state. For Braudel what was remarkable about medieval Europe was that the city had "won hands down" (1988, 511). By contrast, in early modern Europe, the state "regained" its power. To be rather blunt, there never was a struggle between the "city" and the "state." Rather, there were struggles among and within various social groups in their pursuit for recognition, differentiation, and domination. Forms such as cities, states, empires, federations, and kingdoms are technologies of such struggles and for the most part they embody a combination of various forms of capital (e.g., symbolic, economic, martial, social, cultural) available to groups in their struggles. But such forms do not act upon themselves or other forms. They are assembled to mobilize various strategies and to deploy technologies of citizenship. In early modern Europe the transformations of the city have to be told from the point of view of the rise and consolidation of the nobility and its transformation into an aristocracy that, on the one hand, strengthened the emerging absolutist state form, and, on the other hand, held its grip on power as oligarchies in early cities. The eutopolis was dominated by oligarchies from which two consequences flowed: the articulation of the ideal city as a rational order and the articulation of the ideal citizen and his appropriate conduct. The nobility articulated these ideals and invented technologies for inculcating its virtues in other groups, and as we shall see, established its own norms not as universal, but as necessary. How the nobility consolidated its power within both cities and states and how it was able to impose its will on other groups, especially merchants and artisans, by assembling strategies and technologies is of concern if we are to grasp the ideal of citizenship that resulted from these struggles.

Articulating an Ideal Citizen

Throughout the fifteenth and sixteenth centuries, dominant groups in the European city consolidated their power and established either oligarchic or despotic regimes. The brief but ostensibly "revolutionary" usurpation of power by the *popolani* in the Italian cities and by various craft and merchant guilds in other cities had gradually led to the formation of new aristocracies based on landowner and mercantile capital, as well as new forms of social and cultural capital.

Ever since Jacob Burckhardt (1860) advanced his classic argument that both republics and despotic city-states indifferently "discovered the individual" in late fourteenth-century Italy, the characterization of the Renaissance man became immortalized. For Burckhardt the new man was characterized by his learning, his indifference to political affairs, and his cosmopolitanism. For Burckhardt humanists, a group of men— poets, philosophers, writers—who were devoted to classical Greek and Roman cultures, were both the symbol and the driving force not only of the Renaissance, but of modern man. Moreover, for Burckhardt (1872) the Greek man and the Renaissance man became mirror images, so much so that he led his illustrious admirer, Nietzsche, to "recognize the superiority of the Greek man [citizen] and the Renaissance man [citizen]," and wish "to have them without the causes and conditions that made them possible" (1880, §882, 471).

Of course, this nineteenth-century image of the humanist as an apolitical being has now come under intense scrutiny, but the issue is not whether Burckhardt was right to attribute the "discovery of the individual" to the fourteenth and fifteenth centuries and whether that individual was sui generis or a product of social and cultural forces, and thus a myth (Martin 1997). What concerns us here is how the "discovery of the individual" was indeed the invention of a citizen, a new citizen whose sensibilities, virtues, character, orientations, and ways of being no longer corresponded to either the *popolo* or the "old" nobility. That is why Hans Baron advanced the thesis that among the humanists, there was a smaller group of men who constituted themselves as political beings, a group that Baron called the "civic humanists" (Baron 1955, 1988; Hankins 1995). The rise of civic humanism is significant perhaps precisely because it articulated a new image of the citizen, distinguishing him not only from his immediate predecessors, but also reviving an image by reworking and appropriating past Greek and Roman images and by distinguishing the citizen from the vices that surrounded him in the city (Najemy 1992).

Who were the civic humanists? Whether republican or despotic, oligarchic or royal, cities across Europe became the scene for the rise of the professions in administrative, martial, academic, legal, advisory, and tutorial offices without which the formation of aristocracies would have been impossible. That these various pragmatic professionals were also dominant in major fields of thought such as grammar, rhetoric, poetry, history, and ethics often concealed the fact that they were frequently clients for aristocratic publics, among whom were oligarchs, noblemen, rich bourgeois, princes, prelates, curial officials, and administrators, as well as other professional men such as lawyers, notaries, and other literati (Grafton 1991; Grafton and Jardine 1986).

Throughout the fifteenth century, civic humanists as pragmatic professionals were crucial in articulating an image of citizenship, an image that appealed to and was encouraged by their aristocratic publics. This projected image was neither purely contemplative, nor purely active, but was rather an affirmative citizen. Turning toward the major poets of Greece and Rome, such as Homer, Vergil, Horace, Juvenal, and Seneca, they articulated this image as a synthesis of the antique aristocrat and the new aspiring nobility (Grafton 1993; 1997). This citizen was one who conducted himself in public in an eloquent manner, with prudence and sincerity (Martin 1997). Eloquence was perhaps the most significant virtue of the new citizen. In 1436 a Florentine poet could claim that the "best citizen" was the perfect orator, as represented by Cicero. The humanist Frulovisi observed that the eloquent citizen was a precondition of government (Martines 1979, 194). Again, Francesco Patrizi of Siena (1413–94) maintained that "[n]o quality is of more vital concern to the state than public speaking, especially that aspect which relates to civil discussion. For the ends of the state depend upon the ability of men of affairs to persuade others into or out of a proposed course of action" (quoted in Martines 1979, 194–95). Being political required a command of rhetoric and eloquence and was a matter of the application of intellect rather than force. This image was offered directly to the men of affairs as a practical ideal, rather than as an article of faith. Very early in their rise, therefore, aristocracies received the message from the pragmatic professionals that force alone, which they surely commanded through their impressive armies, would not be adequate to establish an effective and durable domination.

Being eloquent did not exhaust the virtues of the new citizen. For he was also prudent and sincere. Prudence dictated that a citizen ought to exercise caution in revealing convictions or feelings. A citizen ought to consider carefully whatever one does or says, attending to the place where one does it, in whose presence, at what time, and for what purposes. Being prudent was a strategy of citizenship insofar as it allowed the citizen to conduct himself properly in the city and in the court. By contrast, being sincere required establishing harmony between deeds and words, actions and feelings. But these strategies were not contradictory or conflicting strategies of conduct, as Martin (1997) contends. Rather, they were strategies that allowed the citizen to conduct himself differently in different contexts. That civic humanists increasingly articulated being political as being active, prudent, and sincere, and that these virtues were associated with being a citizen was interpreted as the "discovery of the individual" itself illustrates how much of history has been written from the perspective of citizens.

At any rate, civic humanists also assembled these strategies and technologies of being political by recreating histories of Greece and Rome. They believed that historians such as Livy, Sallust, Caesar, and Plutarch taught everything from virtue to eloquence, from wisdom to pragmatics (Osmond 1993). They turned history into a pragmatic concern, once again, not as an article of faith, but as prudence. In the life of Greek and Roman cities, the humanists found their own cities; in orators and literati, they found themselves; in public men—rulers, statesmen, orators, professional soldiers—they found their friends, acquaintances, patrons, and again, themselves. They created their own versions of Aristotle, Plato, Demosthenes, Perikles, and Alexander. They felt elective affinities with eminent Roman senators, generals, rhetoricians, and poets (Kallendorf 1995). They wrote the histories of their own cities in light of the histories of Greek and Roman cities. The boundaries between republican Florence and republican Rome were blurred.

That civic humanists were typically clients of aristocracies does not mean that they subserviently produced images for them. They circulated among the dominant social groups and wrote in praise of their own cities, rulers, and patrons, but humanists deliberately cultivated their distinction. That the image of the citizen they articulated was aristocratic was not accidental or natural, but an image of aspiration, rather than reality. Only legally eligible citizens, civic humanists, and the princes and their advisers could aspire to the ideal, but it required cultivating oneself to attain it. The virtue of being political was not a universal virtue; it was only attainable by the well born. The appeal of Greek and Roman images of citizenship, articulated and bequeathed by their patrician vanguards rather than by their peasant or plebeian opponents, was precisely about this point.

The origins of civic humanism have been traced to the universities of the thirteenth and fourteenth centuries, especially in Italian cities such as Bologna, Padua, and Pavia. These universities increasingly produced pragmatic professionals such as jurists, physicians, teachers, and a few philosophers, usually clerics, who carried on the tasks of instruction and reflection. We have noted earlier the tension between these men and their respective cities and communes: in the intensely local life of the commune and its inward concerns, scholars appeared as threatening elements and their "cosmopolitanism" was looked upon skeptically. But the scholars became the real beneficiaries of the consolidation of the power of the nobility and, in fact, lawyers and jurists in particular were instrumental in its rise to dominance. The lawyers, jurists, and notaries conducted the business of government, but were not in a position to challenge the communal or city governments and their small circle of rulers. They began, however, to articulate notions of the duties of citizens, political obligations, civic virtue, and community. In the fourteenth and fifteenth centuries, these notions were not linked up with larger forces. Or as Martines maintains, "So long as the administrative literati, in the give and take of daily discourse, were not driven and stimulated by the citizens around them, driven toward a fresh view of the virtues of political activity and worldly pursuits, so long would that vanguard of men fail to find enough social utility in any garnerings from the literature of antiquity; so long, too, would they have trouble drawing education, politics, eloquence, and classical antiquity into a coherent intellectual program" (1979, 204). While it is impossible to imagine the rise of pragmatic professionals without literary humanists, neither would it be imaginable that these pragmatic professionals could have functioned without generating aristocratic publics, upon whose influence and power they depended. By the early fifteenth century, the governing groups in the city had consolidated their power and articulated strategies of citizenship. Civic humanism articulated and gave expression to these strategies.

The cosmopolitanism of the humanists was not a vice but a virtue for the dominant groups in the city. Most civic humanists were strangers in the sense that they won patronage or major public posts in cities to which they were not native (Martines 1979, 206). While some humanists came from well-established aristocratic families, many were from lesser origins, as the emphasis was on the nobility of work rather than birth. They were typically ambitious, mobile, and combative. The agonistic strategies of eloquence, prudence, and sincerity were not empty ideals, but deployed for accumulating cultural capital. Perhaps we can use that concept with the greatest justification compared with any other group that the city as a difference machine generated, for the civic virtues meant an endowment that had to be acquired by hard work, tenacity, practice, and learning, and which also had to be accredited. As Petrarch (1304–74) confessed, eloquence was a thing of cities, a mode of being political that was valorized only in cities (1924). That the humanists extolled the virtues of professionalism reflected their primary source of capital: they depended on income from chancellery offices, professorships, patronage, and ecclesiastical benefices. They converted their cultural capital into economic capital in the emerging market of professional services that included not only advice for the prince, but the official chronicling of events, advocacy, representation, and, as we shall see, advice on the relationship between political order and spatial order. The humanists were engaged in worldly practices of providing services, and in the process of fostering eloquence and public conduct, they did much to elaborate a view of the dominant groups. For Martines, "Sooner, therefore, and more faithfully than men to the manner born, the professionals—new men, men on the make—were able to articulate the values of elites which they had entered, or to which they aspired, or in whose service their pens were arrayed" (1979, 206). As they articulated a new image of the citizen, the professionals held "lower orders" in the city in contempt and constituted them as vulgar strangers and outsiders. They despised the "crowd" and they affected disdain for all trades, artisans, shopkeeping, and even the practice of law rather than theorizing law. The virtues of eloquence, prudence, and sincerity, with their emphasis on social presence and public appearance, were not virtues available for everyone, but for those endowed or born for them.

It would be a mistake, however, to constitute the civic humanists or their patrons as cohesive classes, let alone ruling classes, as does Martines (1979, 210–14). Rather, there were significant fractures within both the civic humanists and the aristocracy, deriving from their specific positions in the social space (Dewald 1996). In addition, the social relationship between citizens and civic humanists as strangers was agonistic (Rabil 1988). As Martines himself demonstrates, civic humanists often criticized both the wealthy bourgeois and the nobles for not using their wealth prudently and gave advice accordingly. The identity of civic humanists and the citizens was not overlapping, but conflictual and interdependent. The civic humanists were the strangers of the eutopolis. They engaged in debates over the meaning of nobility, about which the nobility was less than happy (Baron 1988; Becker 1968; Brucker 1977; Martines 1979, 212).

By articulating an image of the citizen as a sovereign man, the civic humanists as pragmatic professionals bequeathed a legacy of the sovereign individual, a heroic individual with virtuous eloquence, prudence, sincerity, and nobility as his rank, standing above the herd and vulgar other, which was then interpreted as the discovery of the individual. While articulated in a universal language, it meant and applied to a specific group and its identity. Yet a Greek or a Roman citizen would have considered the image of the citizen an outsider since his virtues were not based on an ideal of heroic or even hoplitic warfare, but on reason, inventiveness, acquisition, and cunning. But the civic humanist ideal of the sovereign and heroic individual had no difficulty seeing itself as a direct descendant and an inheritor of the Greek or Roman citizen.

Statization as a Strategy of Citizenship

Just about the same time that the ideal citizen makes its appearance, the eutopolis becomes a spectacle with the rise of vagrants, poor, vagabonds, beggars—new strangers and outsiders of the eutopolis. The articulation of a new image of the citizen and the "appearance" of new strangers and outsiders in the eutopolis were not separate but interlocked events, both of which were intertwined with the rise of the state.

Another technology that emerged at the same time as the communes and challenged it was the kingship, which derived from the same origins as the city (Strayer 1970). The kingdoms of Europe from the twelfth century onward consolidated large territories under their rule and increasingly became hostile to cities but were enamored by the revenue the cities generated for their war machines. Cities as the seedbed of merchants and artisans, trade and industry generated economic capital. Hence, a tension grew between the emerging states and cities. But, for reasons that are too varied and complex to explore here, the kingdoms of Europe evolved into powerful monarchies and ultimately into modern states. Against monarchical powers, to which they contributed, urban oligarchies did not orient themselves as adversaries, but as allies. By the seventeenth century, urban oligarchies in Europe were in a symbiotic relationship with the state and their royal bureaucracies.

Under what conditions and how the European kingdoms were transformed into the sovereign states of the early modern era, establishing a legal framework of rule, consolidating territories, centralizing power, and monopolizing the means of coercion by building war machines, has been extensively debated (Axtmann 1990; Blickle 1997; Poggi 1978; Reinhard 1996). What is germane for citizenship as alterity is that, regardless of regional variations, the early modern states such as France, England, Spain, Portugal, Holland, and Flanders, as well as German principalities and Italian republics, constituted themselves as rulers of cities and exponentially increased their extraction of economic capital from them. As mentioned earlier, the story of this consolidation of power is often told in narratives of epic struggles between states and cities. Grouping these into geopolitical, economic, systemic, and statist narratives, Charles Tilly argues that they all nonetheless neglected how the citizens of cities contributed to state formation and how this resulted in different paths of transformation of the state in different regions of Europe (1994, 3). Tilly argues that cities shaped the destinies of states in Europe chiefly by serving as containers for the distribution of economic capital, by means of which dominant groups in cities, such as the patriciate including merchants, wealthy artisans, and urban nobles, extended their influence throughout the urban hinterland and across long-distance trade networks. Because cities varied in the composition and power of their dominant groups, their relationship with monarchs differed across Europe. As a result, "The varying intersections between the processes by which capital and coercion concentrated and came under state control help explain the geographic pattern of European state formation, the differential incorporation of urban oligarchies and institutions into consolidated state structure, and the shift in state power from the Mediterranean to the Atlantic" (Tilly 1994, 9).

How wars among the rulers of states and their factions were financed throughout the early modern period sheds light on the relationship between coercion and capital and isolates the way conflicts between dominant groups contributed to the formation of different kinds of states. Although it was possible for a monarch to wage war with his own revenues, it became increasingly difficult to conduct war without borrowing large sums of money from capitalists. Thus the concentration of coercion was dependent in part on the concentration of capital. All makers of war on a large scale conquered or otherwise allied themselves with those who possessed effective means of war: nobility in the noble cavalries, mercenary infantries, clergy, and accumulators of economic capital. The European monarchs needed these groups to effectively dominate workers and peasants as immanent strangers, who were often called upon to pay the final bill of war with their bodies at work or at war. As their demand for revenues and manpower rose, each state also began negotiating with the dominated groups via new institutions such as elections, assemblies, referenda, and consultative devices (Tilly 1994, 11). With whom the states made their strongest bargains depended on the relative strength of the dominated groups vis-à-vis the dominant groups. This created a dilemma for the dominant oligarchies in cities, who as agents of the state strengthened the concentration of coercion in the state and opened the path toward their own domination in the form of increased demands for taxation and revenue from the state. The dominant oligarchs in cities preferred to use their capital toward further capital accumulation rather than in state formation and the financing of war, but without them, they could not have consolidated their dominant position in the first place.

While the way this dilemma led different states along different paths of formation across Europe is a significant story narrated by Tilly and his associates (Tilly 1992; Tilly and Blockmans 1994), for citizenship as alterity in the eutopolis, what this narrative overlooks is precisely how dominant groups established their dominance vis-à-vis the dominated and what strategies and technologies of citizenship they assembled and mobilized. For, as argued above, "cities" and "states" do not act; it is social groups and their agents in pursuit of recognition, differentiation, and domination who act, and in so doing, they mobilize different forms of capital and assemble legal and political technologies such as "cities" and "states." If "cities" were subordinated in early modern Europe, it was not because "states" were ascendant, but because there was a shift in the configurations of power among medieval social groups—patricians, plebeians, clergy, and royal classes—which redefined the nature and relationships between cities and states (Blockmans 1994). The aristocracies found more protection under the auspices of state institutions than was formerly possible in cities and regained the power they had lost to the merchants, artisans, and traders, in short, the workers, peasants, and myriad other groups that emerged in the early modern state.

Expectedly, Weber, in his scattered and few remarks on the eutopolis, considered the rise of the European state and its conquest of the city by the sixteenth century as having actually retarded the growth of capitalism. Since the state required the routinization of administration, the monopolization of violence, and the centralization of power, it resulted in the growth of bureaucracy. Weber drew a parallel between the ancient oriental states and the European states of the sixteenth and seventeenth centuries. In Egypt, as early as the second millennium B.C., the royal clientele had grown into a universally dominant bureaucracy. This bureaucracy and its theocracy throttled the emergence of the free polis in the ancient Near East, and the same happened in Hellenistic kingdoms and the later Roman Empire. He saw the rise of the European state as yet another moment that retarded the growth of capitalism, which always depended on the "free" city. This is, of course, rather an odd interpretation, for Weber, as we have seen, had considered the medieval city as the quintessential type of such a "free city" that had given rise to occidental capitalism. To my knowledge, he never explained how this lag occurred and how eventually capitalism became "reconnected" with the city. This is, in my view, one of the oddest lacunae in Weber's corpus.

At any rate, the grand narrative of the struggle between the city and the state, in addition to neglecting group differentiation within the city, also gives the misleading impression that dominant groups had only to fight against the emerging state when in fact the political order almost always included a variety of powerful magnates and regional powers, which raised as much claim to the city as the state (Friedrichs 1995, 44, 59). Moreover, cities in many parts of Europe did act as though they were states, ruling over villages and smaller cities while deferring to some higher authority within a larger political order. Rather than focusing on these ostensible struggles, my concern here is with how dominant groups conceived their identity and alterity via the eutopolis and how they were able to impose their own vision of themselves and the city on other social groups.

Assembling Noble Selves as Citizens

The remarkable feature of the early modern European city is that its contemporaries regarded its oligarchical character as obvious. It was well understood and accepted by the dominated groups in the city that men, by virtue of their privileges, governed the city and that all must obey "the powers that be." It was assumed that the dominant groups in the city would supply a core of responsible men to fill the offices in city government, men who were sufficiently prosperous to afford to engage in the often time-consuming business of government and skillful enough to conduct themselves in public. Whether as closed as the single group of urban families that dominated Venice between 1381 and 1646 or more open as in English cities, a small circle of families constituted the aristocracies that dominated the eutopolis. We have seen that a key to its success in *consolidating* power was certainly the relationship the aristocracies had with the state. But what was the key to its success in naturalizing its power? How did it ensure that its monopolization of power was considered as eternal?

Of course, merchants, nobles, and wealthy artisans were not the only dominant groups. The professions, such as medicine and jurisprudence, gained increasing prominence in the eutopolis. Always requiring a degree from a respected university in Europe, lawyers and other professionals were typically drawn from the aristocratic families, who used their social and economic capital to allow their sons to acquire cultural capital (Amelang 1984). The aristocrats took these three forms of capital seriously. The possibility of being ennobled or, better still, getting recognized as being inherently noble was symbolically valuable for many members of the aristocracy (Benecke 1971). Yet, being ennobled was not a straightforward affair. Just how this could be achieved was a disputed matter. A fifteenth-century Italian jurist emphasized the need for authorization to define an identity quite effectively: "Nobility is a rank conferred by a sovereign, by which a person is accepted above honest plebeians. . . . No one has rank by his own standing. It is necessary that rank be conferred on him by another" (quoted in Friedrichs 1995, 189). For many aristocratic families, the accumulation of economic capital was a means to achieve noble status or at least social recognition, and they were eager to be acknowledged as belonging to the ranks of nobility (Friedrichs 1995, 188). Similarly, in France, acquiring royal offices in larger cities where the growing state bureaucracies were being established became a popular investment among the aristocracies (190).

The aristocracies of the eutopolis used various forms of classification as agonistic strategies: they ranked, ordered, classified, and placed individuals and families to an extent that was unthinkable in other forms of the city. There were cities, for example, in which the authorities drew up an exact list of all those families whose members were eligible for high office. This was obviously a technology of citizenship, and the process must have been intensely political and contested among the aristocracies. To fill any of the aristocratic seats on the city council, for example, the magistrates in Nuremberg drew up a list in 1521 and summoned forty-three families to a social dance at the city hall. While Nuremberg may have been less subtle than other cities in alienating certain families, in cities across Europe the criteria for eligibility for the city council were often left deliberately vague, thereby making agonistic strategies possible.

In many cities, laborious efforts were undertaken to establish a distinct hierarchy of social ranks. In some cities, the distinction between different ranks was reinforced by sumptuary ordinances, which specified exactly what articles of clothing could be worn by members of each social group (Friedrichs 1995, 140–41; Hunt 1996b). The dominant groups were concerned to mark themselves and others out with special insignia. Obviously, in making their group identity and its alterity visible, they attempted to inscribe the social body with distinction, which otherwise remained vulnerable to appearing arbitrary and invisible.

The magistrates of Frankfurt am Main, for example, issued a new ordinance in 1621 that refined previous practices by dividing the city into five legal "orders." The first order included chiefly the old aristocratic families, who claimed quasi-noble status. Next came nonaristocratic members of the city council, other citizens, and merchants. The third order included distinguished retailers and members of the legal profession. Then came common retailers and craftsmen in a vastly larger category than the first three orders combined. The fifth order classified together unskilled workers and everyone else. The ordinance was further refined in 1671 (describing merchants in more detail) and in 1731 (including merchants in the second order only if they met a specific wealth requirement) (Friedrichs 1995, 141; Soliday 1974, 62–65). As Friedrichs illustrates, in many European cities, formal and informal attempts were made to divide inhabitants into a series of graduated ranks for a variety of purposes. In Venice only three ranks were established: nobility, citizens, and the common people. In the French city of Beauvais, by contrast, the city was divided for political purposes into no less than thirty-one corporate groups: the first six consisted chiefly of civic officials and professionals; the remaining twenty-five were made up of various occupational clusters, beginning with the great cloth merchants and descending downward to the agricultural laborers. While Friedrichs laments that these classifications were not quite precise, that could hardly have been the aim. Rather, just as in the polis, civitas, and Christianopolis, these classifications were stakes in the struggle of various groups for domination and advancing their rights to the city. By mobilizing agonistic strategies such as classification and establishing graduated rank orders where those who claimed noble status always came out on top, followed by officeholders, wealthy merchants and landowners, lesser merchants, artisans and craftsmen and unskilled laborers, dominant groups were etching their dominance in the official records of the city and, no less, in the imagination of the dominated. Such classifications would surely make a vast majority of inhabitants strangers to their own city when they always appeared at the bottom and would surely remind women, immigrants, the poor, vagrants, and beggars that they were outsiders. But the strategies assembled by the aristocracies were by no means limited to official classifications. In fact, these classifications could not be mobilized if the citizens did not assemble solidaristic strategies, such as matrimonialism and ceremonialism, and alienating strategies such as expulsion, branding, systemic violence, and sequestration.

With regard to the solidaristic strategies, it is well known that the nobility took its idleness very seriously and developed various ceremonial and matrimonial practices such as processions, feasts, banquets, hunts, and patronage of the arts, especially music, painting, sculpture, and literature, and held elaborate gatherings, such as dances and balls (Gehl 1993; Trachtenberg 1997). The nobility also developed marriage and concubinage into an art of accumulating social and political capital in the sense that they allowed access to certain networks of power without which success would not be possible (Cox 1995; Friedrichs 1993; Janse 1999; Molho 1994). While social historians have only begun to work on these themes relatively recently, the intense ceremonialism, matrimonialism, and spectacularism of the nobility and its urban styles of life can be fruitfully interpreted as solidaristic strategies and technologies of citizenship that enabled them to constitute themselves distinct from other social groups in the city (Crabb 2000). Unlike solidaristic strategies and technologies that rendered the nobility as a distinct group, its agonistic and alienating strategies and technologies have actually commanded wider attention and also require a brief discussion.

At the Margins of Orders

While idleness was a virtue for the aristocracies in the eutopolis, it was a vice for the poor. The idleness of the aristocrat, seen as freedom from the necessity of having to engage in labor, was ennobling. The rentiers and merchants boasted about their freedom to experience pleasure. The idleness of the poor, interpreted as a refusal to submit to the necessity of working for a living, was demeaning. The concentration of wealth and power in much less than 10 percent of the population and the fairly widespread distribution of poverty in the remainder were two aspects of any given eutopolis (Friedrichs 1995, 152, 226).

In the sixteenth century, new categories were added to the terms of imagining the political and social order of the city: beggars and vagrants. Of course, they did not show up in the classifications that mutually constituted citizens and strangers, but they appeared in documents, edicts, proclamations, records, and legislation that were meant to reform or ban outsiders. Moreover, "beggars" and "vagrants" did exist before the sixteenth century. Remarkably, beggars, for example, were listed not as outsiders, but as citizens in a number of German cities in the fifteenth century and sometimes they even paid taxes; in Cologne an unofficial guild of beggars was organized in the 1450s (Friedrichs 1995, 218). And one needs only to read the fifteenth-century Parisian poet François Villon to get a glimpse of the world of the strangers and outsiders in the city (Holbrook 1972; Villon 1994). But by the sixteenth century, aristocracies began mobilizing alienating strategies toward beggars and vagrants as outsiders. By using branding technologies such as making them wear badges, the deserving poor were given their own badge of honor and distinction. Those who were the undeserving poor, and the mirror opposite of an idle noble, were also marked with whipping, carting, pillorying, and torturing before they were expulsed by being dropped at the gates of the city.

Later in the sixteenth and seventeenth centuries, at about the time when the idle nobles were discovering music and developing a taste for specially commissioned operettas and orchestral works, the idle poor were being either confined or reformed in new workhouses and taught the discipline and skills necessary to become habituated to a more industrious way of life.

The constitution of immigrants as outsiders was a rather more complex issue. Except in some Polish cities, many European cities did not grant citizenship readily. But for wealthy merchants and the respected professions, becoming a citizen was easier than it was for journeymen, apprentices, laborers, and domestic servants (Friedrichs 1995, 238). In fact, wealthy Italian merchants who immigrated to other cities did not even bother requesting citizenship, being content with the privileges afforded by their economic and social capital. Similarly, for lawyers it was relatively easy to circulate among various cities on the basis of the professional services they provided. By contrast, in the eutopolis those who were not Christians always remained outsiders. Muslims and Jews were typically asked to either convert to Christianity or to leave the city. The alienating technologies against the Jews continued from the Christianopolis and were intensified in the eutopolis. Jews were sequestered in that they could live only in cities where their presence was specifically permitted by the authorities. But since the ground rules were constantly being changed, the Jews were often displaced and forced to migrate throughout the early modern era. In almost every city with a substantial population, the Jews lived in their own quarters. In some cities the establishment of a formal ghetto enforced this sequestration. As we have seen earlier, ghettoization as an alienating strategy was first used in Venice, but it was in Frankfurt am Main that the Jews were rigidly confined to a single street surrounded by its own walls and accessible only through its own gates. The Jews were forbidden to leave the ghetto on Sundays and Christian holidays; on other days they could appear in the streets of the city, but only if they had business to do and never in groups of more than two. The Jews were not allowed to touch fruits or vegetables unless they had already paid for the produce. There were numerous other regulations in a similar vein (Friedrichs 1995, 241).

Corporation as a Technology of Citizenship

Among the most fascinating aspects of the eutopolis is the emergence of political and legal discourse about the city (treatises, theories, enactments, legislation, edicts, proclamations, practices, inquiries, surveys), which constituted an ideal of the city. By the fifteenth century, the political and legal discourse on the city reached the conclusion that corporate power not prescribed by the king was neither legitimate, nor legal. It also reached a clear conception of what a corporation was and what legitimate powers it could exercise. This was the de jure corporation. This was what we can call the legal invention of the eutopolis as a corporation (Isin 1992, ch. 2). According to this conception, the corporation was an abstract and subordinate body politic. It was abstract because the obligations and liberties of the people who made up the corporation were distinct from individual obligations and liberties. For example, when a corporation was created, it was thought to have perpetual succession, an attribute that separated the existence of the city from its citizens in the eyes of royal law. Similarly, a corporation could appear before the court and hold landed property distinct from its citizens. It was also abstract because its properties and its very existence were the creation of law—royal law. These de jure characteristics became the basic attributes of an incorporated city in the early modern era. Any group of people who might gather and define themselves as a corporation, exercising powers that were not prescribed by law, was declared illegal, and in time, became unthinkable. As we have seen earlier, in the twelfth, thirteenth, and fourteenth centuries, a variety of groups realized themselves as corporate groups and practised de facto rights to the city. By the eighteenth century, however, European kings and their pragmatic professionals (lawyers, historians, and jurists) had rewritten the history of these groups as corporations, claiming that the kings had always created them. This was a time of edicts and proclamations and these corporate groups had to accept their own histories as rewritten by royal intellectuals.

The articulation of the idea of the corporation as the legal expression of a social group took place in the fourteenth and fifteenth centuries. From that time onward, any group that was not created in law did not have the legitimacy or legality to act as a group. Of course, this does not mean that all social groups heeded this legal change. The realization of the idea of corporation to legislate groups took much longer in practice than the dominant groups would have liked. In fact, the absolute authority to regulate social groups and impose a certain uniformity on them did not crystallize until well into the nineteenth century with the articulation of the modern state. Nonetheless, the legitimation of the authority to impose a political order on a variety of rights, immunities, and privileges of a number of social groups such as guilds, universities, chapters, and associations was a precondition for the rise of the early modern state. While generations of scholars have focused on the absolute origins of the idea of the corporation, the crux of the invention is that to impose an order on medieval particularisms and to consolidate their power, dominant groups of the eutopolis, particularly the urban nobility and merchants, needed such a legal technology. As Reynolds argues, it was not because legal theorists were able to invent the abstract idea of the corporation that the modern state emerged, but because there were rules devised over the centuries to suit the political needs of governments, lawyers, and their masters, which could be assembled into a technology (Reynolds 1995a).

From the point of view of citizenship as alterity, the significant aspect of the invention of the idea of the corporation is that, for the first time in politico-legal history, dominant groups were able to consolidate and maintain their identities, ensure their perpetuity, and legislate rules of conduct and membership via a technology of citizenship that was to prove one of the most permanent for centuries. While citizens of the polis, civitas, or Christianopolis could boast about the unity of their city, as demonstrated by that memorable if unconvincing funeral oration by Perikles in Athens or by the relics of Saint Mark in the facade of the basilica in the piazza San Marco in Venice, the citizens of the eutopolis assembled the city as a legally unified entity. It was a momentous assemblage that would have far-reaching consequences for centuries to come.

The distinction first made by Frederic Maitland between two forms of corporation is still germane: "[I]n the history of medieval Europe we have to watch on the one hand the evolution of groups (in particular, religious groups and groups of burgesses) which in our eyes seem to display all or many of the characteristics of corporations, and on the other hand the play of thought around the idea of an *universitas* which was being slowly discovered in the Roman law books. If the facts were ready for the theory, a theory was being fashioned for the facts, those who were preparing it were Italian lawyers" (Pollock and Maitland 1968, ii, 486). Maitland emphasized that Italian lawyers were increasingly drawing inspiration from Roman law and articulating a conception of groups in law in the fourteenth and fifteenth centuries. During this period royal law invented a technology that radically altered the conception of groups and their legal authority. To put it differently, medieval law and jurisprudence were pressed into the service of dominant groups, which resulted in the invention of the city as a de jure (prescribed and created) corporation.

The primary source for making this distinction was Otto Gierke (Gierke 1868; 1900; 1934; 1939). Gierke traced the growth of the Germanic law of association, based on the concept of the organized group as a corporation. As a result, his attention on the medieval canonists was mainly devoted to expounding the distinction between this Germanic idea of a corporation and the opposing canonist concept of an institution. He found the origins of the corporation in medieval canon law. According to Gierke, in a de facto corporation the principle of unity resided in the actual members, who came together to achieve an end determined by themselves. By contrast, in a de jure institution, the principle of unity, the "end" of association, was imposed "from outside and above." But, as we have seen, the unity of the so-called de facto corporation was as imposed and imagined as the de jure corporation. Yet, Gierke thought, this external principle—in the case of the Church it would be God—was, moreover, the true "right-subject" of the institution, its physical members being mere representatives of the transcendent authority that infused into them unity and a semblance of corporate life. Gierke argued that the doctrines of the medieval canonists were by no means lacking in traces of the "true corporation spirit," which was especially evident in their definition of the whole Church as a corporation. For Gierke these tendencies were quickly overwhelmed by ideas on de jure institutions in the late thirteenth and fourteenth centuries that the canonists applied to the whole Church and to individual churches alike.

Gierke also made a contentious distinction between two opposing theories of the corporate personality. The "properly medieval" doctrine recognized in the corporation a real group will, which was distinct from the wills of individual members. The canonists, Gierke thought, progressed some way toward this conception since they did tend to personify the individual churches. However, this progress was thwarted by the acceptance of Pope Innocent IV's doctrine that the corporate personality was to be defined as a mere *persona ficta*, a fiction of the law subordinate to the whole. Gierke argued that while canon law could not find the constitutive principle of ecclesiastical human groups from within, it *did* have recourse to the idea of creation.

It is this second argument of Gierke that Reynolds (1995a) has justly criticized for its teleological premise. Reynolds argues that those who followed Gierke in discovering the origins of corporate groups in the twelfth and thirteenth centuries are misguided because professional lawyers made such legal arguments about the corporate status of groups much later. For Reynolds many groups that appear in early medieval records as holding rights or owing obligations were quite undefined. In practice people did not worry about whether the citizens of a city were the same as its inhabitants or the members of its guild. What pressed them to begin to reflect upon such questions was the conflict over who had the right to define groups. The dominant groups, whether lay or ecclesiastical, whether kings, nobles, or leading citizens, were always more hostile to demands from the dominated groups who had heavy burdens. The more a group was able to dominate other groups, the less likely they would be to let them off their customary obligations and the less martial or economic capital they could offer in exchange. Associations formed by peasants or craftsmen to demand reductions in dues and services, especially if they were put forward with a show of force or disobedience, were much more likely to seem subversive than were associations of "respectable" citizens who could offer economic capital in exchange. As Reynolds argues, "it was the subversion or rebelliousness that caused trouble, not the mere fact of association, or even of being sworn association, as such" (1995a, 6). The conflicts about groups were not about the right to freedom of association or the legal capacity of the group as a group, but about the legality or subversiveness of what the group was about. Therefore, when formal authorization was explicitly required, it was not the corporate status that needed it, but the exercise of governmental authority. Behind the entire debate about whether or not groups had the right to an abstract corporate status stood the question of the legitimacy of being political.

When Italian jurists such as Bartolus and Baldus began articulating the idea of the corporation, they were legitimating the justification needed to exist as a group. The essence of the legal idea of the corporation is that it is a group that is recognized in law, within a legal system. The Italian lawyers were not inventing ideas out of nothing, but were solving problems that insurgent groups posed to dominant groups. As Martines demonstrates, Florentine lawyers, for example, put their skills to the service of the oligarchy and affiliated their identity with its dominant groups (1968a, 394). As notable citizens and members of the oligarchy, lawyers conducted themselves as makers of the state, adopting its gaze upon political matters: "Casting back and forth in time and weighing things, we may wish to say that lawyers were the architects of the absolute state in northern as in central Italy" (1968a, 475).

As Reynolds argues, "It looks as if in France, Germany, Italy and England, rules about groups developed only in the later middle ages, not because academic lawyers thought out new ideas which then percolated through to practice, but because rulers imposed new controls and professional lawyers found new ways of arguing about them" (1995a, 17). Walter Ullmann illustrated the political nature of the juristic debates over corporations. He argued that during the fourteenth and the fifteenth centuries, jurists and lawyers were beginning to make a distinction between legal and illegal associations (1988). But jurists soon found that Roman law was not clear on whether individuals were at liberty to organize and associate themselves in corporate bodies or whether the legality of an organization depended on an act of a superior authority. Neither of these problems was sufficiently clarified in the Roman texts (Ullmann 1988, 285). The canon law, on the other hand, had important ideas as to the status of human groups within the context of a broader rule. There was, for example, the distinction between permitted or permissible associations and those associations instituted by law for a definite purpose. The concept of a "just cause" hence received an ever-widening interpretation and the legality of a human association was judged by its purpose. The conception, for example, that every organization founded by a just cause was legal was already a core teaching of Pope Innocent IV, who, as previously noted, is often credited with formulating the ideas of the fictitious personality.

Following these principles, medieval jurists and lawyers introduced a scheme of classification of human associations to ascertain their "illegality" and "legality." According to them, the legal associations were (i) tax farming partnerships, trade guilds, charities, universities; and (ii) cities, boroughs, city councils, townships. But their legality derived from their purpose, which was given to them by royal will. They asserted that (i) monopolies, criminal societies, seditious associations; and (ii) leagues and confederations between city-states, federations of cities for the purpose of ousting other cities in politics or economics were illegal associations. Note here that having articulated the legality of a corporation, medieval jurisprudence proceeded to declare federations and leagues of cities illegal. Here legal and illegal came to mean, of course, whether or not the royal authorities prescribed an association. Hence, Ullmann concluded that "the writings of the jurists provide ample testimony of the alarming growth of sectional organizations, and of the people's desire to found associations with more or less justifiable ends" (1988, 291). To put it in other words, if a de facto corporation was deemed unjust by royal authorities it would be declared illegal.

Ullmann also maintained that since corporations began to be considered subordinate, it was not possible to solve the problem of the territorial sovereignty of the state, since the state was also considered in juristic thought as a corporation (1968). This constituted an obstacle as well as an inducement for jurists to reflect on the state, which resulted in a unique formulation of corporation theory. In canon law the corporation was considered as a minor, underaged and incapable of expressing "its" will. "The consequence of this point of view was that, since the corporation could not act on its own accord, just as a minor could not, it had to have a tutor who was also called a procurator or an administrator, whose function differed in no way from that tutor who acted on behalf of an individual minor" (Ullmann 1988, 54). In secular law, which developed against the background of canon law *and* Roman law, the same relation was sustained. In order to have legal status any corporation had to have approbation from the superior. For ecclesiastical bodies, this demand followed logically since, as the whole Church was instituted by divinity, individual bodies could not be created without its authorization. The formulation of the concept of corporation by canonists and secular jurists assisted the process of equating the corporation with a natural person in the shape of a minor. It was now thought that corporations should have, as did their natural counterparts, heads and organs. In ecclesiastical bodies, bishops were heads and the elected monks and priests were the organs. The bishop governed the ecclesiastical body. In charters to cities, a similar formula was used. The mayor represented the body of citizens, who represented the inhabitants of the city. The ideas of representation and corporations therefore presupposed each other. Of course these ideas were formulated in practice over time and only gradually acquired uniformity and coherence. Thus a corporation was called *persona ficta*, a person created by a superior authority "who" in the public sphere had neither an autonomous standing nor enjoyed rights that were not, at least by construction, conferred upon "him" (Ullmann 1988, 58). Baldus (1327–1400), an Italian jurist, expressed it as follows: "[W]e commonly hold that corporations enjoy the rights of a minor and can benefit from restitution. . . . And there is a reason for this, because they are always under the protection and government of administrators, and thus they are equivalent to churches and minors" (quoted in Canning 1987, 196). From the emergence of these ideas in practice until their formulation in juridical political thought, corporations were considered subordinate entities in canon and secular laws, which prompted Ullmann to say that he has "not found one jurist who expressed a different standpoint [in later middle ages]" (1968, 54).

As mentioned earlier, behind the medieval debate about whether or not groups had the right to an abstract corporate status stood the question of the legitimacy of being political. That the corporation was articulated as an *abstract* entity separate from its citizens enabled the dominant groups to usurp the power to consecrate or deny a lesser group the right to constitute itself as a legitimate group. If, as Baldus expressed, "separate individuals do not make up the people, and thus properly speaking the people is not men, but a collection of men into a body which is mystical and taken as abstract, and the significance of which has been discovered by the intellect," it was because certain groups had acquired the dominance to be that intellect to recognize a group as a group (quoted in Canning 1987, 187). Thus, the authority that created a corporation, a king, a bishop, or a lord was also the authority that authorized certain ways of being political: the will to master the city as a difference machine acquired its first legal form and sanction.

Built Virtue as a Technology of Citizenship

As is well known, an entirely new way of conceiving urban space came into being in fifteenth-century Europe. By inventing a new technique—perspective—painters, sculptors, engineers, and architects built an ideal of the city that assembled and expressed the ideals of the citizen and polity and sought to affect it in reality (Damisch 1994; Elkins 1994). What is less emphasized and known is the social and political foundations of the ability to abstract space and realize it. We have seen above how dominant social groups solidified their position during the fifteenth century and were able to impose their authority on the groups they dominated: small traders and merchants, artisans, workers, urban peasants, and seasonal laborers. The dominant groups increasingly articulated, certainly with the assistance of pragmatist professionals, an identity and developed a group consciousness as the fifteenth century crossed into the sixteenth. This identity was not constructed and expressed merely in thought, but also in space. In fact, the consolidation of authority was simultaneous with its dominance in urban space. This took two forms: (i) articulating an ideal of space and its strategic use consonant with the emerging and distinct culture of the urban nobility and creating buildings that reinforced that identity: palaces, halls, churches, courts, and cathedrals, and; (ii) articulating an abstract space in its totality, and imposing a spatial order on other groups to differentiate their spaces from the spaces of nobility.

The first was expressed through the passion for building and redecorating magnificent spaces that marked wealth and status as virtue or what might be called "built virtue." The nobility, with prudent advice from pragmatist professionals, spent lavishly on architectural projects such as churches, chapels, palaces, courts, villas, and new public buildings. This resulted either in the expanding of cities or in the remaking of their existing spaces in a noble image. As Martines notes, the Sienese Francesco di Giorgio was one of the first observers to urge that the houses of merchants and tradesmen be constructed with a clean separation between the rooms intended for private use and those for the conduct of business (1979, 271).

Articulating abstract space with the aid of perspective, the first theorists of space, such as Alberti, Filarete, Francesco di Giorgio, and Leonardo, conceived space in its totality and contemplated the construction of whole cities (Benevolo 1993, 124–59). So was born the interest in "the ideal city": eutopolis. The treatises on the eutopolis were written from the perspective of dominant groups and their image of the city as built virtue. These ideals distinguished carefully among the kinds of spaces fit for noblemen, for professional men, for rich merchants, and for relatively well-off tradesmen. The ideal city appears as a finely differentiated space, distributing various occupations and trades across space according to their position in social space. Thus, because of their attendant sights and smells, tanners and butchers were not allowed to concentrate in the "more honorable" public spaces of the city: the main thoroughfares, the principal public squares, and the areas adjacent to the seats of power. These sites were more appropriate for the silk trades or those who provided for the expensive tastes of the citizen, like the goldsmiths. Leonardo, for example, imagined the city on two levels: the upper city, turned to the sun, for the wellborn; the lower city, with its streets backing onto the upper streets by means of stairs, for the "crowd of paupers." The paupers, workers, and artisans were isolated and marked out in urban space roughly corresponding to their social space. Both Alberti and Leonardo envisaged enclosing the poor in the inner city as a means to protect the wellborn from the eyes and evil influence of the "scoundrel rabble." The eutopolis was an expression of a will to master the city as a difference machine: it took the differences in social space as given; it distributed, encased, and inscribed them in urban space; and it envisaged using urban space for cultivating these differences. The dream of the ideal city was the dream of the mastery of its principles as a difference machine.

While vast public squares, wider and straighter streets, large buildings and spacious interiors with grandiose exteriors expressed the built virtue, they also marked out, enclosed, and isolated the built vice as the spaces of squalor and depravity. The artists, architects, and engineers who articulated the eutopolis were not in a position of exteriority to the nobility or of dominance. Rather, they were both clients of prominent patrons, such as princes, prelates, merchants, and lawyers, and also beneficiaries of these spaces by virtue of their privileged position in the social space. While Martines may be correct to argue that "where reliable information is obtainable, we find artists and writers whose political and social views are indistinguishable from those of their patrons," what is more important is the congruence of the spaces created by these men and their patrons (1979, 274). In fact, in terms of their identity, the professional men were in a position of ambiguous estrangement vis-à-vis the nobility because they held the nobility and its style of life in contempt. Barbari, for example, thought that painters should work for praise, not profit, and held the merchant-citizens in contempt.

The abstract space of the fifteenth century was not just a space seen geometrically from a single viewpoint, perspective; it was also a political space inseparable from a space delineated by openings, angular monumental rectangular forms, vistas that converged on the heroic space of the public man, and the heroic space of the citizen. Through built virtue, dominant groups contrasted themselves with the built vice of dominated groups. The tastes of dominant groups in all their confidence, triumphalism, and celebration were inscribed in urban space, not as a universal ideal of aspiration, but as a badge of distinction from the dominated groups. What distinguished the early modern nobility and its triumphalism was its ability to appropriate the heroic qualities of ancient Greek and Roman heroes in the building of the eutopolis to monumentalize its virtues as ideals *unattainable* to strangers and outsiders.

The spectacularization, monumentalization, and systematization of the built form as agonistic strategies produced various images throughout the sixteenth and seventeenth centuries: More's *Utopia* (1516), Andreä's *Christianopolis* (1619), Bacon's *The New Atlantis* (1622), Campanella's *City of the Sun* (1623), and Harrington's *Oceana* (1656). As Mumford pointed out, that all utopias were articulated as "ideal cities" was not coincidental (1965). While differing in details, form, and emphasis, the agonistic strategies embodied in the eutopolis were unmistakable: that there was a homology between the spatial order and the political order and that the ideal city simultaneously represented and inscribed social differentiation in space. These strategies were articulated in the fifteenth century. But in the sixteenth and seventeenth centuries, these strategies crystallized into new technologies that made the ideal city an apparatus of state building. Examples abound (A. E. J. Morris 1994). The French city Vitry-le-François, designed by Italian engineer Hieronimo Marino, for example, was laid out in 1545 using these technologies with remarkable consistency and transparency (Reps 1965, 6). Built around a main square, Vitry was surrounded by fortifications and marked by prominent public spaces to allow for monumental and spacious buildings. Yet the most flawlessly realized ideal city was probably the Venetian outpost of Palma Nouva, founded in 1593 (Friedrichs 1995, 26). Santa Fé (1492) in Spain, the cities of Nancy (1588) and Charleville (1608) in France, Philippeville (1555) in Belgium, and Coeworden (1597), Klundert (1560s), and Willemstad (1560s) in Holland also displayed similar principles and perfected them: centrality, uniformity, symmetry, order, spaciousness, and movement.

An exploration of various plans proposed for London after the fire of 1666 affords a glimpse of the eutopolis and its fusion of social, political, and spatial orders (Hanson 1989). While none was adopted as such, what unites the plans by Wren, Evelyn, Knight, Hooke, and Newcourt was not so much their combination of orthogonal and radial designs of avenues and interconnecting squares, but the unmistakable relationship they established in their styles to impose the identity of an aristocracy as a totality with interacting segments and parts. The monumental civic square that represented the heroic public man found its counterpart in the uniform residential square that the seventeenth century invented. The ordered civic space found its complement in the ordered residential space. Public space crossed into private space without interrupting its principles of symmetry, openness, and interconnectedness. Yet, the eutopolis found its most potent—both symbolic and material—use in transplanting social and political orders of the Old World into the New World via the colonizing project.

Assembling Bodies via Spaces: Governing Colonies at a Distance

Establishing colonies and the problems associated with their government were not new in sixteenth- and seventeenth-century Europe. We have seen how Greek poleis established colonies and Roman colonies were created as settlements of administration. Many lords, kings, and princes in medieval Europe also established new cities (Beresford 1967; Friedman 1988, 167–99). But there is a fundamental difference between these forms of colonization and their problems of government. Nor were the technologies used in different forms of colonization, such as the orthogonal plan, new or original. What was new to early modern colonization was how the abstract ideals of space, citizen, and body politic were assembled at a distance.

In the early phases of colonization, in the late fifteenth and sixteenth centuries, this assemblage did not unfold following systemic strategies and technologies. But later in the seventeenth century and throughout the eighteenth century, colonizing states such as Spain, France, Holland, and England gradually articulated design strategies and technologies through which establishing spatial orders for producing political and social orders became one of the agonistic strategies of colonization.

The Spanish invented three agonistic strategies: the mission, the *presidio,* and the *cabildo* (Cruz 1988, 165–66). While these strategies had distinct objectives, their larger intentions were similar in that they meant to "transplant" Spanish cultural, linguistic, social, and religious values. The aim of transplantation was neither the reproduction of the old order, as in colonization, nor the creation of an appendage, as in imperialization, but rather the creation of new conditions for breeding new forms of differentiation, groupings, and solidarities. Often the theoretical distinction among these agonistic strategies disappeared in practice. Nonetheless, Spanish colonial practice was very clear that transplanting Spanish culture required establishing cities and breeding new social visions and divisions of the city. The *presidio* was charged with systemic violence: as the martial authority it was responsible for protecting cities. The missions were charged with Christianization: "converting" the natives into Christians. The *cabildos* were the duly constituted municipal governments of cities charged with policing in the sense of maintaining political and social order. The Spanish colonial government was very clear right from the outset that the spatial order of the *cabildos* was the key to the success of colonization and the work of the mission and the *presidio.* It accumulated experience in establishing cities throughout the sixteenth century that was crystallized into one of the most remarkable technologies in the history of colonization: the ordinances of 1573, also known as the Law of the Indies (Nuttall 1922). That the ordinances regulated remarkable details about laying out cities, ranging from lot widths, public buildings and their locations, the layout and spacing of plazas and streets, and the spacing and location of the city, is just as important as their emphasis on differentiating lot spacing and sizing according to the status of settlers (Reps 1965, 28). Of equal importance was the regulation that natives were not allowed in the city until the city had reached a certain level of sophistication, grandeur, and completion: "[S]o that when the Indians see them they will be filled with wonder and will realize that the Spaniards are settling there permanently and not temporarily. They will consequently fear the Spaniards so much that they will not dare to offend them and will respect them and desire their friendship" (quoted in Nuttall 1922).

Reps reckons that the ordinances of 1573 could not have been merely based on earlier experience in the century, but embodied principles articulated by contemporary architects and engineers in Europe, particularly those of Alberti (1965, 31). Be that as it may, it is important to recognize that the ordinances did not only specify a spatial order, but also a political order: each city was envisaged as a corporation, with a council elected according to a specified manner. Cities such as St. Augustine, San Antonio (Texas), Galvez (Louisiana), Pensacola (Florida), Santa Fé (New Mexico), and numerous smaller cities were established with remarkable faithfulness embodying the ordinances of 1573.

Faithfulness, however, does not imply that the Spanish colonial authorities both in Spain and in New Spain desired to create New Spain in the exact image of Spain. As mentioned above, the objective of transplantation was rather to ensure that social relations and the groups that crystallized through such relations in New Spain remained more or less homologous with Spain. That merchants, aristocrats, and notables should be the dominant groups in the city was quite a "natural" assumption from which their instructions issued. But it was understood that the capital allowing the formation of such groups would take different forms. That, therefore, in the late sixteenth and seventeenth century New Spain came to acquire not only a sui generis political and religious culture but also a technical one was probably not much of a surprise to the colonial authorities (Pagden 1987, 85–86). Mexico City, for example, was compared to Rome and Athens and was considered a symbolic and material triumph of the conqueror. In these comparisons it is doubtful that anyone thought that Mexico City was Rome or Athens or even competed with their cultural position. Rather, a magnificent city that was sui generis European was the symbol of its dominant groups' magnificence and image.

Of significance here is that while the solidaristic and agonistic strategies of establishing a political and spatial order were sui generis to Spanish, and to an extent Dutch colonial practices, the British and French were slow to assemble such strategies and technologies. In the early seventeenth century, both the French and the British were content to allow colonists to articulate their identities and follow local and contingent circumstances to establish settlements. The French, for example, developed several cities along the northern and western boundaries of colonial America, which were not laid out according to systemic strategies or technologies. The French were willing to grant certain limited trading rights to companies and let them deal with circumstances prevailing at the time. As a result, early French cities such as Quebec and New Orleans did not necessarily display systemic characteristics to the extent that the Spanish colonial cities did. Similarly, British colonial practices granted almost medieval de facto corporate rights to colonists, primarily in the New England colonies, and allowed them to deal with local exigencies without strategic intervention or articulation.

The reasons for the divergence of colonial practices between the Spanish and Dutch on the one hand, and British and French on the other, are complex. But of pivotal significance here is that the Spanish and the Dutch primarily thought that they were transplanting permanent rather than temporary societies, and this permanence meant producing cities as difference machines to enable group formation and domination. That the task of transplanting fell on the city is hardly surprising as it was seen as a crucible of differentiation. By contrast, the British and the French were not quite certain about the idea of establishing permanent settlements and had not worried about creating either a New France or a New Britain. Yet, by the middle of the seventeenth century, both the French and the British reconceived the role of colonies and articulated a vision for them in their "empires." Along with this vision came strategies and technologies of settlement that were even more elaborate than those of the Spanish and which became ever more sophisticated so that, in the case of the British at least, they could be called a "colonial constitution."

Early in the seventeenth century, in an official expedition, geographer Samuel de Champlain urged the French colonial authorities to adopt a more rigorous approach to colonization, but he was ignored. He managed to persuade the cardinal, however, and consequently a company of the One Hundred Associates was established. This association was charged with bringing about an order through which the French proceeded with colonization and the settlement of cities. Although many of its plans were unrealized, it was able to settle a few thousand settlers according to some recognizable political and spatial order (Harris and Warkentin 1974). It introduced a feudal landholding system—seigneurial tenure—which was a disappearing system in France at that time. Nonetheless, the seigneurial system generated an aristocratic system in which the priest and the *seigneur* became the dominant forces (Grignon 1997). By the 1660s, the spires of the churches and the towers of the fortress of Quebec City (founded in 1608) symbolized these twin powers (Reps 1965, 61).

In the 1660s, France declared Quebec a royal province, revealing a change in its colonizing strategies. Its founding of Louisburg on Cape Breton Island as a typical seventeenth-century eutopolis in 1712 indicated how far the French had moved in the direction of establishing a political and spatial order in New France. Over twenty years, the French invested considerable capital in Louisburg to make it conform to the image of the ideal, which followed the city and fortification layout theories and principles of the French military engineer Sebastian Vauban. With its elaborate fortifications, secured harbor, and orthogonal plan with openings, squares, and an interconnected pattern of streets, Louisburg could easily have been one of the several hundred cities planned or remodeled by Vauban across Europe. While the French did not have a chance to further develop their colonial strategies, British colonial strategies provide ample evidence of how the relationship between spatial and political orders was conceived.

British Colonial Strategies and Technologies

In two stages, from the 1660s to the 1780s and from the 1780s to the 1840s, British colonial strategies developed sui generis technologies of "city planting," a term employed by the colonial officials themselves. How these technologies differed or were inspired from or transferred to other British colonies such as New Zealand, Australia, and later India is beyond the scope of my focus here (Home 1997; Isin 1989). But despite differences in various colonies, the British developed strategies of colonization via founding model cities with an underlying consistency of approach, directed from London, that requires emphasis (Wood 1982). Moreover, these technologies gave the city a corporeal existence that corresponded to its corporate character. It is useful to review the basics of these strategies and technologies, considering how they conceived space as both producing and reproducing social differences, and how the legal corporation as a technology of citizenship realized its potential.

As Home argues, the essential components of British colonization strategies included the deliberate founding of cities in preference to dispersed settlements, the planning and laying out of the city in abstract and in advance of actual settlement, the use of orthogonal layouts, the allotment of public squares, and the reserving of plots for public purposes (1997, 9–15). A technology that assembled these elements together and gave it a coherent form was the Model Township, a design that followed Renaissance and early modern principles. While its size varied through time and across different colonies, the township always embodied the principle of a town at its center, fixed-size lots, some of which were reserved for public purposes, a symbiotic relationship between the town and its surrounding farmsteads *within* the township, and its rectangular layout. The technology of township was first used in planting Ulster in the early seventeenth century, was further developed in founding Charleston and Philadelphia between 1660 and 1685, was further generalized into a formula in settling the royal colonies of the North and South Carolinas and Georgia in the 1730s, and was widely used in settling British North America in the 1780s and Australia and New Zealand in the 1830s.

While the New England colonies were left to their own devices as de facto corporate colonies between the 1630s and the 1660s, British colonial officials became determined to impose an order on the "loose and scattered settlements" and create a "uniform inspection and conduct" (Home 1997, 17). A colonial office, variously called Council of Foreign Plantations, Council or Board of Plantations, and eventually Colonial Office, articulated a conception of spatial order and its corollary political order. The detailed instructions for an expedition in 1669 to the recently created Carolina, for example, included specific details and a plan of how a city should be laid out. The constitution of Carolina set out by its proprietor, Lord Shaftesbury, prescribed a spatial order corresponding to a social division that included the main proprietors, freeholders, and a hereditary aristocracy (Home 1997, 19). Charles Town (later Charleston) was established around 1700 according to these technologies as a quintessential colonial city followed by other proprietors, such as William Penn in founding Philadelphia. In 1730, this model was most clearly realized in the founding of Savannah in Carolina. Before Savannah was conceived, a scheme, Azilia, was proposed that was a prototype of an early modern ideal city. It was envisaged as a frontier city at the Spanish border, and it was to be settled by citizen-soldiers recruited from the poor in Britain. Its center was a grand palace and square. While Azilia was never realized as a eutopolis, Carolina became a royal colony and was instructed to create spatial order according to the township plan. By contrast, a pro-prietor, James Oglethorpe, on the basis of a eutopolis, successfully found-ed the city of Savannah in Georgia. The township was divided into town, garden, and farm lots. There were squares, an orthogonal design, public lands, and a common. The basis of corporate government was founded by dividing the city into wards, each consisting of forty houses.

The articulation of these technologies of creating spatial orders roughly corresponded with the articulation of a political order that began with corporate colonies in New England, continued with the quasi-feudal proprietary colonies of Maryland, Pennsylvania, Virginia, New Jersey, and Maine, and culminated in the royal colonies of North and South Carolina, Georgia, and the conversion of older colonies such as New York and the New England colonies (Isin 1992, 201–3; Teaford 1975). The settlement instructions were always accompanied with de-tailed instructions on incorporation, including the specifics of elections, rights, and duties of the city as a corporate body and politic, guidelines for qualifications to be freemen or freeholders of the city, as well as of the electors and freemen running for office (Williams 1985). There was no doubt in the minds of colonial officials that what they were creating was not an abstract spatial order, but a political order with a corresponding spatial order. This system was continued well after the American Revo-lution and was the spine of the westward expansion of the new United States (Johnson 1976).

Articulating Rights of and to the Colonial City

Because of its uniqueness, the early history of New York illustrates well how a colonial city became the crucible of a difference machine. The Dutch West India Company, a trading post, founded New York in 1626 as New Amsterdam. The Dutch were not certain whether they wanted to colonize the area and establish a permanent settlement, but in the 1630s geopolitical circumstances forced the West India Company to develop New Amsterdam as a city and to give up its monopoly on trade (Burrows and Wallace 1999, 29–30). With the arrival of the director appointed by the company, Stuyvesant, New Amsterdam was being built according to the eutopolic strategies of town settlement as it was becoming a center of trade, particularly the slave trade. By the 1650s New Amsterdam was dominated by new merchants, mostly arriving from Holland. Artisans and workers, not necessarily dominated by the Dutch but also including German and French people, were emerging in workshops and shops owned, operated, or needed by wealthier Dutch merchants. African slaves, as well as being commodities for trade, were also kept as laborers and domestics. The struggle between the emerging merchants and the central colonial authority (symbolized in the person of Stuyvesant) resulted in the establishment of the city as a corporation in 1653 as a technology for mediating their agonistic strategies. To effectuate such mediation, in 1657 the municipal government introduced a two-tiered system of citizenship (Burrows and Wallace 1999, 66). Any native-born residents of the city, anyone who had lived there for at least one year and six weeks, or anyone willing to spend twenty guilders for the privilege was eligible for the small burgher right. This included the right to practice a trade or carry on a business. The great burgher right could be purchased with fifty guilders and qualified anyone to fill any office or dignity of the city. Both burgher rights were open to women. Stuyvesant and nineteen others, including one woman, declared themselves great burghers. An additional 238 persons subsequently received the small burgher right (Burrows and Wallace 1999, 66–67).

Until the 1660s, the city was dominated by citizens with great burgher rights, most of whom were merchants. But the fortunes of this group were threatened by the British conquest of the city in 1664. However, perhaps not surprisingly, the Dutch merchants in the city acquiesced with the British in return for maintaining their great burgher rights to the city. In fact, the prevailing belief was that in liberating themselves from the erratic leadership of the Dutch West India Company, the Dutch merchants and notables could mobilize and accumulate further forms of capital under the "peace and good government" offered by the British. To the chagrin of Stuyvesant, the Dutch West India Company governor and the Dutch notables and merchants decided to surrender the city without firing a shot. The "conquest" afforded New Amsterdam a certain protection from the Indians, as well as a break from boundary disputes with the neighboring British colonies. The new governor, Nicolls, changed the names of both the colony and the city to New York and established New York as a corporate body and politic in 1665. Nicolls replaced the Dutch system of burgomasters with the British one of sheriff, mayor, and aldermen, and retained the authority to directly appoint these officials annually (Archdeacon 1976, 98). While New York was recaptured briefly in 1673 by the Dutch and the old system of government was reintroduced, by 1674 it was again under British rule, this time governed by Andros, who introduced tighter and stricter codes of conduct and rules into the city and ensured that the British began to take over official posts in the city. Andros also introduced the British jury system and made English the language of official business.

When the new governor Dongan was appointed in 1683, the new British notables of the city asked for expanded rights to the city, including the popular election of local officials. That the majority of the city's population was still of Dutch origin shows a remarkable confidence on the part of the British notables in the city. Still, Dongan maintained the power to appoint the chief magistrate, recorder, and treasurer, and only allowed the aldermen to elect the mayor among themselves. The grip of the British notables on power was, however, derailed briefly when the Board of Trade and Plantations created the Dominion of New England in 1688. This would have resulted in a shift of power from New York to Boston, which was declared the seat of government. The Glorious Revolution in England brought an end to this scheme and the British notables in New York looked to consolidate their power in New York. For both the Dutch and the British, the rights *to* the city were implicated in the rights *of* the city in the sense that being constituted as a corporation framed the modalities through which new groups articulated and gained certain rights. Yet, the solidaristic, agonistic, and alienating strategies necessary to constitute selves as citizens are never exhausted by orientations toward institutionalized forms. What strategies and technologies other than the corporation were used by the British colonial notables to differentiate themselves as citizens, and to constitute the Dutch and other merchants and artisans as strangers, and slaves as outsiders *in* the city?

Building on a thorough analysis of two surviving tax lists for 1677 and 1703 in New York, Archdeacon makes use of church records, freemanship lists, customhouse records, and other government documents to examine social differentiation along ethnicity, occupation, residence, and social and political capital (1976). Archdeacon found that by 1703, New York exhibited a high level of social differentiation, a marked concentration of power, and a considerable use of African slaves. The richest 10 percent of the inhabitants owned just under half of all the taxable resources, and less than 3 percent of adult males were considered as being capable of exercising political power, hence being able to constitute themselves as citizens. As in other colonial cities, many wealthier citizens owned slaves, but only a few slaveholders had more than two or three slaves. While Archdeacon interprets this as an indication of their use in domestic labor, Greene reckons that they must have been used as dockworkers and other labor, as evidenced by their concentration among wealthy merchants (1996, 184). Be that as it may, slaves, either as commodities or as labor, were essential for assembling citizens as a distinguished group in the city who were able to mobilize various forms of capital ranging from chattel slaves to religious and symbolic forms of superiority and distinction.

New York was unique in terms of the competition between the Old Dutch and the new British and French Huguenot immigrants, a competition the Dutch gradually lost. The period between 1677 and 1703 witnessed the gradual erosion of the Dutch position in the city. By 1703 the British and French outnumbered the Dutch in the five leading occupations, while the Dutch gravitated toward blacksmithing, carpentry, and cooperage. The relative decline of the Dutch in the ability to mobilize capital and in their position in social space was strengthened by spatial strategies: the British and French minority formed a heavy majority of the inhabitants of the wealthiest and most prestigious zones in 1703, while the Dutch had been largely relegated to more marginal zones and accounted for the vast majority of the poor zones in the city. The struggle over space by the British notables was waged throughout the municipal corporation. For example, the municipality developed municipal plots in the city along the waterfront and the notables were given favorable opportunities to purchase and develop these highly valued lots on fashionable new streets. Dock and Queen Streets were deliberately developed in such a fashion by the municipal government. Moreover, it also guaranteed that these streets would become attractive thoroughfares by requiring that all houses built along the street conform to certain regulated aesthetic criteria (Archdeacon 1976, 84–85).

Blocked in opportunities and marginalized both socially and spatially by various agonistic strategies and technologies successfully used by the British, the Dutch were eventually drawn to an alienating strategy, with a rebellion in the city in 1689 instigated by Jacob Leisler. The intriguing aspect of this rebellion is twofold. First, unlike the uprisings in other British colonies during the last quarter of the seventeenth century, this rebellion represented not the final drive for power by an aspiring British notable group against the imperial power, but rather the futile last gasp of a group becoming estranged from citizenship. While the rebellion was suppressed, the struggle between the Dutch, the British, and the French Huguenots continued until 1712, which marks the second aspect of the struggle. In that year slaves in New York rebelled against oppression, thereby sharpening the difference between the organizing slaves as outsiders and the dominant groups in the city. The differences between the British and the French groups, who constituted the Dutch as strangers, appeared less than the differences between the dominant notables and the oppressed slaves as outsiders of the city (Burrows and Wallace 1999, 148).

The early history of New York City, despite its uniqueness, illustrates something that was widespread not only in the colonial, but also in the European eutopolis: that oligarchization symbolized by the formation of a body corporate and politic restricting rights to the city was a fundamental agonistic strategy. Very few men (and many fewer women) were able to constitute themselves as being political either by holding offices or by making themselves present in public. Archdeacon estimates that only 6.5 percent of inhabitants managed to hold some offices in the early history of New York. These men were drawn from wealthy merchants or governing groups, originally Dutch and later British and French. For Archdeacon, "The purpose of government was largely administration of the status quo rather than the enactment of legislation, and accordingly, officials did not propose far-reaching social programs which might excite the voters" (1976, 153). The real struggle for power was between various factions of the notables, between merchants and planters, and they fought each other viciously for power and its spoils.

After the American colonies won independence in the 1780s, the settling of British North America followed but also systematized the strategies and technologies of citizenship that were articulated in colonial America, particularly in royal colonies (Sebert 1980). However, the colonial officials were startled by the fact that despite persistent efforts to invent and implement these strategies and technologies, the colonists had not necessarily constituted themselves as British subjects, but had developed distinct and antagonistic identities. Perhaps because of this diagnosis, the strategies and technologies of citizenship in colonial America between the 1660s and 1780s received relatively less attention (Constable 1994). Nonetheless, in what may be one of the most fascinating and intense periods of othering and citizenship, between the 1780s and 1830s, there were numerous debates, correspondences, rethinking, and experimentation about the best ways to establish that elusive relationship between political and spatial order in British North America. British colonial officers and other notables experimented with various strategies and technologies, interpreting and transforming the colonial American experiences, inventing new ways of governing themselves and others, and in the process, articulating new ways of being political. The struggles over governing towns and cities, constituting and differentiating various groups within them, allocating rights, and responding to problems of government were paramount in the early years of colonization (Isin 1992, chaps. 4, 5). These governmental practices were intensified briefly by the rebellions in Toronto and Montreal in 1837 and 1838, respectively, to be followed by a remarkable commission led by Lord Durham, which urged new governmental strategies and technologies (Ajzenstat 1988; Durham 1837; Martin 1972). Of significance in terms of the legacy of the colonial eutopolis was the rise of the new professions, which constituted building, regulating, and monitoring the city as their fields of expertise. By the middle of the nineteenth century, as Home illustrates, the new British Empire was not built merely in a top-down manner but by colonial agents, who in their increasingly professional capacities and identities left an indelible mark on the city. Certain professions, notably the land surveyors, engineers, doctors, architects, and planners, found that the empire offered them wider scope and opportunity than they might have had at home (Home 1997, 37). As fascinating and neglected as it is, the constitution of British North American cities as difference machines and the strategies and technologies of citizenship involved in their production is beyond the scope of my focus here.

Eutopolis as Realized Utopia

Between the fifteenth and the late eighteenth centuries, European countries and their colonies unfolded many strategies and technologies of citizenship, such as the invention of the corporation or of perspective; the elaboration of instructions on how to create new cities in the New World and restructure them in the Old; the various detailed classifications and rankings of groups in cities; the laws, norms, and regulations of the conduct of both the dominant and dominated groups; and the rewriting of the histories of Athens and Rome to generate affinities between them and the nobles. These strategies and technologies do not easily fit grand narratives of the rise of the state and mercantile capitalism, the routinization of administration, the rationalization of conduct, the centralization of power, and the monopolization of violence or coercion. While there are no direct causal relationships, it is inconceivable that neither mercantile capitalism nor the state would have been possible without various strategies and technologies of citizenship through which dominant groups, including merchants, aristocrats, wealthier artisans, and the members of the pragmatic professions, lawyers, notaries, and clerks, could establish their domination in the city, codify it in law, and inscribe it in the spaces of the city. While strangers and outsiders, such as artisans in European cities and the slaves in the New World, rebelled, resisted, and attempted to establish themselves as citizens, we have no evidence of any of these attempts reaching the level of organization of the demes or the *popolo*. The aristocracy, defined broadly and including the landowners, merchants, and wealthier artisans, with its twin sources of economic capital—land and trade—and abundance of martial capital, was able to establish a dominance in the eutopolis that would certainly have appeared impressive to Roman patricians or even Greek aristocrats. The dominated groups were not able to transform their objective conditions in the social space and combine them into subjective resources to mount an effective resistance against or even challenge the aristocratic oligarchies. The secret of this effective dominance is embedded and embodied in the eutopolis. That Weber focused exclusively on the similarities between the polis and Christianopolis to account for the rise of capitalism in the occident and completely ignored the eutopolis, which in fact was the site of the emergence of capitalism, is not accidental. For the eutopolis unsettles the orientalist narrative that attributes the origins of capitalism to autonomous occidental cities without oligarchies. The eutopolis, with its centralized oligarchies inextricably interwoven with state institutions, provided an inverse image of the free occidental cities, ostensibly the seedbed of capitalism. If Weber had chosen to confront the eutopolis, his orientalism would have come up against the intensely oligarchic, centralized, and fissiparous cities of both Europe and its colonies.

Metropolis

Sansculottes
Savages
Flâneurs
Intellectuals
Africans

I am a temporary and not at all discontented citizen
Of a metropolis considered modern because all known taste has been eluded
In the furnishings and the outsides of the houses,
As well as in the plan of the city.
Here you will find no trace of a single monument to superstition.
—Arthur Rimbaud, *City*

The official acropolis outdoes
The most colossal conceits of modern barbarity.
How can I describe the dull daylight of unchanging gray skies,
The imperial effect of these buildings, the eternally snow-covered ground? . . .
How far above or below the acropolis is the rest of the city?
For the stranger in our time, recognition is impossible.
—Arthur Rimbaud, *Cities II*

Early in 1848 Alexis de Tocqueville rose in the Chamber of Deputies to express a sentiment that most Europeans and Americans shared: "We are sleeping on a volcano. . . . Do you not see that the earth trembles anew? A wind of revolution blows, the storm is on the horizon" (quoted in Hobsbawm 1975, 21). At about the same time, two German exiles, the thirty-year-old Karl Marx and the twenty-eight-year-old Friedrich Engels, were outlining the principles of the working-class revolution about which Tocqueville was warning his own class. A few weeks earlier Marx and

Engels had been asked to draft a program for the German Communist League, which was published in London on February 24, 1848, as the *Manifesto of the Communist Party*. Within weeks of the Tocqueville speech and within hours of the publication of the *Manifesto*, the French monarchy was overthrown by insurrection, the republic proclaimed, and the European revolutions of 1848 had begun. Within weeks, the revolutions spread from Paris to Berlin, Vienna, Milan, Prague, and Belgrade and severely threatened to topple state governments. Yet, within months, the revolutions of 1848 were declared a failure and the bourgeoisie consolidated and strengthened its grip on state power. But the language of "revolutions" dominated the long nineteenth century of the metropolis. The groups that created and structured the space of the modern metropolis can be seen via the three moments of its crystallization: 1789, 1848, and 1871. That all three moments are intertwined with revolutions—successful or failed—is not an accident. The metropolis was born of revolutions. But, perhaps more importantly, the revolutionaries also gave us new images of the polis and the civitas being born of revolutions.

Worker-Citizens, Dangerous Classes, Insurgent-Citizens

The invention of citizenship in the years leading up to the Revolution of 1789 in France is well known (Fitzsimmons 1993). It has also been well articulated how this new conception of citizenship was founded on the model of the bourgeois man: a masculine conception associated with property rights (Brubaker 1992, 35–49; Godineau 1998; Gutwirth 1993; Hufton 1992). This bourgeois conception of citizenship was best expressed much later, in a debate in the assembly on April 18, 1832, when it was argued that "[w]orkers are outside political life, outside the city. They are the barbarians of modern society. They should enter this society, but only be admitted to it after passing through the novitiate of owning property" (quoted in Merriman 1991, 59). What is less known is how this new conception of the citizen was briefly subverted in the formation of the sansculottes as a group. As in all struggles, the Revolution of 1789 was fought within, for, and via the city (Andrews 1985). That the sansculottes were able to constitute themselves as citizens was radical because it was a reversal and overturning of the bourgeois conception of citizenship on at least two grounds: the inclusion of women and the abolition of the difference between active and passive citizenship.

But who were the sansculottes? Answering that question is difficult because it is tangled up, as Furet (1981, 6–7) illustrated, with the contested interpretations of the Revolution itself. The successful segments of the bourgeoisie regarded the sansculottes as the criminal urban mob (see Rudé 1988, 94–95). A later generation of historians considered them as violent outcasts, lacking revolutionary consciousness (Soboul 1964, 1968). Furet and Richet (1970, 22) even called their existence into question, arguing that they were the creation of the Jacobins, as auxiliaries to the bourgeoisie. The sansculottes have also been revived as popular (Williams 1969) or cultural (Harris 1981; Levy 1981) revolutionaries, as insurgents (Rose 1983; Sonescher 1984), and even as postmodern guerrillas (Gandelman 1989). That generations of historians reinvented the sansculottes and their role in the Revolution is precisely what makes this group interesting from the perspective of investigating citizenship as alterity.

The sansculottes were the ill-clad and ill-equipped volunteers of the revolutionary army, who later constituted themselves as the radical democrats of the Revolution. While the group included for the most part poorer men, during the Reign of Terror educated public functionaries styled themselves *citoyens sans-culotte* ("citizens sansculotte"). The distinctive costume of the typical sansculotte was the *pantalon* (long trousers)—in place of the *culotte* worn by the upper classes—as well as the *carmagnole* (short-skirted coat), the red cap of liberty, and *sabots* (wooden shoes). The influence of the sansculottes ceased with the reaction that followed the fall of Robespierre (July 1794), and the name itself was proscribed. That the Revolution took a further radical turn in 1793, from being a bourgeois revolution to being a radical democracy with the Jacobins and that this would not have been possible without the urban sansculottes is what makes the interpretation of the sansculottes a treacherous terrain. While the laboring poor and the peasantry provided the muscle power for the Revolution, the sansculottes were mostly an urban movement of workers, small craftsmen, shopkeepers, artisans, small entrepreneurs, and the like. The sansculottes were organized in the sections of Paris and the local political clubs, and provided the most potent striking force of the Revolution, in demonstrations, riots, and construction of barricades. The sansculottes were also effective in articulating their ideals and ideas through journalists, writers, and poets, positioning themselves between the bourgeoisie and the proletarians against the aristocracy (Blavier 1993). In 1793–94, when the sansculottes briefly seized power, they themselves articulated an image of a golden urban past with small craftsmen, farmers, and artisans unexploited by bankers, merchants, and bureaucrats (Levy 1981).

1789: The Sansculottes as Worker Citizens

It has been difficult to account for the sansculottes. For some time now, the heroic image of the sansculotte has prevailed. For Soboul (1964; 1968) and others (Rose 1983; Williams 1969), the artisan earning his living by work with his hands was the supreme citizen-worker of the revolutionary order, who alone could be counted on to defend the republic under siege from adversaries within and without. But Potofsky argues that before the sansculottes forged a group identity, the image of the revolutionary citizen had undergone four transformations in the early period of the Revolution (Potofsky 1993). Emerging out of the need to rebuild Paris in a bourgeois image, the workers, professionals, and artisans in building and construction trades established relationships between their identity and citizenship. In 1789–90, almost all construction projects in Paris had come to a halt. At first, the builders of Paris appealed to the need for work for destitute-citizens of the city via public works to rebuild the nation. Most destitute-citizens were employed in "charity workshops." This image of destitute-citizens along with charity workshops increasingly came under attack and was rapidly replaced by an image of the builder-citizen as constructing the nation with his industry, and a distinction was made between the industrious and the idle poor, who depended on workshops (Stuurman 1996). The former organized themselves as builder-citizens and claimed economic and social rights to perform "work for the nation." Citizenship meant the enjoyment of these rights by participating as economic beings, rather than as dependent workshop workers (Potofsky 1993, 188). In 1790, architects working for a new bureau established to build projects in Paris outlined a blueprint that had a twofold objective: building a network of boulevards and monuments to rejuvenate the nation and occupying in a useful manner the artisans and workers of Paris. To strengthen the appeal for funding to employ the able-bodied and the skilled, the architect-authors of the blueprint sought to expose the corruption of the indigent and the poor, who entered the charity workshops. They contrasted the sterile labor performed by the indigent poor with that of the skilled laborer, arguing that supporting the charity workshops would breed the dangerous classes. There was then a distinction made between stultifying and edifying labor. The blueprint aimed to "breathe new life into such professional and mechanical crafts, to engage in grand public enterprises" and it claimed that "[a]rchitecture is, of all the crafts, the one that employs the most extended influence " (quoted in Potofsky 1993, 190). The building professions therefore began to forge a special niche as professional-citizens in the new republic. They were no longer at one with the great majority of the impoverished but virtuous poor; rather, they distinguished themselves by their particularly competitive yet cooperative labor as more dignified and more deserving than the poor.

It was the new professional-citizens who articulated the ideal that the civic virtue of the republic had to be inscribed in space by monumental projects. None other than building a symbolic version of the agora, the marketplace of the polis, where its political assemblies met, could inspire this. This was at once the most eminent, symbolic, and material representation of the new republic and its image of the citizen. The building of the Panthéon in Paris was its crystallization. But its building was more than the erection of a monument, even as a symbol. It was the introduction of a new division of labor, where the skilled professionals competed with each other according to rational rules introduced in direct contradistinction to the methods of building that marked the ancien régime. The projection of the new image of the citizen onto the building site was accomplished in several ways: traditional hierarchies between masters and journeymen were jettisoned, and technical experts replaced elite craftsmen; a rugged system of petitioning for work introduced political virtue as a theory of employment; and the organization of labor was made according to rational routines (Potofsky 1993, 193). Soon, however, political virtue was replaced with that of civic virtue and civic virtue with that of professional virtue, in which skill and talent defined the revolutionary citizen. The meritocracy inherent in building the nation was portrayed as a form of citizenship based on talent alone, stripped of political or civic virtue. Potofsky concludes from this that "[t]he pamphlets and petitions by builders reveal that the central sans-culotte polemic—the glory of those who work with their hands—was arrived at only after the meandering and sometimes contradictory career of images of the citizen-worker in the early period" (1993, 196). But we can also argue that the sansculotte image of the citizen was formed as a radical reversal of the professional-citizen image of the bourgeois man and that it destabilized that virtuous image, which then gave rise to the problematizations of the sansculottes.

The sansculottes made up perhaps half to two-thirds of Paris in 1793–94 (Rose 1983, 7). They were artisans, small masters and merchants, journeymen, apprentices, shopkeepers, laborers, and peasants. While some held modest property, most did not. On the eve of the Revolution, artisans were organized in about forty-four guilds and corporations, grouped under mercers, hosiers, drapers, goldsmiths, grocers, and wine merchants. Rose notes that there were widespread strikes by Parisian journeymen and apprentices for better conditions or more pay during the eighteenth century, and the repetitious vehemence of royal and other official condemnations of illegal organizations and assemblies suggests that the frequency and extent of such activity was growing just before the Revolution (13).

Before they articulated a group identity, these variegated segments supported and incorporated the objects, ideas, and slogans of the revolutionary bourgeoisie and they acknowledged its leadership when they took up arms in July 1789 (Rose 1983, 18). In a remarkably short period of time, however, these segments were transformed into the sansculottes and articulated sui generis strategies and technologies of citizenship. While they certainly drew upon their experience of the guild and corporate existence that the European artisan had been familiar with, they also invented new ways of being political. Without getting into their role in the Revolution and without aiming to give a precise definition, the making of the sansculottes roughly followed the following trajectories (Andrews 1985; Rose 1983; Soboul 1964, 1968). For the purpose of elections to the Estate General in the spring of 1789, Paris was divided into sixty districts. On April 21, 1789, the electors of the Third Estate met across Paris, devising rules, regulations, and principles for conducting their assemblies. They also established a network of communication that made it possible to exchange and share experiences (Rose 1983, 25). This organization without doubt was crucial for the crystallization of the collective energies that led to the Revolution. The district assemblies were the seedbed of the formation of a bourgeois class consciousness and included vast numbers of lawyers and other professionals, merchants, manufacturers, and officeholders (Rose 1983, 32–33). While artisans did not attend these assemblies in any numbers, this organizational network was later to prove the basis of their becoming political. The political crisis of July precipitated the intervention of artisans, laborers, and the poor into politics. By that time the pattern of participation had changed radically to include artisans, merchants, laborers, and other poor in the district assemblies, which played a decisive role in the Revolution (Rose 1983, 54–55). Nonetheless, in 1790 the National Assembly banned the districts and replaced them with sections. It also created a municipal council of representatives with limited powers. It placed property restrictions on participation in the section assemblies and forbade their permanence. The section boundaries were deliberately drawn to impede political continuity between districts and sections, and to break up the existing leadership. The distinction introduced between "active" citizens with property and "passive" citizens without drew widespread criticism from those artisans and the laboring poor who had taken an active role in the Revolution through the district assemblies. It was obvious that the incipient bourgeoisie was intent on keeping a tight control of, but at the same time harnessing the energies of, the very movement that helped it seize power. The sansculottes were immanent strangers in the bourgeois metropolis.

The sansculottes had fought against the aristocracy and royal absolutism. They furnished the revolutionary bourgeoisie with the indispensable manpower for bringing down the ancien régime and for routing the coalition. But they were also opposed to the bourgeoisie. Ultimately, they could not change the direction of the Revolution, but they did pursue their own objectives and articulate a program that was different from that of the bourgeoisie. The sansculottes claimed rights to the taxation of foodstuffs and over regulation regarding their commerce. They also claimed rights to work and education. Thus they articulated values hostile to the bourgeoisie and its ideals (Andrews 1985; Levy 1981).

The history of the sansculottes is always written from the point of view of their failure to accomplish their objective: to seize power and institute radical democracy. Their ostensible failure is attributed to their lack of a broad vision of principles (Hobsbawm 1962, 88–89, 91–94) or their intolerant, essentialist, and violent tendencies (Baumann 1998, 62–83). While it would be interesting to bring these views into critical attention by illustrating that both the bourgeoisie and later working-class movements actually incorporated the ideals, tactics, and organizations of the sansculottes, the intriguing aspect of the sansculottes for citizenship as alterity is how the sansculottes formed an identity, articulated their ideals, used symbols, organized their practices, and created material and symbolic spaces in the city. In other words, my concern here is to investigate how the sansculottes were implicated in strategies and technologies of otherness that constituted them as strangers to bourgeois citizens and how they appropriated and transformed some of these strategies and technologies to constitute themselves as citizens by claiming their rights to Paris.

The sansculottes were not a firmly defined group and the way they identified themselves changed rapidly. In 1792 they constituted themselves primarily against the aristocracy. By 1793 they also displayed intense hostility toward the bourgeoisie. Leaders such as Babeuf spoke of the unpropertied sansculottes with fear and admiration (Levy 1981). The clearest description of this comes from a report read to the Convention: "[W]hen we speak of the sans-culottes, we do not mean all the citizens, except for the nobles and aristocrats, but men who have nothing, to distinguish them from men who have something" (quoted in Soboul 1968, 21). In this formulation, the sansculottes were considered those artisans who manufacture things as opposed to bankers, financiers, merchants, monopolists, and lawyers. This definition was contradicted by more factions of the sansculottes, who included artisans and shopkeepers with property (Andrews 1985). Soboul argues that the sansculottes did not develop a class consciousness because they were divided into divergent and contradictory factions. If the Declaration of the Rights of Man and Citizen was the voice of the bourgeoisie, the sansculottes aimed to push the declaration into radical democracy. That the state should guarantee every citizen the means of subsistence was radical. The sansculottes were not opposed to the right to property, but to its use as an exclusive basis for citizenship rights. As they contemplated methods to curb this use, they began articulating principles that went against the bourgeois property rights that were entrenched in the declaration. Yet none of this was radical enough for Soboul, who wanted to see a working-class consciousness in the sansculottes (1968, 55).

As we have seen earlier, Soboul argued from a Marxist perspective that the sansculottes were not original in their ideas and that they lacked coherent social thought. He saw the sansculottes as a group without class consciousness, their uniting principle being merely opposition to aristocracy. According to Soboul, since the sansculottes were made up of heterogeneous members of artisans and shopkeepers, intellectuals and artists, some workers in industrial factories in Paris, and a few former aristocrats, they could not have developed a class consciousness. Their aspirations remained contradictory and indefinite. Nonetheless, even Soboul conceded that the originality and inventiveness of the sansculottes were in the specific strategies and technologies of citizenship that they developed.

The sansculottes were not only opposed to the aristocracy and the bourgeoisie, but also to commercial capital. They succeeded in their demands to close the Paris stock exchange on June 27, 1793. They also succeeded, in August of the same year, in banning all financial companies (Soboul 1968, 66). They were also in the forefront of the food riots (Rudé 1988, 88–89). Similarly, the sansculottes also demanded the right to work and education, organizing curriculum in sections, territorial units through which they were organized. Their insistence on limited property rights, their demands for action against monopolies in state enterprises, and their demands for the organization of a fiscal policy, for public assistance, and for education, which would have equalized incomes, made the sansculottes a threat to the bourgeois order (Soboul 1968, 92). But these characterized their social ideal of citizenship.

For the sansculottes used the insurrection as a strategy for popular sovereignty, which was expressed through the sections. It meant refusing to obey laws that they did not accept, reasserting their sovereign rights, and insisting on their elected representatives rendering an account of their activities and fulfilling the decision of the sections (Soboul 1968, 129). The call to arms was the ultimate manifestation of popular sovereignty and insurrection. The sansculottes developed certain rites and rituals by which the sections issued the call to arms. The atmosphere surrounding the call embodied a symbolic as well as a material exaltation. The closing of the city gates, the beating of drums, the ringing of bells (tocsin), with all the attendant excitement, contributed to mass exaltation and also to the feeling among the sansculottes that they were participating in something that was bigger than their individual selves or of becoming political (Soboul 1968, 131).

The sansculottes articulated three strategies: transparency, radical activism, and systemic violence. They demanded that decisions be made in public and be transparent to the citizens. In 1792 the sansculottes invaded the general assemblies and were not content to play the role of spectator. As a material expression and an embodiment of this intolerance toward spectatorship, platforms were erected in the assembly halls of one section and were crowded by the citizens. From that moment forward, the section deliberated in the presence of the citizens. The sansculottes also advocated a radical activism. They rediscovered fraternization and its most potent symbol, the oath (Soboul 1968, 145). Some sections in Paris issued proclamations of brotherhood, followed by the oath and kiss of peace. The sansculottes fraternized in bodies: if a section was threatened by their political adversaries who supported the bourgeoisie, another section would unite with it to maintain the sansculotte majority in the assembly.

The sansculottes were intent on involving all citizens in politics, unable to conceive of anyone being indifferent or neutral. If the sansculottes could not persuade, they were severe in their condemnation and oppression of those who did not become political in the way they envisaged. In 1793, the calls for attendance at meetings of the assemblies were accompanied by threats against indifference. They devised mechanisms to punish those who did not become political. A section proclaimed that those who missed three successive sessions of the general assembly would be declared bad citizens. In their intense efforts to politicize various groups, the sansculottes also increasingly identified their adversaries within the revolutionary movement: merchants, lawyers, officers, notaries, and other wealthier groups in the city. As a result, the difference between the individualism of the bourgeoisie and the group-oriented sansculottes became wider and deeper. While the sansculottes did not find any contradiction in collectively signed petitions, the bourgeoisie became increasingly agitated against such petitions (Soboul 1968, 150). On May 10, 1791, the Constituent Assembly banned collective petitions, but the sections of the sansculottes continued to present them.

The sansculottes considered violence as the legitimate recourse against their adversaries or those who refused to become political in the way they envisaged (Soboul 1968, 158). But such violence was not random or accidental. It was political and collective and thus systemic (Singer 1990). It was used in their fight against the aristocracy. It was used against the bourgeoisie to make their claims to rights to the city.

Among the solidaristic technologies the sansculottes developed were a specific dress code and principles of conduct and language. A red cap and a pike became symbols of the militant sansculottes. They insisted on wearing the red cap after 1789 during the general assemblies and there was a bitter struggle between the bourgeoisie and the sansculottes over the practice (Harris 1981). While the revolutionary bourgeois never accepted the cap, the sansculottes continued to wage a battle to maintain its continued use on the one hand, and to restrict its use to only legitimate patriots on the other (Soboul 1968, 223–25). On December 8, 1792, the general assembly of a section ordered its president to wear a red cap during meetings. The following day all officers of the section wore one. As Soboul says, "Henceforth, the red cap was to be the sans-culottes' symbol of political power and a target of sarcasm and attack from the moderates" (1968, 224).

The pike was as much the emblem of the militant sansculottes as the red cap. It became a symbol of people in arms and was a demonstration of popular sovereignty achieved by insurrection. It was celebrated as the weapon of the masses par excellence. On September 21, 1792, a victorious revolutionary declared that "too long has this terrible weapon been neglected; the aristocrats purposely discredited it, nevertheless it is only with pike in hand that the French people were reborn; it is only the pike of the sans-culottes which gave us our liberty" (quoted in Soboul 1968, 227).

The sansculottes used language as an articulate solidaristic technology that expressed their own cultural distinctions against those of the aristocracy or the bourgeoisie (Sonescher 1984). On December 14, 1790, a section endorsed certain principles on the basis of an article entitled "On the Influence of Words and the Power of Language" (Soboul 1968, 228–29). With their dress, language, and appearance code, the sansculottes began making claims to areas in Paris that were occupied by either the aristocracy or the bourgeoisie. They began wandering out of their usual taverns and cafés into boulevards and made themselves public in areas formerly reserved for the wealthy and distinguished citizens of Paris. According to a contemporary account, "such poorly dressed people, who would formerly have never dared show themselves in areas frequented by people of fashion, were walking among the rich, their heads as high as theirs . . . there was an air of contentment in the crowd, and a stranger would never have guessed that these people were forced to make many sacrifices on account of the critical situation" (quoted in Soboul 1968, 234). This was a powerful symbolic and material expression of becoming political and claiming rights to the city as the sansculottes transformed themselves from strangers into citizens.

While most our discussion has focused on the Parisian sansculottes, sansculottism itself was not limited to Paris. While most developed and documented in Paris, the sansculotte movement was widespread in French provincial cities (Margadant 1992, 164; Williams 1969, 3–18) and in English cities such as Sheffield, Norwich, London, Birmingham, Leeds, Coventry, Leicester, and Manchester (Thompson 1965, 171; Williams 1969, 58–80), as well as in German and Italian cities. Throughout European cities as well as in revolutionary America, the republican virtue that the sansculottes articulated was very different from the one the bourgeoisie articulated. While the sansculottes made the bourgeois revolution possible with their political ideals and practices, there were fundamental differences between their ideals and those of the bourgeoisie. It would be interesting to find out if this was the reason Weber was never interested in the sansculottes, especially in his essay on the city. After all, the sansculottes drew from their artisanal roots and the guild tradition, organized in political clubs and societies, and "illegitimately" usurped power, though they did not explicitly appeal to the images of the *popolo* as their historical ancestor. These uncanny historical resemblances should have caught his attention even if the early modern or modern city was not his object of analysis. Be that as it may, a more germane issue here is that the sansculottes illustrate how the dominant images of being political have been usurped by the victorious, who, inscribing themselves as the revolutionaries in historical imagination, devalorized the minute, diversified, multiple, and effective practices that strangers and outsiders used to create new political spaces, from the streets to theatres.

1848: Civilizing the Savages / Of Being Dangerous

In the early nineteenth century, at a time when the ideal of the bourgeois citizen was articulated as the vanguard of civility, the working classes came under increasingly intense attention from the bourgeois gaze: within a few decades, while nobody could remember the rugged image of the sansculotte as the worker-citizen, the working classes were being categorized as "dangerous classes." How to civilize the savage became the problematic of an enormous number of surveys, pamphlets, statistics, researches, and parliamentary reports in French, German, British, American, and other European cities. Steadily increasing until the 1848 revolutions, the discourse on the laboring classes literally exploded after 1848, now being also linked to the revolutionary activities, hence the distinction that was made between the dangerous and the laboring classes. Many savages in the metropolis lived on the margins of the law because they were born, mated, procreated, and sometimes even died unrecognized and unregistered by it. To civilize the savage meant bringing him under the law and subjecting him to discipline.

Until 1848, it was quite common to categorize the laboring classes as barbarians, savages, vagrants, nomads, or the mob. In a survey published in 1840 on the laboring classes in England and France, Eugéne Buret observed that "[i]solated from the nation, outlawed from the social and political community, alone with their needs and miseries, they struggle to extricate themselves from this terrifying solitude and, like the barbarians to whom they have been compared, they are perhaps meditating invasion" (quoted in Chevalier 1958, 360). What these categories shared was that the laboring classes were outsiders in both social and spatial senses. As far as the bourgeois was concerned, the laboring classes were and remained at the edge of the city in precisely the same way that outsiders remained as social outcasts. As for their situation in social space, "These are the men who form not the bottom, but the dangerous part, of great congested masses; there are the men who deserve the name, one of the worst stigmatized in history, mark you, of mob" (quoted in Chevalier 1958, 364). By 1848, the nomads, savages, vagrants, and mob were grouped into one convenient class: the dangerous class. The sharp distinction drawn after 1848 between the laboring classes, with appropriate conduct, habitus, and disposition, and the dangerous classes, with their short temper, moblike mentality, and nomadism, articulated the difference between good versus bad manners, which the bourgeoisie transformed into an agonistic strategy. The dangerous classes were dangerous precisely because they defied discipline and were not only intransigent, but transient. None other than Baron Haussmann singled out this aspect of the danger: "Paris belongs to France, not to Parisians by birth or choice who live there and especially not to the mobile population in its lodging houses ... ; this 'mob of nomads,' to use an expression for which I have been reproached, but which I maintain is correct, the best of whom move to the great city in search of fairly regular work, but with the intention of returning in due course to their place of origin where their true ties persist" (quoted in Chevalier 1958, 365). As Chevalier emphasized, the bourgeoisie constituted the residents of the city as outsiders precisely because they posed a threat to the bourgeois political order (see Himmelfarb 1991).

But the dangerous classes were not only transient, intransigent, and nomadic; they were also ugly, smelly, dirty, and disgusting, "so brutal, ignorant, vain people, so disagreeable to rub shoulders with, so repulsive when seen close up" (quoted in Chevalier 1958, 413). For the bourgeois identity it became crucial to distinguish itself from the laboring and dangerous classes, not only by economic and social status, but also by cultural capital: manners, physique, smell, appearance, and language. In fact, in the self-image of the bourgeois, they acquired wealth and status because they were well mannered and groomed. As Corbin (1986) illustrated, the bourgeoisie paid increasing attention to "social" odors. Throughout the nineteenth century, odor became an index by which to differentiate oneself. The absence of intrusive odor enabled an individual to distinguish himself from the laboring classes, stinking like death, and at the same time to implicitly justify the treatment meted out to them. As Corbin says: "Emphasizing the fetidity of the labouring classes, and thus the danger of infection from their mere presence, helped the bourgeois to sustain his self-indulgent, self-induced terror, which dammed up the expression of remorse" (1986, 143). This gave rise to the notion that making the laboring classes odorless would promote discipline and a work ethic among them. The unpleasant odor of the laboring classes remained a stereotype for at least a quarter of a century until the discipline started to bear fruit when the laboring classes began aspiring to become odorless selves. How was this accomplished?

Throughout the century, studies poured forth describing the condition of the working classes, ranging from their most intimate habits to statistical characteristics of the group as a whole (Ashforth 1976; also see Rose 1985). These studies and reports were supplemented with various reform proposals, projects, and commissions to transform the dangerous classes into laboring classes: the institutions that Foucault (1961; 1975) explored, such as prisons, hospitals, asylums, schools, and workhouses, became the spatial and social symbols of the bourgeois political order and its identity, which was defined against and qua the identity of the working classes (see Dean 1991).

Were these categories, practices, and institutions of the bourgeoisie passively accepted by the working classes (plural) or was the working class (singular) present in its own making on its own terms, as Thompson (1965) argued? According to Chevalier, "There is no doubt that 'savages,' 'barbarians' and 'vagrants' were intended as terms of abuse, but they were not really insults since the laboring classes themselves accepted the terms and acquiesced in the opinion implied in them; their opinion was not so very different" (1958, 394). Nonetheless, the working-class identity was formed and forged out of variegated practices and struggles against the bourgeoisie by calling into question its mentalities, conceptions, and categories. We have already alluded to the 1848 revolutions in Europe, which were based on working-class movements such as Chartism in England and Jacobinism in France. The radical democratic demands of these movements for citizenship rights and constituting workers as legitimate holders of citizenship in the 1830s and 1840s were a testimony of the working class constituting itself.

Of particular interest here is a novel published in installments in Paris newspapers in 1842 and 1843 that, originally intended as a description of the wretched condition of the dangerous classes, became one of the most popular books among the working classes. Eugène Sue (1804–57) started out *The Mysteries of Paris* as a description of the barbarians in Paris: "We have trembled for the colonists and the town dwellers, to think that so near them there lived and roamed those barbaric tribes sundered so far from civilization by their sanguinary customs" (quoted in Chevalier 1958, 403). But he added, "Only the barbarians of whom we are speaking are in our midst; we can brush elbows with them if we venture into the dens in which they live, where they meet to plot murder and robbery and to share out their victims' spoils. These men have manners of their own, women of their own, a language of their own, a mysterious language replete with baleful images, metaphors dripping blood. Like the savages, these people usually address each other by nicknames borrowed from their energy, their cruelty or certain material qualities or defects" (quoted in Chevalier 1958, 403–4). That the novel became very popular and even a sensation among the laboring classes as it proceeded is quite well known (Lehan 1998, 55; Merriman 1991, 15). What is less known is what Chevalier claims: far less as a result of a decision by its author than owing to a collective pressure, which imposed a transformation more and more strongly with every installment, the novel was at least partly written by the laboring classes. On the basis of correspondence that was kept and archived, Chevalier argues that the pressure was exerted by the effect of popular opinion, which singled out its characters, directed their fate, decided the plot, and intervened daily in the shaping of the narrative, either through threatening or admiring letters, or by the great wave of demands protesting the disappearance of a character, deploring the inaccuracy of some trait of manners, or deprecating some solution. The novel about the dangerous classes was transformed from installment to installment into a novel of the working class by its active engagement. Chevalier says that "[t]his intervention could easily be traced in detail by making a chronological study of the correspondence and the serial and by comparing the successive editions of the novel" (1958, 405). The work of the dangerous classes had become the work of the laboring classes, but of laboring classes that had retained many of the physical and ethical features of the dangerous classes, the same language, ugliness, violence, and incivility. Lehan thinks that Marx was actually critical of Sue (1998, 405). But the opposite was true: for Marx a new class consciousness was being formed and he thought that Sue had captured an expression of this consciousness. This explains why Marx was quite sympathetic toward Sue, but fiercely critical of the interpretation of a Young Hegelian of Sue's novel (Marx 1845, 55–77). "Herr Szeliga makes mysteries out of real trivialities. His art is not that of disclosing what is hidden, but of hiding what is disclosed" (56). Marx was more critical of how German Hegelians misunderstood Sue than of the content of *Mysteries*. In fact, he found Sue's descriptions of Parisian working classes concrete and grounded. What he took issue with was that Sue did not understand the underlying causes of the miseries he so accurately described. As a result, according to Marx, the proposals of Sue to reform legal practices, penal codes, and education to improve the condition of the working classes were misplaced and utopian (Kramer 1988, 159).

If the working classes were working out agonistic strategies and making claims to the representation of their selves in literary space, they were also making claims to various spaces of the city. Exploring marginal spaces and identities in nineteenth-century French cities, Merriman argues that while "marginality" existed before the nineteenth century, it was then defined via the views of the bourgeoisie. Considering marginality in both a social and a geographic sense, Merriman defines it as being "on or beyond the fringe of bourgeois society, and at or beyond the frontiers of its urban world" (1991, 3). He argues that social marginality was expressed in a spatial marginality in that the peripheries of cities were where social marginality concentrated. In the 1830s and 1840s, the discourse that focused on the dangerous classes always identified them with the faubourgs or suburbs. Throughout the nineteenth century, the bourgeoisie in French cities increasingly took control of the center and displaced strangers and outsiders to the outer edges of the city. The dangerous classes as the new barbarians were "gathered on the edge of the capital, and of other cities as well. The result of this awareness, indeed fear, was an expansion of not only police activities but of the reach of the police into the outskirts of French towns and cities, and ultimately, in the case of large cities, the imposition of order, the conquest through incorporation of suburbs seen as threatening" (Merriman 1991, 8). What was the source of this fear? The bourgeoisie saw the faubourgs as the spaces of the "floating worlds" of the criminals, ragpickers, vagabonds, beggars, paupers, prostitutes, and outcasts. But Merriman argues that behind this facade of fear of the unknown, there was a much better understood danger diagnosed by the bourgeoisie of the faubourgs: they were the spaces in which the rising working classes became conscious of themselves as a class, established neighborhood and workplace solidarities, and organized with more established groups of artisans and workers of the center (22–23). In other words, the inhabitants of the faubourgs used their spaces as solidaristic strategies and began constituting themselves as political beings. The faubourgs and open spaces around the city provided strategic places for workers to gather to discuss demands and articulate claims, beyond the prying eyes of the state and the police. What really made the faubourgs threatening was that their spatial marginality became a source for articulating the social differentiation between the workers and the bourgeois of the center: "For within the faubourgs, social solidarities developed, and were expressed and reaffirmed by festivals, songs, strikes, and political movements" (23).

While prominent in all large French cities, the stigma of the faubourgs as spaces of insurrection was particularly strong in Paris. Before the 1848 revolutions the bourgeoisie had been shaping the city to its own image and displacing various groups toward the edges of the city. While scholars dispute how complete the embourgeoisement of Paris was by 1871, the role of Haussmann and Napoleon III is indisputable (Hall 1998, 730; Jordan 1995; Pinkney 1955). The Haussmannization of Paris has been well studied, ranging from interpretations of it as a spatial fix to invest excess capital or as a massive workfare project to that of imposing a social order or guarding the city against demonstrations and insurrections (Benevolo 1993, 169–88; Sennett 1994, 329–32). Nevertheless, the imposing of a political and social order on the faubourgs and bringing them into the orbit of the government of Paris was perhaps among the most important of its achievements. The Haussmannization of Paris meant bringing the dangerous classes into the orbit of government and transforming them into laboring classes. As Harvey observed, "While it would be untrue to say that Haussmann created spatial segregation in the city, his works coupled with the land-use sorting effect of rent in the context of changed land and property markets did definitely produce a greater degree of spatial segregation, much of it based on class distinctions" (1985, 167). That with the 1871 insurrection this objective seemed unfulfilled matters little. As Merriman suggests, the Paris Commune of 1871 can be interpreted as "the revenge of the expelled" (1991, 80). The support for the Commune ran deepest at the edges (Gould 1995, 175).

1871: Insurgent Identities

The Paris Commune was a paradoxical insurgence. It was certainly not a carnival. Some twenty-five thousand insurgents were dead on the streets of Paris in May 1871, more than in any of the battles of the war between France and the emerging Germany. Yet it also developed certain carnivalesque features (Christiansen 1994; Gullickson 1996; Johnson 1996; Ross 1988). More than any known revolution, the Commune was a question of the rapid, dizzying transformation of everyday life, a dramatic upheaval in everyday experiences of time and space, identity and language, work and pleasure. The peculiarity of the Commune baffled both the insurgents and its interpreters. While the insurgents included many types of workers, the dominant group among them was the artisans, not the organized proletariat of Paris. Thus, a remnant sansculottism was definitely prevalent among the insurgents. It was also a revolution that was organized to seize, transform, and defend a place, a city, where men and women lived, congregated, and deliberated. Unlike the 1848 revolutions across European metropolises, the identity of the insurgents was an amalgam of craft, neighborhood, workplace, and other loyalties. The citizen emerged as the favorite identification for insurgents, indicating a double overturn and appropriation of the city and its symbols. What interpellated the dominated groups in Paris into insurgence was precisely the besieged bastion of their city, a space that once belonged to and had been made by them.

While both 1848 and 1871 were revolts instigated by workers, there were essential differences between them in Paris. The 1848 revolution was based on class consciousness and the conviction of its participants was principally directed toward the replacement of capitalism with a social order ruled by and for the working class (Gould 1995, 4). By contrast, 1871 revolutionaries scarcely made an appeal to the overthrow of capitalism and instead conceived of themselves primarily as inhabitants of Paris in revolt against injustice, symbolized but not exhausted by the state. The dominant slogan of the 1848 revolution was the "right to work" and it was instigated against the closures of charity workshops. Thus, the struggle was focused on districts where artisans were concentrated. In 1871, the focus of conflict was not any particular neighborhood or district, but the entire city, and the insurgents came from outside the city walls. These two Parisian revolutions, therefore, began differently, ended differently, and were understood by their protagonists as thoroughly different kinds of struggles. They were struggles whose protagonists understood themselves differently (Gould 1995, 7). And yet, Gould argues, both revolts have been constituted by the class-based interpretations of Harvey (1985) and Castells (1977) as being essentially worker revolts, intent upon overthrowing capitalism. By neglecting forms of identification other than class, these interpretations missed that there were essential differences between 1848 and 1871 and, as a result, they could not shed light on them as distinct urban social movements. Even Castells in his later work, when he abandoned class-based analysis, still succumbed to explaining 1871 as a search for an "urban meaning" (1983, 15–26). According to Gould, in 1848 insurgents in Paris formed their identities on the basis of class. The vast majority of them were wage earners and this was central to participation in the revolution: they justified their actions using a language that explicitly tied their grievance to and articulated their claims against capitalism. By contrast, the 1871 insurgents drew their identity from the city: when massive numbers of Parisians joined insurgent battalions and risked their lives on the barricades, they did so for specific reasons that had much more to do with their self-conception as inhabitants of a city than with their self-conception as workers. This argument, however, besides being another way of expressing essentially the same argument that Castells did later, commits an error in attributing causal powers to space: why should insurgents draw their identity from being inhabitants of a place? How did they *become* inhabitants of that place? Can one attribute an identity to all Parisians? While the sources of the 1871 insurrection can be seen against the remnant sansculottism and its artisanal foundations in guilds, to attribute unities and coherence to the Commune runs the risk of missing the specific strategies and technologies of citizenship inherited, devised, used, and bequeathed by the insurgents. While Gould's argument is important in documenting the effects of changes that took place in Paris between 1850 and 1870 on the Parisian political and social order and how different groups and their identities were formed in the process, it falls into an explanatory trap.

The poetry of Rimbaud was much more perceptive and is more revealing than the words of modern interpreters. It was formed in this dizzying and transformative event, where the constant movement of transgression, of the dismantling and remapping of political and spatial orders took place (Ross 1988; Thum 1994, 111–12). Kristin Ross identifies the two most significant aspects of the Commune as embodied in Rimbaud's poetry: a new understanding of space and of citizenship. She notes that Rimbaud's poetry is "the invitation to conceive of space *not* as a static reality but as active, generative, to experience space as created by an interaction, as something that our bodies reactivate, and that through this reactivation, in turn modifies and transforms us" (1988, 35). This relational conception of space is consistent with how the insurgents created a political space during their occupation of Paris for seventy-two days. The use of "occupation" may be surprising here since the insurgents were residents of Paris. But as we have seen earlier, the rise of the bourgeoisie throughout the nineteenth century was inscribed into the spaces of the city of Paris, the culmination of which was the social and spatial order imposed by Haussmannization, which gradually displaced working classes from the center of the city toward its northeastern edges. As Ross says, "The workers' redescent into the centre within a tradition of popular insurgency, and in part from their desire to reclaim the public space from which they had been expelled, to reoccupy streets that once were theirs" (1988, 41). The workers were occupying the space of citizens, the circumscribed proper place of the dominant social order, and making claim to that space as its strangers and outsiders.

With respect to citizenship, the Commune, unlike the 1848 revolutions, did not embrace a right to work, but questioned how work was defined by the bourgeois morality. It envisaged a new conception of work, or at least, it articulated the need to reconceptualize work. Many pamphlets and proclamations written during the Commune used recurring themes of work and property. The Communards questioned property as the basis of citizenship and articulated that "active citizenship" did not need to be tied to occupation or property. Instead, being political in the sense of conducting oneself with critical judgment in public space was deemed the source of citizenship (cf. Potofsky 1993).

At the time of the Commune Rimbaud said in a letter: "I will be a worker: that's what holds me back when a wild fury drives me toward the battle in Paris, where so many workers are still dying while I am writing to you! Work, now? Never, never. I'm on strike." Rimbaud would be a worker, but not then. He was on strike because the new conception of work had not yet arrived. When it finally does, Rimbaud would work; he would be a worker (Ross 1988, 59). Similarly, in a pamphlet that was to have an enormous influence second only to *The Communist Manifesto*, Paul Lafargue called into question the right to work as an expression of bourgeois morality and instead defended a right to laziness (1880). By proclaiming the right to laziness, Lafargue aimed to call into question the association between productivity and formal work that went back to 1789. For Ross, "The interest in Lafargue lies particularly in his refusal to participate in the construction of the 'good worker,' that image type central to pre-Commune moralizing discourse directed at workers by right-wing philanthropists, moralists, and factory managers" (1988, 62). Lafargue protested that by seeking the right to work in factories, the laborers in June 1848 "have delivered up to the barons of industry their wives and children" (1880, 16). Narrating a critical history of capitalism, Lafargue argued that at the beginning the bourgeois man possessed reasonable and agreeable habits. He was against the corrupt noble virtues of idleness, consumption, and vanity. He was frugal, provident, and thrifty. But overaccumulation of capital for more than a century throughout Europe spoiled the original virtues of the bourgeois man and he became unproductive, consumptive, vainglorious, and complacent. The more the bourgeois man preached a Christian ascetic morality of work to the working classes and complained about their laziness, the less he became productive. It is in this sense that the working class had to assert its right to laziness not in the sense of a right to idleness: "If, uprooting from its heart the vice which dominates it and degrades its nature, the working class were to arise in its terrible strength, not to demand Rights of Man, which are but the rights of capitalist exploitation, not to demand the Right to Work, which is but the right to misery, but to forge a brazen law forbidding any man to work more than three hours a day, the earth, the old earth, trembling with joy would feel a new universe leaping with her"

(Lafargue 1880, 56). But how could the working class accomplish this? It must "trample under foot the prejudices of Christian ethics, economic ethics and free-thought ethics . . . concocted by the metaphysical lawyers of the bourgeois revolution" (29).

What Lafargue wished was to appropriate the derogatory words used by the bourgeoisie to describe the dangerous classes, such as barbarians, nomads, savages, or pagans, and transform them into positive categories, indicating nomad or savage morality. This refusal to accept categories as given is an effective strategy of reversal: what was considered as nomadic, savage, and outsider by a bourgeois morality became a recognized insider, a citizen. In "Bad Blood" Rimbaud explodes: "I am well aware that I have always been of inferior race," reveling in the fact that he inherited all sorts of "vice." He says "priests, professors, and doctors, you are mistaken in delivering me into the hands of the law. I have never been one of you; I have never been a Christian; I belong to the race that sang on the scaffold." That race Rimbaud identifies with "owes its existence to the Declaration of the Rights of Man," the marginal and the excluded, its other, its alterity. In Rimbaud the subaltern figures of the serf, the leper, the reiter, the witch, the ragpicker, the vagabond, are implicitly opposed to the canonical trio of "priests, professors and doctors." This is where poetics becomes political in the sense that it reverses categories of otherness. Throughout the nineteenth century there were many instances where strangers and outsiders constituted themselves as citizens and created spaces in the metropolis to enact these claims (Epstein 1994; Vernon 1993; Winter 1993). Yet, we seem to hear more about the adventures of the flâneurs than about these characters and their practices. Why?

Flâneurs as Professional Strangers

Such agonistic strategies were only partially successful and the defeat of the working classes was more common than their victory. After 1871, a new political and spatial order was imposed on the metropolis. If Paris was the epitome of this order, it was because it was in Paris that this order was so vehemently contested. But the bourgeoisie was able to cultivate an order in metropolises everywhere in Europe and America. With its great boulevards planted with trees and flanked by service roads, its airy apartment buildings, its parks, its lights and sewers, the metropolis emerged toward the end of the nineteenth century as the crowning achievement and symbol of the bourgeoisie. "The City Beautiful," as it was crystallized in a movement, was an expression of the cultivation of a particular type of aesthetic on the city that combined concerns about the "moral health" of the working classes with their physical health. Metropolises everywhere bore witness to the success of the cultivation of a new political and social order on urban space. In this new order there was no more ambiguous identity than that of the flâneur: while it appears as the figure of an intensely autonomous persona, it turns out that it finds itself in a particular way of being political, of being in the city.

While *flânerie,* the activity of strolling and looking that is carried out by the flâneur, was originally tied to nineteenth-century Paris, the figure of the flâneur is now understood as someone who conducts himself in public space. The flâneur of nineteenth-century Paris received his most famous eulogy in the poetics of Charles Baudelaire (Benjamin 1973; Burton 1994; Tester 1994b; Thum 1994). Ostensibly, the flâneur of Baudelaire belonged neither to the bourgeoisie nor to the working or laboring classes, but somehow was of them. But a closer look reveals something else.

For Baudelaire we must take on the city not by dealing with it, not by trying to make sense out of chaos, but by espousing the anonymity and the disconnection it suggests by losing ourselves in its midst (Blanchard 1985, 75). Baudelaire was anxious to eradicate any trace of a resident past. "The city is the place of a present where to be oneself means first to be confronted with the other" (Blanchard 1985, 76). The city is a stage, a spectacle through which the flâneur walks, observes, and loses himself. Walking through the city the flâneur is attuned to the way the city begins and ends before his very eyes and to those who appear on the stage. As Tester puts it, the flâneur is "the man *of the* crowd as opposed to the man *in* the crowd" (1994a, 3). To the flâneur those who appear in the crowd are types or characters, not real individuals. Never does the flâneur know them personally. He recreates his encounter with these types even long after the encounter. The flâneur is at once an observer and the observed, a subject and an object: "There is nothing more interesting than this reflection of the pleasures of the rich in the depths of poor people's eyes" (Baudelaire 1905, 19). The city is made for and lives in the present. The best description of the city is one that integrates separate views of the city taken by a moving observer in the midst of a moving city. Such is the spectacle and stage of the flâneur. Ceaselessly moving with the city itself, the flâneur is interested in the appearance of events and types, or rather, types through events through which he also makes his own appearance, formation, becoming. As Blanchard observes, the secret of Baudelaire's poetics is the city's secret: "[W]hat the city has in store, it surrenders only to those who dare become its accomplices and exchange their memories of the ones it offers them" (1985, 86). Baudelaire establishes a distance between the flâneur and the city. His choices of characters and places do not in any way indicate a privileged knowledge of the city on his part. They indicate that with the mysterious and manifold types and objects in the city, the flâneur has dared to enter into a relationship for which he does not wish to be held responsible: "Take heed, I beg, of this fact, that the spirit of mystification which, in certain people, is not the result of over work, or of a combination, but of a fortuitous inspiration, seems by the intensity of the desire, to be part of that state of mind which doctors call hysteria and people more thoughtful than doctors, demonism, and impels us unresisting, to commit many dangerous and unconventional actions" (Baudelaire 1905, 11–12). Since the flâneur walks through the surface of the city, without any claim to its depth, his relationship to objects and types is ephemeral. There are only loose references to objects: a boulevard, a park, a street, without actually describing or naming them, and thus implying that what happened on that street, that boulevard, is an instance of an event or appearance, but not the event or the appearance. This emphasis on the surface, distance, and detachment led Sartre to criticize Baudelaire with bad faith since his flâneur is unable to make a commitment (Sartre 1950). The flâneur is unable to identify with anything or anybody and is associated with the leisurely pace of a man with time on his hands who is contemptuous of both labor and capital. As Blanchard puts it, "To Baudelaire, who preaches a philosophy of self-survival in the city, groups are worthless until one can isolate from them one or two people with whom to set up an imaginary relationship. The flâneur seeks to approach—never to master—the other, the unknown, through a one-to-one relation with separate persons. . . . He wishes to retain the freedom of a man walking the boulevards and feeling allegiance to no one, while refusing to make the choices this freedom allows" (1985, 94). The poet as flâneur is a sovereign individual: he can be what he wills to be; he can put on masks and make the faces of strangers hide the sordid secrets of their souls. "The poet is the maker of the order of things" (Tester 1994a, 5).

Was the flâneur a sovereign artist, as contemporary interpretations imply? Is the account of the flâneur of himself an adequate account of his identity? We would answer these questions negatively and instead interpret the flâneur as a professional stranger. Baudelaire himself dropped a clue: "The crowd is his domain, just as the air is the bird's, and water that of the fish. His passion and his *profession* is to merge with the crowd" (emphasis added, 1863, 399). The flâneur may have perfected the profession of being both a stranger and a citizen simultaneously. The sources for questioning the flâneur as a sovereign individual are twofold. First, of course, this is the bourgeois conception of negative freedom. While the image of the city in Baudelaire may not correspond to the officially sanctioned view held by his bourgeois contemporaries, as Thum (1994, 53) argued, it is impossible to detach the image of the man who roams about the city from the prosperous bourgeois man in his leisure. To share the bourgeois view of the city, one does not have to see it only in a positivistic manner, but also as an aspiration toward the ways in which the bourgeois man experiences his freedom in the city. Second, it also derives its possibility from the professional strangers of the nineteenth century. As we have seen, the professional strangers were those casual laborers and a variety of transient characters who came in and out of the city, pursuing opportunities, taking up odd and seasonal jobs, sometimes begging or stealing, all in all surviving in the floating worlds at the edges of the city (Merriman 1991, 6, 16, 42). These transient characters also blended into bohemian characters, such as artists, poets, painters, writers, and performers. In 1850 Gustave Courbet, for example, idealized himself as leading the life of a savage, no doubt a reference to the characterization of the dangerous classes at the time, and as an independent vagabond life of the gypsy (Merriman 1991, 11). By the 1880s, many artists had appropriated or subverted the metaphor of the gypsy or bohemian as an identity of the artistic avant-garde. They dreamed of themselves as nomads and gypsies in the world, sharing characteristics with them while simultaneously also living the lives of bourgeois men. Of course, these sources of the identity of the flâneur were contradictory, but gave it the ambiguous and mysterious character it acquired.

If the flâneur, while on the one hand benefiting from the image of the ideal bourgeois citizen and on the other from the floating and transient character of the quintessential city dweller, was a professional stranger, it is not adequate to interpret the flâneur as the man of the public who knows himself to be of the public (cf. Tester 1994a, 7). The flâneur may be of the crowd, but the public is *not* a crowd. The public is constituted in modernity precisely as that space in which the citizen conducts himself as a political being. The flâneur constitutes himself as an apolitical being, or at least, in appearance or on the surface. But that act itself becomes a particular way of being political. The activity of the sovereign spectator in going about the city in order to find the things that will occupy his gaze and thus complete his otherwise incomplete identity is a way of being political, but overturns the principle of being a citizen into a being hiding from itself and losing himself in the crowd.

The flâneur as professional stranger was in turn a source for another ambiguous modern identity that is intertwined with the modern metropolis: the intellectual as both the antithesis and the completion of the flâneur as professional stranger. In fact, in developing one of its most effective strategies, autonomy, modern intellectuals as a social group relied on the images of the professional strangers.

Cosmopolitanism of Intellectuals

If we define intellectuals to include all those professions and occupations not involved in manual labor, then we can claim that we have encountered the intellectual before the metropolis. The philosopher-king of the polis and the Roman lawyer of the civitas can be considered instances of the intellectual at work. We can also see the intellectual at work in the Christianopolis, attending to matters of law, theology, and medicine, with a degree from a reputable European university such as Bologna, Paris, Cambridge, or Oxford (Le Goff 1985). He was also at work as an engineer or architect in the eutopolis, serving as an adviser to the prince. But to define intellectuals by essential or universal attributes is to miss not only their historical specificity but also, as in other types of strangers and outsiders that form the alterity of citizenship, their group foundations, and the strategies and technologies within which they are implicated. Before the metropolis, intellectuals never defined themselves as a group with their own symbols, organizations, rituals, and consciousness. The intellectual is a uniquely modern identity of the metropolis.

The origins of the modern intellectual are usually traced back to the late nineteenth century and to a specific event: the Dreyfus Affair in France (Jennings 1993b). It is through this event that the intellectual was viewed not only as one engaged in intellectual labor, but also as one with relative autonomy from the state and society, endowed with a critical capacity for independent judgment. The scene was Paris in the 1890s and a Jewish army officer, Dreyfus, was charged with treason. When it became obvious that the officer was likely not guilty as charged, a group of academics, poets, painters, writers, actors, and journalists took a position in the political order by rendering a judgment on the injustice of the charge, thereby forming the identity of the intellectual. What is significant here is neither the details nor the eventual outcome of the specific affair, but how it served to spark a moment where various intellectual laborers were interpellated into a specific standpoint. But for this to happen, social networks must already have existed as resources for various intellectuals to draw upon in order to articulate themselves as a group with a particular way of life and being in the city.

We have alluded above to the emergence of professional strangers—vagabonds, beggars, itinerant and seasonal laborers, prostitutes, and other forms of marginal identities—who moved about in the floating worlds of the outskirts of Paris in the 1830s and 1840s. We have also alluded to the fact that the emerging bourgeois sphere of arts and sciences enabled certain artists, writers, and poets to identify with the floating world of professional strangers as both the milieu and the object of their art and thought. It was this milieu and object that made Baudelaire, Mallarmé, Verlaine, Rimbaud, Hugo, Sue, and Balzac possible. It was this milieu that enabled these artists to identify with their objects and to define themselves as bohemian, gypsy, or vagabond, despite the fact that their position in social space and their habitus was in fact ambiguously bourgeois (Seigel 1986). In attempting to come to terms with their own stranger or outsider status in the bourgeois city, they appealed to the position of professional strangers who had already formed an identifiable, albeit ambiguous, position in the social and spatial order of the metropolis. Nonetheless, this milieu and object was a source for them to articulate this ambiguous identity into a form of artist-citizenship in which their claim to the public sphere did not necessarily draw upon the possession of property, as in the case of bourgeois citizens or manual workers such as artisans and laborers, but upon the possession of an intellect and an ability to exercise *autonomous* and *critical* judgment via their art and thought.

Juxtaposed onto these networks and using them as resources were numerous émigré intellectuals from across Europe who were drawn to Paris precisely because of its reputation for these networks and resources. As we shall see, the modern metropolises such as Paris, London, Milan, Chicago, New York, and San Francisco were not destinations for just the floating worlds of professional strangers, but also for immigrants and exiles from across Europe. For Kramer (1988), Paris of the 1830s and 1840s was such a milieu, where exilic intellectuals found these networks congenial for developing their identities as outsiders. Kramer argues that the experience of being an outsider has been an essential aspect of intellectual production. While being an outsider or stranger is possible within one's own nation or culture, a specifically exilic experience has been significant in the intellectual formation of Herodotus and Ovid, Dante and Erasmus, through to Dostoyevsky, Joyce, and Thomas Mann. The modern metropolis, however, became an important milieu for émigré intellectuals, drawing upon an exile tradition that can only be found in the city. While Amsterdam, Zurich, London, and New York were such metropolises, Paris attracted more émigré intellectuals than any other metropolis in the world (Kramer 1988, 6). These émigré intellectuals introduced a certain cosmopolitanism that also changed the floating world of professional strangers by giving a more universal rather than parochial interpretation to it. By providing a distinctive position to the outsider, the émigré experience in the modern metropolis helped articulate the position of the intellectual as a distant, autonomous but critical persona. Occupying a space on the margins of both sending and receiving cultures, the émigré was able to articulate the position of the intellectual as a desired liminality. "Along with this new perspective on the self, exiles often gain insights into the collective consciousness of their society and historical epoch" (Kramer 1988, 10). Their interaction with the social networks of professional strangers helped them recognize the unconscious social and ideological ranks and habitus that created order and meaning in their native culture, but remained hidden for the agents who never left home. This exilic experience illustrates that identity never exists in any pure or complete form and that it always depends on interactions with other referents on the outside or margin; identity always evolves against its alterity. That this was so—that identity is formed against difference—is not only obvious to us in the early twenty-first century, but was increasingly important in European thought with the growing contact between people from various nations across Europe. It was even more obvious in the history of expatriated intellectuals. While everyone in the modern metropolis confronted difference, exiles faced the question most acutely and explicitly. The point made by Kramer (1988, 230), that the persistence of the notion of estrangement and alienation in the work of young Marx can be associated with his exilic experience in Paris in the 1840s, is poignant (Namier 1944).

That the metropolis was crucial both as a milieu of and object for the formation of intellectuals is not an original argument (Charle 1993; Prigge 1992). But how the spaces of the metropolis were generated— the Latin Quarter in Paris and French quarters in almost every other metropolis—and how these spaces articulated networks, contacts, and associations alongside the bourgeois spaces of salons, cafés, publishing outlets, bookshops, and newspapers nonetheless engendered different and alternative conceptions of identity that challenged the bourgeois conception of citizenship (Sennett 1994, 345–46; Haine 1996). While Habermas (1962) focuses on the formations of the public sphere as solidaristic strategies and technologies of bourgeois citizenship, Foucault (1967) focuses on the alienating strategies and technologies of otherness. What is perhaps now needed is a focus on agonistic strategies and technologies that formed the bourgeois and its others within the same space.

Yet, the formation of this critical space was only an aspect of the formation of an intellectual identity. Another and perhaps equally important aspect is studied by Christophe Charle (1987; 1990) and Ringer (1992). Charle suggests that the formation of a consciousness of intellectuals as a group arose out of the formation of elites within the bourgeoisie as a dominant class: politico-administrative, academic, and business elites. While the bourgeoisie inherited from the aristocracy lineage as its principal method of social reproduction and dominance, the formation of these three elite factions within the bourgeoisie shifted the emphasis of social reproduction from lineage to ability and merit. For these groups meritocracy became the main solidaristic strategy, which was effectuated by cultural capital rather than by merely economic capital. Between 1880 and 1890, these groups became increasingly dominant both within the state and within corporations. Remarkably, the milieu and object of these elites were the same as the floating worlds of the professional strangers: as administrators, social workers, planners, and, above all, as experts, their identities were formed qua this milieu and object. Admittedly, their orientation toward this milieu was even more ambiguous than those of the bohemian artists and thinkers; still, this was the field in which they articulated their identities and completed their disciplinary professionalization. Moreover, their distance from the bourgeoisie was more pronounced in their positions as autonomous experts or independent savants. All this became crystal clear when in 1898, at least in Paris, intellectuals signed a manifesto using that category to define themselves and in order to bring the miscarriage of justice regarding the Dreyfus Affair to the attention of the entire nation. It was this manifesto that set the pattern for the later enactment of intellectuals in the political order (Jennings 1993a, 14).

It is through these diverse and distinct but overlapping worlds that intellectuals were able to articulate themselves as a group with a certain ethic of responsibility and an ethic of conviction when confronted with the Dreyfus Affair. But similar formations occurred in various metropolises across Europe and America: Amsterdam, Vienna, London, Berlin, New York, Chicago, and Rome experienced the rise of critical spaces that were at once a milieu and an object of professional strangers, which en-

abled the formation of groups defined as intellectuals. It is this deep ambiguity of intellectuals in the political and spatial order that has been the
source of incessant classification struggles ever since the late nineteenth
century. It is this sense of deep ambiguity of being strangers within the
gates of the metropolis that intellectuals and intelligentsia share with immigrants. This ambiguity was most viciously and clearly played out in
the American metropolis.

Strangers within Our Gates: Estranging Immigrants, Americanizing Outsiders

The American city was always a supreme assemblage, a difference machine: its formation was coincident with the eutopolis as realized utopia.
It always assembled together various groups and then sequestered, distributed, concentrated, and intensified their formation. We have seen the
struggle between the Dutch and the British merchants in New York, and
between the merchants and the artisans in Boston and Philadelphia. But
"America" was formed against groups that did not have much to do with
the metropolis until the late nineteenth century. The first were the aboriginal groups. From the very early settlement until the late nineteenth
century, the struggle between the European settlers and aboriginal groups
proceeded as the latter were constructed as heathens, barbarians, or savages who needed to be civilized or Christianized (Axtell 1992). By the late
nineteenth century, through a protracted and demoralizing battle, aboriginal groups in America were defeated; they were neither civilized nor
assimilated, but sequestered in space, away from view or concern of the
colonial metropolis.

The second group was the slaves. By the 1660s, the British colonies, especially in the south, were cut from their original sources of labor due to
the Navigation Laws and the changing British colonial policy, leading them
to turn to the slave trade from Africa (Morgan 1975; Wood 1974). Unlike
indentured servants, who were enslaved for a definite period and freed
later, slaves were a permanent source of cheap labor on southern plantations. While before the 1660s, neither Virginia nor Maryland (the original
southern colonies) had formally recognized slavery, after that decade they
and other southern colonies introduced slave codes to regulate and institutionalize slavery. By the eighteenth century, new laws made the freedom of
slaves impossible and slaves were denied the right to hold property and to
testify in court. Slaves were firmly entrenched in law as property.

Both groups and their differences from the white "race" were constituted as objects of contempt, inferiority, and disgust. Neither Africans nor aboriginals were Christians and, orientalism being inapplicable, racialization became the main alienating strategy through which the differences were evaluated as savagery and barbarity, which eventually constituted skin color as the common cause of such savagery and inferiority. While both Africans and, to a much lesser extent the aboriginals, could be seen taking up occupations in cities, becoming carpenters, coopers, tailors, cooks, blacksmiths, and servants, their contact with the city remained minimal throughout the eighteenth and early nineteenth centuries, except as passing commodities traveling from Liverpool and Bristol to Boston and New York. Until then, the relationship between the aboriginals and the Africans and whites was conflictual and beleaguered. Between the aboriginal nations and the whites there was a prolonged and tortured battle from the 1660s to the 1860s, which eventually resulted in the formation of reservations and sequestering as alienating technologies. Between Africans and the settlers, the conflict never ceased despite the appalling alienating strategies and technologies of oppression, enslavement, confinement, and systemic violence used by the settlers. Nonetheless, Africans developed solidaristic strategies, including resistance via oral history and maintaining many of their cultural symbols and practices. They also devised reverse alienating strategies through rebellions and revolts on many occasions against slavery, the most famous of which was the 1739 Stono Rebellion in South Carolina. As a result, they began to develop an African American culture that was a hybrid of the two. For example, as a solidaristic strategy they accepted Christianity and blended it with their own customs to create a synthetic and sui generis African American religion. The African and aboriginal oppression in America illustrates that even under severely cruel conditions, groups are able to maintain, strengthen, and expand their identities and enact forms of resistance and affirmation (Levine 1977). Yet, until both these groups encountered the metropolis, they did not articulate these strategies into claims about citizenship.

The constitution of the aboriginals and the Africans in America as its most distant and yet symbiotic alterity was neither accidental nor incidental (Smith 1997). That this was so, however, is not an issue we shall focus on here. Rather, this historical perspective was necessary to understand the moment when both the aboriginals and the Africans, along with immigrants, became the strangers of the metropolis in the late nineteenth century.

Between the 1870s and the 1920s, the American metropolis assembled one of the most rapid and massive movements of people in human history.

During this time, more than 27 million immigrants arrived in America, the majority of whom settled in New York, Chicago, Philadelphia, Boston, New Orleans, San Francisco, and Detroit. While the earlier waves of immigration to American cities included European peoples, such as the Irish, Scots, English, French, Dutch, and German, this wave of immigrants that made the American metropolis consisted largely of Italians, Slavs, Jews, Mexicans, Asians, Hungarians, Greeks, Armenians, Syrians, Turks, Christian Arabs, and Latin Americans (Dinnerstein, Nichols, and Reimers 1996, 125–26). By 1870, the percentage of foreign-born inhabitants of American metropolises was already exceptionally high and it remained so throughout the era of the metropolis: 44.5 percent in New York, 35.1 percent in Boston, 48.4 percent in Chicago, 44.5 percent in Detroit, 49.3 percent in San Francisco, and 20 percent in Los Angeles (Gibson and Lennon 1999). By 1930, 75 percent of New York was inhabited by immigrants and their children. Italians and Eastern European Jews made up the majority, but every other group, ranging from Arabs to Yugoslavs, also settled there. By 1900, Germans constituted 35 percent of Chicago, Irish 17 percent, and Scandinavians 14 percent.

The stories of this exodus or assemblage and its causes have been narrated by generations of historians in different ways. That it was inextricably associated with capitalism is beyond doubt. The modern capitalism that uprooted peasants and drew them to European cities, dispossessed artisans of their craft and condemned them to workhouses and factories was also responsible for the assemblage that was the American metropolis. The dispossessed and uprooted looked not only to European metropolises, but also to American metropolises for opportunity. This was, however, accompanied by the voracious appetite of American capitalism for cheap labor. Neither immigration nor modern American capitalism would have been possible without each other (Bodnar 1985). The dominant groups in the American metropolis thus developed agonistic technologies of citizenship to assemble immigrants in the metropolis at a distance. The immigration agent was such a technology, either working for companies or as an independent supplier (such as the padroni for Italian, Greek, and Syrian immigrants), roaming Europe to recruit immigrants. Some traveled to Europe to recruit immigrant-workers, while others operated from the United States. They negotiated deals with employers, sent the workers off to their destinations, and even collected and distributed the salaries of workers after deducting their service fees. Some padroni also provided housing, wrote letters, and interpreted the social and cultural norms and rules of conduct on behalf of their clients. If the immigrants were lucky, the padrone was fair; if not, they were in the hands of a scoundrel who exacerbated the already exploited life and opportunities of the immigrant. The padroni were supplemented with American labor agents, who also served similar purposes, including providing scabs and strikebreakers drawn from new immigrants.

To survive in the metropolis, the family became the most significant solidaristic technology for immigrants. The work was the work of the family. The husband, wife, children, and even members of the extended family combined forces to devise matrimonial strategies to make ends meet. The 1910 census recorded over two million child laborers. But the division of labor within the family varied between ethnic groups. In Chicago and New York, Italian females made up the majority of workers in the garment industry. Dutch and Greek women typically stayed and worked at home. Irish, German, Scandinavian, and Slavic women did both factory and domestic work. French-Canadian women did not work as domestics but as factory workers. Low wages for long hours in abysmal surroundings was the common experience of immigrants, both men and women. The miserable working conditions stimulated the development of a working-class consciousness and its corresponding organizations, but ethnic identifications made matters more complicated than that of European metropolises. In the 1870s, the two big labor organizations, the Knights of Labor and the American Federation of Labor, were unable to come to terms with the different views and needs of immigrant or African workers and so devised agonistic strategies toward them.

While the immigrants flowed into the metropolis, African Americans also began an exodus from the South to the northern metropolises after 1880, but especially after 1910. The abolition of slavery and the failure to provide land for the freedmen made it impossible for African Americans to maintain their subsistence (Karst 1989, 43–61). While the slaves had begun leaving plantations and arriving in cities such as New Orleans even before the 1880s, the exodus in the 1880s and 1910s was incomparable to any prior experience. Between 1880 and 1920, more than 350,000 freed Africans arrived in both New York and Philadelphia, some 200,000 in Chicago, and more then 50,000 in both Boston and Detroit (Dinnerstein, Nichols, and Reimers 1996, 140).

It is well known that most Africans and immigrants, regardless of their cultural backgrounds, joined the ranks of the working class and, in spite of the predominant images of mobility, never moved beyond that status (Bodnar 1985, 169; Dinnerstein, Nichols, and Reimers 1996, 144). Moreover, immigrants and Africans typically constituted the lower ranks of the working class, not only by virtue of their lower wages, but also by the stigmatization and racialization they endured. And within African and immigrant groups, the status of women ranked even lower in terms of their position in the division of labor and the social and symbolic status associated with it. Nevertheless, both Africans and immigrants, men as well as women, contested their dominated status and developed sui generis solidaristic and agonistic strategies, contesting and overturning agonistic strategies that constituted them as inferior beings, making claims to citizenship, and winning rights that established the framework for citizenship in the twentieth century.

The turn-of-the-century strategies that constructed immigrants as strangers subject to assimilation and civilization and Africans as outsiders subject to exclusion also included orientalization. These strategies were mobilized on the basis of an ostensible superiority of the Anglo-Saxon race and its ineluctable instinct for freedom and democracy and they were clearly cognizant of the changing character of the immigrants: "A line drawn across the Continent of Europe from north-east to south-west, separating the Scandinavian Peninsula, the British Isles, Germany and France from Russia, Austria-Hungary, Italy and Turkey, separates countries not only of distinct races but also of distinct civilizations. It separates Protestant Europe from Catholic Europe; it separates countries of representative institutions and popular government from absolute monarchies. It separates lands where education is universal from lands where illiteracy predominates; it separates manufacturing countries, progressive agriculture and skilled labour from primitive hand industries, backward agriculture and unskilled labour; it separates an educated, thrifty peasantry from a peasantry scarcely a single generation removed from serfdom; it separates Teutonic races from Latin, Slav, Semitic and Mongolian races" (quoted in Woodsworth 1909, 164). This was how group boundaries within the American metropolis were drawn across Europe, marking immigrants with attributes according to those boundaries. In addition, racialization and stigmatization were used as agonistic strategies based on attributing differences in institutions and practices to race and ethnicity as represented in dichotomies, such as educated versus illiterate and manufacturing versus unskilled industries.

Many Americans were convinced that "[e]mphatically too many people are now coming over here; too many of an undesirable sort. In 1902 over seven-tenths were from races who do not rapidly assimilate with the customs and institutions of this country" (quoted in Woodsworth 1909, 161). This was a commonly held assumption that followed from the earlier sentiment that boundaries marking out immigrants related to the boundaries that marked them out in their origins, and that those boundaries determined their disposition and ability to assimilate. Of course, assimilation is the second implicit assumption in the passage.

In 1894 the *Report of the Associated Charities of Boston* asserted that "[t]he recent immigrants have been, generally speaking, much inferior to those who came in earlier times. They are lowering the average standard of citizenship in our country, and such immigration must be checked before we can adequately deal with the problems of pauperism and crime in our cities" (quoted in Woodsworth 1909, 187). Ultimately, the fear and anxiety about the strangers within the gates of the American metropolis was about "whether this sweeping immigration is to foreignize us, or we are to Americanize it. Our safety demands the assimilation of these strange populations, and the process of assimilation becomes slower and more difficult as the proportion of foreigners increases" (quoted in Woodsworth 1909, 232).

As is well documented, these views of the immigrant as the stranger were not isolated or random, but systematic and widespread constructions. Nor were they limited to the racist and bigoted few. The rapid arrival of immigrants into the midst of the American metropolis pitted various groups against each other and fractured their identities, alliances, and loyalties. The American labor movement, for example, despite the fact that many immigrants had become active in it, adopted an agonistic and often alienating orientation toward the immigrant. Unlike the immigration before the 1880s, many immigrants were absorbed into unskilled jobs in the manufacturing industries (Bodnar 1985, 65). John Mitchell, president of the American Federation of Labor, spoke against immigration in 1909, arguing that it depressed the wage rates of American workers (Dudley 1990, 150–57). But his opposition went much deeper than concern for the depressing effect of surplus labor that immigration would generate. He believed that the new immigrants did not make good labor activists. Earlier immigrants were "sturdy, adventurous pioneers." But the new immigrant was not a "constructive factor in the development of a new and high civilization." Mitchell claimed that "[l]arge numbers of the immigrants of recent years regard our country simply as a foraging ground, in which they expect to make a 'stake,' and when they have done so, to return to their own countries and spend the remainder of their lives there; and this 'stake' is too often accumulated by eating and living in a manner destructive of physical and social health" (quoted in Dudley 1990, 153). Aware that this view might be interpreted as a prejudice, Mitchell argued that "[t]he American wage earner, be he native or immigrant, entertains no prejudice against his fellow from other lands; but as self-preservation is the first law of nature, our workmen believe and contend that their labour should be protected against the competition of an induced immigration comprised largely of men whose standards and ideals are lower than our own" (quoted in Dudley 1990, 154).

The massive assemblage of Africans and immigrants in the metropolis, the dominated position in which they found themselves, and the strategies and technologies they encountered in the face of symbolic and material exploitation manifested themselves, partly as a material resource and partly as a symbol of isolation and marginalization, in one of the most ubiquitous strategies in the metropolis that was simultaneously solidaristic and agonistic: segregation. Concentrating in areas of the metropolis where the cheapest residences were available and using this concentration as a resource for establishing networks of survival was certainly behind the phenomenon of segregation. Nevertheless, just as important was that spatial segregation reinforced the marginalization and isolation of Africans and immigrants in the social order since neither the bourgeoisie nor the members of the emerging disciplinary professions wanted to maintain any proximity with the "wretched" and "dangerous" classes swarming the metropolis. Segregation in the spatial order, therefore, occupied an ambiguous position and became the object of both admiration and disgust on the part of reformers, social workers, entrepreneurs, and the emerging disciplinary professions: public health officials, engineers, and planners. Spatial labels that served as indexes of both social and spatial situation, such as "Niggertown," "Nigger Hill," "Dutch Hill," or "Chinatown," became agonistic ways of representing spaces in the metropolis. It also mobilized statistical and social research as instances of this classification struggle. In the 1870s and 1880s, the Bureau of Census surveyed the American metropolis, looking for ways of reining the masses into categories based on such characteristics as occupation, national origin, and previous conditions of servitude (Ryan 1997, 187). By designating African American as "Colored," the Census Bureau incorporated strategies of racialization by grouping and classifying people according to their "race" (Nobles 2000).

Perhaps it was such representations of immigrants that led generations of historians to assume that immigrants were not essential and active agents of the labor movement in the American metropolis. We have alluded to the fact that the labor movement was unable to come to terms with Africans and immigrants. But there is also evidence that both

Africans and immigrants were crucial members of the trade unions, contributing to the movement not only by their activism, but also by importing the solidaristic and agonistic strategies of the European working-class movements. As Bodnar reports, during the 1880s, Irish dockworkers in New York City and northern New Jersey used the "boycott" as a tool to pressure employers to accept labor demands. The term was adopted by the Irish National Land League to describe an identical tactic used against landlords in rural Ireland (Bodnar 1985, 90). Bodnar concludes that "communal solidarity was characteristic of much immigrant labour activity in both the nineteenth and twentieth centuries and usually resulted in protest and violence which involved all family and community members" (1985, 91). Similarly, in the 1880s, German workers dominated the labor movement among the skilled craftsmen. In fact, American capitalists were quite cognizant of the fact that immigrants were not easily disciplined into the obedient and acquiescent manners of routine work process. They assembled various strategies and technologies of citizenship in the name of Americanizing or civilizing workers, but in fact they were to discipline them. While much has been said about the Ford Motor Company's "Five Dollar Day" as a measure of making consumers out of workers, the fact that it was conceived to reform the morals of immigrant workers is less discussed (Meyer 1981). Ford instituted a sociological department that investigated the morals of immigrants to adjudicate whether they could be certified to qualify for the wage. The department sent (sociological) investigators into immigrant homes to ascertain the extent to which immigrants conformed to the values Ford set out as appropriate (Bodnar 1985, 98). The technologies of citizenship introduced by Ford and its sociological department were only some of many that were initiated by American companies to effectuate agonistic strategies, such as Americanization, moralization, racialization, and routinization of the conduct of immigrants.

While exposed to and implicated in these strategies and technologies, neither African nor immigrant workers were passive agents. There are numerous instances of institutions, symbols, practices, organizations, and narratives that attest to the vital and strong solidaristic strategies that many African immigrant workers forged in the city. As mentioned, they were certainly not as cool to the trade unions and the labor movement as has been assumed. Moreover, immigrant workers instituted strong and durable practices of group solidarity that contributed to the formation of their own group identities, but also to that of the working class. The immigrants and Africans did not readily submit to the specter of

Americanization, but overturned and supplanted various strategies of assimilation (Dinnerstein, Nichols, and Reimers 1996, 160). Through establishing cultural and social networks, both Africans and immigrants constituted their identities and consciousness in newspapers, music, clubs, bars, associations, and various charities (Spencer 1997). Various immigrant groups became active in municipal politics, the most famous being the Irish at the turn of the twentieth century in Chicago, Boston, New Orleans, and San Francisco.

Moreover, the various ways of being political invented by Africans and immigrants were not restricted to municipal politics in the metropolis. As Mary Ryan (1990; 1997) illustrates, both Africans and immigrants, women and men, made their presence public in the metropolis via parades, protests, picnics, marches, street theaters, and gatherings. Italian and Jewish theater in San Francisco and New York in the 1880s, and the "Harlem Renaissance" of Africans in music, literature, and poetics in the 1900s explored themes that rejected the virtues of citizenship that Americanization and racialization imposed. In fact, it was the accomplishments of Africans and immigrants as the strangers of the metropolis that made the metropolis a vibrant and vital political, social, and cultural space and bequeathed a strong legacy of strategies and technologies of citizenship to the cosmopolis of the late twentieth century. Many of their accomplishments served as resources for new identifications, new groupings, and new strengths for articulating different ways of being political, such as the movements for civil, women's, gays and lesbians', and environmental rights (Isin and Wood 1999; Siemiatycki and Isin 1998).

Governing Strangers and Outsiders via Municipalization

It perhaps makes sense that in 1848 Marx should not only see "modernity" from the perspective of two classes locked in a struggle, but should see "[t]he history of all hitherto existing society [as] the history of class struggles." While Marx admitted that "[i]n the earlier epochs of history, we find almost everywhere a complicated arrangement of society into various orders, a manifold gradation of social rank," he believed that the epoch of the bourgeoisie had simplified the class antagonisms, saying that "[s]ociety as a whole is more and more splitting up into two great hostile camps, into two great classes directly facing each other: bourgeoisie and proletariat." For Marx, when such classes stood against each other in the earlier epochs of history, as did freemen and slave, patrician and plebeian, lord and serf, guild-master and journeymen, each time their fight ended "either in a revolutionary reconstitution of society at large, or in the common ruin of the contending classes." Marx wanted to historicize 1848 as a point of no return and no alternative: that society was either to be reconstituted or ruined. As has been argued, however, neither patricians nor plebeians, neither guild-masters nor journeymen were ever so clearly constituted as hypothetical and practical classes simultaneously. What was a strategic interpretation did not render a sound historical judgment. That by the 1840s the two revolutions—industrial and French—seemed to have consolidated the two opposing classes in the way Marx envisaged was, to an extent, a success of the bourgeoisie in distinguishing itself and reducing the complex terrain into a plane of laboring and dangerous classes. To claim its rights to the city was crucial in this bourgeois success. The metropolis was a strategic space whose appropriation became decisive for accumulating capital and whose spatialization became crucial for accumulating men: the transformation of what was then constituted as the dangerous classes as outsiders into laboring classes as strangers (Valverde 1996). Municipalization of government was the most significant strategy in governing citizens, strangers, and outsiders of the modern metropolis and embodied simultaneous nationalization *and* localization of discipline, loyalty, virtue, and subsidiarity (see Isin 2000a).

The modern conception of municipal government constituted the city as a space of discipline and liberty at the same time, which was captured by perhaps one of the most revealing phrases, "local self-government" or "local democracy" (Beetham 1996; Loughlin 1986). Municipalization of government involved two seemingly contradictory movements. First, it expressed autonomy exercised by municipal governments, where cities were accorded powers to manage their "local" affairs. It was a political space in which the bourgeois *man*, as owner of property and head of household, was habituated into conducting himself in the democratic sphere and practicing his citizenship. Second, municipalization of government constituted and disciplined groups into useful habits (Munro 1926, 50–51). The technologies of power to which historians have given some attention more recently, including hospitals, workhouses, prisons, schools, policing, and correctional institutions, were in fact activated, operated, and maintained by municipalization of government. There is a telling symbolism in the fact that Tocqueville came to America to study the penitentiary system and wrote an influential book about the need for municipalization of government (Beaumont and Tocqueville 1833; Tocqueville 1835). If liberty was an expression of the emancipation of bourgeois *man* from the shackles of aristocracy, it also embodied a new tangled web of obligations for citizens, strangers, and outsiders alike, implicating them in intricate solidaristic, agonistic, and alienating strategies that municipalization operationalized and effectuated. While the nineteenth century invents the liberty of bourgeois *man* (never specified but always universalized), this intricate web of rights and obligations problematized conduct and games of domination and differentiation in very complex manners. For laboring men and women, children, youth, the poor, the destitute, and the mentally ill, the world of freedom was as abstract as the new brave world of wealth, colonialism, and imperialism (Valverde 1998). "The free citizen was one who was able and willing to conduct his or her own conduct according to the norms of [bourgeois] civility; the delinquent, the criminal, the insane person, with their specialized institutions of reformation, were the obverse of this individualization and subjectivization of citizenship" (Rose 1999, 233).

While the way this tension between liberty and order was addressed followed different trajectories in Canadian, French, German, British, and American forms of municipalization, broadly speaking, the strategies and technologies of citizenship were comparable (see Munro 1918, 1926). This reflected the increasing nationalization of disciplinary professionalization, which brought together various professions in assemblages, enabled them to exchange experiences, and systematized the professions into various fields of knowledge, the disciplines. It is the disciplinary character of knowledge that gave it a universal, comparable, and scientific authority. Nonetheless, while American municipal government showed the most entrepreneurial élan, the French and British metropolises had to deal with the oligarchization of past municipal governments, which required the heavier hand of states to create new spaces of discipline *and* freedom via legislation (Cohen 1998).

Municipal government orientations toward various groups were therefore a question of governability in the interests of order and liberty simultaneously (Rose 1996b). Associated with the question of governability was that of disciplinary professionalization, which relied on expertise in the sense of an authority arising out of a claim to knowledge, neutrality, and efficacy. Through the increasing deployment of statistical and other forms of knowledge, the rising disciplinary professions described and reconstructed in detail how the lifestyles of various groups (e.g., the mentally ill, immigrant, hysterical women, unruly children) and working classes departed from expected and useful norms. The disciplinary professions became mediating and effective agents for articulating the virtues of bourgeois citizenship, and these virtues were deployed as yardsticks for assessing the conduct of those who lacked them. But the disciplinary professions achieved more than mediating bourgeois values of citizenship to its strangers and outsiders: they also scientized and theorized their transformation into virtuous citizens by applying expertise and knowledge. The rise of correctional sites as technologies of citizenship, such as hospitals, workhouses, prisons, schools, housing projects, and other institutions, marked the characteristic form of disciplinary professionalization. What made these strategies and technologies governmental rather than philosophical was the wish to be practical, to connect up with various procedures and apparatuses of correction, inculcation, and disposition. Similarly, what made these strategies and technologies of citizenship different from those devised in the eutopolis was that citizenship was constituted as an attainable goal for strangers and outsiders, rather than an unattainable ideal.

As disciplinary professions assembled strategies and technologies of citizenship via municipalization of government and effectively mediated the virtues of citizenship with the viciousness and barbarism of strangers and outsiders (hence becoming effective civilizing agents), they also constituted various disciplinary fields by scientizing guilds of expertise and fraternization, carving out an indispensable function for the professions in capitalism. Yet, to assume a straightforward causal homology between professionalization and capitalism overlooks the fact that these strategies and technologies embody their own histories and develop their own rationalities, which may or may not link up with capitalism. Also, as much as capitalism needed professions as agents of strategies and technologies of citizenship, professions also made capitalism possible. Well before the rise of factory discipline, for example, the early modern workhouses made a major contribution to the discipline of the working classes. The laboring men and women were not simply found in cities looking for jobs; they were assembled into a class by strategies and technologies of citizenship. Through these strategies and technologies, different governmental authorities sought to enact programs in relation to different groups and classes and the resistances and oppositions anticipated or encountered (Burchell 1996; Rose 1996b, 1996c). These strategies and technologies did not derive from a formula, but were invented throughout the late eighteenth and nineteenth centuries in Europe and America. The resistance and oppositions were many and opportunities for becoming political, assembling solidaristic, agonistic, and alienating strategies and technologies, and creating spaces for dissent were made possible by those who were constituted as strangers and outsiders of the metropolis (Brophy 1997).

Cosmopolis

Immigrants
Homeless
Squeegeers
Refugees

Between the 1940s and the 1990s, millions of immigrants arrived in European, American, Canadian, and Australian metropolises, transforming them into cosmopolises. But this transformation was more than a quantitative explosion of "difference." It came at a time when the bourgeois strategies of nationalization, rendering an order of differences to create a "people," came up against new solidaristic and agonistic strategies and technologies, new forms of capital, and new struggles. Cosmopolis was crystallized at the intersection of these new strategies, capitals, groups, and enactments of new ways of being political. While the grand narratives of postmodernization and globalization dominated categories of perception and expression, they were nonetheless the symptoms of a reconfiguration of the dominant and dominated groups of the city. While the early twentieth century was marked by embourgeoisement, by the middle of the century disciplinary professionalization was already giving way to entrepreneurial professionalization, breeding new characters in the theater of the metropolis. Unlike the disciplinary professions, whose primary strategy was statization, the entrepreneurial professions were both of and beyond the state. While the investigations of the cosmopolis can certainly proceed with analyses of social movements that introduced radically new ways of being political (Eder 1993; Foweraker and Landman 1997; Magnusson 1996), the movement that has received the least attention is professionalization. The genealogical investigations of the cosmopolis focus on various solidaristic, agonistic, and alienating strategies invented by entrepreneurial practices deployed by many new as well as old professions to articulate new ideals of citizenship, new tables of virtues and vices, and new ways of being political.

Professions and Disciplines: Articulating a New Ideal of the Citizen

Already in the late nineteenth century, Otto Gierke and Émile Durkheim believed that the modern nation-state could not survive without finding a meaningful solidaristic order somewhere between the state and the individual. They believed that for socialization, the state was too remote from "individuals" and its connections with them too superficial, irregular, and tenuous. For them this was the reason why, when the state becomes the dominant form of association, it inevitably disintegrates. In this view, the nation-state as a political association cannot be sustained unless there exists between the state and individuals a whole range of secondary groups with which individuals associate and identify. These groups must be close enough to the individual to cultivate loyalty and engage them in everyday practices, and in so doing to absorb them into everyday social and political life (Durkheim 1894, liv). The political question for them was how to encourage the formation of such groups (Durkheim 1890, 96; Gierke 1868).

For both Gierke and Durkheim, on the basis of historical experience, there were only two kinds of social groups that could fulfil such needs. They both recognized that groups based on territorial associations, such as cities, villages, and towns, were organized as self-governing municipalities and constituted the traditional basis of European states, political representation and social engagement. Gierke believed that the future of the state was dependent on these intermediate territorial groups (1868). By contrast, Durkheim believed that territorial groups no longer had the importance they once had because individuals were mobile and lacked loyalties to place. The ties that had united the members of self-governing municipalities were external and not permanent. There was something artificial about such groups. For Durkheim the durable social groups, those to which individuals devote their whole lives regardless of their place, those for which they may have the strongest attachment, were increasingly the professional groups. At the turn of the twentieth century, then, Durkheim envisaged that the professions would become the basis of being political as well as the social structure in the future (1890, 96–97).

Whether the professions have fulfilled this role is a matter of debate (Freidson 1994; Halliday 1983; Krause 1996). It is remarkable, however, how Durkheim perceived the transformations in capitalism and its association with entrepreneurial professionalization in the late nineteenth century. Unlike Marx, Weber, or Simmel, Durkheim made prescient observations about the formation of the professions and their role in the state. Since he made these observations, the importance of territorialization and municipalization of government have steadily declined, but the importance of professionalization has increased. Nonetheless, although Durkheim envisaged the professions as aspatial forms of loyalty and solidarity, the professions actually contributed to the formation of new spaces within the state and were intricately bound up with cities. As Thomas Bender argued, subsequent research on the professions rarely paid attention to the relationship between the professions and the city (1979; 1998). But this relationship, which may be the defining aspect of the cosmopolis, is fundamental for investigating the articulation of new strategies and technologies of citizenship, and the formation of different social groups and identities associated with them.

The professions developed four solidaristic and agonistic strategies for claiming rights to the city throughout the twentieth century: spatialization, socialization, objectification, and habitation (Blau, La Gory, and Pipkin 1983; Hillier and Hanson 1984, 188–90; Knox 1988; Larson 1993; Ley 1996; Smith 1996; Zukin 1995). We shall return to each of these later when discussing the cosmopolis, professions, and disciplines, but we shall first establish relations between guilds, professions, and citizenship and then investigate how the transformations in strategies and technologies from disciplinary to entrepreneurial professionalization have affected citizenship.

Guilds, Professions, Citizenship

As a solidaristic strategy, each profession finds its origins somewhere among the Mayan astronomers, Egyptian scribes, Mesopotamian priests, Greek philosophers, or Roman lawyers. If we recognize the professions as providers of "expert advice" undertaking "intellectual" labor, such claims are probably credible. But if we recognize a profession by its formalization of knowledge, organization of an association, monopolization of a market, and centralization of accreditation, then these strategies of professionalization emerged only recently. While both views of the professions as eternal and sui generis modern groups have been influential, until recently the historical affinities between the guilds and the professions have been neglected. The relative decline in the autonomy, status, and power of especially the public professions in the past few decades, however, refocused attention on the historic similarities between the guilds and the professions. As a result, the view held by Gierke and Durkheim that there were no groups between the individual and the modern state has, if it ever was justifiable, become untenable.

While the history of modernity is written with the grand narrative that all associations and guilds were abolished between the state and the individual (hence the worries of Gierke and Durkheim), the professions had been forming new and powerful guilds since the fifteenth century. "The record shows clearly that the professions were not a product of the industrial revolution" (Krause 1996, 11). As is well known, modern capitalism and the state were hostile to guilds and attacked their privileges. By the nineteenth century, all guilds and associations were regulated by the state and their powers were radically curtailed. But at the same time the professions were developing guildlike strategies and technologies for inculcating certain forms of conduct. The university is a case in point, which survived both capitalism and the state throughout the twentieth century. A reason for this, as we have seen earlier, is that universities were cosmopolitan in character by virtue of Latin being the universal language of instruction and fellowship. But the other, perhaps more important, reason is that the university became articulated in the rise of the new guilds: the professions. The new disciplines that were organized in the universities in the late nineteenth and early twentieth centuries were closely allied with the new professions.

Thus, recent historical studies have rejected the assumption, held by Carr-Saunders (1933) and subsequent scholarship, that the professions were a product of the industrial revolution after 1860. Since the 1970s, the sociology of the professions has rejected the functionalist scholarship and adopted the historicized and politicized approaches represented by neo-Marxist and neo-Weberian approaches in the United States and Britain. In France, the work of Bourdieu (Bourdieu 1979, 1989; Bourdieu and Passeron 1970) has critically brought the study of the professions and knowledge formation into the study of professionalization. Similarly, the historiography of the professions also underwent changes when historians joined the debate with sociologists. Anglo-Saxon, French, and German studies on the professions critiqued the functionalist and evolutionist approaches to the formation of the professions (Burrage and Torstendahl 1990; Cocks and Jarausch 1990; Corfield 1995; Geison 1984; Malatesta 1995; Prest 1981, 1987b). While Italy initially remained an outsider to these developments, recently Malatesta (1995) has brought Italy into the fold. For Malatesta the formation of modern professions was not necessarily associated with industrialization in a straightforward sense.

Rather, the system that arose in medieval Italian cities was the fruit of a union between systematic knowledge, professions, and governing groups, and has been an enduring feature of the Italian professions until today (Malatesta 1995, 7). Similarly, Prest (1987a), for example, illustrates that law, clergy, and medicine were fairly well formed in early modern England and that there is a continuity between the professions before and after the industrial revolution. Nonetheless, the most obvious contrast is their organization. If what distinguishes a profession from any other occupation is the ability of its membership to determine, directly or indirectly, who may pursue that particular vocation, then there were either very few or very many professions in early modern England. Few, if we consider legal or medical professions as prototypes, but many if we include all the craft guilds and trading companies whose members sought to maintain monopolies in various localities. "The historical puzzle is to explain, if possible without embroiling ourselves in unprofitable debate about the attributes or definition of a true profession, why the national occupational monopoly form (represented by the guilds) shrank and withered on the vine" (Prest 1987a, 14). The difficulty the guilds faced was how to expand their boundaries beyond the city. Yet lawyers and doctors were able to organize beyond the city fairly quickly.

For Moore, too, the affinities between medieval guilds and contemporary professional associations are unmistakable. The guilds developed practices of apprenticeship, provided for a graded career as proficiency increased, and regulated technical and personal conduct for their members (Moore 1970, 43–47, 114). In the nineteenth century the guilds were idealized primarily to show that they either were or were not precursors of trade unions. Throughout the twentieth century, scholars uncritically accepted the decline of the guilds as a sign of the rise of capitalism and placed the professions above the crafts. A sharp distinction was thus drawn between the professions and the guilds. As a result, the history of the professions took very little account of the social and ethical traditions of the craft and merchant guilds in the formation of the professions (Pelling 1987, 96). But the guilds developed strategies and technologies thought to be definitive of the professions: they specialized, were self-regulating, were recognized authorities, were the source of criteria of qualifications, and regulated their markets (Pelling 1987, 98).

The assumption that the early modern professions were merely clients of the aristocracy has been questioned as well. The professions exercised power and influence and were a meritocratic force in their own right, which we have seen earlier as pragmatic professionalization (Corfield

1995, 244). While the existence of professional knowledge-brokers did not end or exclude other sources of authority, knowledge did become a significant source of authority. The professions neither constituted an intelligentsia nor represented the entire social spectrum that was designated under the term *middle class* but, nevertheless, they developed into groups with authority (Corfield 1995, 246).

To sum, in European and American history, all occupations were once organized as guilds with some form of legal corporate status. Beginning in the late seventeenth century, first in England and later in France and America, a few dominant occupations established themselves as more learned, more honorable, and more autonomous and began to distinguish themselves as professions. Over succeeding generations, the English word *profession* came to be used less as a synonym of occupation than as a reference to this group of occupations. When the professions became the subject of study in the twentieth century, three categories of occupations dominated: a group whose claims to professional status were never disputed, a larger group whose claim to professional status was contested, and a vast majority of nonlabor and labor occupations that never claimed professional status and were never offered it (Burrage 1990, 151). The study of organized professions and organized labor thus defined two distinct boundaries, which rarely informed each other. Burrage, however, argues that the professions and labor organizations not only share the same lineage with guilds, but also borrowed from each other both solidaristic and agonistic strategies and technologies. The patterns of divergence and convergence between these two forms of association are not a difference in kind at all, but historically contingent differences in strategies and technologies.

This renewed focus on the affinities between the guilds and the professions allows us to make a crucial connection between citizenship and the professions, especially in the period between 1870 and 1920. During that period, driven largely by the managerial revolution that swept capitalism in America and Europe (Taylorism and Fordism), various white-collar occupations were either created or vastly expanded in number. Growing legions of salaried men, and increasingly women, were employed by the industrial and public corporations, insurance companies, retail establishments, and municipal, state, and federal governments, which hired large numbers of managers and professionals to organize their affairs. The white-collar worker replaced the industrial worker as a symbol of changes that affected social life. Many observers began to associate these changes with the rise of a "new middle class." The "old middle class" of independent craftsmen and artisans continued to exist, but salaried workers soon outnumbered them and became the core of a new social transformation. The formation of the new professions and disciplines was an essential element in this process. The new professions, such as social work, personnel management, business administration, accounting, planning, architecture, and public health, were the symbols and embodiments of this transformation. Others, such as engineering, law, and medicine, flourished and grew rapidly with the growing demand for professional services. The professions embodied crucial elements of the new type of white-collar occupation: the importance of licensing, the rising educational qualification for white-collar work, the stronger linkages between educational credentials and careers, the rapid specialization of knowledge, and the functional differentiation of work tasks and routines. It is in this period that cultural capital increasingly played a significant role in enabling groups to differentiate themselves from the entrepreneurs, artisans, merchants, and workers and to constitute themselves as citizens. By the 1920s, although wealth and income—economic capital— still remained the primary determinants of group differentiation, cultural capital increasingly mediated access to economic capital. This is why the system of higher education played a particularly important role in the accumulation of cultural capital and the strengthening of occupational boundaries. The formation of research universities in the 1870s and 1880s altered the parameters of the production and distribution of knowledge. Older traditions of scholarly inquiry changed in the wake of the genesis of specialized academic disciplines, which were organized via professional associations. It is in this period that the close affinity between organized disciplines in the universities and the pragmatic demands of the professions was firmly established. The rising demand for white-collar workers coincided with the introduction of courses and degrees in new fields.

The modern professions and disciplines have always been implicated in the question of government (Abbott 1988). They became implicated in governing conduct by contributing to the problem of government by virtue of their own demands, by articulating and mobilizing the demands of other social groups, and by solving problems via the expertise they provided. The professions and disciplines founded associations as solidaristic strategies, standardized and tightened the requirements for admission to practice, shifted professional education from apprenticeship to specialized academic institutions, secured various forms of state-sponsored occupational licensing as agonistic strategies, and established their jurisdictions by fighting off outside competitors as alienating strategies. The professions and disciplines were neither homogeneous, nor equal in terms of the success of these strategies. Following Larson (1977), these strategies take two forms: reproducing its membership (autonomy) and consolidating its jurisdiction (heteronomy). It is, therefore, more appropriate to regard the language and the instrument of professionalization—licensing, academic certification, state protection, and collective action through associations—as a series of strategies and technologies very much in the manner of the guilds. These strategies and technologies have been used by a wide range of occupations to establish their markets, to increase their public authority, and to enhance their status and rights.

As discussed earlier, Durkheim suggested that a new social solidarity can be found in the professions between the state and the individual (Halliday 1987, 17). For other early scholars of the professions, such as T. H. Marshall, the professions had the capacity to engender a new stability and affiliation (Halliday 1987, 18; Marshall 1939). For Carr-Saunders, the professions were a means to establish a proper balance between power and knowledge (Carr-Saunders and Wilson 1933; Halliday 1987, 19). Since secularization in the modern world would not allow authority to be vested in traditional religion, Parsons believed that only expertise would be able to solve modern problems (Halliday 1987, 20; Parsons 1939, 1968). But none of these scholars made a connection between the professions and citizenship, despite the fact that during the twentieth century, professions in America and Europe merged features of two classical conceptions of guilds. First, they adopted some features, including self-regulation, solidarity, and intermediate association. Second, they developed, in a modern guise, the monopolistic inclinations of medieval guilds (Halliday 1987, 23). It is these guildlike features that make the professions of interest to our genealogical investigations on citizenship as alterity. A close examination of strategies and technologies of the formation of the professions reveals remarkable similarities to the development of citizenship as guild membership, understood as a group defined with and against other groups.

If we examine the formation of professional groups through their bodies and societies since the late nineteenth century, we see these similarities. These bodies and societies, offering a membership within a club, have certain expectations of their members, which reflect the more general characteristics claimed by professionals in addition to the specific requirements of each group. That the four fundamental solidaristic strategies of the professions—calling, expertise, knowledge, and autonomy—are essentially the same as those of the guilds, whether warrior or artisan, is notable. A *calling* has a twofold orientation. While it is based on a discipline or a body of knowledge, it also embodies a professional ethic that entices an individual to that body of knowledge. A profession cannot establish its legitimacy without a claim to represent, to have a level of mastery over, and to practice a particular discipline, vocation, or calling. Higher education qualifications and credentials usually represent *expertise* as flowing from this claim. Professions are also founded upon a body of *knowledge:* a claim to inculcate high-level intellectual skills that show an ability to grasp new events quickly and to respond effectively. Professions have always intentionally separated themselves from manual or routine labor precisely on this claim. Finally, the identity of any profession would be incomplete without a claim to *autonomy,* independence or discretion within the work situation. Although professionals negotiate with their patrons (state and/or corporation), clients, and publics, their claim to professionalism as their sui generis ethic involves their autonomy before, after, and during the provision and delivery of services. Whether professionals work as salaried employees or as independent consultants, such a claim to autonomy constitutes their fundamental and inviolable claim.

Via these solidaristic strategies, professions have developed a particular professional ethic that is shared by the existing or aspiring professions. The professional ethic involves valorization of technical and theoretical expertise and the authority, trust, and status flowing from such expertise; the establishment and the exercise of trust as a basis for client-patron relationships; adherence to professional standards often, but not always, represented by the granting of a license to practice; independence, autonomy, and discretion; and specific attitudes toward work, clients, and peers involving dedication, reliability, flexibility, and creativity in relation to problems to be solved.

Of course, this professional ethic is as much an ethos as a strategy of recruitment. That a profession involves technically and culturally valued knowledge and requires special education justifies it as a formally licensed practice via negotiations between the state and an occupational association (Freidson 1994, 17–18; Mann 1993, 564). But, following Weber, to interpret this as "social closure," a close fraternity, is, once again, to invoke logics of exclusion (Ellul 1964, 162). To interpret autonomy (involving claiming rights to regulate its own members, including entry and credentialing) and heteronomy (involving negotiations with its patrons, clients, and publics) as closure or exclusion is misleading because these strategies prescribe certain forms of professional conduct and are open to those who are willing to cultivate these virtues in themselves and conduct themselves accordingly. As we have seen, this is very different from the pragmatic professional ethic in the eutopolis, when virtue was available to only those who inherited it. The disciplinary professional ethic, by contrast, emphasized ability, merit, and conduct. What is decisive about the modern professions from the point of view of citizenship is their agonistic openness for those who are willing to cultivate themselves according to their ethical principles of conduct. The fundamental difference between pragmatic and disciplinary professionalization is that while civic humanists in the fifteenth century articulated the virtues of the citizen as being unattainable by anyone but the well born, the virtues articulated by the nineteenth-century citizens are attainable by anyone as long as they are desired.

The development of solidaristic, agonistic, and alienating strategies has required the development of a sui generis professional ethic, principles and norms that members adhere to and uphold. While each profession develops an identity and norms of conduct, the articulation of these principles also results in a broadly acceptable and commensurable professional ethic across various professions because the work of the professions, their clients, their patrons, and the publics always involves the members of other professions. This intensely specific *and* universal ethic is the basis of *modern* professional-citizenship, which renders the professional ethic and its virtues as universal norms of conduct and where those who either fail or refuse to uphold these virtues are constituted as strangers and outsiders subject to reformation, cure, incarceration, imprisonment, and the like.

Disciplinary Professionalization

The formation of the professions in the twentieth century had two significant moments of transformation, which paralleled the shifts in the study of professions. In the early twentieth century, the study of professions was dominated by functionalism. Studies such as those by Carr-Saunders (1928; 1933), Parsons (1939), and Marshall (1939) focused on the functional aspects of the professions in terms of their objectives, organization, and membership. Their taxonomic approach, which persisted well into the 1960s (Goode 1960), emphasized the occupational basis of the professions and was concerned with occupational classification (Katz 1972). These studies came under attack in the 1970s for being descriptive rather than analytical. The critique focused on the negligence of the unequal power relationship between the professions and their clients, between the professions and the state, and among the professions themselves. The critique also focused on the static and evolutionary conceptions of the professions, ignoring the formation of the professions as a politico-economic process. Finally, functionalist studies were criticized for ignoring the relationship between the formation of professions and social classes (Johnson 1972). The impact of C. Wright Mills in changing the conception of professions was significant. His early studies on the rise of white-collar occupations and the power elite brought a new class perspective to bear on the formation of the professions (Mills 1951, 1956; Mills and Gerth 1942).

By the 1970s, new studies of the professions were focusing on the complex economic and political transformations involving class, state, and capitalism. Some focused on professionals constituting a new middle class, perhaps a contradictory class situation in advanced capitalism (Wright 1985). Others such as Gouldner (1979) and Konrád and Szelényi (1979) claimed that the professionals actually constituted a new class on its way to power. Still others such as Bell (1973; 1979) and Perkin (1989) claimed that in fact the rise of professions spelled an end to class-divided societies and became the dominant ideal of postmodern or postindustrial societies (Frow 1993, 1995; Szelényi and Martin 1990). Whether these groups constitute a broader class, between capital and labor, has been debated throughout the century (Szelényi and Martin 1990; Vidich 1995). Each successive wave of "classification struggles" has identified it with a label and occupational groups that ostensibly composed it. In recent years, there has been a move away from defining these new groups as a new class and toward an analysis of various professions and paraprofessions that typically occupy the new class positions. The emerging view is that because the new class is sufficiently divided among different professions, it is more fruitful to analyse it as constituent fields, rather than as one homogeneous class. Thus, the emphasis has shifted from its supposed unity to the multifarious and fluid occupations that constitute the old as well as the new professions (Longhurst and Savage 1996). Brint (1994), for example, argues that public sector professionals and private sector professionals (which Bourdieu conflates in *Distinction*) have developed different ways of being political. Similarly, Freidson argues that professional and paraprofessional occupations (which Bourdieu also conflates) or the old professions (law, medicine, academe) and the newly organized professions (accountancy, brokerage, information technology specialists) command different resources and have different powers (1994,

114). He also argues that professionals have not developed the class solidarity that was anticipated by earlier studies, but that they do display disciplinary and occupational solidarity (1994, 100). While earlier studies have undoubtedly raised significant issues, the shift toward grand themes of capitalism, state, and class diverted crucial attention from the solidaristic, agonistic, and alienating strategies and technologies through which the professions claim their autonomy and authority. Thus, more recent studies that focus on the professions as groups with distinct strategies and technologies of marketization, habitation, and cultivation of conduct are more useful in investigating how different professions appropriate capital and realize themselves as groups, rather than as a homogeneous class (Freidson 1994; Katz 1972; Kellner and Berger 1992; MacDonald 1995; Perkin 1996). From the point of view of citizenship as alterity, the question is less to explain the professions, let alone predict their trajectories, than to investigate how the professions have articulated an ideal of citizenship and constituted their strangers and outsiders by various strategies and technologies of citizenship.

Let us recall the two moments of the transformation of the professions in the twentieth century mentioned earlier, that which occurred after the 1940s and the other since the 1970s. Between the 1940s and the 1970s, the rise of disciplinary professions was significant: occupations such as medicine, law, journalism, planning, advising, policy, consulting, administration, adjudication, negotiation, inspection, investigation, and caregiving all developed strategies and technologies of citizenship that acquired state sponsorship. By contrast, since the 1970s, the rise of entrepreneurial professions such advertising, accounting, programming, management, and design has been prominent. The impact of this change on the labor force has been well documented. Many studies confirm that while managers and professionals composed about 5 percent of the labor force in the early decades of the twentieth century, by the 1990s they constituted about 30 percent of the labor force in western states. Castells (1996, 303), for example, estimates that of the total labor force, the professional, managerial, and technical occupations accounted for 29.7 percent in the United States (1991), 30.6 percent in Canada (1992), 32.08 percent in Britain (1990), 25.9 percent in France (1989), and 26.7 percent in West Germany (1987). While there is some diversity, Castells notes that there has been a common trend toward the increase of the relative weight of the professional-managerial occupations in all these states (218). Recent comparative studies confirm this trend in occupational structure (Clement and Myles 1994; Esping-Andersen 1993; Wright

1997). Similarly, the professional business services sector has grown significantly (Goldthorpe 1982; Lash and Urry 1987). The sector now accounts for about 30 percent in European and American labor markets and its growth has been consistently higher than the general rate of growth in GDP in major economies (Scott 1998).

This context is useful in investigating why modern disciplinary professions came under increasing attack from various governments for their strategies of closure, privileges, and monopoly of expertise. Various governments attacked the very heart of the modern professional ethic and its autonomy. Initially, these were interpreted as symptoms of the proletarianization of the professions in the sense that professionals were being increasingly absorbed into corporate and government bureaucracies, losing their autonomy and becoming more like salaried workers without any appreciable control of their work situation (Derber 1982). Later, the attacks on the professions were also interpreted as the death of the last vestiges of the guilds (Krause 1996). More recently, however, it became obvious that the attacks on the professions were only on certain of its segments, targeted not toward the professions as such, but toward the prevailing professional ethic, and, after twenty years, they were only partially successful (Burrage 1997; Marquand 1997; Perkin 1996). It now appears that "globalization" and "postmodernization" were inextricably linked to a shift from disciplinary to entrepreneurial professionalization (Bender 1979). It is this moment that constitutes an object of investigation for an analysis of the relationship between the cosmopolis and citizenship.

Entrepreneurial Professionalization

While cultural capital became a crucial element of disciplinary professionalization at the turn of the twentieth century, a century later, entrepreneurial professionalization in advertising, design, law, information, accounting, and marketing is related to the transformations of forms of cultural capital in professional services. As well, more and more professional commodities and services are being produced for consumers across a range of sectors, deliberately inscribed with particular meanings and associations, and produced and circulated with conscious tactics to generate desire for them among consumers. Also, industrial production itself has now come to crucially depend on such professional services. The importance of both the disciplinary and entrepreneurial professions is that they link production to consumption and cultures of production to the production of culture (Isin and Wood 1999, 125–38).

Various new occupations are making claims to autonomy, legitimacy, and credentialism, such as marketing, advertising, entertainment, new communications media, fashion, and design, and constituting themselves as professions. These occupations are rapidly emerging across various sectors providing professional goods and services, which cover a vast territory of activities, from advertising through to legal work, software design, and network design. These different fields vary dramatically in terms of their structure, as do the structures of firms competing in them. It is estimated that professional services include seven major sectors, which account for approximately 75 percent of the entire spectrum, with the remaining segment composed of a disparate collection of activities including talent agencies and architectural consulting. These major sectors are: (i) investment banking services (e.g., sales, trading, brokering services, and fund management); (ii) auditing, tax, and accountancy advisory services; (iii) commercial legal services; (iv) marketing, advertising, and communications services; (v) management and information technology consulting services; (vi) recruitment, placement, and personnel services; and (vii) market research services. Each sector includes various segments, ranging from small, flexible firms to major international corporations. Nevertheless, while the image of independent professionals dominates these sectors, in reality they are dominated by multinational service firms, in which the majority of new professionals are employed (Schmidt 2000). For example, in audit and accountancy services, five major firms dominate the world market. In advertising, more than half of world expenditure is concentrated in the hands of ten agencies (Scott 1998, 10). Typically, professional service firms organize in local, regional, and global networks. That local professional service firms generated more revenue in 1997 than regional and global firms combined shows how much of the work of globalization gets done in cities (Bourdieu 1979, 359; Scott 1998, 14).

While entrepreneurial professionalization and its strategies and technologies have not received much attention, we can turn briefly to Perkin, who provided one of its most sustained, if flawed, analyses (1989; 1996). Originally taking England as his focus, Perkin interpreted the nineteenth century as a struggle between three ideals: the aristocratic ideal of the landowning class, the entrepreneurial ideal of the manufacturing class, and the working-class ideal of the small but growing proletariat. According to Perkin, the central theme of early nineteenth-century English history may be found in the victory of the entrepreneurial ideal over the other two. By the middle of the century its triumph was complete. In that very moment, however, the seeds of its own decline were already being sown. For within the entrepreneurial ideal there had always been a tension between the interests of economic capital on the one hand, and those of the rising professions and cultural capital on the other. Paradoxically, the victory of the entrepreneurial ideal made it possible for the professions to break away from the entrepreneurial ideal. They did this in the name of an alternative professional ideal, which held that "trained and qualified expertise rather than property, capital or labour should be the chief determinant of status and power in society" (Perkin 1969, 258).

For Perkin the professional ideal succeeded in the early twentieth century much as the entrepreneurial ideal had triumphed in the early nineteenth. Just as the professional ideal became dominant, despite the continuing existence of social classes and continuing recourse to the rhetoric of class struggle, the divisions between these classes became gradually less significant, but the differences between various professional groups increased and their interests diverged. But just as the entrepreneurial ideal had started to decline at the very moment of its triumph, so the professional ideal began to lose its glitter when it had achieved moral hegemony. As "society" became more professionalized, with an ever increasing number of professional groups, the groups concerned found themselves engaged in a kind of auction in which they had to bid against each other for their share of resources. Group after group invented reasons why it was essential for the taxpayer to finance public services to meet social needs that same group had identified. The welfare state became ever more hungry for resources as an ever larger number of professional groups sought to expand their boundaries. As the economic climate grew colder and resources became scarcer, the professional groups began to bifurcate, much as the entrepreneurial groups had bifurcated in the nineteenth century. Professionals employed in the private sector came to see the profession-induced growth of the public sector as a threat to their interests; little by little, they began to desert the professional ideal in the name of which their growth had taken place. And, by an extraordinary paradox, they did so under the banner of a new version of the entrepreneurial ideal of the early nineteenth century.

For Perkin this is the foundation of the rise of new regimes of government since the 1970s, which have proclaimed their adherence to the entrepreneurial ideal of the early nineteenth century and announced their intention to reconstruct society in accordance with laissez-faire values. While their opponents assume that the new regimes mean what they proclaim, in reality they camouflage their own social interests, which are different from those of the early nineteenth-century capitalists, whose claims were justified by the entrepreneurial ideal in its original form. The bourgeoisie as owner-managers of economic capital risked their own capital, hired their own labor, invested their own energies, and took their own decisions; the entrepreneurial ideal of that era represented the interests of the bourgeoisie. In the twentieth century, however, professionals became salaried employees, skilled in the service and management of large, hierarchically organized bureaucracies that dominate markets, quite unlike the competitive market of the early nineteenth century. The new regimes appeal to laissez-faire not because they really want to return to the nineteenth century, but because laissez-faire values are the best available strategy for defeating their public sector opponents.

This account is compelling because it highlights the struggle for domination among various professional groups, rather than between two or three classes. But it is also inadequate because it has almost nothing to say about solidaristic and agonistic strategies and technologies invested by professional groups to constitute themselves as virtuous citizens and others as irrational, inexpert, and unproficient beings (Marquand 1997). Just reflecting on the meaning attributed to "unprofessionalism" may itself indicate the need to focus on the struggle between professional groups and their strangers and outsiders. By focusing exclusively on yet another grand narrative of an epic struggle between two major groups of professionals—public and private—Perkin shifts emphasis away from specific strategies and technologies through which the professions reinvent themselves, constitute their virtues as norms for aspiration, and differentiate themselves from others whom they manage to constitute as strangers and outsiders for their lack of these virtues. Without taking into account these strategies and technologies, the formation of new professional groups and their struggles become either unintelligible or irrationally driven by greed and power.

The primary focus of entrepreneurial professionalization has been to "re-engineer" the welfare state: privatizing public utilities and welfare functions; marketizing health services, social insurance, and pension schemes; marketizing colleges and universities; introducing new forms of professional management into the public service modeled upon the methods in the private sector; establishing new contractual relations between agencies and service providers and between professionals and clients; and placing a new emphasis on the personal responsibilities of individuals, their families, and their communities for their own future well-being and upon their own obligation to take active steps to secure this. My point is that a transformation from disciplinary to entrepreneurial professionalization has not only engendered the formation of new groups, but also new rationalities of government—the deliberations, strategies, tactics, and technologies employed by authorities for making up and acting upon various groups to ensure effective government (Rose 1996a).

As entrepreneurial professionalization has invented new strategies and technologies, it has gradually displaced the bourgeois work ethic with a consumption ethic. As Rose argues, this ethic cultivates a new image of the citizen: "The primary image offered to the modern citizen is not that of the producer but of the consumer. Through consumption we are urged to shape our lives by the use of our purchasing power. We are obliged to make our lives meaningful by selecting our personal lifestyle from those offered to us in advertising, soap operas, and films, to make sense of our existence by exercising our freedom to choose in a market in which one simultaneously purchases products and services, and assembles, manages, and markets oneself. The image of the citizen as a choosing self entails a new image of the productive subject" (1990, 102–3). The most significant agonistic strategies of entrepreneurial professionalization included marketization, privatization, responsibilization, and individualization. To interpret these strategies as the decline of government has been a major mistake as various studies have shown that, first, despite severe reductions in the public sector, government spending as a percentage of gross domestic product has actually continued to increase (Burrage 1997), and, second, legislation has increased exponentially (Loughlin 1996). While entrepreneurial professionalization may have changed modalities and domains of government by virtue of new strategies and technologies, that does not mean that the will to govern and its practices have declined.

Moreover, entrepreneurial professionalization has restructured the relationship between knowledge and being political. While disciplinary professionalization had given a central role to knowledge by virtue of raising claims to truth and validity in fields such as education, health, and planning, the legitimacy and authority of new knowledges do not derive from their truth and validity, but from their ability to gauge performance (Rose 1996b, 1996c). The shift of focus from disciplinary occupations of law, medicine, and academe to new occupations involving consultancy, accountancy, and audit is associated with that change (Starr 1987). If the modes of production of knowledges that activated disciplinary strategies and technologies of citizenship were verity, validity, and reliability, the new modes of production are enumeration, calculation, monitoring, and evaluation (Stehr 1994). Modern universities that educated and trained cadres of disciplinary professionals in law, medicine, and administration are now shifting to entrepreneurial occupations. In addition, the new occupations shift their focus from the patient, the ill, and the poor to the client and consumer, who are constituted as autonomous individuals capable of making the right choices (Brint 1994). Entrepreneurial professionalization constitutes the individual not as a subject of intervention, but as an active agent of decisions and choice: risk reduction becomes an individual, rather than a collective, responsibility. This is a significant change in the production of subjectivities in that instead of disciplines, the field of choices and its structure become a contested arena of political struggle. This is partly why the new media have come to play such a significant role in politics (Morley and Robins 1995). Solidaristic and agonistic technologies associated with these strategies involve quasi-autonomous "nongovernmental" organizations and the shifting of responsibilities from governmental agencies and authorities to organizations without electoral accountability and responsibility (e.g., the "privatization" of "public" utilities, civil service, prisons, insurance, and security). For both citizens and authorities this opens up the delivery of services as an agonistic game in which to compete, rather than as a solidaristic expectation. As individuals are now constituted as active purchasers and enterprisers in pursuit of their own choices, vouchers in education, housing, and other services replace "paternal" forms of distribution. Just as avoiding risk becomes the responsibility of individuals as authors of their own destiny, ill-fate and misfortune also become the responsibility of individuals: the unemployed, the homeless, and the poor are constituted as responsible for their own condition.

What Brint (1994, 204) has characterized as a change from "social trustee professionalism" to "expert professionalism" or what can be considered as a transformation from disciplinary to entrepreneurial professionalization does not eradicate or lessen the powers of modern occupations, but reveals how the invention of new fields of expertise also restructure old occupations.

As both disciplinary and entrepreneurial professions invent and assemble unique solidaristic, agonistic, and alienating strategies and technologies of citizenship, they nonetheless rely upon three common strategies: mediatization, concealment, and universalization.

First, arising from the mobilization of cultural capital, the professions produce categories and objects of perception that permeate social life. The mediatization of entertainment, sports, and news spectacles, produced by professionals, disseminates certain ethics and orientations toward the world, which are then incorporated by other groups as ways of seeing not only the world, but also themselves in that world. Those who adopt, possess, or invent different ways of seeing and being in the world become strangers and outsiders. Second, disciplinary and entrepreneurial professions constitute themselves as both interpreters and legislators of the social issues they have mediatized. This twofold orientation often conceals the difference between the targets and the benefits of government. The targets of government arise when the professions are implicated in questions of government by virtue of strategies and technologies they propose for solving these questions. The benefits of government also arise when the professions propose solutions, but with the aim of establishing their professions, or specific segments of them, as legitimate, useful, and productive pursuits. To put it another way, it is very difficult to untangle strategies and technologies that professions assemble to form and govern themselves from those assembled to constitute and govern others. Third, as the professions govern themselves, they reorient virtues that arise from governing themselves toward governing others. Thus, the virtues of being a professional gradually permeate the virtues of being a citizen and the vices of being a stranger, an outsider, and an alien. If a significant number of entrepreneurial professionals find that their cultural capital enables them to be flexible in their routine production of services, "being flexible" becomes gradually mediatized into a new way of being in a "postmodern" world. Virtues that arise from professional conduct become universalized as virtues of being.

These unique and common strategies and technologies of citizenship arising from entrepreneurial professionalization await genealogical investigations, but our focus here shifts to the cosmopolis, where the professions claim their rights to the city.

Cosmopolis, Professions, Citizenship

The professions, like the guilds, develop spatial strategies and technologies to realize themselves in material space. First, *spatialization:* their jurisdictions, often negotiated with the state and constructed through their clients and publics, constitute a contested space over which they stake their authority. It is within this space that they negotiate their autonomy and heteronomy. Durkheim thought that the solidaristic strategies of the professions were aspatial. That thought can be called into question. While their jurisdictions typically may not overlap with the existing boundaries of cities and regions, the organization and functioning of the professions have involved intensely spatial strategies and technologies. Second, *socialization:* the agonistic strategies and technologies that the professions and disciplines practice require "assemblages," such as conferences, workshops, shows, symposia, and colloquia, that by and large take place in cities and that assemble together their members, clients, patrons, and publics. The members of the professions assemble in these events to socialize, network, habituate, exchange knowledge, and emulate certain practices. But they also construct their markets, clients, patrons, and publics through these assemblages. Any occupational group aspiring to constitute itself as a profession would need a strong presence in such assemblages. The city is therefore not only a strategic space of production and consumption of professional services, skills, and expertise, but also a space for the reproduction of professionalism as its habitus. To construct these markets, the professions must display their knowledges to establish the distinction of their expertise in intensely agonistic strategies. Third, *objectification:* the city itself is an object of professional expertise, engendering design, planning, engineering, and building professions. We have seen earlier how disciplinary professions constituted designing spaces conducive to appropriate working-class conduct as their specific claim to expertise. We shall see later how entrepreneurial professions have constituted generating healthy and civil habitats as their expertise. Fourth, *habitation:* the city is also a "natural" habitat for the members of the professions. The professions seek their rights to the city not only as their market and jurisdiction, but also as their habitat in the sense that they appropriate spaces in the city for the accumulation of economic, symbolic, and cultural capital (Featherstone 1992, 1995; Zukin 1995). The relationship between the city as their natural habitat and the professional ethic is an ambiguous, or even an enigmatic relationship.

Given these strategies, it is not surprising to observe that as the authorities that grant rights and regulate obligations to professional bodies are becoming increasingly global, the professions are increasingly organized locally through cosmopolises. That several professions including law, accountancy, architecture, and engineering are authorized globally but organized locally is becoming apparent (Aharoni 1993; Brennan 1979; Dezalay and Sugarman 1995; Halliday and Karpik 1997; Larson 1993; Perkin 1996). Accordingly, the solidaristic and agonistic strategies that the professions articulate increasingly implicate their identities in international and global networks. But this does not mean that the new professionals form a cosmopolitan or transnational "elite." While professions are being reorganized globally, they still need municipal and national jurisdictional regulation, networks, credentialing, and training (Beaverstock 1996). Moreover, some professions such as primary and secondary teaching, nursing, and counseling are authorized and organized locally and inculcate localizing virtues among their members. Nonetheless, quite similar to the cosmopolitanism of the mercenaries and artisans in the ancient polis or the lawyers in Christianopolis or the engineers and architects in the eutopolis, the new professions are broadening their networks and constructing transnational markets and publics of authority. The consequence of this, while still incipient, cannot be underestimated for citizenship. The professions are acquiring certain forms of authority as globally organized entrepreneurial guilds. While there has been considerable debate over the "globalization" or "postmodernization" of citizenship, so far the relationship between entrepreneurial professionalization and globalization has not been adequately explored by empirical research (Bourdieu and Wacquant 1999).

These issues have become increasingly relevant in the literature on the global city, though processes of professionalization have remained latent in it. While the debate originally focused on the organization of international finance in cities, it has gradually included labor markets and immigration (Friedmann 1986, 1995; Friedmann and Wolff 1982; Sassen 1991). Most cogently, Saskia Sassen argued that introducing the city into the analysis of globalization "allows us to recover the concrete, localized processes through which globalization exists and to argue that much of multiculturalism in large cities is as much a part of globalization as is international finance" (1996b, 208).

The city under globalization is generally defined as a node within a network of flows of capital and labor (Castells 1996, 384; Sassen 1991, 3–4). These flows permeate the established boundaries of the nation-state and build intensities that do not map onto these political boundaries. Thus, for Sassen, "The space constituted by the global grid of cities, a space with new economic and political potentialities, is perhaps one of the most strategic spaces for the formation of transnational identities and communities. This is a space that is both place-centered in that it is embedded in particular and strategic locations; and it is transterritorial because it connects sites that are not geographically proximate yet are intensely connected to each other" (1996b, 221). Or in the words of Castells, "The global city is not a place, but a process. A process by which centers of production and consumption of advanced services, and their ancillary local societies, are connected in a global network, while simultaneously downplaying the linkages with their hinterlands, on the basis of information flows" (1996, 386).

By serving as concentrations of the *servicing* and *financing* of international trade, investment, and headquarter operations, the city becomes a focus of the globalization of labor (Sassen 1996b, 210). Thus, "Understanding [immigration and ethnicity] as a set of processes whereby global elements are *localized*, international labor markets are constituted, and cultures from all over the world are de- and re-territorialized, puts them right there at the center along with internationalization of capital as a fundamental aspect of globalization" (220). The city therefore becomes a new site of conflicts over resources, representation, and rights: "The city has indeed emerged as a site for new claims: by global capital which uses the city as an 'organizational commodity,' but also by disadvantaged sectors of the urban population, which in large cities are frequently as internationalized a presence as capital" (208). We therefore "see a new geography of centrality and marginality. The downtowns of global cities and metropolitan business centers receive massive investments in real estate and telecommunications while low-income city areas are starved for resources. Highly educated workers employed in leading sectors see their incomes rise to unusually high levels while low- or medium-skilled workers in those same sectors see theirs sink" (214).

While this debate has been useful in drawing attention to the relationship between globalization and the city, it has relied upon a simple class conflict: the dominant, often called the elites, are employed in professional-managerial occupations, especially in the financial sector, and the dominated are employed in clerical and manual occupations. As Kofman argues, the debate has been marked by a reductionist view that sees city centers "as the battleground between the upper middle classes, on the one hand, and the younger, educated countercultures that occupy the interstices of the urban fabric, on the other," adding that cities "also house areas of immigrant concentrations" (1998, 284). For Kofman, "Whatever theoretical framework is followed, the core idea is a restructuring of capitalism that expels the middle strata from the city and leads, on the one hand, to the expansion of higher-level professional and managerial classes and, on the other, to increasingly precarious and informal activities at the lower end, filled disproportionately by women and immigrants" (279).

Indeed, this core idea seems to have pervaded the debate right from its inception (Knox 1993). For Friedmann and Wolff, "The primary social fact about world city formation is the polarization of its class divisions" (1982, 322). But what kind of divisions? It seems that there is a "global" or "transnational" elite that controls the global city (Castells 1989, 1996; Cox 1997; Friedmann 1995, 25–26; Sassen 1991). Or, in Sassen's words,

"New conditions of growth have contributed to elements of a new class alignment in global cities—[composed] of a high-income stratum and a low-income stratum" (1991, 13). Or, in Castells's words, "Articulation of the elites, segmentation and disorganization of the masses seem to be the twin mechanisms of social domination in our societies. Space plays a fundamental role in this mechanism. In short: elites are cosmopolitan, people are local" (1996, 415).

Similarly, the city is marked by increasing inequities in life opportunities. "We can see this effect, for example, in the unusually sharp increase in the starting salaries of business and law school graduates who succeed in entering top firms, and in the precipitous fall in the wages of low-skilled manual workers and clerical workers" (Sassen 1996b, 211). These income disparities translate into social disparities: while there are new city users who make claims on the city and constitute strategic spaces of the city in their image, there are those who use urban political violence to make their claims on the city, claims that lack the de facto legitimacy enjoyed by the new city users. "These are claims made by actors struggling for recognition and entitlement, claiming their right to the city" (222).

For Sassen, "The center now concentrates immense economic and political power, power that rests on the capability for global control and apability to produce superprofits. And actors with little economic and traditional political power have become an increasingly strong presence through the new politics of culture and identity, and an emergent transnational politics embedded in the new geography of economic globalization. Both actors, increasingly transnational and in contestation, find in the city the strategic terrain for their operations. But it is hardly the terrain of a balanced playing field" (223–24). For Castells, "The new managerial-technocratic-political elite does create exclusive spaces, as segregated and removed from the city at large as the bourgeois quarters of the industrial society, but, because the professional class is larger, on a much larger scale" (1996, 401). For Lash and Urry, "[T]he new lower class represents a sort of structural downward mobility for substantial sections of the organized-capitalist working class, as well as a set of structural social places in which large numbers of immigrants flow. . . . The new lower class takes its place at the bottom of a restructured stratificational ladder in which the hierarchy of capital and labour is replaced by a three-tiered ordering—a mass class of professional-managerial types (alongside a very small capitalist class), a smaller and comparatively under-resourced working class, and this new lower class" (1994, 145–46).

These metaphors of hierarchy, center, stratification, polarization, elites, and even class are inadequate for interpreting the cosmopolis as a space through which various groups struggle to constitute themselves, to gain recognition, and to accumulate different forms of capital, and for interpreting how they are implicated in various strategies and technologies of citizenship. The way each group struggles for or against dominance varies from city to city precisely because the combination of different forms of capital that are accessible or available varies from city to city and from neighborhood to neighborhood. As we shall see below, four professions that have undergone transformations—law, accountancy, academe, and architecture—appropriate the city and articulate their rights to it with different combinations of spatialization, socialization, objectification, and habitation strategies.

Dealing in Virtue: Postmodern Podestà

As we have seen, law was already a guildic profession in Christianopolis. It was a strategic profession for the patriciate to maintain its dominance (Berman 1983). We have also seen the *podestà*, that unique Italian legal technology that arbitrated conflicts within cities among various groups and their rival factions. Law has always been able to legitimate itself on the basis of its disinterestedness and objectivity and its arbitration function has served its purpose well. We have also seen above the importance of the statization of law and its implication in the question of governability. Law and the state implicated each other perhaps more than any other profession in modernity. Yet, law has been one of the most successful professions under the pressures of globalization and postmodernization. At one level, this is not surprising since law was inherently cosmopolitan in its origins. However, its statization made the legal profession an intensely national rather than a transnational profession. But in the last two decades law has been intensely globalized and now some speak about the rise of a transnational legal order (Arthurs 1997).

There is a growing literature on the globalization of law, but Yves Dezalay demands our attention for his latent account of how the work of the globalization of law gets done in cities. For Dezalay, while it is true that economic and cultural globalization is restructuring the professions and the ways in which the "elites" operate in them, the result is not a depoliticization, but a new form of politicization where the production and marketing of expertise become new stakes (1995, 1). The market for expertise in national and international regulation is going through a tremendous growth. By selling their services as consultants, the merchants of norms and rules successfully conceal that this growth ensures their own prosperity and invests in their own future. "Who better than they to guide enterprises through the complex quagmire of rules and institutions, national as well as international, that overlap and very often clash?" (2–3). However, the authority of the legal experts in international relations reflects in effect what they can command within their own national spheres as well as in their international networks (4). This is why "globalization" is as much an agonistic strategy as a description of reality. Dezalay urges that one can no longer study the emergence of norms or, more broadly, the regulation of economic activity, without taking into account the transformation of the mode of the production of law. In other words, "analyses of regulation and the sociology of the professions can no longer continue to co-exist in ignorance of one another as they have done until recently" (6).

For Dezalay and Garth, globalization does not merely take place within transnational space, which is, in fact, a virtual space that provides strategic opportunities for competitive struggles engaged in by "national" actors. Taking as their focus the globalization of the legal profession in commercial arbitration, Dezalay and Garth explore how this specific professional market has been constructed since the 1970s. The outlines of their analysis are familiar to students of the legal profession, especially in the last few decades: that international commercial arbitration took off in the 1970s, forcing legal firms to compete in the international arena; that multinational firms prefer to resolve their disputes via private arbitration rather than meeting each other in their respective national courts; and that by the 1990s international commercial arbitration had become one of the major businesses. Yet the way they analyze these transformations and their dynamics has two principal consequences for citizenship: the competitive strategies constitute a specific conception of strangers and outsiders that goes well beyond national boundaries and even cultures; and these strategies are articulated in and through a few cosmopolises well suited to attract major arbitration business.

Working as "merchants of law" and "moral entrepreneurs," international arbitrators engage in mostly glamorous and very well paid cases in cosmopolises such as Paris or Geneva and lead distinct, professional lifestyles. Like the *podestà* of Italian cities in the twelfth century, they deal in virtue in that they are selected for their judgment, neutrality, and expertise. Their symbolic and cultural capital includes academic standing, practical experience, training in alternative dispute resolution, connections to business and political power, and proficiency and skill in both syntactical and tactical aspects of arbitration practice (Dezalay and Garth 1996,

19). For Dezalay and Garth, "The competition, however, is not simply a matter of striving for business by offering better services. International commercial arbitration is a symbolic field, and therefore the competitive battles that take place within it are fought in symbolic terms among moral entrepreneurs" (33). The struggles for legitimacy and credibility result not only in constructing markets and careers, but also in enhancing the legitimacy and credibility of international legal practices and their institutions.

The two key sources of conflict in these struggles are between grand notables and upstart technocratic professionals and between academics and practitioners. The grand notables are the European legal elites, imbued with traditional values and academic distinction for whom arbitration is a duty, not a career. The young technocrats are drawn largely from large and growing Anglo-American law firms, who see an expanding market for their professional services and emphasize their technical expertise, gained mostly in large American law schools. They are critical of idealism and the traditionalism of the grand notables and see themselves as entrepreneurs. Dezalay and Garth quote a leading member of the new generation whose words succinctly articulate not only the transformation in the international legal field, but also the broader transformation of the professions from the disciplinary to the entrepreneurial professional ethic we discussed earlier: "[T]he age of innocence has come to an end ... [and] the subject has inevitably lost some of its charm. Once the delightful discipline of a handful of academic *aficionados* on the fringe of international law, it has become a matter of serious concern for great numbers of professionals determined to master a process because it is essential to their business. They labor, but not for love" (1996, 37). Obviously, this conflict spills over to the conflict between academics, who are most interested in building a body of international commercial law, the *lex mercatoria,* and practitioners, who promote the virtues of solid case law and thorough analysis of "facts."

But both of these struggles are relational in the sense that each group needs the other. While routinizing charisma, the young generation still appeals to the grand notables and their sense of craft. Similarly, practitioners still need the appeal of academic learning symbolized by degrees and publications. The opposition and dependence between these different groups structures the field of arbitration, creating a dynamic that has allowed the field to expand. These struggles also structure the patterns through which specific legal cultures and cities are articulated into the field. The ascendance of Paris as the premier center of international arbitration, for example, may appear paradoxical. As we have seen, being associated with insurgency and revolution, Paris developed a rather uneasy and distant relationship with economic capital. French legal culture and international business culture do not seem like good partners. Not anymore. As Dezalay and Garth illustrate, Paris, where the International Chamber of Commerce is located, has become a major center for international commercial arbitration. While the reasons are complex, not surprisingly they are connected to its relations with London. Since 1979, London has been spearheading a major transformation of English law and radically internationalizing it. To compete with the ascendancy of London, American legal firms have chosen Paris for their European operations for historical and cultural reasons. Similarly, cities such as Stockholm, Cairo, and Hong Kong began playing new roles in attracting international arbitration business. Although not explicitly argued by Dezalay and Garth, it becomes obvious that the markets and careers for international commercial arbitration and the legal field with which it is associated are made in the cosmopolises. Or more accurately, the cosmopolis is that space through which transnational professionals construct their markets and, in turn, by which transnational professionals are being produced.

Obviously, this is a simplistic account of both Dezalay and Garth, as well as the transnationalization of law. But it does illustrate how important it is to approach the cosmopolis not as an already constituted container through the established categories of perception, such as "globalization" and "postmodernization," but as a difference machine being assembled by groups that are constructing it both as a symbolic and a material space through various strategies and technologies of otherness that constitute new forms of citizenship.

Auditing Auditors: Accountability

We have seen above how the Florentine *popolo* had demanded an audit of the fiscal administration of the city. While hardly resembling the conditions that led to such demands, one of the most significant beneficiaries and instigators of entrepreneurial professionalization has been the accounting profession. For Michael Power, the "audit explosion" in the 1980s and early 1990s, when the word *audit* began to be used in Britain with growing frequency in a wide variety of contexts, is a symptom of this change. During this period, in addition to its traditional use to indicate financial audit, the word acquired broader meaning, encompassing a variety of fields such as environmental audit, management audit, forensic audit, data audit, intellectual property audit, medical audit, teaching audit, and performance audit (Power 1997, 3). Power argues that audit is as much an idea as a concrete technology and that is why its usage remains ambiguous. The audit society refers to the tendencies revealed by these commitments, rather than an objectively definable state of affairs. The ambiguity of auditing is not a methodological problem, but a substantive fact (6). The audit explosion has its roots in a programmatic restructuring of organizational life and a new rationality of government. The audit increasingly creates a society where trust gives way to distrust and judgment becomes routinized, managerial, and abstract. Other cultures of performance evaluation that do not fit the image of abstract, systematic, and impartial auditing are distrusted. But Power shows that auditing is just as biased and selective as other systems of evaluation and that the effectiveness of auditing itself needs to be evaluated (13). The audit explosion is far from contributing to democracy. Many audit reports communicate little more than the fact that an audit has been done and the reader is left to decode specialized and cautious expressions of opinion. Rather than providing a basis for informed dialogue and discussion, audits demand that their efficacy be trusted. "The audit society is a society that endangers itself because it invests too heavily in shallow rituals of verification at the expense of other forms of organizational intelligence" (123).

Maybe so. But to interpret the proliferation of auditing technologies as heralding a new "society" is a mistake in that it conflates technologies that professions assemble to form and govern themselves with those they assemble to constitute and govern others: auditing technologies that promise efficiency, productivity, and accountability are as much about achieving these objectives as about valorizing these technologies to claim expertise and authority. In fact, the more accountants valorize accountability, the less they themselves become so since there are no technologies forthcoming to audit the auditors. The global growth of accountancy should therefore be interpreted as much as the success of these technologies as their failure (Hanlon 1994, 1997). Or, rather, the success that defines these technologies may be their incessant failure as a provocation to government. That accountancy has been transformed into a major global industry in the past two decades and has experienced a major monopolization and centralization ought to be interpreted against this background. Accordingly, that five or six multinational firms dominate the entire global industry in accountancy and consultancy services and that these firms organize through the cosmopolis by constructing markets for their services, recruiting and reproducing professionals and constructing publics, are matters awaiting further genealogical investigations.

Homo Academicus: Professionalizing Disciplines

Those who can undertake such investigations are themselves increasingly interpellated into entrepreneurial professionalization (Bourdieu and Wacquant 1999). Earlier we have seen that medieval universities engendered a peculiar form of cosmopolitanism. Situated within the intensely localized loyalties and bonds of medieval cities such as Paris, Bologna, Oxford, and Cambridge, scholars were nonetheless drawn from various cities across Europe. The scholars were therefore regarded skeptically as strangers of the city, without any apparent internal bonds with it. Yet they did have internal bonds with the city and the intensely competitive culture of the city would not have survived without the lawyers, theologians, and later humanists that the universities produced. We have seen, for example, the role of the *podestà* in Italian cities in resolving conflicts and its "postmodern" counterpart more recently. We have also seen how the modern university adjusted and responded to the growth of the professions between the 1880s and the 1920s and became the site of the production of professional knowledge and the reproduction of the professional ethic and ideal via disciplines. For Bender this was also the period in which civic professionalism was replaced by disciplinary professionalism, through which the professions severed their ties to the city and aligned themselves with the state (1979). While the modern university was typically located in the city, it was not of the city in the sense that it turned its back to the city (Bender 1998). This was in a sense a reflection of its ambiguous roots: unlike other professions, the academic profession, while its claim to capital rests on its ability to educate and train professionals, is also a profession in itself (Burrage, Jarausch, and Siegrist 1990). By turning away from the city and aligning itself with the state, the academic profession aligned its productive function with disciplinary professionalization rather than its civic role, its heteronomy rather than its autonomy.

While this served the university well in terms of accumulating different forms of capital between the 1940s and the 1970s, since then entrepreneurial professionalization has transformed the university dramatically. Like their counterparts in the professions, some disciplines have done quite well adjusting to entrepreneurial professionalization. Traditional disciplines such as law (as we have seen above) and architecture (as we shall see below) responded exceptionally well to "globalization." Also, various disciplines in engineering and the sciences have become increasingly globalized. But certain subjects in law, medicine, and especially the social sciences and humanities, born of disciplinary professionalization, are struggling with their identities. While this is most visible in Britain and America, other states are following suit. For Bender, for the university to become of the city its distinctive culture must be brought into dialogue with the city (1998, 24–25). "By reorienting academic culture from the nation to the metropolis, and from national cultures to the metropolitan cultures in which universities are deeply implicated, one might thereby acquire important new resources for the making of the pluralized public culture that must be constructed in the coming generation" (27). While there are signs of a reorientation of the university to the city, unfortunately this is happening via entrepreneurial professionalization. As the universities are pressured to adjust from disciplinary to entrepreneurial professionalization, both from within and without, they are inventing globalizing strategies by making links with their host cities as agents for the incubation of knowledge products (Currie and Newson 1998). There has been a large literature on the incubating role of universities and cities in encouraging high-technology firms and the "knowledge economy" (Castells and Hall 1994). Each university is attempting to develop expertise in professional fields and collaborate with firms to marketize its knowledge, especially in biotechnological, environmental, and high-tech industries. Traditional universities such as Cambridge and Oxford are rapidly turning into incubators of entrepreneurial professionalization, as reflected in the host cities and the universities themselves, and in the shifting of investment away from the modern disciplines. Thus, entrepreneurial professionalization is engendering a new relationship between the city and the university as both increasingly become focused on expertise rather than discipline (Rhoades and Slaughter 1998; Slaughter and Leslie 1997). It is also engendering new images of academics as "public" intellectuals who, in one version, become comfortable with the marketization of knowledge through advising, consulting, or mediating their expertise in cameo appearances on radio and television, and, in another version, as intellectuals who symbolically identify themselves with strangers and outsiders (nomads, bohemians, immigrants, refugees), while enjoying all the privileges that their professional-citizen status brings (Pels 1999).

Building Thoughts, Architecting Citizens

Architecture and its allied professions in building cities such as planning, design, engineering, and construction are of special concern because they directly take the city as their object of expertise (see Blau, La Gory, and Pipkin 1983; Knox 1988). For Larson, "This is not only because a majority of architects work in cities but also because it is in cities that architecture, in theory, becomes public—a public space, a public good, and publicly visible" (1993, 70). As we have seen, nationalization and statization were effective strategies in the formation of modern architecture in Europe and America (see also Larson 1983). After the French, American, and industrial revolutions, architecture was organized rather rapidly as a profession. The transformations of architecture broadly parallel the other professions, such as the academic and legal professions. Modern architecture was a nationalist project. The ascendant bourgeoisie in the nineteenth century sought to establish a visible identity for itself in a space dominated by the lineages of the aristocracy and monarchy. In Europe and its colonies, bourgeois architects built an elegant New World in their image. The main professional battle architecture waged was against engineering, which became the flagship profession for embodying and displaying the marvels of industrial capitalism via magnificent constructions ranging from bridges to buildings. Henceforth architecture had to contend with the difference machine and its acknowledged symbolic master, the engineer. For architecture to establish an identity for itself, it had to shift its emphasis away from technological skills to design and style, away from mechanics to aesthetics (Larson 1993, 25). This shift enabled the profession to reinvent a past that connected it with the disciplinary professionalism of the mid-nineteenth century and the concern with the condition of the working classes and their housing. But it was not until the 1920s and 1930s that this new identity was forged successfully. Much has been written about the causes of the rise of modernism in architecture in Europe and its transplantation to America. For Larson (1993) the important point is that modernism in architecture originated as a social democratic project and was deeply embedded in the rise of the modern welfare state. From Le Corbusier and Walter Gropius to Alvar Aalto and Ludwig Mies van der Rohe, modern architects cast their projects in the service of the state and capitalism and expressed in them a desire to help construct a new society and a new way of life: virtues of disciplinary professionalization (Larson 1993, 31–32). Modernist architecture constituted urban space as a totality and was concerned with its radical transformation in the service of a new society: this was the reincarnation of the dream of the ideal city as the dream of the mastery of its principles as a difference machine.

If the origins of modernism in Europe were social democratic, its Americanization after the Second World War was another story. The uses of modernism to build massive housing projects, glass towers, and suburbs are considered a subversion of modernism (Ghirardo 1996). Nonetheless, the professional ethic that motivated these projects, building a society anew, was similar.

These technocratic, rational, and patronizing strategies for building cities carried within themselves the seeds of their destruction. The modernism of Europe in the 1920s had sought to blend aesthetic innovation with economic rationality, overcoming the dominated role of the architect in bourgeois culture. But in the 1950s the architect was transformed into an expert in aesthetics and social engineering. Beginning in the 1960s, architects and their allied professions came under attack from both within and without. From within, a new generation of architects realized both the consequences of a modernist professional ethic and the blockages it created via its failures, which became all too visible in American and European cities. From without, critics such as Jane Jacobs and Lewis Mumford, despite their differences, expressed the increasing realization that the disciplinary professions had a totalizing effect on the city.

By the 1970s this critique crystallized in postmodernism as a movement. Like early modernism, early postmodernism was carrying promising premises: it reacted against the rationalizing and totalizing discourses of modernism, its patronizing, disciplinary professional ethic, its elitism, and its disregard for the spontaneity, diversity, organicism, and disorder of the city. But this critique overlapped and coincided with the shift toward entrepreneurial professionalization. This coincidence and overlap should not be interpreted in any simple cause and effect manner, but rather as the complex articulation between entrepreneurial professionalization and other movements, which simultaneously contributed to the acceleration of both. By the 1990s, the underlying professional ethic of architecture was transformed from building cities to that of building objects and from planning to design. Larson provides an account of how the shift in its professional ethic was accompanied by shifts in the organizations and associations of architecture (1993, 52–59). Above all, the most important consequence of postmodernization and the globalization of architecture has been its renewed emphasis on clientelism, functionalism, polysemism, and symbolism: in its transformation from disciplinary professionalization, where it promised a new social order, to entrepreneurial professionalization, where it was primarily concerned with aestheticization, architecture became oriented toward its clients and their fragmented desires and objectives (Stevens 1998). The profession was now infused with a new functionalism through which it promised to respond to the needs of its clients, protesting against any unitary or unified ethics or purpose. Instead it sought multiple and playful meanings and began seeing its value in building objects with aesthetic and symbolic, as well as functional value for clients. There was accordingly a massive change in the clientele of architecture from state institutions to corporations.

The study of architecture as a profession understood not simply as art, but as a social and politically embedded group has begun astonishingly recently (Stevens 1998, 17). There are rational reasons behind this lack of interest in architecture as a profession, reasons that stem from one of its most effective strategies for constituting itself as an autonomous art (see also Crinson and Lubbock 1994; Ghirardo 1991). To adequately understand the cosmopolis and how specific groups articulate claims to it, it will be necessary to undertake genealogical investigations into how architecture constitutes itself as a profession, how it develops strategies and technologies of citizenship, and how it constitutes the city simultaneously as its object, habitat, jurisdiction, and socialization, as well as how it constitutes itself, strangers, and outsiders.

Becoming Strangers: Encounters with Citizens

As the professions restructure themselves, incorporate newer occupations, and establish rights to the city, they constitute their strangers and outsiders by inventing new agonistic and alienating technologies of citizenship. Many groups have been classified, labeled, problematized, and constituted as objects of sympathy, empathy, hatred, reformation, elimination, fear, danger, virtue, vice, regulation, incorporation, assimilation, segregation, and emulation by governing authorities with claims to expertise. That these strategies and technologies of citizenship are closely associated with a particular will to govern has been emphasized effectively (Cruikshank 1999; Rose 1999). That, however, these strategies and technologies arise in the context of and are inextricably associated with the constitution of the professions as the new guilds and of professionals as the new virtuous citizens through the cosmopolis is my specific concern. While some scholars focus on technologies of citizenship without focusing on their embeddedness in games of citizenship such as domination, subjectification, and estrangement, others focus on the formation of these groups through "insurgent practices," valorizing them without illustrating their embeddedness in these strategies and technologies of citizenship. Both approaches, therefore, effectively assume that the formation of the professions and their strangers and outsiders are separate domains. While the new strangers and outsiders of the cosmopolis may be refusing to appropriate the imposed language of journalists, intellectuals, professionals, managers, and academics, instead inventing new languages and dialects and hence developing agonistic strategies, these strategies are not divorced from their encounters with the professions and their strategies and technologies of citizenship (Holston 1998). It has been widely discussed that new cultural politics of ecological and feminist movements, gay and lesbian rights, immigrants, and the poor are among the new agents claiming new rights to the city (Beall 1997; Wekerle 1999; Brown 1997). Also, that new diasporas of immigrant groups are emerging in the cosmopolis, advancing claims for citizenship understood as the rights to the city itself has been documented (Isin 2000b). Finally, it has also been emphasized that, across the globe, new networks are emerging, which once again are passing through regulations and impositions and creating their own rather loosely defined, fluid, inventive, and *cosmopolitan* networks (Riberio 1998). These developments eventuated the use of the term *cosmopolis* as an image that mirrors the city as a space of "diversity" (Soja 2000, 229–32).

For Sandercock, the image of cosmopolis suggests diversity, which is partly a consequence of the transnationalization of labor (Sandercock 1998, 204). For Holston, this "includes both highly skilled and unskilled immigrants: it produces a new set of class fractions in the city of high-income capital managers and the low-income manual and service workers who attend them" (Holston and Appadurai 1996, 198). But Holston emphasizes that "both the elite and the subaltern mark urban space with new and insurgent forms of the social—that these forms are not, in other words, limited to the latter" (Holston 1998, 48 n. 8). "Among the most vocal critics of liberal citizenship in this sense are groups organized around specific identities—the kind of prior differences liberalism relegates to the private sphere—which affirm the importance of these identities in the public calculus of citizenship" (Holston and Appadurai 1996, 193). Thus, they affirm the "right to difference" as an integral part of the foundation of citizenship. For Holston, "Although this kind of demand would seem contradictory and incompatible with citizenship as an ideology of equality, there is nevertheless a growing sense that it is changing the meaning of equality itself. What it objects to is the equation that equality means sameness" (Holston and Appadurai 1996, 195). With these struggles, "right becomes more of a claim upon than a possession held against the world. It becomes a claim upon society for the resources necessary to meet the basic needs and interests of members rather than a kind of property some possess and others do not. It is probably the case that this change applies mostly to socio-economic and political rights rather than to civil rights. . . . But in terms of rights to the city and rights to political participation, right becomes conceived as an aspect of social relatedness rather than as an inherent and natural property of individuals" (Holston and Appadurai 1996, 197). Formal citizenship is neither necessary nor a sufficient condition for substantive citizenship. The new claims to citizenship are new, and not only because they force the state to respond to new social conditions. They are also new because they create new kinds of right, based on the exigencies of lived experience, outside of the normative and institutional definitions of the state and its codes (Holston 1998, 52).

While the city becomes an arena where these new forms of citizenship are created, it is also a war zone for this very reason: the dominant classes meet the advance of these new citizens with new strategies of segregation, privatization, and fortification (Holston 1998, 52; Holston and Appadurai 1996, 200). "These sites vary with time and place. Today, in many cities, they include the realm of the homeless, networks of migration, neighbourhoods of Queer Nation, constructed peripheries in which the poor build their own homes in precarious material and legal conditions, ganglands, fortified condominiums, employee-owned factories, squatter settlements, suburban migrant labour camps, sweatshops, and the zones of the so-called new racism. They are sites of insurgence because they introduce into the city new identities and practices that disturb established histories" (Holston 1998, 48) "These insurgent forms are found both in organized grassroots mobilizations and in everyday practices that, in different ways, empower, parody, derail, or subvert state agendas. They are found, in other words, in struggles over what it means to be a member of the modern state—which is why I refer to them with the term *citizenship*. Membership in the state has never been a static identity, given the dynamics of global migrations and national ambitions. Citizenship changes as new members emerge to advance their claims, expanding its realm, and as new forms of segregation and violence counter these advances, eroding it. The sites of insurgent citizenship are found at the intersection of these processes of expansion and erosion" (Holston 1998, 47–48).

For Sandercock, "A new city is emerging, and it is not one with which the modernizers identify. This is the city of cultural difference" (1998, 175). "We need to start understanding our cities as bearers of our intertwined fates. We need to formulate within our city a shared notion of a common destiny. We need to see our city as the locus of citizenship, and to recognize multiple levels of citizenship as well as multiple levels of common destiny, from the city to the nation to transnational citizenship possibilities. We need to see our city and its multiple communities as spaces where we connect with the cultural other who is now our neighbour" (182–83). "The modern project of the nation state emphasized unity and sameness over difference and diversity. The rise of multiculturalism as a political force is a sign of the failure of that modernist project. The cities and regions of the future must nurture difference and diversity through a democratic cultural pluralism" (183). "If cultural imperialism and systemic violence are features of contemporary global urban and regional changes, then a politics of difference is a prerequisite for confronting these oppressions. A politics of difference is a politics based on the identity, needs, and rights of specific groups who are victims of any faces of oppression" (185). "A rejection of the ideal of the homogeneous community as part of the future cosmopolis leads us into an investigation of the idea of *multiple publics,* together constituting some form of civic culture, as a basis for the survival of a culturally pluralist form of cities and regions" (195). For Sandercock, cosmopolis is "an always unfinished and contested construction site, one characterized above all by its space for difference" (199). "At the moment these global forces and top-down processes are increasing economic, social, and cultural polarization in an overall climate of increasing uncertainty and decreasing legitimacy of governments everywhere. In response, mobilized communities within civil society launch struggles for livelihood, in defence of life space, and in affirmation of the right to cultural difference" (217).

These images sharply contrast with the images of the underclass that have dominated the debate over cities, particularly American cities, in the 1980s and 1990s. While contested, the category of "underclass" included individuals inside cities but outside mainstream society, such as the poor, street criminals, drug addicts and drunks, hustlers and prostitutes, drifters and the homeless, and deinstitutionalized mental patients. While originally the focus was the Africans in American cities (Massey and Denton 1993; Wilson 1987), it was broadened to include other groups in other cities (L. Morris 1994). Further investigating the classification struggles over the concept of the underclass would itself be revealing, but it is sufficient to stress that these groups were not regarded as active groups making and claiming demands for citizenship. Rather, the prevailing image is one of oppression, powerlessness, marginalization, and outcasting. The contrast between these two images of marginal groups in the cosmopolis is striking.

Which image prevails as the dominant representation of the cosmo-

polis is itself an object of and stake in struggles that configure the cosmopolis. These struggles for recognition and becoming political are not isolated or independent from the rise of the new professions and their rights
to the city. The city as a difference machine constitutes these spaces and
identities in simultaneous, fragmented, contradictory, and paradoxical
ways (Ruddick 1996). While immigrants may be struggling for citizenship
rights, they may also become a target and an object of analysis of various
professional knowledges that constitute them as oppressed subjects. The
struggles of gays and lesbians may be absorbed into professional knowledges that constitute them as normalized and subservient identities
(Phelan 2001). The terrain is complex and variegated, rather than that implied by rigid and dichotomous views. Yet the dominant instinct in the
literature has been to create these dichotomies, oppose them against each
other, and invoke logics of exclusion. What does a "right to difference"
mean, as though difference is that which exists before an encounter? As has
been argued, the dominant groups and the subaltern are not mutually exclusive groups that preexist each other, but their presence is interdependent, mutual, and symbiotic. The constitution of strangers and outsiders in
the cosmopolis is inextricably bound up with how the professions constitute themselves and their objects in discourse, how they articulate their
difference from strangers and outsiders and invest that difference with
social and symbolic capital, and how they produce and reproduce spaces.
The "immigrants," "homeless," "beggars," "criminals," "squeegeers," and
"hooligans" do not exist outside the city, but are assembled in the city in
their encounters and confrontations with the professions and the strategies and technologies of citizenship they have articulated.

Immigrants

Since the 1970s, the changing nature of immigration in American and
European cosmopolises has been similar to that of the late nineteenth century waves we discussed earlier. This time, however, the origins of immigrants shifted from southern Europe to Asia, India, and the Middle East.
This shift has resulted in the rise of new conflicts, tensions, and definitions
of otherness. Complicating these have been significant transformations in
forms of capital: labor markets in which immigrants find themselves and
the forms of capital that ensure success in these markets are very different
from the late nineteenth- and early twentieth-century conditions of the
metropolis. These conditions obviously vary in different cosmopolises depending on their articulation into transnational markets and networks.
Here the question becomes what forms of capital immigrants bring from

their original milieu and what sorts of capital are valorized in their new cities. Given that cultural capital has become the main determinant of group differentiation, and that the conversion of cultural capital is most difficult from one milieu to another, immigrants may find themselves in dominated as well as dominant situations. The conditions also vary with immigration policies and other policies of states in which these cosmopolises are situated. These two variables affect the solidaristic and agonistic strategies and technologies available to immigrants to establish themselves as being political in the cosmopolis, to articulate and claim rights, and to constitute themselves as citizens (Soguk 1999).

While there is a vast literature on the question of immigration, Sassen (1988; 1996a; 1998; 1999) has established the most cogent relationship between the cosmopolis and immigration. For Sassen (1988) the patterns of immigration are associated with the mobility of labor and capital and the dynamics of advanced capitalism. If the increasing immigrant labor in service jobs in cosmopolises in the developed world is one aspect of this dynamic, the increasing number of manufacturing jobs in the developing world cosmopolises is another (1988, 53). While these patterns are complex and varied, empirical evidence indicates that, typically, immigrants do not participate in the professions. There are two broad reasons. First, immigrants are more often drawn to low-skill, low-wage service jobs. Second, the successful closure of the professions of their markets and jurisdictions ensures low levels of immigration among professionals or their exclusion from local markets. In other words, the professional strategies of spatialization and marketization render the movement of immigrants in labor markets more difficult. While there is an increasing pressure toward liberalization of professional markets, as mentioned above, so far the professions have successfully protected their markets and their spatialization (Kofman 2000; OECD 1995, 1997). More recent immigration policies favor the importation of professional immigrants but because of the closed nature of the professions, the immigrants are not employed in their fields of expertise and are mostly unable to transfer their credentials and skills. As a result, immigrants occupy either positions in the paraprofessions or unskilled occupations in the service economy (Siemiatycki and Isin 1998). Or, worse, unable to articulate and claim their rights, they may be employed in high-tech sweatshops (Laws 1997). While these strategies of marketization and spatialization are effectuated through various governmental authorities responsible for regulating immigration, they are realized in the cosmopolis.

Evidence from European and American cosmopolises reveals an ambiguous but dominated position for immigrants in the cosmopolis. While immigrants and professionals occupy opposite spaces both spatially and socially, this "polarization" is not a straightforward or rigid matter. There are some immigrants who, by virtue of their ability to convert cultural capital to economic capital or vice versa, have been able to occupy dominant spaces (Li 1998). But, at the same time, the overall trend has been one of diminishing opportunities for the majority of immigrants. William Clark, for example, considers the question of whether immigrants are beginning to create a new urban underclass (Clark 1998). Between 1970 and 1990, in American cities such as Los Angeles, New York, Dallas, Miami, Chicago, Phoenix, Philadelphia, Detroit, and Seattle, differentials in skill and education levels between immigrants and native-born have translated into real wage differentials (Clark 1998, 376). Accordingly, poverty levels are much higher among immigrants than native-born and highest among the recent immigrants (378). Similar sharp differentiation between immigrants and citizens has been noted for Canadian cities such as Toronto, Montreal, and Vancouver (Ley 1996; Murdie 1996; Siemiatycki and Isin 1998). While Canadian cosmopolises do not yet display the same level of spatial and social differentiation as their American counterparts, increasingly the difference between American and Canadian cosmopolises is one of degree rather than kind (Levine 1995).

Although European cosmopolises display similar transformations, for a variety of complex historical reasons, different regimes accommodate and recognize citizenship rights-claims by certain immigrant groups more than others (Soysal 1994; Vertovec 1998). This results in a real variation among European cosmopolises. Nonetheless, social and spatial differentiations between immigrants and professionals have become apparent. But these patterns of differentiation are more complex than the dualities implied by rich versus poor or possessed versus dispossessed categories. In Milan, Turin, and Genoa, for example, the professional-managerial groups have clearly established themselves in the historic city and created exclusive spaces through their exclusive position in social space (Petsimeris 1998). An examination of maps of concentration among professionals and immigrant workers in these cities reveals not only the concentration of immigrants in new service jobs, but also the spatial isolation of these two groups from each other (Petsimeris 1998, 462). Catherine Rhein (1998) illustrates that since the 1970s, professional-managerial groups have taken over the historic city center in Paris and displaced immigrants to working-class suburbs (just as the bourgeoisie had taken over the center and displaced the working and dangerous classes in the early nineteenth century). As in Italian cities, immigrants are disproportionately concentrated in low-skill, low-wage service jobs, whereas citizens are increasingly concentrated in professional and managerial jobs (Maspero 1994; Rhein 1998, 438). Similarly, in other European cosmopolises such as Amsterdam, Brussels, Frankfurt, Düsseldorf, London, and Manchester, new patterns of social and spatial differentiation have been noted between immigrants and non-immigrants (Badcock 1997; Musterd and Ostendorf 1998; O'Loughlin and Friedrichs 1996).

To recognize this ambiguous location of immigrants in the cosmopolis, we ought to investigate how immigrants are constituted as strangers (Soguk 1999). While on the one hand they are objects of agonistic and alienating strategies, such as stigmatization, deportation, xenophobia, hatred, marginalization, and violence resulting in social, economic, and spatial segregation and isolation, on the other hand, they are incessantly in demand in labor markets for specific tasks in the division of labor, for achieving a general downward pressure on wages and for engendering flexible patterns of employment (Laws 1997). Similarly, while on the one hand there are continuing debates over immigration quotas, on the other hand, immigrant groups are also being constructed as objects of sympathy, affection, and even emulation resulting in hybridity (Stasiulis 1997). Honig argues that the valorization of immigrants as the founders of settler nations often leads to a backlash against them when they conduct themselves in ways that are not acceptable to citizenship. As Honig says, "[T]he liberal xenophilic deployment of the foreigner as the truest citizen (because the only truly consenting one) actually feeds the xenophobic backlash against the nonconsenting immigrant—the illegal alien—to whom we supposedly do not consent and who does not consent to us" (1992, 16). While it is important to question images of the immigrant that mobilize the virtuous citizen, it is a mistake to draw a sharp distinction between immigrants as consenting citizens and illegal aliens as nonconsenting citizens. For immigrants also engage in practices that dissent from accepted norms and question the dominant images of the virtuous citizens. These are not paradoxical or contradictory aspects of immigration in the cosmopolis, but a reflection of how immigrants, constituted as strangers, are necessary for the functioning, organization, and appropriation of the cosmopolis by the professions.

Homeless

The appearance of the category "homeless" should also be seen within the context of transformations from disciplinary to entrepreneurial professionalization. As we have seen, "individuals without a permanent address" due to economic or social conditions or exceptional circumstances have existed in different forms and have been categorized differently in different types of cities. Their appearance in discourse in the seventeenth century in the form of vagabonds and vagrants and as objects of punishment, and in the nineteenth century in the form of dangerous classes and as objects of discipline, were closely linked with changing regimes of government and professionalization. They constituted different forms of danger and hence were regarded, reformed, and objectified differently. As both Morris (1994) and Daly (1996, 51–88) observed, to grasp the issue of "homelessness" that burst into imagination in the 1980s and accelerated in the 1990s, these historical lineages need to be traced. While as a problematized subject much has been written about homelessness, from the point of view of citizenship as alterity, the "homeless" can be considered a kind of stranger. What made the reappearance in discourse of those who were constituted as strangers with a new category in the late twentieth century was that it was no longer possible to regard them as idle and lazy outcasts, deserving to be punished, or as subjects lacking moral certitude for work, deserving to be disciplined. Rather, from the perspective of entrepreneurial professionalization, the question was how to engage them in their own government as active subjects. Unlike the vagrant, vagabond, or pauper, or the dangerous class, "homelessness" refers to the lack or absence of something: a home. But with its presence, a person can move from that category into another and perhaps transform himself into, say, a consumer. That is why the homeless person is constituted, on the one hand, as an unfortunate individual who found himself in this condition, and, on the other, as a subject who needs to become entrepreneurial and active and move out of this subject position. That is why the homeless have not been constituted as "the evicted," signifying a victimized status (Deutsche 1996, 54–56). To constitute himself as a citizen, not as a rights-bearing subject demanding and making claims, but as an active subject, the homeless person is interpellated into becoming an active consumer via various projects, programs, and policies.

Beggars, Squeegeers, Refugees, Hooligans

The beggars, squeegeers, and hooligans among "us" are other categories of alterity that allow citizens to constitute themselves as bearers of virtue (Dean 1999). While disciplinary professionalization was oriented toward various groups as objects of cure, correction, and rehabilitation, entrepreneurial professionalization aims for neither reformation, nor salvation, but for interpellating these subjects as responsible agents of their destiny. Among the agonistic strategies that have proven most effective has been the responsibilization of subjects to enable or empower them to constitute themselves as citizens. The case of beggars and squeegeers shows that the ability of "marginalized" social groups to articulate a language of citizenship and claim rights comes up against the professional discourse that constitutes them not as rights-bearing subjects, but as objects of nuisance. While it may be possible to interpret beggars and squeegeers as insurgent practices, perhaps it is more important to empirically investigate how they have been constituted as objects of nuisance and cleansing, and how they have been incorporated into governmental practices by entrepreneurial professionalization and by being encouraged to consider themselves as entrepreneurs, rather than rights-bearing citizens, to avoid becoming objects of nuisance. Squeegeers, for example, are prompted into believing that they are entrepreneurs of the streets and that their practices can be made legitimate, productive, and legal only if they agree to certain rules and regulations in return for some money to set up their business. Similarly, beggars are prompted into schemes such as replacing them with collection boxes or as virtuous entrepreneurs selling magazines about "big issues." In their everyday struggles, every marginalized, stigmatized, and dominated social group is invited, interpellated, incited, and cajoled into making such bargains to constitute themselves as active citizens under terms and conditions that they may not have articulated. Whether the homeless, squeegeers, and beggars can develop solidaristic strategies and overturn agonistic strategies within which they are implicated is an open question when they increasingly face alienating strategies and technologies of cleansing, removal, dispersal, banishment, imprisonment, and harassment.

While squeegeers are constituted as strangers, incited to conduct themselves as citizens whose virtues are defined by professionals, refugees are constituted as quasi-permanent outsiders and are interpreted as the worst kind of beggars (Soguk 1999). While squeegeers find themselves implicated in agonistic strategies and technologies, refugees are increasingly subjected to alienating strategies and technologies such as vouchers and dispersal: refugees in various cosmopolises are issued vouchers and dispersed in urban space, keeping them outside the formal economy and avoiding their spatial congregation, thus denying them political visibility (Spencer 1994). While today these outsiders are categorized as "refugees," in the late nineteenth century the category "hooligans" originated as the antithesis of citizens to designate working-class immigrants from southern Europe, distinguishing them from "respectable" working-class members who were able to conduct themselves as citizens (Schwarz 1996, 118). By contrast, today "hooligans" are constituted as permanent outsiders who are unreformable and unalterable, and thus either unwilling or incapable of conducting themselves as citizens. This, in turn, justifies implicating "potential hooligans" in alienating technologies such as intimidation, deportation, banning, surveillance, and immobilization.

Associated with this entrepreneurial professionalization, which aims to inculcate its virtues in various groups, is the broader aestheticization of everyday life in the city (Featherstone 1992). As professions increasingly make the city their habitat and refashion it in their image, their sense of aesthetics and civility defines what city life is about (Smith 1996). As with every social group rising in dominance, the professions see their own aesthetic as natural, normal, and legitimate. Hence their sense of civility and conduct of self in public permeates and interpenetrates into a universal sense of what it means to conduct oneself in public as a citizen. Unlike the bourgeoisie, the professions do not have an agonistic relationship with intellectuals and intelligentsia and thus their ability to dominate discourse by virtue of the command of symbolic capital is more powerful than any other group. It is this command that takes over subjects such as beggars and squeegeers as objects of government, but instead of eliminating, incarcerating, or correcting them, it constitutes them as active subjects of their own making, a twofold solidaristic strategy of citizenship that inculcates a professional ethic of conduct while simultaneously valorizing that ethic by consecrating professionals as agents of virtue.

The Need *for* Strangers and Outsiders

Whether the strangers and outsiders of the cosmopolis can activate "insurgent practices," or get connected up with the entrepreneurial professionalization that constitutes them as active subjects of their own making, or engage in autonomous and transversal practices of becoming political by refusing to constitute themselves via the gaze of the dominant groups and thereby define new rights and responsibilities, remains, as ever, to be seen. It is important, however, that insurgent citizenship should be seen in the context of the changing strategies and technologies of citizenship, rather than opposing insurgent practices against an imaginary global or transnational elite or immediately giving them the badge of authenticity and effectiveness without empirically investigating the strategies and technologies of citizenship within which they are implicated.

"Beggars," "homeless," or "squeegeers" arise from encounters with these strategies and technologies: as the professions *habitate* the city, they occupy certain neighborhoods and transform them in their own image of civility and urbanity; as they *objectify* the city, they mobilize the fears and anxieties of manifold other groups about the declining morality, increasing crime, dilapidation, and the need to regenerate, renovate, and reinvent the city as solutions or cures to the problems thus articulated; as they *socialize* through the city, forming networks of association, collegiate, and symposia, they mobilize other groups as clients, patrons, beneficiaries, objects, or some combination thereof to realize themselves as legitimate and necessary groups; as they *spatialize* their jurisdictions, markets, and spheres of authority, they outcast, exclude, and ban some from these spaces and include, valorize, and enable others in them. It is from these very specific encounters that these categories arise and become objects of identification or dissociation. These strategies and technologies of citizenship always mobilize and assemble a combination of solidaristic, agonistic, and alienating forms, often overlapping, tangled up and fluid. The disciplinary ethic implicates youth in agonistic strategies of reform and cure, while the entrepreneurial ethic constitutes them as agents of responsibility and freedom. The entrepreneurial ethic constitutes beggars as responsible agents, while the disciplinary ethic regards them as victims needing affection and care. To constitute the cosmopolis as an object of analysis means empirically investigating the formation and realization of these groups via each other, the changes they bring about in the content and extent of citizenship, and how they claim the city as a political space where new rights of citizenship are being negotiated.

Becoming Political

Being political means being implicated in strategies and technologies of citizenship as otherness. When social groups succeed in inculcating their own virtues as dominant, citizenship is constituted as an expression and embodiment of those virtues against others who lack them. To put it another way, citizenship is that particular point of view of the dominant, which constitutes itself as a universal point of view—the point of view of those who dominate the city and who have constituted their point of view as natural by representing the city as a unity. But the strategies of universalization are not universal and have differed widely among various historical groups. Becoming political is that moment when the naturalness of the dominant virtues is called into question and their arbitrariness revealed. When the ancient Greek women questioned the concept of masculine nobility as the natural attribute of warrior-aristocrats and instituted new ways of being citizens, when Roman plebeians questioned the alleged superiority of the patricians and conducted themselves as citizens in their own assemblies, when the medieval *popolo* challenged the patricians and constituted the city differently, or when the sansculottes claimed themselves as legitimate citizens with and against the bourgeoisie, these acts were being rendered political, not in the name of establishing their natural superiority, but in exposing the arbitrary foundations of such superiority. Nor were these acts political in the way being political was envisaged by their dominant others, citizens. Rather, these acts redefined the ways of being political by developing symbolic, social, cultural, and economic practices that enabled them to constitute themselves as political agents under new terms, taking different positions in the social space than those in which they were previously positioned.

Becoming political is that moment when a rank established between the superior versus inferior, high versus low, black versus white, noble versus base, good versus evil, is reversed, transvalued, and redefined, and the ways of being political are rethought. Becoming political is that moment when freedom becomes responsibility and obligation becomes a right, and involves arduous work upon oneself and others, building solidarity and alterity simultaneously. All domination is arbitrary and its success depends on its ability to conceal its arbitrariness. That is why becoming political should be seen neither as wide as encompassing all ways of being (conflating being political with being social), nor as narrow as restricting it to being a citizen (conflating polity and politics). The moment the dominated, stigmatized, oppressed, marginalized, and disfranchised agents expose the arbitrary, they realize themselves as groups and constitute themselves as political. Becoming political is that moment when one constitutes oneself as a being capable of judgment about just and unjust, takes responsibility for that judgment, and associates oneself with or against others in fulfilling that responsibility. Becoming political is that moment when beings develop a mastery of strategies and technologies that implicated them in certain ways of being political and begin to transform these ways in different directions than their intended aims and trajectories. Thus, citizenship at any given moment and space cannot be defined without investigating strategies and technologies as modes of being political that implicate beings in solidaristic, agonistic, and alienating orientations of being political, constituting them as citizens, strangers, outsiders, and aliens. Ways of being political combine these modes and orientations through which beings are constituted as citizens, strangers, outsiders, and aliens.

The history of citizenship has often been narrated by dominant groups who articulated their identity as citizens and constituted strangers, outsiders, and aliens as those bête noire who lacked the properties they defined as essential for citizenship. The dominant views on citizenship derive not from those who questioned and attempted to overturn its values, but from those who were its benefactors and inheritors. Nevertheless, the attempt in *Being Political* was not to rewrite the history of citizenship from the viewpoint of the oppressed, marginalized, and disfranchised, if indeed such an enterprise is possible. But it was to write histories of citizenship from the point of view of its alterities in the sense of recovering those solidaristic, agonistic, and alienating moments of reversal and transvaluation, where strangers and outsiders constituted themselves as citizens or insiders and in so doing altered the ways of being political. It was to glean from those moments the universal but particular strategies and tragedies, tactics and errors that becoming political involves.

As Rancière recognized, being political provokes acts of speaking against injustice and vocalizing grievances as equal beings. But is becoming political that moment "when the natural order of domination is interrupted by the institution of a part of those who have no part" (1995, 11, 123)? As Žižek indicated, by reproducing excluded/invisible and included/visible dichotomies, this concept of the political disavows its own conditions of possibility as a subversive or transversal act (1999, 234). For Žižek a "truly subversive political intervention" strives to question the order of things in which the visible and the invisible are integral parts (1999, 235). Yet, Žižek himself depoliticizes becoming political as that "moment in which a particular demand is not simply part of the negotiation of interests but aims at something more, and starts to function as the metaphoric condensation of the global restructuring of the entire social space" (1999, 208). While Žižek is right to recognize that becoming political is that moment of questioning the part that a being occupies in social space and is not simply an interruption by those beings who have no part, he depoliticizes those acts of becoming political by restricting the political to those "revolutionary" actions that seek universal restructuring. This restriction of the properly political to acts of a "revolutionary" character is itself a political strategy that is driven by a will to derive the particular from the universal. That strategy served occidental citizens well as they inculcated their vision of politics in others by valorizing the unity, harmony, and congruity of the city.

Yet, to begin with the beginning, the Greek polis had neither the political nor the spatial unity, harmony, or congruity that was ascribed to it by either those citizens who were trying to shape it to their own image or, more importantly, by those later citizens, be they civic humanists in the fifteenth century or the bourgeoisie in the eighteenth century, who were appropriating it. Rather, the polis was thoroughly fissiparous with the presence of multiple groups with multiple desires and identifications. At the intersection of these multiplicities, citizens, women, peasants, slaves, merchants, metics, and artisans confronted, defined, struggled against, or allied with each other, assembled strategies and technologies, and mobilized different forms of capital. When certain ways of being political had undergone change, when virtues became vices and vices virtues, those citizens who were accustomed to their privileges, benefits, and symbols lamented their transvaluation and announced that politics and the polis were dead—a nostalgic reaction that was to return eternally. What did Nietzsche find so alluring in warrior-citizens, who, when challenged, yearned for the bygone days of glory and whose noblest voice was the beloved Theognis? Was Nietzsche ironic or nostalgic when he wanted to have the Greek citizen and the Renaissance citizen without the causes and conditions that made them possible? That different ways of being political were being invented through *collegia,* associations, and clubs, and that new ways of orienting toward the polis, such as Stoic cosmopolitanism, were experimented with was of little concern to aristocrat-citizens or peasant-citizens, who were now being estranged by being implicated in transversed strategies and technologies of citizenship.

Even the Roman civitas was so differentiated that it required the invention of a war machine to impose a unity on it—to no avail. Neither plebs nor slaves rested with being governed in the name of their inferior nature and identity. Instead, by destabilizing and denaturalizing, they contested the authorities and configured practices, ranging from secession to revolt, that constituted them differently. Jews and Pauline Christians inherited these practices, appropriated them, and assembled sui generis strategies and technologies of citizenship. It is questionable to refer to civitas in the singular, as though it were ever a unified and harmonious political, social, or spatial order. Quite the contrary. It is in the incredibly complex strategies and technologies of otherness embodied in the civitas that its image becomes visible. This is important to recognize because the images of being political given to us by the austere Roman citizen conducting himself in the Senate sharply contrasts with the images of being political given by mothers contesting census classification to protect their sons, widows contesting property qualifications, and clients and slaves claiming rank and order in the streets of Rome. These acts of being political were just as constitutive of Roman political life as the actions of citizens in the Senate.

Similarly, even after the granting of charters, the Christianopolis contained multiple and overlapping networks of power and jurisdiction within itself. Before even the rise of the craft guilds, there were various lesser associations, bishoprics, and parishes, as well as other groups in the city, scattered across space but claiming certain liberties of governing themselves. That artisans, lesser merchants, and workers were constituted as the strangers of the commune was evident in the fact that while they were not members of the commune, as inhabitants of the city they were obligated to pay taxes to the commune and serve in its militia. That merchants, artisans, and other groups struggled to speak for the whole city as a unified order, claiming to represent its interests, was a reasonable agonistic strategy. What is not reasonable is to interpret this strategy as evidence of the unity of the city. The use of the term *citizenship* in charters to have themselves defined by higher authorities as citizens was not accidental, for the patriciate of the commune constituted themselves, though not with a clear and consistent language, as the citizens of the city and as distinguished from strangers and outsiders. The European and colonial unfolding of strategies and technologies of citizenship between the fifteenth and the late eighteenth centuries (such as the invention of the corporation or of perspective); the elaboration of instructions on how to create new cities in the New World and restructure them in the Old; the various detailed classifications and rankings of groups in cities; the laws, norms, and regulations of the conduct of both the dominant and the dominated groups; and the rewriting of the histories of Athens and Rome to generate affinities between them and the nobles do not easily fit grand narratives of the rise of the state and mercantile capitalism, the routinization of administration, the rationalization of conduct, the centralization of power, and the monopolization of violence or coercion. Even the way the bourgeoisie constituted itself in the metropolis as the virtuous citizens and assembled effective strategies and technologies of citizenship that sequestered, disciplined, cajoled, incited, encouraged, incarcerated, stigmatized, classified, and labeled workers, Africans, immigrants, and criminals does not fit into a formula of the irresistible rise of capitalism. That the bourgeoisie, unlike early modern aristocracies, engaged in agonistic strategies and enabled strangers and outsiders to constitute themselves as citizens were its distinguishing characteristics.

Whether it was the women, peasants, Pauline Christians, *popolo,* artisans, sansculottes, vagabonds, Jews, workers, Africans, or immigrants, there were always spaces for becoming political and engaging and transversing strategies and technologies of citizenship inventively and imaginatively. But none of these enactments and struggles can or should be interpreted as either continuous or "revolutionary." First, if there is any apparent continuity that citizenship stands for, then it derives from its historically constructed character: that time and again groups that established their rights to the city constituted themselves as direct inheritors of historical forms of citizenship. Second, we ought to remember that the fundamental images of being political given to us derive from a particular interpretation of historical forms of citizenship in the age of revolutions in the late eighteenth and early nineteenth centuries. The two images of revolution that have dominated our perceptions of the city were narrated by the citizens who constituted themselves as revolutionary. That the merchants, organized in guilds, constituted themselves as citizens and usurped powers from the landowning nobility in the eleventh and twelfth centuries gave us the first image of the revolution as the communal movement. That in the mid-thirteenth century many artisans, also organized in guilds, challenged the patriciate, as the dominant merchants were designated, and gained access to power and participation in the city gave us the second image of revolution. So, according to these images, the European city, as a species belonging to the genus of the occidental city, goes through the stages of "evolution" that culminate in "democratic" government, which is its true differentia. If this narrative now appears doubtful and suspiciously parallels the narratives of revolution from the aristocracy to the demos in the polis and from patricians to plebeians in the civitas, it is not because there are inherent stages that cities go through, but because the later "revolutionaries" drew these parallels by appropriating the images of citizenship from the polis and civitas and because modern historians either reproduced or appropriated these narratives. We have every reason to deconstruct these narratives, not because they give us false images, but because we must know what these images mobilize.

To claim that the ancient Greeks and Romans invented politics will now perhaps appear as an ambiguous and imprecise statement. More precisely, they may have invented antipolitics and noncitizenship. Associated with these inventions were various forms of otherness through which various groups identified themselves and others and engaged in a combination of violent, inventive, symbolic, and outright malicious struggles over these categories and their content. While "citizenship" stood for the most privileged of these categories, the claims to its privileges and to the rights consecrated by it were objects of struggles among various groups that were constituted as its others. That certain groups who constituted themselves as capable of being political, in the sense of being endowed with the capacity to be governed by and govern other citizens and being differentiated from strangers and outsiders, implied a game that could only be played with and against others. It was by no means a game of the dominant few, though the dominant citizens certainly wished to present it that way. The images of the city that emerge from these genealogical investigations are protean entities with fragmented, segmented, and fractionalized orders, rather than unified, harmonious, and centralized orders. These images were both premises and conclusions of these investigations: while a critique of synoecism and orientalism engendered different images of the city, these images were given concrete forms and instances.

To put it bluntly, the occidental city was never a confraternity. Rather, it was a difference machine that simultaneously assembled and dispersed various groups and their differentiations across social and material space, enabling them to govern themselves and others by using various solidaristic, agonistic, and alienating strategies. While the city was not a confraternity, there were various orders of fraternization and confraternization as solidaristic and agonistic strategies that always formed from struggles among these groups. Nor was the ancient city a rationalized order dissolving kinship and tribal ties. Citizenship always included kinship or tribal identifications and networks, which served as the basis of solidaristic, agonistic, and alienating strategies.

These are very different images of the city than those we have been given by citizens, who, for *strategic* reasons, preferred to claim to represent the city as a unified order, when that representation was in fact something contested. Every group that constituted itself as the dominant group in the city also claimed to represent the city as a unified order. Thus, the image of the city as a unified order has acquired an ontological superiority over its protean, fragmented, and fractious realities. But this is neither a falsehood nor an intentional misrepresentation. Rather, it is a solidaristic and agonistic strategy that enabled dominant segments of dominant groups to constitute themselves as virtuous, righteous, and moral agents, justified in inculcating their vision of the city in other groups. That this vision never remained uncontested was the space that enabled various strategies of becoming political.

To reach these general conclusions, we proceeded with genealogical investigations that made crucial distinctions between solidaristic, agonistic, and alienating strategies and technologies on the one hand, and between citizens, strangers, outsiders, and aliens on the other. Failing to make these distinctions results in succumbing to logics of exclusion and enclosure, binary oppositions such as friend versus enemy, or us versus them, or "we" versus Other, and conflating various uses and mobilizations of strategies and technologies of citizenship. With these distinctions we developed a critique of synoecism and orientalism. By first outlining the grand narratives of the overthrow of kingships and revolutions in the means of warfare leading to the invention of the city and citizenship and hence politics, we critiqued them by highlighting how these narratives are mobilized by a particular perspective of establishing essential differences between occidental and oriental cities. But we did not remain at the level of critique and proceeded with positive genealogical investigations once we became skeptical of these grand narratives. These investigations of how various technologies of citizenship were mobilized, how various forms of capital were appropriated, how various strategies of solidarity, agon, and alienation were deployed, and how spaces were created for the formation of group identities are meant only as illustrations of how we can think differently about the city and citizenship. We no longer have to think of citizenship as a consequence of a revolution, whether against kingship or against aristocracy, as Fustel de Coulanges thought in his *Ancient City* (1864); nor do we need to think of such unified cities as the "patrician city" or the "plebeian city," as Max Weber did in his *The City* (1921). Nor, perhaps most importantly, do we need to believe without qualifications that being political was necessarily synonymous with being a citizen.

That the fundamental image of being political given to us derives from a particular interpretation of historical forms of citizenship in the age of revolutions in the late eighteenth and early nineteenth centuries explains the revolutionary accounts of citizenship. For that particular interpretation valued epic struggles between classes, glorious symbols of democratization, and unified polities. Yet none of these struggles were revolutionary in the sense of being spontaneous, radical, and rapid overthrows. Rather, moments of becoming political were polyvalent, multiple, minor, and tactical engagements with strategies and technologies of citizenship. Nor is there an unbroken continuity between historical and contemporary forms of citizenship. If there is, it is symbolically produced as a solidaristic and agonistic strategy, rather than given in reality. Instead of seeing citizenship as an unbroken continuous or revolutionary history, *Being Political* constituted it as a principle that assembles various strategies and technologies of domination, power, and government. If citizenship appears to be continuous it is because dominant groups have always found it imperative to establish their historicity. The very continuity of citizenship is immanent in its principle of generating alterity.

Becoming political can perhaps be defined as acts of transfiguration and transvaluation by noncitizens. In the end, we may owe the existence of politics not to citizens, but to strangers, outsiders, and aliens. In their inventive practices of transfiguration and transvaluation, declaring certain forms and ways of being as intolerable and problematizing their relationship to themselves and others, noncitizens may have invented the city-citizen game. When kings or philosopher-kings managed to impose their vision of the world, they generally aimed to end politics.

Central to *Being Political* is the fact that at the root of our conception of citizenship lies the invention of the occidental city. By abandoning the frame of reference that contrasted the occidental with oriental cities and their conceptions (or lack thereof) of citizenship and instead focusing on the configuration of power and group formations within Western cities, it is possible to change our perspective on citizenship. Rather than seeing "citizenship" as a stable and original innovation and the city as at once its symbol and domain, we can see it as an unstable and invented tradition through which certain groups have established their dominance and constituted themselves as citizens of a domain that valued their existence and devalued that of those who were constituted as its strangers and outsiders.

These genealogical investigations may enable us to think about citizenship differently today. The interpretation of the professions as the new guilds in the cosmopolis and the cosmopolis as the space through which a new political and social order (cosmos) is created is but an invitation to see citizenship differently. It may enable us to see categories such as immigrants, squeegeers, the homeless, and others not as excluded or given, but as articulated against their others, citizens. It may also enable us to see "globalization" and "postmodernization" not as given and immutable phenomena, but as strategies deployed by the professions as dominant groups to constitute their strangers, outsiders, and aliens, who, while being implicated in these strategies, also attempt to capture and transverse them. The city is a difference machine because these "characters" are not formed outside the machine and encounter each within the city, but the city assembles, generates, distributes, and differentiates these differences, incorporates them within strategies and technologies, and elicits, interpellates, adjures, and incites them. The city is not a container where differences encounter each other; the city generates differences and assembles identities. The city is a difference machine insofar as it is understood as that space which is constituted by the dialogical encounter of groups formed and generated immanently in the process of taking up positions, orienting themselves for and against each other, inventing and assembling strategies and technologies, mobilizing various forms of capital, and making claims to that space that is objectified as "the city." The city is a crucial condition of citizenship in the sense that being a citizen is inextricably associated with being *of* the city. Throughout the centuries struggles over citizenship have always taken place "over" the city. The city is neither a background to these struggles *against which* groups wager, nor is it a foreground *for which* groups struggle for hegemony. Rather, the city is the battleground *through which* groups define their identity, stake their claims, wage their battles, and articulate citizenship rights, obligations, and principles. The city as an object of thought and experience emerges out of these practices and has neither the unity nor the cohesion that has been attributed to it. The city as a difference machine relentlessly provokes, differentiates, positions, mobilizes, immobilizes, oppresses, liberates. Being political means being of the city. There is no political being outside the machine.

Long ago Socrates already thought that the rivalry between poetics and philosophy was ancient. If philosophy stood as a metaphor for the rational and natural language of citizenship, poetics perhaps stands as the metaphor for the language of becoming political. It arises at a moment when it becomes possible to conceive of oneself differently, to reorient oneself toward the other, and to reconstitute identity qua alterity. Poetics is both the embodiment and the creator of such moments when new spaces open up and allow agents to constitute or reconstitute themselves as political, as legitimate agents of their own formation and their relationships with others. Hesiod, Villon, Rimbaud, Hikmet, Brecht are those moments where the relationship between citizenship and alterity is transfigured. Hannah Arendt captured this when she discussed Brecht's poetry. For Arendt, Brecht's "fundamental bitterness is directed against the world of victors and vanquished—a world in whose history the cause of the defeated was always excluded from human memory because the victors wrote history. What rouses him to anger is not so much poverty, oppression, and exploitation, but rather the fact that the poor, the oppressed, and the exploited have never been able to make their voices heard, that their voices have been irrevocably stifled, that the insult of oblivion is always added to the injury of defeat and misfortune" (1950, 49–50). While Benjamin (1966, 60–61) was perceptive when he recognized that Brecht constituted the city as a battlefield, his observation that "Brecht is probably the first important poet who has something to say about urban man" (1966, 61) is questionable, as we have seen throughout this book the immanent associations of polis, poetics, and politics. Yet, the fundamental question about poetics is not that it is "political" in the simple sense of serving particular interests but in the sense of creating, embodying, and transmitting a perspective from which good from evil, noble from base, virtue from vice, honor from dishonor, greatness from pettiness, magnificence from poverty are made distinguishable, and by virtue of that fact they are also made questionable and contestable (Badiou and Rancière, 1992). These forms of alterity are created dialogically and are open to reversals, reinterpretations, and contestation. It was through these complex and open solidaristic and agonistic strategies that poetics became political, and it was these uncertain possibilities that frightened Plato, the ultimate philosopher-king, and led him to expel the poets from the city.

Bibliography

Abbott, Andrew Delano. 1988. *The System of Professions: An Essay on the Division of Expert Labor.* Chicago: University of Chicago Press.

Aharoni, Yair. 1993. "Globalization of Professional Business Services." In *Coalitions and Competition: The Globalization of Professional Business Services,* edited by Y. Aharoni. London: Routledge.

Ajzenstat, Janet. 1988. *The Political Thought of Lord Durham.* Montreal and Kingston: McGill-Queen's University Press.

Allen, John. 1999. "Spatial Assemblages of Powers: From Domination to Empowerment." In *Human Geography Today,* edited by D. Massey, J. Allen, and P. Sarre. Cambridge: Polity.

Amelang, James S. 1984. "Barristers and Judges in Early Modern Barcelona: The Rise of a Legal Elite." *American Historical Review* 89, no. 5: 1264–84.

Andreau, Jean. 1993. "The Freedman." In *The Romans,* edited by A. Giardina. Chicago: University of Chicago Press.

Andrews, Richard Mowery. 1985. "Social Structures, Political Elites and Ideology in Revolutionary Paris, 1792–94." *Journal of Social History* 19, no. 1: 71–112.

Archdeacon, Thomas J. 1976. *New York City, 1664–1710: Conquest and Change.* Ithaca: Cornell University Press.

Arendt, Hannah. [1950] 1962. "The Poet Bertolt Brecht." In *Brecht: A Collection of Critical Essays,* edited by P. Demetz. New York: John Wiley.

Aristotle. 1984. *The Athenian Constitution.* Translated by P. J. Rhodes. London: Penguin.

———. 1995. *Politics.* Translated by E. Barker. Edited by R. F. Stalley. Oxford: Oxford University Press.

Arthurs, Harry W. 1997. "Globalization of the Mind: Canadian Elites and the

Restructuring of Legal Fields." *Canadian Journal of Legal Studies* 12, no. 2: 219–34.

Ashforth, David. 1976. "The Urban Poor Law." In *The New Poor Law in the Nineteenth Century,* edited by D. Fraser. London: Macmillan.

Axtell, James. 1992. *Beyond 1492: Encounters in Colonial North America.* Oxford: Oxford University Press.

Axtmann, Roland. 1990. "The Formation of the Modern State: A Reconstruction of Max Weber's Arguments." *History of Political Thought* 11, no. 2: 295–311.

Bachelard, Gaston. [1964] 1994. *The Poetics of Space.* Boston: Beacon Press.

Badcock, B. 1997. "Restructuring and Spatial Polarization in Cities." *Progress in Human Geography* 21, no. 2: 251–62.

Badiou, Alain, and Jacques Rancière. 1992. *La Politique Des Poètes: Pourquoi Des Poètes En Temps De Détresse?, Bibliothèque Du Collège International De Philosophie.* Paris: A. Michel.

Ballard, Adolphus, ed. 1913. *British Borough Charters, 1042–1216.* Cambridge: Cambridge University Press.

Balsdon, John Percy Vyvian Dacre. 1979. *Romans and Aliens.* Chapel Hill: University of North Carolina Press.

Banti, Luisa. 1976. *Etruscan Cities and Their Culture.* Translated by E. Bizzari. London: Batsford.

Barber, Benjamin. 1974. *The Death of Communal Liberty.* Princeton, N.J.: Princeton University Press.

Baron, Hans. 1955. *Humanistic and Political Literature in Florence and Venice at the Beginning of the Quattrocento: Studies in Criticism and Chronology.* Cambridge: Harvard University Press.

———. 1988. *In Search of Florentine Civic Humanism: Essays on the Transition from Medieval to Modern Thought.* 2 vols. Princeton, N.J.: Princeton University Press.

Bartelson, Jens. 1995. *A Genealogy of Sovereignty.* Vol. 39 of *Cambridge Studies in International Relations.* Cambridge: Cambridge University Press.

Baudelaire, Charles. [1863] 1972. "The Painter of Modern Life." In *Selected Writings on Art and Artists,* edited by P. E. Charvet. Harmondsworth: Penguin.

———. 1905. *Poems in Prose.* Translated by A. Symons. London: Mathews.

Baumann, Fred E. 1998. *Fraternity and Politics: Choosing One's Brothers.* Westport, Conn.: Praeger.

Beall, Jo, ed. 1997. *A City for All: Valuing Difference and Working with Diversity.* London: Zed Books.

de Beaumont, Gustave, and Alexis de Tocqueville. [1833] 1964. *On the Penitentiary System in the United States and Its Application in France.* Carbondale: Southern Illinois University Press.

Beaverstock, J. V. 1996. "Subcontracting the Accountant! Professional Labour Markets, Migration, and Organisational Networks in the Global Accountancy Industry." *Environment and Planning A* 28: 303–26.

Becker, Howard Saul. 1966. *Outsiders: Studies in the Sociology of Deviance.* New York: Free Press.

Becker, Marvin B. 1965. "A Study in Political Failure: The Florentine Magnates, 1280–1343." *Medieval Studies* 27: 246–308.

———. 1968. "The Florentine Territorial State and Civic Humanism in the Early Renaissance." In *Florentine Studies: Politics and Society in Renaissance Florence,* edited by N. Rubinstein. Evanston, Ill.: Northwestern University Press.

Beetham, David. 1996. "Theorising Democracy and Local Government." In *Rethinking Local Democracy,* edited by D. S. King and G. Stoker. Basingstoke: Macmillan.

Bell, Daniel. 1973. *The Coming of the Post-Industrial Society.* New York: Basic Books.

———. 1979. "The New Class: A Muddled Concept." In *The New Class?,* edited by B. B. Briggs. New Brunswick, N.J.: Transaction Books.

Bender, Thomas. 1979. "The Cultures of the Intellectual Life: The City and the Professions." In *New Directions in American Intellectual History,* edited by J. Higham and P. K. Conkin. Baltimore: The Johns Hopkins University Press.

———. 1998. "Scholarship, Local Life, and the Necessity of Wordliness." In *The Urban University and Its Identity: Roots, Location, Roles,* edited by H. van der Wusten. Dordrecht, Netherlands: Kluwer.

Benecke, Gerhard. 1971. "Ennoblement and Privilege in Early Modern Germany." *History* 56: 360–70.

Benevolo, Leonardo. 1993. *The European City.* Oxford: Butterworth.

Benjamin, Walter. [1966] 1973. "Commentaries on Poems by Brecht." In *Understanding Brecht.* London: Verso.

———. 1973. *Charles Baudelaire: A Lyric Poet in the Era of High Capitalism.* London: New Left Books.

Beresford, Maurice W. 1967. *New Towns of the Middle Ages: Town Plantation in England, Wales and Gascony.* London: Lutterworth.

Berman, Harold J. 1983. *Law and Revolution: The Formation of Western Legal Tradition.* Cambridge, Mass.: Harvard University Press.

Bernal, Martin. 1994. "The Image of Ancient Greece as a Tool for Colonialism and European Hegemony." In *Social Construction of the Past: Representation as Power,* edited by G. C. Bond and A. Gilliam. London: Routledge.

Black, Anthony. 1984. *Guilds and Civil Society in European Political Thought from the Twelfth Century to the Present.* Ithaca: Cornell University Press.

Blanchard, Marc Eli. 1985. *In Search of the City: Engels, Baudelaire, Rimbaud.* Saratoga, Calif.: Anma Libri.

Blau, Judith R., Mark La Gory, and John Pipkin, eds. 1983. *Professionals and Urban Form.* Albany: State University of New York Press.

Blavier, Yves. 1993. "Les Derniers Sans-Culottes." *Gavroche* 12, no. 72: 18–21.

Blickle, Peter. 1997. *Resistance, Representation, and Community.* Oxford: Oxford University Press.

Blockmans, Willem Pieter. 1994. "Voracious States and Obstructing Cities: An Aspect of State Formation in Preindustrial Europe." In *Cities and the Rise of States in Europe, A.D. 1000 to 1800,* edited by C. Tilly and W. P. Blockmans. Boulder, Colo.: Westview Press.

Bodnar, John E. 1985. *The Transplanted: A History of Immigrants in Urban America.* Bloomington: Indiana University Press.

Boholm, Åsa. 1990. *The Doge of Venice: The Symbolism of State Power in the Renaissance.* Gothenburg: University of Gothenburg.

Bourdieu, Pierre. [1979] 1984. *Distinction: A Social Critique of the Judgement of Taste.* Cambridge: Harvard University Press.

———. [1980] 1990. *The Logic of Practice.* Stanford, Calif.: Stanford University Press.

———. [1981] 1991. "Political Representation: Elements for a Theory of the Political Field." In *Language and Symbolic Power.* Cambridge, Mass.: Harvard University Press.

———. [1983] 1986. "The Forms of Capital." In *Handbook of Theory and Research for the Sociology of Education,* edited by J. G. Richardson. New York: Greenwood Press.

———. 1987. "What Makes a Social Class? On the Theoretical and Practical Existence of Groups." *Berkeley Journal of Sociology* 32: 1–18.

———. [1988] 1991. *The Political Ontology of Martin Heidegger.* Stanford, Calif.: Stanford University Press.

———. [1989] 1996. *The State Nobility: Elite Schools in the Field of Power.* Translated by L. C. Clough. Oxford: Polity.

———. 1991. "On Symbolic Power." In *Language and Symbolic Power.* Cambridge, Mass.: Harvard University Press.

———. 1993. *The Field of Cultural Production.* Edited by R. Johnson. New York: Columbia University Press.

———. [1994a] 1998. *Practical Reason: On the Theory of Action.* Stanford, Calif.: Stanford University Press.

———. 1994b. "Rethinking the State: Genesis and Structure of the Bureaucratic Field." *Sociological Theory* 12, no. 1: 1–18.

———. [1997] 2000. *Pascalian Meditations.* Translated by R. Nice. Stanford, Calif.: Stanford University Press.

Bourdieu, Pierre, and Jean Claude Passeron. [1970] 1990. *Reproduction in Education, Society and Culture.* Translated by R. Nice. London: Sage.

Bourdieu, Pierre, and Loïc J. D. Wacquant. 1992. *An Invitation to Reflexive Sociology.* Chicago: University of Chicago Press.

———. 1999. "On the Cunning of Imperialist Reason." *Theory, Culture & Society* 16, no. 1: 41–58.

Bowsky, William M. 1967. "Medieval Citizenship: The Individual and the State in the Commune of Siena, 1287–1355." In *Studies in Medieval and Renaissance History.* Lincoln: University of Nebraska Press.

Braudel, Fernand. 1977. *Capitalism and Material Life, 1400–1800.* Glasgow: Collins.
————. 1988. *The Structures of Everyday Life.* Vol. 1 of *Civilization and Capitalism 15th–18th Century.* New York: Harper and Row Publishers.

Brennan, W. John, ed. 1979. *The Internationalization of the Accountancy Profession: A Collection of Views.* Toronto: Canadian Institute of Chartered Accountants.

Brint, Steven. 1994. *In an Age of Experts: The Changing Role of Professionals in Politics and Public Life.* Princeton, N.J.: Princeton University Press.

Brophy, James M. 1997. "Carnival and Citizenship: The Politics of Carnival Culture in the Prussian Rhineland, 1823–1848." *Journal of Social History* 30, no. 4: 873–904.

Brown, Michael. 1997. *Replacing Citizenship.* New York: Guilford Press.

Brown, Peter Robert Lamont. 1978. *The Making of Late Antiquity.* Cambridge, Mass.: Harvard University Press.

Brubaker, Rogers. 1992. *Citizenship and Nationhood in France and Germany.* Cambridge, Mass.: Harvard University Press.

Brucker, Gene A. 1977. *The Civic World of Early Renaissance Florence.* Princeton, N.J.: Princeton University Press.

Brunt, Peter Astbury. 1971. *Social Conflicts in the Roman Republic.* New York: Norton.

Burchell, Graham. 1996. "Liberal Government and Techniques of Self." In *Foucault and Political Reason,* edited by A. Barry, T. Osborne, and N. Rose. Chicago: University of Chicago Press.

Burckhardt, Jacob. [1860] 1981. *The Civilization of the Renaissance in Italy.* Oxford: Phaidon Press.
————. [1872] 1998. *The Greeks and Greek Civilization.* Translated by S. Stern. New York: St. Martin's Press.

Burford, Alison. 1972. *Craftsmen in Greek and Roman Society.* Ithaca, N.Y.: Cornell University Press.

Burkert, Walter. [1984] 1992. *The Orientalizing Revolution: Near Eastern Influence on Greek Culture in the Early Archaic Age.* Translated by W. Burkert and M. E. Pinder. Cambridge, Mass.: Harvard University Press.

Burrage, Michael. 1990. "Beyond a Sub-Set: The Professional Aspirations of Manual Workers in France, the United States and Britain." In *Professions in Theory and History: Rethinking the Study of the Professions,* edited by M. Burrage and R. Torstendahl. London: Sage.
————. 1997. "Mrs. Thatcher against the 'Little Republics': Ideology, Precedents, and Reactions." In *Lawyers and the Rise of Western Political Liberalism: Europe and North America from the Eighteenth to Twentieth Centuries,* edited by T. C. Halliday and L. Karpik. Oxford: Oxford University Press.

Burrage, Michael, Konrad Jarausch, and Hannes Siegrist. 1990. "An Actor-Based Framework for the Study of the Professions." In *Professions in Theory and History: Rethinking the Study of the Professions,* edited by M. Burrage and R. Torstendahl. London: Sage.

Burrage, Michael, and Rolf Torstendahl, eds. 1990. *Professions in Theory and History: Rethinking the Study of the Professions.* London: Sage.

Burrows, Edwin G., and Mike Wallace. 1999. *Gotham: A History of New York City to 1898.* New York: Oxford University Press.

Burton, Joan B. 1995. *Theocritus's Urban Mimes.* Berkeley, Calif.: University of California Press.

Burton, Richard D. E., ed. 1994. *The Flâneur and His City: Patterns of Daily Life in Paris, 1815–1851.* Durham: University of Durham.

Canning, Joseph P. 1987. *The Political Thought of Baldus De Ubaldis.* Cambridge: Cambridge University Press.

Carr-Saunders, A. M. 1928. *Professions: Their Organization and Place in Society.* Oxford: Oxford University Press.

Carr-Saunders, A. M., and P. A. Wilson. 1933. *The Professions.* Oxford: Oxford University Press.

Cartledge, Paul. 1993. *The Greeks: A Portrait of Self and Others.* Oxford: Oxford University Press.

Castells, Manuel. 1977. *The Urban Question: A Marxist Approach.* London: Edward Arnold.

———. 1983. *The City and the Grassroots.* Berkeley and Los Angeles: University of California Press.

———. 1989. *The Informational City: Information Technology, Economic Restructuring and the Urban Regional Process.* Oxford: Blackwell.

———. 1996. *The Rise of Network Society.* Vol. 1 of *The Information Age: Economy, Society and Culture.* Cambridge, Mass.: Blackwell.

Castells, Manuel, and Peter Hall. 1994. *Technopoles of the World: The Making of the Twenty-First Century Industrial Complexes.* London: Routledge.

Chadwick, John. 1976. *The Mycenaean World.* Cambridge: Cambridge University Press.

Charle, Christophe. 1987. *Les Élites De La République, 1880–1900.* Paris: Fayard.

———. 1990. *Naissance Des «Intellectuels», 1880–1900.* Paris: Les Éditions de Minuit.

———. 1993. "Academics or Intellectuals? The Professors of the University of Paris and Political Debate in France from the Dreyfus Affair to the Algerian War." In *Intellectuals in Twentieth-Century France: Mandarins and Samurais,* edited by J. Jennings. New York: St. Martin's Press.

Chevalier, Louis. [1958] 1973. *Labouring Classes and Dangerous Classes in Paris During the First Half of the Nineteenth Century.* Translated by F. Jellinek. London: Routledge.

Childe, Gordon. 1985. *What Happened in History.* London: Penguin.

Christiansen, Rupert. 1994. *Paris Babylon: The Story of the Paris Commune.* New York: Viking.

Christie, Neil, and S. T. Loseby, eds. 1996. *Towns in Transition: Urban Evolution in Late Antiquity and the Early Middle Ages.* Aldershot: Scolar Press.

Clark, William A. V. 1998. "Mass Migration and Local Outcomes: Is International Migration to the United States Creating a New Urban Underclass?" *Urban Studies* 35, no. 3: 371–83.

Clarke, J. J. 1997. *Oriental Enlightenment: The Encounter between Asian and Western Thought.* London: Routledge.

Clement, Wallace, and John Myles. 1994. *Relations of Ruling: Class and Gender in Postindustrial Societies.* Montreal and Kingston: McGill-Queen's University Press.

Cobban, Alan B. 1975. *The Medieval Universities: Their Development and Organization.* London: Methuen.

Cobb-Stevens, Veda, Thomas J. Figueira, and Gregory Nagy. 1985. "Introduction." In *Theognis of Megara: Poetry and the Polis,* edited by T. J. Figueira and G. Nagy. Baltimore: The Johns Hopkins University Press.

Cocks, Geoffrey, and Konrad Hugo Jarausch, eds. 1990. *German Professions, 1800–1950.* New York: Oxford University Press.

Cohen, William B. 1998. *Urban Government and the Rise of the French City: Five Municipalities in the Nineteenth Century.* New York: St. Martin's Press.

Colognesi, L. Capogrossi. 1995. "The Limits of the Ancient City and the Evolution of the Medieval City in the Thought of Max Weber." In *Urban Society in Roman Italy,* edited by T. Cornell and K. Lomas. New York: St. Martin's Press.

Connolly, William E. 1993. *The Terms of Political Discourse.* 3d ed. Princeton, N.J.: Princeton University Press.

Constable, Marianne. 1994. *The Law of the Other: The Mixed Jury and Changing Conceptions of Citizenship, Law, and Knowledge.* Chicago: University of Chicago Press.

Corbin, Alain. 1986. *The Foul and the Fragrant: Odor and the French Social Imagination.* Cambridge, Mass.: Harvard University Press.

Corfield, P. J. 1995. *Power and the Professions in Britain, 1700–1850.* London: Routledge.

Cox, Robert. 1997. "Economic Globalization and the Limits of Liberal Democracy." In *The Transformation of Democracy?,* edited by A. McGrew. London: Open University Press.

Cox, Virginia. 1995. "The Single Self: Feminist Thought and the Marriage Market in Early Modern Venice." *Renaissance Quarterly* 48, no. 3: 513–81.

Crabb, Ann. 2000. *The Strozzi of Florence: Widowhood and Family Solidarity in the Renaissance.* Ann Arbor: University of Michigan Press.

Crinson, Mark, and Jules Lubbock. 1994. *Architecture-Art or Profession?: Three Hundred Years of Architectural Education in Britain.* Manchester: Manchester University Press.

Cruikshank, Barbara. 1999. *The Will to Empower: Democratic Citizens and Other Subjects.* Ithaca, N.Y.: Cornell University Press.

Cruz, Gilberto Rafael. 1988. *Let There Be Towns: Spanish Municipal Origins in*

Texas and the Southwest, 1610–1810. College Station: Texas A&M University Press.

Currie, Jan, and Janice Angela Newson, eds. 1998. *Universities and Globalization: Critical Perspectives*. Thousand Oaks, Calif.: Sage.

Daly, Gerald P. 1996. *Homeless: Policies, Strategies, and Lives on the Street*. London: Routledge.

Daly, Lowrie John. 1961. *The Medieval University, 1200–1400*. New York: Sheed and Ward.

Damisch, Hubert. [1994] 1987. *The Origin of Perspective*. Translated by J. Goodman. Cambridge, Mass.: MIT Press.

Davies, John K. 1997. "The 'Origins of the Greek *Polis*': Where Should We Be Looking?" In *The Development of the Polis in Archaic Greece*, edited by L. G. Mitchell and P. J. Rhodes. London: Routledge.

Dean, Mitchell. 1991. *The Constitution of Poverty: Toward a Genealogy of Liberal Governance*. New York, N.Y.: Routledge.

———. 1994. *Critical and Effective Histories: Foucault's Methods and Historical Sociology*. London: Routledge.

———. 1999. *Governmentality: Power and Rule in Modern Society*. London: Sage.

Deleuze, Gilles, and Félix Guattari. [1980] 1987. *A Thousand Plateaus*. Minneapolis: University of Minnesota Press.

Dench, Emma. 1995. *From Barbarians to New Men: Greek, Roman, and Modern Perceptions of Peoples of the Central Apennines*. Oxford: Oxford University Press.

Derber, Charles. 1982. "The Proletarianization of the Professional: A Review Essay." In *Professionals as Workers*, edited by C. Derber. Boston: G. K. Hall.

Deutsche, Rosalyn. 1996. *Evictions: Art and Spatial Politics*. Cambridge, Mass.: MIT Press.

Dewald, Jonathan. 1996. *The European Nobility, 1400–1800*. Cambridge: Cambridge University Press.

Dezalay, Yves. 1995. "Introduction: Professional Competition and the Social Construction of Transnational Markets." In *Professional Competition and Professional Power: Lawyers, Accountants and the Social Construction of Markets*, edited by Y. Dezalay and D. Sugarman. London: Routledge.

Dezalay, Yves, and Bryant G. Garth. 1996. *Dealing in Virtue: International Commercial Arbitration and the Construction of a Transnational Legal Order*. Chicago, Ill.: University of Chicago Press.

Dezalay, Yves, and David Sugarman, eds. 1995. *Professional Competition and Professional Power: Lawyers, Accountants and the Social Construction of Markets*. London: Routledge.

Dinnerstein, Leonard, Roger L. Nichols, and David M. Reimers. 1996. *Natives and Strangers: A Multicultural History of Americans*. 3d ed. New York: Oxford University Press.

Donlan, Walter. 1997. "The Relations of Power in the Pre-State and Early State Polities." In *The Development of the Polis in Archaic Greece,* edited by L. G. Mitchell and P. J. Rhodes. London: Routledge.

Drews, Robert. 1983. *Basileus: The Evidence for Kingship in Geometric Greece.* New Haven, Conn.: Yale University Press.

Dudley, William, ed. 1990. *Immigration: Opposing Viewpoints.* San Diego, Calif.: Greenhaven Press.

Durham, Lord. 1837. *Report on the Affairs of the British North America.* Edited by P. Lucas. 3 vols. Oxford: Oxford University Press.

Durkheim, Emile. [1890] 1992. *Professional Ethics and Civic Morals.* London: Routledge.

———. [1894] 1984. *The Division of Labor in Society.* Translated by W. D. Halls. Edited by L. Coser. New York: Free Press.

Eder, Klaus. 1993. *The New Politics of Class: Social Movements and Cultural Dynamics in Advanced Societies.* London: Sage.

Eldem, Edhem, Daniel Goffman, and Bruce Alan Masters. 1999. *The Ottoman City between East and West: Aleppo, Izmir, and Istanbul.* New York: Cambridge University Press.

Elias, Norbert. [1976] 1994. "Introduction: A Theoretical Essay on Established and Outsider Relations." In *The Established and the Outsiders: A Sociological Enquiry into Community Problems.* London: Sage.

Elias, Norbert, and John L. Scotson. 1994. *The Established and the Outsiders: A Sociological Enquiry into Community Problems.* 2d ed. London: Sage.

Elkins, James. 1994. *The Poetics of Perspective.* Ithaca: Cornell University Press.

Elliott, John Hall. 1990. *A Home for the Homeless.* 2d ed. Minneapolis: Fortress Press.

Ellul, Jacques. 1964. *The Technological Society.* New York: Vintage.

Eph'al, E. 1978. "The Western Minorities in Babylon in the Sixth–Fifth Centuries B.C." *Orientalia* 47: 74–90.

Epstein, James. 1994. *Radical Expression: Political Language, Ritual, and Symbol in England, 1790–1850.* New York: Oxford University Press.

Esping-Andersen, Gosta. 1993. "Post-Industrial Class Structures: An Analytical Framework." In *Changing Classes,* edited by G. Esping-Andersen. London: Sage.

Featherstone, Mike. 1992. "Postmodernism and Aestheticization of Everyday Life." In *Modernity and Identity,* edited by S. Lash and J. Friedman. Oxford: Blackwell.

———. 1995. *Undoing Culture: Globalization, Postmodernism and Identity.* London: Sage.

Ferenczy, Endre. 1976. *From the Patrician State to the Patricio-Plebeian State.* Translated by G. Dedinsky. Amsterdam: Adolf M. Hakkert Publisher.

Fine, John V. A. 1983. *The Ancient Greeks: A Critical History.* Cambridge, Mass.: Harvard University Press.

Finer, S. E. 1997a. *Ancient Monarchies and Empires.* Vol. 1 of *The History of Government from the Earliest Times.* Oxford: Oxford University Press.

———. 1997b. *The Intermediate Ages.* Vol. 2 of *The History of Government from the Earliest Times.* Oxford: Oxford University Press.

Finley, M. I. 1981. "The Ancient City: From Fustel De Coulanges to Max Weber and Beyond." In *Economy and Society in Ancient Greece.* New York: Viking.

———. 1983. *Politics in the Ancient World.* Cambridge: Cambridge University Press.

Fitzsimmons, Michael P. 1993. "The National Assembly and the Invention of Citizenship." In *The French Revolution and the Meaning of Citizenship,* edited by R. Waldinger, P. Dawson, and I. Woloch. Westport, Conn.: Greenwood Press.

Foucault, Michel. [1961] 1973. *Madness and Civilization.* Translated by R. Howard. New York: Vintage Books.

———. 1967 [1998]. "Different Spaces." In *Aesthetics, Method, and Epistemology,* edited by P. Rabinow. New York: New Press.

———. 1975 [1979]. *Discipline and Punish: The Birth of the Prison.* Translated by A. Sheridan. New York: Vintage Books.

———. 1982. "Afterword: The Subject and Power." In *Michel Foucault: Beyond Structuralism and Hermeneutics,* by H. L. Dreyfus and P. Rabinow. Chicago: University of Chicago Press.

———. [1984] 1988. *The Care of Self.* New York: Pantheon.

———. 1988. "Technologies of the Self." In *Technologies of the Self: A Seminar with Michel Foucault,* edited by L. H. Martin, H. Gutman, and P. H. Hutton. Amherst: University of Massachusetts Press.

Foweraker, Joe, and Todd Landman. 1997. *Citizenship Rights and Social Movements: A Comparative and Statistical Analysis.* Oxford: Oxford University Press.

Freidson, Eliot. 1994. *Professionalism Reborn: Theory, Prophecy, and Policy.* Cambridge: Polity Press.

Friedman, David. 1988. *Florentine New Towns: Urban Design in the Late Middle Ages.* Cambridge, Mass.: MIT Press.

Friedmann, John. 1986. "The World City Hypothesis." *Development and Change* 17, no. 1: 69–83.

———. 1995. "Where We Stand: A Decade of World City Research." In *World Cities in a World System,* edited by P. L. Knox and P. J. Taylor. Cambridge: Cambridge University Press.

Friedmann, John, and G. Wolff. 1982. "World City Formation: An Agenda for Research and Action." *International Journal of Urban and Regional Research* 6: 309–44.

Friedrichs, Christopher R. 1995. *The Early Modern City, 1450–1750.* London: Longman.

Friedrichs, Rhoda L. 1993. "Marriage Strategies and Younger Sons in Fifteenth-Century England." *Medieval Proposography* 14: 53–69.

Frijhoff, Willem. 1999. "Foucault Reformed by Certeau: Historical Strategies of Discipline and Everyday." In *Cultural History after Foucault*, edited by J. Neubauer. New York: Aldine de Gruyter.

Frow, John. 1993. "Knowledge and Class." *Cultural Studies* 7, no. 2: 240–81.

———. 1995. *Cultural Studies and Cultural Value*. Oxford: Oxford University Press.

Furet, François. 1981. *Interpreting the French Revolution*. Cambridge: Cambridge University Press.

Furet, François, and Denis Richet. [1965] 1970. *French Revolution*. Translated by S. Hardman. London: Weidenfeld & Nicolson.

Fustel de Coulanges, Numa Denis. [1864] 1978. *The Ancient City: A Study on the Religion, Laws, and Institutions of Greece and Rome*. Translated by W. Small. New York: Doubleday Anchor Books.

Gandelman, Claude. 1989. "Scatological Semiotics: The Revolution as Defecatory Process." *American Journal of Semiotics* 6, no. 4: 13–31.

Gehl, Paul F. 1993. *A Moral Art: Grammar, Society, and Culture in Trecento Florence*. Ithaca: Cornell University Press.

Geison, Gerald L., ed. 1984. *Professions and the French State, 1700–1900*. Philadelphia: University of Pennsylvania Press.

Geremek, Bronislaw. [1971] 1987. *The Margins of Society in Late Medieval Paris*. Translated by J. Birrell. Cambridge: Cambridge University Press.

Ghirardo, Diane Yvonne. 1991. *Out of Site: A Social Criticism of Architecture*. Seattle: Bay Press.

———. 1996. *Architecture after Modernism*. London: Thames and Hudson.

Giardina, Andrea. 1993. "Roman Man." In *The Romans*, edited by A. Giardina. Chicago: University of Chicago Press.

Gibson, Campbell J., and Emily Lennon. 1999. *Historical Census Statistics on the Foreign-Born Population of the United States: 1850–1990*. Washington, D.C.: U.S. Census Bureau.

Gierke, Otto. [1868] 1990. *Community in Historical Perspective*. Translated by M. Fischer. Edited by A. Black. Cambridge: Cambridge University Press.

———. 1900. *Political Theories of the Middle Age*. Translated by F. W. Maitland. Cambridge: Cambridge University Press.

———. 1934. *Natural Law and the Theory of Society, 1500–1800*. Cambridge: Cambridge University Press.

———. 1939. *The Development of Political Theory*. London: Unwin.

Godineau, Dominique. 1998. *The Women of Paris and Their French Revolution*. Berkeley and Los Angeles: University of California Press.

Golden, Mark, and Peter Toohey, eds. 1997. *Inventing Ancient Culture: Historicism, Periodization, and the Ancient World*. London: Routledge.

Goldthorpe, John H. 1982. "On the Service Class, Its Formation and Future."

In *Social Class and the Division of Labour,* edited by A. Giddens and
    G. Mackenzie. Cambridge: Cambridge University Press.
Goode, William J. 1960. "Encroachment, Charlatanism and the Emerging
    Professions: Psychology, Medicine and Sociology." *American Sociological
    Review* 25: 902–14.
Goodich, Michael, ed. 1998. *Other Middle Ages: Witnesses at the Margins of
    Medieval Society.* Philadelphia: University of Pennsylvania Press.
Gottdiener, Mark. 1984. "Debate on the Theory of Space: Toward an Urban
    Praxis." In *Cities in Transformation,* edited by M. P. Smith. London: Sage.
———. 1994. *The Social Production of Urban Space.* 2d ed. Austin: University of
    Texas Press.
Gould, Roger V. 1995. *Insurgent Identities: Class, Community, and Protest in Paris
    from 1848 to the Commune.* Chicago: University of Chicago Press.
Gouldner, Alvin W. 1979. *The Future of Intellectuals and the Rise of the New Class.*
    New York: Oxford University Press.
Grafton, Anthony. 1991. *Defenders of the Text: The Traditions of Scholarship in an
    Age of Science, 1450–1800.* Cambridge, Mass.: Harvard University Press.
———. 1993. *Rome Reborn: The Vatican Library and Renaissance Culture.*
    Washington D.C.: Library of Congress, and New Haven: Yale University
    Press, in association with Biblioteca apostolica vaticana.
———. 1997. *Commerce with the Classics: Ancient Books and Renaissance Readers.*
    Ann Arbor: University of Michigan Press.
Grafton, Anthony, and Lisa Jardine. 1986. *From Humanism to the Humanities:
    Education and the Liberal Arts in Fifteenth- and Sixteenth-Century Europe.*
    London: Duckworth.
Greene, Jack P. 1996. "Coming to Terms with Diversity: Pluralism and Conflict
    in the Formation of Colonial New York." In *Interpreting Early America:
    Historiographical Essays.* Charlottesville: University Press of Virginia.
Grignon, Marc. 1997. *Loing Du Soleil: Architectural Practice in Quebec City
    During the French Regime.* New York: Lang.
Gullickson, Gay L. 1996. *Unruly Women of Paris: Images of the Commune.* Ithaca,
    N.Y.: Cornell University Press.
Gutwirth, Madelyn. 1993. "*Citoyens, Citoyennes:* Cultural Regression and the
    Subversion of Female Citizenship in the French Revolution." In *The French
    Revolution and the Meaning of Citizenship,* edited by R. Waldinger, P. Dawson,
    and I. Woloch. Westport, Conn.: Greenwood Press.
Habermas, Jürgen. [1962] 1989. *The Structural Transformation of the Public
    Sphere: An Inquiry into a Category of Bourgeois Society.* Cambridge, Mass.:
    MIT Press.
Haine, W. Scott. 1996. *The World of the Paris Café: Sociability among the French
    Working Class, 1789–1914.* Baltimore: The Johns Hopkins University Press.
Hall, Edith. 1989. *Inventing the Barbarian: Greek Self-Definition through Tragedy.*
    Oxford: Oxford University Press.

Hall, Peter Geoffrey. 1998. *Cities in Civilization: Culture, Innovation, and Urban Order.* London: Weidenfeld & Nicolson.

Halliday, Terence C. 1983. "Professions, Class and Capitalism." *Archives Européens de Sociologie* 24: 321–46.

———. 1987. *Beyond Monopoly: Lawyers, State Crises, and Professional Empowerment.* Chicago: University of Chicago Press.

Halliday, Terence C., and Lucien Karpik. 1997. "Postscript: Lawyers, Political Liberalism, and Globalization." In *Lawyers and the Rise of Western Political Liberalism: Europe and North America from the Eighteenth to Twentieth Centuries,* edited by T. C. Halliday and L. Karpik. Oxford: Oxford University Press.

Hankins, James. 1995. "The 'Baron Thesis' after Forty Years and Some Recent Studies of Leonardo Bruni." *Journal of the History of Ideas* 56, no. 2: 309–38.

Hanlon, Gerard. 1994. *The Commercialisation of Accountancy: Flexible Accumulation and the Transformation of the Service Class.* Houndmills, Basingstoke: St. Martin's Press.

———. 1997. "A Shifting Professionalism: An Examination of Accountancy." In *The End of the Professions?: The Restructuring of Professional Work,* edited by P. J. Broadbent, M. Dietrich, and J. Roberts. London: Routledge.

Hanson, Julienne. 1989. "Order and Structure in Urban Design: The Plans for the Rebuilding of London after the Great Fire of 1666." *Ekistics* 56, no. 334/5.

Harré, Rom. 1993. *Social Being: A Theory for Social Psychology.* 2d ed. Oxford: Blackwell.

Harris, Jennifer. 1981. "The Red Cap of Liberty: A Study of Dress Worn by French Revolutionary Partisans, 1789–94." *Eighteenth-Century Studies* 14, no. 3: 283–312.

Harris, R. C., and J. Warkentin. 1974. *Canada before Confederation: A Study in Historical Geography.* New York: Oxford University Press.

Hartog, François. 1988. *The Mirror of Herodotus: The Representation of the Other in the Writing of History.* Berkeley and Los Angeles: University of California Press.

Harvey, David. 1982. *The Limits to Capital.* Chicago: University of Chicago Press.

———. 1985. "Paris, 1850–1870." In *Consciousness and the Urban Experience.* Baltimore: The Johns Hopkins University Press.

———. 1996. *Justice, Nature and the Geography of Difference.* Cambridge, Mass.: Blackwell.

Harvey, David W. 1993. "From Space to Place and Back Again: Reflections on the Condition of Postmodernity." In *Mapping the Futures: Local Cultures, Global Change,* edited by J. Bird, B. Curtis, T. Putnam, G. Robertson, and L. Tickner. London: Routledge.

Heller, Agnes. 2000. "The Absolute Stranger: Shakespeare and the Drama of Failed Assimilation." *Critical Horizons* 1, no. 1: 147–67.

Hillier, Bill. 1989. "The Architecture of the Urban Object." *Ekistics: The Problems and Science of Human Settlements* 56, no. 334–35: 5–21.

———. 1996. *Space Is the Machine: A Configurational Theory of Architecture.* Cambridge: Cambridge University Press.

———. 1999. "The Need for Domain Theories." *Environment and Planning B: Planning & Design* 26, no. 2: 163–67.

Hillier, Bill, J. Hanson, and H. Graham. 1987. "Ideas Are in Things: An Application of the Space Syntax Method to Discovering House Genotypes." *Environment and Planning B: Planning & Design* 14, no. 4: 363–85.

Hillier, Bill, and Julienne Hanson. 1984. *The Social Logic of Space.* Cambridge: Cambridge University Press.

Hilton, Rodney H. 1992. *English and French Towns in Feudal Society: A Comparative Study.* Cambridge: Cambridge University Press.

Himmelfarb, Gertrude. 1991. *Poverty and Compassion: The Moral Imagination of the Late Victorians.* New York: Knopf.

Hobsbawm, E. J. [1962] 1977. *The Age of Revolution, 1789–1848.* London: Abacus.

———. [1975] 1977. *The Age of Capital, 1848–1875.* London: Abacus.

Holbrook, Sabra. 1972. *A Stranger in My Land: A Life of François Villon.* New York: Farrar Straus and Giroux.

Holston, James. 1998. "Spaces of Insurgent Citizenship." In *Making the Invisible Visible: A Multicultural Planning History,* edited by L. Sandercock. Berkeley and Los Angeles: University of California Press.

Holston, James, and Arjun Appadurai. 1996. "Cities and Citizenship." *Public Culture* 8, no. 2: 187–204.

Home, Robert K. 1997. *Of Planting and Planning: The Making of British Colonial Cities.* London: Spon.

Honig, Bonnie. 1998, "How Foreignness 'Solves' Democracy's Problems." *Social Text* 16, no. 3: 1–27.

Hufton, Olwen H. 1992. *Women and the Limits of Citizenship in the French Revolution.* Toronto: University of Toronto Press.

Hughes, Diane Owen. 1985. "Earrings for Circumcision: Distinction and Purification in the Italian Renaissance City." In *Persons in Groups: Social Behavior as Identity Formation in Medieval and Renaissance Europe,* edited by R. C. Trexler. Binghamton, N.Y.: Medieval & Renaissance Texts & Studies.

Hunt, Alan. 1996a. *Governance of the Consuming Passions: A History of Sumptuary Law.* London: Macmillan.

———. 1996b. "Governing the City: Liberalism and Early Modern Modes of Governance." In *Foucault and Political Reason,* edited by A. Barry, T. Osborne, and N. Rose. Chicago: University of Chicago Press.

Hyde, J. K. 1973. *Society and Politics in Medieval Italy: The Evolution of the Civil Life, 1000–1350.* London: Macmillan.

Isin, Engin F. 1989. *The Birth of the Modern City in British North America: An*

Introduction. Toronto: University of Toronto, Centre for Urban and Community Studies.

———. 1992. *Cities without Citizens: Modernity of the City as a Corporation.* Montreal: Black Rose Books.

———. 2000a. "Introduction: Democracy, Citizenship and the City." In *Democracy, Citizenship and the Global City,* edited by E. F. Isin. London: Routledge.

———, ed. 2000b. *Democracy, Citizenship and the Global City.* London: Routledge.

Isin, Engin F., and Patricia K. Wood. 1999. *Citizenship and Identity.* London: Sage.

Jacobs, Jane. 1969. *The Economy of Cities.* New York: Random House.

Janse, Antheun. 1999. "Marriage and Noble Lifestyle in Holland in the Late Middle Ages." In *Showing Status: Representation of Social Positions in the Late Middle Ages,* edited by W. Blockmans and A. Janse. Turnhout, Belgium: Brepols.

Jennings, Jeremy. 1993a. "Mandarins and Samurais: The Intellectual in Modern France." In *Intellectuals in Twentieth-Century France: Mandarins and Samurais,* edited by J. Jennings. New York: St. Martin's Press.

———, ed. 1993b. *Intellectuals in Twentieth-Century France: Mandarins and Samurais.* New York: St. Martin's Press.

Johnson, Hildegard Binder. 1976. *Order upon the Land: The U.S. Rectangular Land Survey and the Upper Mississippi Country.* New York: Oxford University Press.

Johnson, Martin Phillip. 1996. *The Paradise of Association: Political Culture and Popular Organizations in the Paris Commune of 1871.* Ann Arbor: University of Michigan Press.

Johnson, Terence. 1972. *Professions and Power.* London: Macmillan.

Jones, Philip James. 1997. *The Italian City-State: From Commune to Signoria.* Oxford: Oxford University Press.

Jordan, David P. 1995. *Transforming Paris: The Life and Labors of Baron Haussmann.* New York: Free Press.

Jordan, William Chester. 1998. "Home Again: The Jews in the Kingdom of France, 1315–1322." In *The Stranger in Medieval Society,* edited by F. R. P. Akehurst and S. C. Van D'Elden. Minneapolis: University of Minnesota Press.

Kallendorf, Craig. 1995. "From Virgil to Vida: The Poeta Theologus in Italian Renaissance Commentary." *Journal of the History of Ideas* 56, no. 1: 41–62.

Karskens, Machiel. 1991. "Alterity as Defect: On the Logic of the Mechanism of Exclusion." In *Alterity, Identity, Image,* edited by R. Corbey and J. Leerssen. Amsterdam: Rodopi.

Karst, Kenneth L. 1989. *Belonging to America: Equal Citizenship and the Constitution.* New Haven, Conn.: Yale University Press.

Käsler, Dirk. 1979. *Max Weber: An Introduction to His Life and Work.* Oxford: Blackwell.

Katz, M. B. 1972. "Occupational Classification in History." *Journal of Inter-disciplinary History* 3: 63–88.

Keaveney, Arthur. 1987. *Rome and the Unification of Italy.* London: Croom Helm.

Kellner, Hansfried, and Peter L. Berger. 1992. *Hidden Technocrats: The New Class and New Capitalism.* New Brunswick, N.J.: Transaction Books.

King, Richard. 1999. *Orientalism and Religion: Postcolonial Theory, India and the Mystic East.* London: Routledge.

Knox, Paul L. 1993. "Capital, Material Culture and Socio-Spatial Differentiation." In *The Restless Urban Landscape*, edited by P. L. Knox. Englewood Cliffs, N.J.: Prentice-Hall.

———, ed. 1988. *The Design Professions and the Built Environment.* London: Croom Helm.

Kofman, Eleonore. 1998. "Whose City? Gender, Class and Immigrants in Globalizing European Cities." In *Cities of Difference*, edited by R. Fincher and J. M. Jacobs. New York: Guilford.

———. 2000. "The Invisibility of Skilled Female Migrants and Gender Relations in Studies of Skilled Migration in Europe." *International Journal of Population Geography* 6: 45–59.

Konrád, György, and Iván Szelényi. 1979. *The Intellectuals on the Road to Class Power.* Translated by A. Arato and R. E. Allen. New York: Harcourt Brace Jovanovich.

Kramer, Lloyd S. 1988. *Threshold of a New World: Intellectuals and the Exile Experience in Paris, 1830–1848.* Ithaca: Cornell University Press.

Krause, Elliott A. 1996. *Death of the Guilds: Professions, States, and the Advance of Capitalism, 1930 to the Present.* New Haven, Conn.: Yale University Press.

Kristeva, Julia. 1991. *Strangers to Ourselves.* Translated by L. S. Roudiez. New York: Columbia University Press.

Ladner, Gerhart B. 1967. "Homo Viator: Medieval Ideas on Alienation and Order." *Speculum: A Journal of Medieval Studies* 42, no. 2: 233–59.

Lafargue, Paul. [1880] 1907. *The Right to Be Lazy and Other Studies.* Translated by C. H. Kerr. Chicago: C. H. Kerr.

Lansing, Carol. 1991. *The Florentine Magnates: Lineage and Faction in a Medieval Commune.* Princeton, N.J.: Princeton University Press.

Larson, Magali Sarfatti. 1977. *The Rise of Professionalism: A Sociological Analysis.* Berkeley and Los Angeles: University of California Press.

———. 1983. "Emblem and Exception: The Historical Definition of the Architect's Professional Role." In *Professionals and Urban Form*, edited by J. R. Blau, M. La Gory, and J. Pipkin. Albany: State University of New York Press.

———. 1993. *Behind the Postmodern Facade: Architectural Change in Late Twentieth-Century America.* Berkeley and Los Angeles: University of California Press.

Lash, Scott, and John Urry. 1987. *The End of Organized Capitalism.* London: Polity.

————. 1994. *Economies of Signs and Space*. London: Sage.

Laws, Glenda. 1997. "Globalization, Immigration, and Changing Social Relations in U.S. Cities." *The Annals of the American Academy of Political and Social Science* 551 (May): 89–104.

Le Goff, Jacques. [1985] 1993. *Intellectuals in the Middle Ages*. Translated by T. Lavender. Oxford: Blackwell.

Lefebvre, Henri. [1974] 1995. *The Production of Space*. Translated by D. Nicholson-Smith. Oxford: Blackwell.

————. 1996. *Writings on Cities*. Translated by E. Kofman and E. Lebas. Oxford: Blackwell.

Lehan, Richard Daniel. 1998. *The City in Literature: An Intellectual and Cultural History*. Berkeley and Los Angeles: University of California Press.

Lévêque, Pierre, Pierre Vidal-Naquet, and David Ames Curtis. 1996. *Cleisthenes the Athenian: An Essay on the Representation of Space and Time in Greek Political Thought from the End of the Sixth Century to the Death of Plato*. Translated by D. A. Curtis. Atlantic Highlands, N.J.: Humanities Press.

Lévinas, Emmanuel. 1969. *Totality and Infinity: An Essay on Exteriority*. Translated by A. Lingis. Pittsburgh: Duquesne University Press.

————. 1978 [1991]. *Otherwise Than Being or Beyond Essence*. Translated by A. Lingis. Dordrecht: Kluwer.

————. 1999. *Alterity and Transcendence*. London: Athlone Press.

Levine, Lawrence W. 1977. *Black Culture and Black Consciousness: Afro-American Folk Thought from Slavery to Freedom*. Oxford: Oxford University Press.

Levine, Marc V. 1995. "Globalization and Wage Polarization in U.S. and Canadian Cities: Does Public Policy Make a Difference?" In *North American Cities and the Global Economy*, edited by P. K. Kresl and G. Kappert. Thousand Oaks, Calif.: Sage.

Levy, R. P. 1981. "Babouvism and the Parisian Sans-Culottes." *Journal of European Studies* 11, no. 3: 169–83.

Ley, David. 1996. *The New Middle Class and the Remaking of the Central City*. New York: Oxford University Press.

Li, Wie. 1998. "Anatomy of a New Ethnic Settlement: The Chinese *Ethnoburb* in Los Angeles." *Urban Studies* 35, no. 3: 479–501.

Liebeschuetz, Wolfgang. 1992. "The End of the Ancient City." In *The City in Late Antiquity*, edited by J. Rich. London: Routledge.

Lintott, Andrew William. 1999. *The Constitution of the Roman Republic*. Oxford: Oxford University Press.

Lomas, Kathryn. 1998. "Roman Imperialism and the City in Italy." In *Cultural Identity in the Roman Empire*, edited by R. Laurence and J. Berry. London: Routledge.

Longhurst, Brian, and Mike Savage. 1996. "Social Class, Consumption and the Influence of Bourdieu: Some Critical Issues." In *Consumption Matters*, edited by S. Edgell, K. Hetherington, and A. Warde. Cambridge, Mass.: Blackwell.

Loraux, Nicole. 1986. *The Invention of Athens: The Funeral Oration in the Classical City.* Translated by A. Sheridan. Cambridge, Mass.: Harvard University Press.

Loughlin, Martin. 1986. *Local Government in the Modern State.* London: Sweet & Maxwell.

———. 1996. *Legality and Locality: The Role of Law in Central-Local Government Relations.* Oxford: Clarendon Press.

Love, John. 1991. *Antiquity and Capitalism: Max Weber and the Sociological Foundations of Roman Civilization.* London: Routledge.

———. 2000a. "Max Weber's *Ancient Judaism.*" In *The Cambridge Companion to Weber,* edited by S. P. Turner. Cambridge: Cambridge University Press.

———. 2000b. "Max Weber's Orient." In *The Cambridge Companion to Weber,* edited by S. P. Turner. Cambridge: Cambridge University Press.

Luscombe, David. 1992. "City and Politics before the Coming of the *Politics:* Some Illustrations." In *Church and City, 1000–1500,* edited by D. Abulafia, M. Franklin, and M. Rubin. Cambridge: Cambridge University Press.

MacDonald, Keith M. 1995. *The Sociology of the Professions.* London: Sage.

MacDowell, Douglas M. 1978. *The Law in Classical Athens.* London: Thames and Hudson.

Magnusson, Warren. 1996. *The Search for Political Space: Globalization, Social Movements, and the Urban Political Experience.* Toronto: University of Toronto Press.

Mahon, Michael. 1992. *Foucault's Nietzschean Genealogy: Truth, Power, and the Subject.* Albany: State University of New York Press.

Maisels, Charles Keith. 1990. *The Emergence of Civilization: From Hunting and Gathering to Agriculture, Cities, and the State in the near East.* London: Routledge.

Malatesta, Maria. 1995. "The Italian Professions from a Comparative Perspective." In *Society and the Professions in Italy, 1860–1914,* edited by M. Malatesta. Cambridge: Cambridge University Press.

Mann, Michael. 1986. *A History of Power from the Beginning to A.D. 1760.* Vol. 1 of *The Sources of Social Power.* Cambridge: Cambridge University Press.

———. 1993. *The Rise of Classes and Nation-States, 1760–1914.* Vol. 2 of *The Sources of Social Power.* Cambridge: Cambridge University Press.

Manville, Philip Brook. 1990. *The Origins of Citizenship in Ancient Athens.* Princeton, N.J.: Princeton University Press.

Margadant, Ted W. 1992. *Urban Rivalries in the French Revolution.* Princeton, N.J.: Princeton University Press.

Marquand, David. 1997. "Professionalism and Politics: Towards a New Mentality?" In *The End of the Professions?: The Restructuring of Professional Work,* edited by P. J. Broadbent, M. Dietrich, and J. Roberts. London: Routledge.

Marshall, T. H. 1939. "The Recent History of Professionalism in Relation to

Social Structure and Social Policy." *Canadian Journal of Economics and Political Science* 5: 325–40.

Martin, Ged. 1972. *The Durham Report and British Policy: A Critical Essay.* Cambridge: Cambridge University Press.

Martin, John. 1997. "Inventing Sincerity, Refashioning Prudence: The Discovery of the Individual in Renaissance Europe." *American Historical Review* 102, no. 5: 1309–17.

Martines, Lauro. 1963. *The Social World of the Florentine Humanists, 1390–1460.* London: Routledge.

———. 1968a. *Lawyers and Statecraft in Renaissance Florence.* Princeton, N.J.: Princeton University Press.

———. 1968b. "Political Conflict in the Italian City States." *Government and Opposition* 3: 88–91.

———. 1979. *Power and Imagination: City-States in Renaissance Italy.* New York: Knopf.

———, ed. 1972. *Violence and Civil Disorder in Italian Cities, 1200–1500.* Berkeley and Los Angeles: University of California Press.

Marx, Karl. [1845] 1975. "The Holy Family: Critique of Critical Criticism." In *Collected Works.* New York: International Publishers.

———. 1852. "The Eighteenth Brumaire of Louis Bonaparte." In *Selected Writings,* edited by D. McLellan. Oxford: Oxford University Press.

———. [1867] 1967. *Capital: A Critical Analysis of Capitalist Production.* Edited by F. Engels. New York: International Publishers.

———. 1963. *Early Writings.* Translated by T. B. Bottomore. Edited by T. B. Bottomore. New York: McGraw-Hill.

Maspero, François. 1994. *Roissy Express: A Journey through the Paris Suburbs.* Translated by P. Jones. London: Verso.

Massey, Douglas S., and Nancy A. Denton. 1993. *American Apartheid: Segregation and the Making of the Underclass.* Cambridge, Mass.: Harvard University Press.

McDonald, William A., and Carol G. Thomas. 1990. *Progress into the Past: The Rediscovery of Mycenaean Civilization.* 2d ed. Bloomington: Indiana University Press.

McKechnie, Paul. 1989. *Outsiders in the Greek Cities in the Fourth Century B.C.* London: Routledge.

McRee, Benjamin R. 1994. "Unity or Division? The Social Meaning of Guild Ceremony in Urban Communities." In *City and Spectacle in Medieval Europe,* edited by B. A. Hanawalt and K. L. Reyerson. Minneapolis: University of Minnesota Press.

Mead, George Herbert. 1932. *The Philosophy of the Present.* Edited by Paul Carus Foundation. Chicago: Open Court.

Meeks, Wayne A. 1983. *The First Urban Christians: The Social World of the Apostle Paul.* New Haven, Conn.: Yale University Press.

————. 1993. *The Origins of Christian Morality: The First Two Centuries.* New Haven, Conn.: Yale University Press.

Meier, Christian. 1990. *The Greek Discovery of Politics.* Translated by D. McLintock. Cambridge, Mass.: Harvard University Press.

Merriman, John M. 1991. *The Margins of City Life: Explorations on the French Urban Frontier, 1815–1851.* Oxford: Oxford University Press.

Meyer, E. A. 1990. "Explaining the Epigraphic Habit in the Roman Empire." *Journal of Roman Studies* 80: 74–96.

————. 1993. "Epitaphs and Citizenship in Classical Athens." *Journal of Hellenistic Studies* 103: 99–121.

Meyer, Stephen. 1981. *The Five-Dollar Day: Labor Management and Social Control in the Ford Motor Company 1908–1921.* Albany: State University of New York Press.

Mills, C. Wright. 1951. *White Collar: The American Middle Classes.* Oxford: Oxford University Press.

————. 1956. *The Power Elite.* London: Oxford University Press.

Mills, C. Wright, and H. H. Gerth. 1942. "A Marx for the Managers." *Ethics: An International Journal of Legal, Political and Social Thought* 52, no. 2.

Mitchell, Richard E. 1990. *Patricians and Plebeians: The Origins of the Roman State.* Ithaca, N.Y.: Cornell University Press.

Mitteis, Heinrich. 1972. "Über Den Rechtsgrund Des Satzes 'Stadtluft Macht Frei.'" In *Die Stadt Mittelalters: Recht Und Verfassung,* edited by C. Haase. Darmstadt: Wissenschaftliche Buchgesellschaft.

Molho, Anthony. 1994. *Marriage Alliance in Late Medieval Florence.* Cambridge, Mass.: Harvard University Press.

Molotch, Harvey. 1976. "The City as a Growth Machine: Toward a Political Economy of Place." *American Journal of Sociology* 82: 309–30.

————. 1999. "Growth Machine Links: Up, Down, and Across." In *The Urban Growth Machine: Critical Perspectives Two Decades Later,* edited by A. E. G. Jonas and D. Wilson. Albany, N.Y.: State University of New York Press.

Momigliano, Arnaldo. [1970] 1977. "The Ancient City of Fustel De Coulanges." In *Essays in Ancient and Modern Historiography.* Oxford: Blackwell.

Moore, Wilbert Ellis. 1970. *The Professions: Roles and Rules.* New York: Russell Sage Foundation.

Morgan, Edmund Sears. 1975. *American Slavery, American Freedom: The Ordeal of Colonial Virginia.* New York: W. W. Norton.

Morley, David, and Kevin Robins. 1995. *Spaces of Identity: Global Media, Electronic Landscapes and Cultural Boundaries.* London: Routledge.

Morris, A. E. J. 1994. *History of Urban Form: Before the Industrial Revolutions.* 3d ed. London: Longman.

Morris, Ian. 1997. "The Art of Citizenship." In *New Light on a Dark Age: Exploring the Culture of Geometric Greece,* edited by S. H. Langdon. Columbia, Mo.: University of Missouri Press.

Morris, Lydia. 1994. *Dangerous Classes: The Underclass and Social Citizenship.* London: Routledge.

Mouffe, Chantal. 1998. "Carl Schmitt and the Paradox of Liberal Democracy." In *Law as Politics: Carl Schmitt's Critique of Liberalism,* edited by D. Dyzenhaus. Durham, N.C.: Duke University Press.

Mumford, Lewis. 1961. *The City in History: Its Origins, Its Transformations, and Its Prospects.* London: Harcourt Brace Jovanovich.

———. 1965. "Utopia, the City, and the Machine." *Daedalus* 94 (spring): 682.

Munro, William Bennett. 1918. *The Government of European Cities.* New York: Macmillan.

———. 1926. *The Government of American Cities.* 4th ed. New York: Macmillan.

Murdie, Robert. 1996. "Economic Restructuring and Social Polarization in Toronto." In *Social Polarization in Post-Industrial Metropolises,* edited by J. V. O'Loughlin and J. Friedrichs. Berlin: Walter de Gruyter.

Murray, Oswyn. 1990. "Cities of Reason." In *The Greek City: From Homer to Alexander,* edited by O. Murray and S. Price. Oxford: Oxford University Press.

———. 1993. *Early Greece.* 2d ed. Cambridge, Mass.: Harvard University Press.

Musterd, Sako, and W. J. M. Ostendorf, eds. 1998. *Urban Segregation and the Welfare State: Inequality and Exclusion in Western Cities.* London: Routledge.

Nafissi, M. R. 1998. "Reframing Orientalism: Weber and Islam." *Economy and Society* 27, no. 1: 97–118.

Nagy, Gregory. 1985. "Theognis and Megara: A Poet's Vision of His City." In *Theognis of Megara: Poetry and the Polis,* edited by T. J. Figueira and G. Nagy. Baltimore: The Johns Hopkins University Press.

———. 1997. "The Shield of Achilles: Ends of the *Iliad* and the Beginnings of the Polis." In *New Light on a Dark Age: Exploring the Culture of Geometric Greece,* edited by S. H. Langdon. Columbia, Mo.: University of Missouri Press.

Najemy, John M. 1992. "In Search of Florentine Civic Humanism: Essays on the Transition from Medieval to Modern Thought." *Renaissance Quarterly* 45, no. 2: 340–50.

Namier, Lewis Bernstein. [1944] 1962. *1848: The Revolution of the Intellectuals.* Oxford: Oxford University Press.

Nicholas, David. 1997a. *The Growth of the Medieval City: From Late Antiquity to the Early Fourteenth Century.* London: Longman.

———. 1997b. *The Later Medieval City, 1300–1500.* London: Longman.

Nicolet, Claude. 1980. *The World of the Citizen in Republican Rome.* Translated by P. S. Falla. Berkeley and Los Angeles: University of California Press.

———. 1993. "The Citizen; the Political Man." In *The Romans,* edited by A. Giardina. Chicago: University of Chicago Press.

Nietzsche, Friedrich. [1880] 1967. *The Will to Power.* Translated by W. Kaufman and R. J. Hollingdale. Edited by W. Kaufman. New York: Vintage Books.

van Nijf, Onno M. 1997. *The Civic World of Professional Associations in the Roman East.* Amsterdam: J. C. Gieben.

Nobles, Melissa. 2000. *Shades of Citizenship: Race and the Census in Modern Politics.* Stanford, Calif.: Stanford University Press.

Nuttall, Zelia. 1922. "Royal Ordinances Concerning the Laying out of New Towns." *The Hispanic American History Review* 5: 249–54.

O'Loughlin, John V., and Jürgen Friedrichs, eds. 1996. *Social Polarization in Post-Industrial Metropolises.* Berlin: Walter de Gruyter.

Ober, Josiah. 1996. "How to Criticize Democracy in Late Fifth- and Fourth-Century Athens." In *Athenian Revolution: Essays on Ancient Greek Democracy and Political Theory.* Princeton, N.J.: Princeton University Press.

OECD. 1995. *Liberalisation of Trade in Professional Services.* Paris: Organisation for Economic Co-operation and Development.

———. 1997. *International Trade in Professional Services: Advancing Liberalisation through Regulatory Reform.* Paris: Organisation for Economic Co-operation and Development.

Ogden, Daniel. 1997. *The Crooked Kings of Ancient Greece.* London: Duckworth.

Osborne, Robin. 1985. *Demos: The Discovery of Classical Attika.* Cambridge: Cambridge University Press.

———. 1996. *Greece in the Making, 1200–479 B.C.* London: Routledge.

Osborne, Thomas, and Nikolas Rose. 1999. "Governing Cities: Notes on the Spatialisation of Virtue." *Environment and Planning D: Society and Space* 17: 737–60.

Osmond, Patricia J. 1993. "Sallust and Machiavelli: From Civic Humanism to Political Prudence." *Journal of Medieval and Renaissance Studies* 23, no. 3: 407–38.

Pagden, Anthony. 1987. "Identity Formation in Spanish America." In *Colonial Identity in the Atlantic World, 1500–1800,* edited by N. P. Canny and A. Pagden. Princeton, N.J.: Princeton University Press.

Palmer, Leonard Robert. 1963. *The Interpretation of Mycenaean Greek Texts.* Oxford: Oxford University Press.

Parsons, Talcott. 1939. "The Professions and Social Structure." *Social Forces* 17: 457–67.

———. 1968. "Professions." In *International Encyclopedia of the Social Sciences,* edited by D. L. Sills. New York: Free Press.

Patterson, Orlando. 1991. *Freedom in the Making of Western Culture.* New York: Medieval Academy of America.

Pearsall, Derek. 1998. "Strangers in Late-Fourteenth Century London." In *The Stranger in Medieval Society,* edited by F. R. P. Akehurst and S. C. Van D'Elden. Minneapolis: University of Minnesota Press.

Pelling, Margaret. 1987. "Medical Practice in Early Modern England: Trade or Profession?" In *Professions in Early Modern England,* edited by W. Prest. London: Croom Helm.

Pels, Dick. 1999. "Privileged Nomads: On the Strangeness of Intellectuals and the Intellectuality of Strangers." *Theory, Culture & Society* 16, no. 1: 63–86.

Perkin, Harold. 1969. *Origins of Modern English Society.* London: Routledge.

———. 1989. *The Rise of Professional Society: England since 1880.* London: Routledge.

———. 1996. *The Third Revolution: Professional Elites in the Modern World.* London: Routledge.

Petit-Dutaillis, Charles Edmond. [1947] 1978. *The French Communes in the Middle Ages.* Translated by J. Vickers. Amsterdam: North-Holland.

Petrarch, Francis. 1924. *The Life of Solitude.* Translated by J. Zeitlin. Urbana, Ill.: University of Illinois Press.

Petsimeris, Petros. 1998. "Urban Decline and the New Social and Ethnic Divisions in the Core Cities of the Italian Industrial Triangle." *Urban Studies* 35, no. 3: 449–65.

Phelan, Shane. 2001. *Sexual Strangers: Gays, Lesbians, and Dilemmas of Citizenship.* Philadelphia: Temple University Press.

Pinkney, David H. 1955. "Napoleon III's Transformation of Paris: The Origins and Development of the Idea." *The Journal of Modern History* 27, no. 2: 125–34.

Pirenne, Henri. 1925. *Medieval Cities: Their Origins and the Revival of Trade.* Princeton, N.J.: Princeton University Press.

Poggi, Gianfranco. 1978. *The Development of the Modern State: A Sociological Introduction.* Stanford, Calif.: Stanford University Press.

de Polignac, François. 1995. *Cults, Territory, and the Origins of the Greek City-State.* Translated by J. Lloyd. Chicago: University of Chicago Press.

Pollock, Frederick, and Frederic William Maitland. 1968. *The History of English Law.* 2 vols. Cambridge: Cambridge University Press.

Potofsky, Allan. 1993. "Work and Citizenship: Crafting Images of Revolutionary Builders, 1789–1791." In *The French Revolution and the Meaning of Citizenship,* edited by R. Waldinger, P. Dawson, and I. Woloch. Westport, Conn.: Greenwood Press.

Powell, Anton. 1988. *Athens and Sparta: Constructing Greek Political and Social History from 478 B.C.* London: Routledge.

Power, Michael. 1997. *The Audit Society: Rituals of Verification.* Oxford: Oxford University Press.

Prest, Wilfrid R. 1987a. "Introduction: The Professions and Society in Early Modern England." In *Professions in Early Modern England,* edited by W. R. Prest. London: Croom Helm.

———. 1987b. *Professions in Early Modern England.* London: Croom Helm.

———, ed. 1981. *Lawyers in Early Modern Europe and America.* New York: Holmes & Meier Publishers.

Prigge, Walter. 1992. *Städtische Intellektuelle: Urbane Milieus Im 20. Jahrhundert.* Frankfurt am Main: Fischer Taschenbuch Verlag.

Raaflaub, Kurt A. 1997. "Soldiers, Citizens, and the Evolution of the Early Greek Polis." In *The Development of the Polis in Archaic Greece,* edited by L. G. Mitchell and P. J. Rhodes. London: Routledge.

Rabil, Albert J. 1988. "The Significance of 'Civic Humanism' in the Interpretation of the Italian Renaissance." In *Renaissance Humanism: Foundations, Forms and Legacy,* edited by A. J. Rabil. Philadelphia: University of Pennsylvania Press.

Rancière, Jacques. [1995] 1999. *Disagreement: Politics and Philosophy.* Translated by J. Rose. Minneapolis: University of Minnesota Press.

Ravid, Benjamin. 1999. "Curfew Time in the Ghetto of Venice." In *Medieval and Renaissance Venice,* edited by E. E. Kittell and T. F. Madden. Urbana, Ill.: University of Illinois Press.

von Reden, Sitta. 1998. "The Well-Ordered Polis: Topographies of Civic Space." In *Kosmos: Essays in Order, Conflict, and Community in Classical Athens,* edited by P. Cartledge, P. Millett, and S. von Reden. Cambridge: Cambridge University Press.

Reinhard, Wolfgang, ed. 1996. *Power Elites and State Building.* Oxford: Oxford University Press.

Reps, John W. 1965. *The Making of Urban America: A History of City Planning in the United States.* Princeton, N.J.: Princeton University Press.

Reynolds, Susan. 1977. *An Introduction to the History of English Medieval Towns.* Oxford: Oxford University Press.

———. 1995a. "The History of the Idea of Incorporation: A Case of Fallacious Teleology." In *Ideas and Solidarities of the Medieval Laity: England and Western Europe.* Aldershot: Variorum.

———. 1995b. "Medieval Urban History and the History of Political Thought." In *Ideas and Solidarities of the Medieval Laity: England and Western Europe.* Aldershot: Variorum.

———. 1997. *Kingdoms and Communities in Western Europe, 900–1300.* 2d ed. Oxford: Oxford University Press.

Rhein, Catherine. 1998. "Globalisation, Social Change and Minorities in Metropolitan Paris: The Emergence of New Class Patterns." *Urban Studies* 35, no. 3: 429–47.

Rhoades, Gary, and Sheila Slaughter. 1998. "Academic Capitalism, Managed Professionals, and Supply-Side Higher Education." In *Chalk Lines: The Politics of Work in the Managed University,* edited by R. Marin. Durham, N.C.: Duke University Press.

Riberio, Gustavo Lins. 1998. "Cybercultural Politics: Political Activism at a Distance in a Transnational World." In *Cultures of Politics/Politics of Cultures: Re-Visioning Latin American Social Movements,* edited by S. E. Alvarez, E. Dagnino, and A. Escobar. Boulder, Colo.: Westview Press.

Richards, Jeffrey. 1991. *Sex, Dissidence, and Damnation: Minority Groups in the Middle Ages.* London: Routledge.

Ringer, Fritz K. 1992. *Fields of Knowledge: French Academic Culture in Comparative Perspective, 1890–1920.* Cambridge: Cambridge University Press.

Robbert, Louise Buenger. 1999. "Domenico Gradenigo: A Thirteenth-Century Venetian Merchant." In *Medieval and Renaissance Venice,* edited by E. E. Kittell and T. F. Madden. Urbana, Ill.: University of Illinois Press.

Robertson, George I. C. 1997. "Evaluating the Citizen in Archaic Greek Lyric, Elegy and Inscribed Epigram." In *The Development of the Polis in Archaic Greece,* edited by L. G. Mitchell and P. J. Rhodes. London: Routledge.

Rodinson, Maxime. [1966] 1974. *Islam and Capitalism.* Translated by B. Pearce. London: Penguin.

Romano, Dennis. 1987. *Patricians and Popolani: The Social Foundations of the Venetian Renaissance State.* Baltimore: The Johns Hopkins University Press.

Rörig, Fritz. [1932] 1967. *The Medieval Town.* Translated by D. Bryant. Berkeley and Los Angeles: University of California Press.

Rose, Michael E., ed. 1985. *The Poor and the City: The English Poor Law in Its Urban Context, 1834–1914.* Leicester: Leicester University Press.

Rose, Nikolas. 1990. *Governing the Soul: The Shaping of the Private Self.* London: Routledge.

———. 1996a. "The Death of the Social? Re-Figuring the Territory of Government." *Economy and Society* 25, no. 3: 327–56.

———. 1996b. "Governing 'Advanced' Liberal Democracies." In *Foucault and Political Reason,* edited by A. Barry, T. Osborne, and N. Rose. Chicago: University of Chicago Press.

———. 1996c. "Government, Authority and Expertise in Advanced Liberalism." *Economy and Society* 22, no. 3: 283–99.

———. 1999. *Powers of Freedom: Reframing Political Thought.* Cambridge: Cambridge University Press.

Rose, R. B. 1983. *The Making of the Sans-Culottes: Democratic Ideas and Institutions in Paris, 1789–92.* Manchester: Manchester University Press.

Ross, Kristen. 1988. *The Emergence of Social Space: Rimbaud and the Paris Commune.* Minneapolis: University of Minnesota Press.

Rotz, Rhiman A. 1976. "Investigating Urban Uprisings with Examples from Hanseatic Towns, 1374–1416." In *Order and Innovation in the Middle Ages: Essays in Honor of Joseph R. Strayer,* edited by W. C. Jordan, B. McNab, and T. F. Ruiz. Princeton, N.J.: Princeton University Press.

Ruddick, Susan. 1996. "Constructing Difference in Public Spaces." *Urban Geography* 17, no. 2: 132–51.

Rudé, George F. E. 1988. *The French Revolution.* New York: Weidenfeld & Nicolson.

Ryan, Mary P. 1990. *Women in Public: Between Banners and Ballots, 1825–1880.* Baltimore: The Johns Hopkins University Press.

———. 1997. *Civic Wars: Democracy and Public Life in the American City During the Nineteenth Century.* Berkeley and Los Angeles: University of California Press.

Said, Edward S. 1978. *Orientalism*. New York: Random House.

Saller, Richard P. 1988. "Roman Class Structures and Relations." In *Civilization of the Ancient Mediterranean: Greece and Rome*, edited by M. Grant and R. Kitzinger. New York: Scribner.

Sandercock, Leonie. 1998. *Towards Cosmopolis: Planning for Multicultural Cities*. New York: Wiley.

Sartre, Jean Paul. 1950. *Baudelaire*. Translated by M. Turnell. New York: New Directions.

Sassen, Saskia. 1988. *The Mobility of Labor and Capital: A Study in International Investment and Labor Flow*. Cambridge: Cambridge University Press.

———. 1991. *The Global City: New York, London, Tokyo*. Princeton, N.J.: Princeton University Press.

———. 1996a. *Losing Control?: Sovereignty in an Age of Globalization*. New York: Columbia University Press.

———. 1996b. "Whose City Is It? Globalization and the Formation of New Claims." *Public Culture* 8: 205–23.

———. 1998. *Globalization and Its Discontents*. New York: New Press.

———. 1999. "Whose City Is It? Globalization and the Formation of New Claims." In *Cities and Citizenship*, edited by J. Holston. Durham, N.C.: Duke University Press.

Saunders, Peter. 1981. *Social Theory and the Urban Question*. 2d ed. New York: Holmes and Meier.

Saxonhouse, Arlene W. 1992. *Fear of Diversity: The Birth of Political Science in Ancient Greek Thought*. Chicago: University of Chicago Press.

Sayer, R. Andrew. 1992. *Method in Social Science: A Realist Approach*. 2d ed. London: Routledge.

Schmidt, Jeff. 2000. *Disciplined Minds: A Critical Look at Salaried Professionals and the Soul-Battering System That Shapes Their Lives*. Lanham, Md.: Rowman & Littlefield.

Schmitt, Carl. [1932a] 1996. *The Concept of the Political*. Chicago: University of Chicago Press.

———. [1932b] 1996. "Strong State and Sound Economy." In *Carl Schmitt and Authoritarian Liberalism*, edited by R. Cristi. Cardiff: University of Wales Press.

Schmitt-Pantel, Pauline. 1990. "Collective Activities and the Political in the Greek City." In *The Greek City: From Homer to Alexander*, edited by O. Murray and S. Price. Oxford: Oxford University Press.

Schofield, Malcolm. 1991. *The Stoic Idea of the City*. Cambridge: Cambridge University Press.

———. 1999. *Saving the City: Philosopher-Kings and Other Classical Paradigms*. London: Routledge.

Schwarz, Bill. 1996. "Night Battles: Hooligan and Citizen." In *Modern Times:*

Reflections on a Century of English Modernity, edited by M. Nava and
A. O'Shea. London: Routledge.

Scott, John. 1996. *Stratification and Power: Structures of Class, Status and
Command*. Cambridge: Polity.

Scott, Mark C. 1998. *The Intellect Industry: Profiting and Learning from Professional
Services Firms*. Chichester, N.Y.: Wiley.

Scully, Stephen. 1990. *Homer and the Sacred City*. Edited by G. Nagy. Ithaca,
N.Y.: Cornell University Press.

Sebert, L. M. 1980. "The Land Surveys of Ontario, 1750–1980." *Cartographica*
17, no. 3: 65–106.

Seigel, Jerrold E. 1986. *Bohemian Paris: Culture, Politics, and the Boundaries of
Bourgeois Life, 1830–1930*. New York: Viking.

Sennett, Richard. 1994. *Flesh and Stone: The Body and the City in Western
Civilization*. New York: Norton.

Sherwin-White, A. N. 1973. *The Roman Citizenship*. 2d ed. Oxford: Oxford
University Press.

Siemiatycki, Myer, and Engin F. Isin. 1998. "Immigration, Diversity and Urban
Citizenship in Toronto." *Canadian Journal of Regional Science* 20, nos. 1, 2:
73–102.

Simmel, Georg. [1908a] 1971. "Domination." In *On Individuality and Social
Forms*, edited by D. N. Levine. Chicago: University of Chicago Press.

———. [1908b] 1997. "The Sociology of Space." In *Simmel on Culture: Selected
Writings*, edited by M. Featherstone and D. Frisby. London: Sage.

———. [1908c] 1971. "The Stranger." In *On Individuality and Social Forms*,
edited by D. N. Levine. Chicago: University of Chicago Press.

———. [1922] 1955. "The Web of Group-Affiliations." In *Conflict and the Web
of Group-Affiliations*. New York: Free Press.

Singer, Brian C. J. 1990. "Violence in the French Revolution: Forms of Ingestion/
Forms of Compulsion." In *The French Revolution and the Birth of Modernity*,
edited by F. Fehér. Berkeley and Los Angeles: University of California Press.

Skinner, Quentin. 1978. *The Foundations of Modern Political Thought*. 2 vols.
Cambridge: Cambridge University Press.

Slaughter, Sheila, and Larry L. Leslie. 1997. *Academic Capitalism: Politics, Policies,
and the Entrepreneurial University*. Baltimore: The Johns Hopkins University
Press.

Smith, Neil. 1996. *The New Urban Frontier: Gentrification and the Revanchist
City*. New York: Routledge.

Smith, Neil, and Cindi Katz. 1993. "Grounding Metaphor: Towards a Spatialized
Politics." In *Place and the Politics of Identity*, edited by M. Keith and S. Pile.
London: Routledge.

Smith, Rogers M. 1997. *Civic Ideals: Conflicting Visions of Citizenship in U.S.
History*. New Haven, Conn.: Yale University Press.

Snodgrass, Anthony M. 1964. *Early Greek Armour and Weapons: From the End of the Bronze Age to 600 B.C.* Edinburgh: University Press.
———. 1980. *Archaic Greece: The Age of Experiment.* London: J. M. Dent & Sons.
Soboul, Albert. 1964. *The Parisian Sansculottes and the French Revolution, 1793–4.* Translated by G. Lewis. Oxford: Oxford University Press.
———. [1968] 1972. *The Sans-Culottes: The Popular Movement and Revolutionary Government, 1793–1794.* Translated by R. I. Hall. Garden City: Anchor Books.
Soguk, Nevzat. 1999. *States and Strangers: Refugees and Displacements of Statecraft.* Minneapolis: University of Minnesota Press.
Soja, Edward W. 1989. *Postmodern Geographies: The Reassertion of Space in Critical Social Theory.* London: Verso.
———. 1996. *Thirdspace.* Oxford: Blackwell.
———. 2000. *Postmetropolis: Critical Studies of Cities and Regions.* Oxford: Blackwell.
Soliday, Gerald Lyman. 1974. *A Community in Conflict: Frankfurt Society in the Seventeenth and Early Eighteenth Centuries.* Hanover, N.H.: University Press of New England.
Sonescher, Michael. 1984. "The Sans-Culottes of the Year II: Rethinking the Language of Labour in Revolutionary France." *Social History* 9, no. 3: 301–28.
Southall, Aidan William. 1998. *The City in Time and Space.* Cambridge: Cambridge University Press.
Soysal, Yasemin. 1994. *Limits of Citizenship: Migrants and Postnational Membership in Europe.* Chicago: University of Chicago Press.
Spencer, Jon Michael. 1997. *The New Negroes and Their Music: The Success of the Harlem Renaissance.* Knoxville: University of Tennessee Press.
Spencer, Sarah. 1994. *Strangers & Citizens: A Positive Approach to Migrants and Refugees.* London: IPPR/Rivers Oram.
Springborg, Patricia. 1992. *Western Republicanism and the Oriental Prince.* Cambridge: Polity Press.
Starr, Chester G. 1961. "The Decline of the Early Greek Kings." *Historia* 10: 129–38.
———. 1986. *Individual and Community: The Rise of the Polis, 800–500 B.C.* New York: Oxford University Press.
Starr, Paul. 1987. "The Sociology of Official Statistics." In *The Politics of Numbers,* edited by W. Alonso and P. Starr. New York: Russell Sage Foundation.
Stasiulis, Daiva K. 1997. "International Migration, Rights, and the Decline of 'Actually Existing Liberal Democracy.'" *New Community* 23, no. 2: 197–214.
de Ste. Croix, G. E. M. 1981. *The Class Struggle in the Ancient Greek World.* Ithaca, N.Y.: Cornell University Press.
Stehr, Nico. 1994. *Knowledge Societies.* London: Sage.
Stevens, Garry. 1998. *The Favored Circle: The Social Foundations of Architectural Distinction.* Cambridge, Mass.: MIT Press.

Strayer, Joseph R. 1970. *On the Medieval Origins of the Modern State*. Princeton, N.J.: Princeton University Press.

Stuurman, Siep. 1996. "Productive Virtue: The Language of Citizenship and the Idea of Industrial Civilization." *European Legacy* 1, no. 1: 329–35.

Swanson, Heather. 1989. *Medieval Artisans: An Urban Class in Late Medieval England*. Oxford: Blackwell.

Szelényi, Iván, and Bill Martin. 1990. "The Three Waves of New Class Theories and a Postscript." In *Intellectuals and Politics*, edited by C. C. Lemert. London: Sage.

Tait, James. 1936. *The Medieval English Borough*. Manchester: Manchester University Press.

Tajfel, Henri. 1981. *Human Groups and Social Categories: Studies in Social Psychology*. Cambridge: Cambridge University Press.

———. 1982. "Instrumentality, Identity and Social Comparisons." In *Social Identity and Intergroup Relations*, edited by H. Tajfel. Cambridge: Cambridge University Press.

Tandy, David W. 1997. *Warriors into Traders: The Power of the Market in Early Greece*. Berkeley and Los Angeles: University of California Press.

Teaford, Jon C. 1975. *The Municipal Revolution in America: Origins of Modern Urban Government, 1650–1825*. Chicago: University of Chicago Press.

Tellegen-Couperus, Olga. 1990. *A Short History of Roman Law*. London: Routledge.

Tenenti, Alberto. 1973. "The Sense of Space and Time in the Venetian World of the Fifteenth and Sixteenth Centuries." In *Renaissance Venice*, edited by J. R. Hale. Totowa, N.J.: Rowman and Littlefield.

Tester, Keith. 1994a. "Introduction." In *The Flâneur*, edited by K. Tester. London: Routledge.

———, ed. 1994b. *The Flâneur*. London: Routledge.

Thébert, Yvon. 1993. "The Slave." In *The Romans*, edited by A. Giardina. Chicago: University of Chicago Press.

Thomas, Carol G. 1982. *The Earliest Civilizations: Ancient Greece and the near East, 3000–200 B.C.* New York: University Press of America.

Thomas, Carol G., and Craig Conant. 1999. *Citadel to City-State: The Transformation of Greece, 1200–700 B.C.E.* Bloomington: Indiana University Press.

Thompson, E. P. 1965. *The Making of the English Working Class*. London: Gollancz.

Thum, Reinhard H. 1994. *The City: Baudelaire, Rimbaud, Verhaeren*. New York: Lang.

Tilly, Charles. 1992. *Coercion, Capital, and European States, A.D. 990–1992*. Cambridge, Mass.: Blackwell.

———. 1994. "Entanglements of European Cities and States." In *Cities and the Rise of States in Europe, A.D. 1000 to 1800*, edited by C. Tilly and W. P. Blockmans. Boulder, Colo.: Westview Press.

Tilly, Charles, and Willem Pieter Blockmans, eds. 1994. *Cities and the Rise of States in Europe, A.D. 1000 to 1800.* Boulder, Colo.: Westview Press.

Tocqueville, Alexis de. [1835] 1945. *Democracy in America.* New York: Alfred A. Knopf.

Trachtenberg, Marvin. 1997. *Dominion of the Eye: Urbanism, Art, and Power in Early Modern Florence.* Cambridge: Cambridge University Press.

Trexler, Richard C. 1980. *Public Life in Renaissance Florence.* New York: Academic Press.

———. 1993a. "Florentine Prostitution in the Fifteenth Century: Patrons and Clients." In *The Women of Renaissance Florence.* Binghamton, N.Y.: Center for Medieval and Early Renaissance Studies.

———. 1993b. "Neighbors and Comrades: The Revolutionaries of Florence, 1378." In *The Workers of Renaissance Florence.* Binghamton, N.Y.: Center for Medieval and Early Renaissance Studies.

———. 1994. "Charity and the Defense of Urban Elites in the Italian Communes." In *Dependence in Context in Renaissance Florence.* Binghamton, N.Y.: Center for Medieval and Renaissance Studies.

Tully, James. 1999. "The Agonic Freedom of Citizens." *Economy and Society* 28, no. 2: 161–82.

Turner, Bryan S. 1974. *Weber and Islam: A Critical Study, International Library of Sociology.* London: Routledge & Kegan Paul.

———. 1996. *For Weber: Essays on the Sociology of Fate.* 2d ed. London: Sage.

Tyerman, Christopher. 1998. *The Invention of the Crusades.* Houndmills, Basingstoke: Macmillan Press.

Ullmann, Walter. 1966. *The Individual and Society in the Middle Ages.* Baltimore: The Johns Hopkins University Press.

———. 1967. "The Rebirth of the Citizen on the Eve of the 'Renaissance' Period." In *Aspects of the Renaissance,* edited by A. R. Lewis. Austin: University of Texas Press.

———. 1968. "Juristic Obstacles to the Emergence of the Concept of State in the Middle Age." *Annali di Storia diritto* 12–13: 43–64.

———. 1975. *Law and Politics in the Middle Ages.* Ithaca, N.Y.: Cornell University Press.

———. 1988. "The Medieval Theory of Legal and Illegal Organizations." In *Law and Jurisdiction in the Middle Ages,* edited by G. Garnett. London: Variorum Reprints.

Urry, John. 1996. "The Sociology of Space and Time." In *The Blackwell Companion to Social Theory,* edited by B. S. Turner. Oxford: Blackwell.

van Uytven, Raymond. 1999. "Showing Off One's Rank in the Middle Ages." In *Showing Status: Representation of Social Positions in the Late Middle Ages,* edited by W. Blockmans and A. Janse. Turnhout, Belgium: Brepols.

Valverde, Mariana. 1996. "'Despotism' and Ethical Liberal Governance." *Economy and Society* 25, no. 3: 357–72.

————. 1998. "On Governing through Habits." *Studies in Law, Politics, and Society* 27 (October): 34–51.

Ventris, Michael, and John Chadwick. 1956. *Documents in Mycenaean Greek*. 2d ed. Cambridge: Cambridge University Press.

Vernant, Jean-Pierre. 1962 [1992]. *The Origins of Greek Thought*. Ithaca: Cornell University Press.

————. [1974] 1988. "The Class Struggle." In *Myth and Society in Ancient Greece*. New York: Zone Books.

Vernon, James. 1993. *Politics and the People: A Study in English Political Culture, C. 1815–1867*. Cambridge: Cambridge University Press.

Vertovec, Steven. 1998. "Multicultural Policies and Modes of Citizenship in European Cities." *International Social Science Journal* 50, no. 2: 187–99.

Veyne, Paul. 1976. *Bread and Circuses: Historical Sociology and Political Pluralism*. Translated by B. Pearce. London: Penguin.

————. 1993. "Humanitas: Romans and Non-Romans." In *The Romans*, edited by A. Giardina. Chicago: University of Chicago Press.

Vidal-Naquet, Pierre. 1986. *The Black Hunter: Forms of Thought and Forms of Society in the Greek World*. Translated by A. Szegedy-Maszak. Baltimore: The Johns Hopkins University Press.

————. 1995. *Politics Ancient and Modern*. Translated by J. Lloyd. Cambridge: Polity.

Vidich, Arthur J., ed. 1995. *The New Middle Classes*. New York: New York University Press.

Villon, François. 1994. *Complete Poems*. Translated by B. N. Sargent-Baur. Toronto: University of Toronto Press.

Waley, Daniel Philip. 1988. *The Italian City-Republics*. 3d ed. London: Longman.

Walker, R. B. J. 1993. *Inside/Outside: International Relations as Political Theory*. Cambridge: Cambridge University Press.

Weber, Max. [1905] 1930. *The Protestant Ethic and the Spirit of Capitalism*. Translated by T. Parsons. London: Unwin.

————. [1909] 1976. *The Agrarian Sociology of Ancient Civilizations*. Translated by R. I. Frank. London: New Left Books.

————. [1916] 1951. *The Religion of China*. Translated by H. H. Gerth. New York: Free Press.

————. [1917] 1958. *The Religion of India*. Translated by H. H. Gerth and D. Martindale. New York: Free Press.

————. [1918] 1994. "Socialism." In *Political Writings*, edited by P. Lassman and R. Speirs. Cambridge: Cambridge University Press.

————. [1921] 1978. *Economy and Society: An Outline of Interpretive Sociology*. Edited and translated by G. Roth and C. Wittich. 2 vols. Berkeley and Los Angeles: University of California Press.

————. [1927] 1981. "Citizenship." In *General Economic History*. London: Transaction Publishers.

Weinbaum, Martin. 1937. *The Incorporation of Boroughs*. Manchester: Manchester University Press.

Wekerle, Gerda R. 1999. "Gender Planning as Insurgent Citizenship: Stories from Toronto." *Plurimondi* 1, no. 2: 105–26.

Whittaker, Richard. 1995. "Do Theories of the Ancient City Matter?" In *Urban Society in Roman Italy*, edited by T. Cornell and K. Lomas. New York: St. Martin's Press.

Williams, Gwyn A. 1969. *Artisans and Sans-Culottes: Popular Movements in France and Britain During the French Revolution*. New York: Norton.

Williams, John C. 1985. "The Invention of the Municipal Corporation: A Case Study in Legal Change." *American University Law Review* 34: 369–438.

Wilson, S. G. 1995. *Related Strangers: Jews and Christians, 70–170 C.E.* Minneapolis: Fortress Press.

Wilson, William J. 1987. *The Truly Disadvantaged: The Inner City, the Underclass, and Public Policy*. Chicago: University of Chicago Press.

Winter, Bruce W. 1994. *Seek the Welfare of the City: Christians as Benefactors and Citizens*. Grand Rapids, Mich.: William B. Eerdmans.

Winter, James H. 1993. *London's Teeming Streets: 1830–1914*. London: Routledge.

Wirth, Louis. [1927] 1964. "The Ghetto." In *On Cities and Social Life: Selected Papers*. Chicago: University of Chicago Press.

———. [1945] 1964. "The Problem of Minority Groups." In *On Cities and Social Life: Selected Papers*. Chicago: University of Chicago Press.

Wittfogel, Karl A. 1957. *Oriental Despotism: A Study of Total Power*. New Haven, Conn.: Yale University Press.

Wood, David J. 1982. "Grand Design on the Fringes of Empire: New Towns for British North America." *Canadian Geographer* 26, no. 3: 243–54.

Wood, Ellen Meiksins. 1988. *Peasant-Citizen and Slave: The Foundations of Athenian Democracy*. London: Verso.

Wood, Peter H. 1974. *Black Majority: Negroes in Colonial South Carolina from 1670 through the Stono Rebellion*. New York: Knopf.

Woodsworth, James S. [1909] 1972. *Strangers within Our Gates*. Toronto: University of Toronto Press.

Wright, Erik Olin. 1985. *Classes*. London: Verso.

———. 1997. *Class Counts: Comparative Studies in Class Analysis*. Cambridge: Cambridge University Press.

Žižek, Slavoj. 1999. *The Ticklish Subject: The Absent Centre of Political Ontology*. London: Verso.

Zukin, Sharon. 1995. *The Cultures of Cities*. Oxford: Blackwell.

Index

Engin F. Isin is associate professor in the urban studies program at York University, Toronto. He is the author of *Cities without Citizens* and (with Patricia Wood) *Citizenship and Identity*, and the editor of *Democracy, Citizenship, and the Global City*.